D0933241

Appalachia Inside Out

VOLUME I

Conflict and Change

Weeks-Townsend Memorial Library
Union College
Barbourville, KY 40906

Appalachia Inside Out

A Sequel to *Voices from the Hills*

VOLUME I

Conflict and Change

Editors

Robert J. Higgs
Ambrose N. Manning
Jim Wayne Miller

Associate Editors

Laura L. Higgs
Cindy Hyder Tipton
Annie H. Michal
Douglas Powell

The University of Tennessee Press • Knoxville

810.80327568
A646
v.1
c.2

To the pioneers of modern Appalachian consciousness:

Harriette Arnow
Harry Caudill
Wilma Dykeman
Loyal Jones
James Still
Jesse Stuart
Cratis Williams

Copyright © 1995 by The University of Tennessee Press / Knoxville.
All Rights Reserved. Manufactured in the United States of America.

Cloth: 1st printing, 1995.
Paper: 1st printing, 1995; 2nd printing, vol. 1, 1997.

The paper in this book meets the minimum requirements of the American National Standard
for Permanence of Paper for Printed Library Materials. ∞ The binding materials have been
chosen for strength and durability.

     Printed on recycled paper.

LIBRARY OF CONGRESS CATALOGING IN PUBLICATION DATA

Appalachia inside out/editors, Robert J. Higgs, Ambrose N. Manning, Jim Wayne Miller;
associate editors, Laura L. Higgs [et al.]—1st ed.
              p.   cm.
        "A sequel to Voices from the hills."
        Includes bibliographical references and index.
        Contents: v. 1. Conflict and change—v.2. Culture and custom.
        ISBN 0-87049-873-8 v. 1 (cloth: alk. paper)
        ISBN 0-87049-874-6 v. 1 (pbk.: alk. paper)
        ISBN 0-87049-875-4 v. 2 (cloth: alk. paper)
        ISBN 0-87049-876-2 v. 2 (pbk.: alk. paper)
1. Mountain Life—Appalachian Region, Southern—Literary collections.
2. American literature—Appalachian Region, Southern.
3. Appalachian Region, Southern—Civilization.
I. Higgs, Robert J., 1932–   . II. Manning, Ambrose N. III. Miller, Jim Wayne.
PS554.A65   1995
810.8'0327568—dc20   94-18718
                                                          CIP

Contents

Volume 1

Conflict and Change

VIII

Volume 2

Culture and Custom

Introduction

In this sequel to *Voices from the Hills,* published twenty years ago, we are attempting to reflect a proliferation of imaginative and critical writing about Appalachia that some students of the region speak of as a "renaissance." While gathering work for this sequel, we have also kept before us certain critiques of *Voices*: C. Hugh Holman's view that the selections in *Voices* failed to connect Appalachia with the rest of the South, and W. H. Ward's concern about the overall quality of selections.

Certainly we have considered the literary quality of every selection; however, the main task before us has not been to argue the literary parity or superiority of selections. Rather, we have sought to identify writing that both represents and reveals the culture of the Appalachian region. At the same time, in *Appalachia Inside Out* we have endeavored to show Appalachia's relationships to neighboring regions, as seen in the chapter "Exile, Return, and Sense of Place." As much as *Voices* attempted to identify a corpus of writing distinguishable as *Appalachian* literature, this sequel undertakes to show the literature of the region in the context of the American experience and indeed the human experience.

Just as we cannot define precisely where Appalachia begins and ends geographically, neither can we say exactly where the region's literature and criticism thereof begin and end. This linkage between "inside" and "outside" seems in keeping with some current critical theory. The title, *Appalachia Inside Out,* further refers to an effort to look not only at the visible Appalachia but also at underlying influences and at relationships in the region between the dark and the light, the ugly and the beautiful, the upside down and the right side up, the "antisigodlin" and the "plumb straight" and angles in between. Although there is considerable overlap between what Henry Shapiro calls the "otherness" of the myth of Appalachia and the otherness of the myth of progress of mid-America, each offers a valuable critique of the other.

Like the issues of gender and ethnicity, the question of region has entered the debate over what constitutes the canon of American, and even southern, literature. *Appalachia Inside Out* engages this issue of region, which major American literature texts, focusing as they usually do upon major authors and literary movements, fail substantially to address. It is our belief that, if self-knowledge is the goal of humanistic learning, then literature should reflect some understanding of the self not only in the abstract but also on native or familiar ground.

We extend thanks to the staff of the Charles Sherrod Library at East Tennessee State University, especially Dr. Fred Borchuck, head librarian, and Beth Hogan of Interlibrary Loan, for supporting this project in innumerable ways. We are grateful, too, for the support of Jean Haskell Speer, director of the Center for Appalachian Studies and Services at ETSU, and of Dr. Styron Harris, chair, Department of English at ETSU. We would like to express a hearty and grateful tribute to Reny Higgs and Mary Manning who contributed many hours in indexing and proofreading.

Special recognition goes to Deanna Bryant, who not only typed both volumes on disks but also served as factotum for the project, coordinating assignments in editing and rewriting, securing permissions, and typing. If there was one point at which all the aspects of such a huge undertaking came together, it was Deanna's desk. Despite the constant workload imposed upon Deanna, from her there never was heard a discouraging word. She kept a faithful and reliable hand on the helm throughout the voyage. We are grateful for her professional service and her inspiration. Hers is a truly pioneering spirit, appropriate to this task.

Chapter I

Roots, Exploration, and Settlement

Introduction

The exploration and settlement of Appalachia have provided abundant material for historians, fiction writers, and poets. Legendary, even mythical, figures have emerged from the process of taming the hill country, and the mountaineer as an American archetype has passed into the popular consciousness.

Serious investigation of the region has entered its third generation, passing from early gentleman historians to professional historians, who in turn paved the way for cultural historians and theoreticians. The question "How did this society develop?" has become "Why did this society develop as it has?" as scholars in recent times have sought answers in the beginnings, in the European conquest and settlement of the Appalachian mountains. In these mountains newcomers, already on the fringe of their original culture, displaced by war, economic conditions, or ambition, first carved a niche for themselves in a generally hostile setting and then established their culture throughout the region.

In truth, however, the "settlement" of the Appalachians continues to this day. The frontier has not moved so much as changed; the "pioneering" aspect of the region now lies in the seemingly inevitable growth of industry and technology, which brings new sorts of settlers, new conflicts and tensions. If the pioneers of the eighteenth century looked ahead, their descendants today look back to determine where they, or the stock they arose from, have been. What was once the frontier of white settlement, the land of the future, now in many ways is a land of the past, quaint to some, backward to others. In this light, the study of the frontier may seem only a sentimental backward glance, unless one realizes, with the region's scholars, that in Appalachia, just as elsewhere, an examination of origins can suggest future directions.

H. Tyler Blethen

H. Tyler Blethen earned his master's and Ph.D. degrees from the University of North Carolina at Chapel Hill. He is professor of history at Western Carolina University, Cullowhee, North Carolina, and has been director of that university's Mountain Heritage Center since 1985. Co-author of *From Ulster to Carolina: The Migration of the Scotch-Irish to Southwestern North Carolina* (1983), which accompanied a permanent museum exhibition funded by the National Endowment for the Humanities, and *A Mountain Heritage: The Illustrated History of Western Carolina University* (1989), he has also published numerous articles on Scotch-Irish ethnicity and on regional and Southern Appalachian history.

The Scotch-Irish Heritage of Southern Appalachia

Appalachia has traditionally been perceived as a region settled and overwhelmingly shaped by people of Scotch-Irish ancestry. Most Appalachians, when asked about ancestry, will assert that some of their kin were Scotch-Irish, or "Arsh." Many authors have cited a wide range of songs, stories, beliefs, behaviors, speech patterns, etc., as proof that Appalachia's culture can be traced back to Ireland.[1] Some have used this cultural heritage to affirm, even to romanticize, the uniqueness of Appalachia as a place where time has stood still, where remnants of old traditions such as violence, kinship ties, fundamentalist religion, and a powerful sense of place have survived.[2]

To what extent can the roots of Appalachian people and culture be traced back across the Atlantic to Ireland? How powerfully did an Irish heritage shape the new frontier society in the Southern Highlands? Such an examination must begin with the realization that not all Appalachians share Scotch-Irish ancestry. Earlier studies that used surname analysis to calculate the Scotch-Irish percentage of the post-Independence population at 60 to 70 percent have been challenged by recent findings informed by a more sophisticated understanding of the massive historical migration of surnames throughout the British Isles and Ireland. Such movement makes it difficult to link surnames to specific localities (e.g., the most common Irish surname in the nineteenth century was Smith), so estimates have been revised downwards, with some placing the Scotch-Irish portion as low as 20 to 35 percent.[3] Certainly many other ethnic groups settled in the mountains, the earliest of whom were Native Americans. European immigrants included significant numbers of English, Germans, French, Welsh, and Italians, and people of African descent also settled

Printed by permission of the author.

throughout the region. So Southern Appalachia, since the Revolution, has been shaped by ethnic and cultural diversity. But even the lowest estimates of Scotch-Irish ancestry still acknowledge this as the largest single group in Appalachia, and as such it played a powerful role in shaping the region's culture.

The roots of the Scotch-Irish are found in that cultural region whose shores bounded the northern part of the Irish Sea: northern Ireland (known as Ulster), southwestern Scotland (called the Lowlands), and northwestern England. Throughout that region many different peoples, mostly Celtic and English, sometimes with but often without the approval of their respective rulers, met, traded, fought, and settled for centuries. It was a frontier area, sometimes marked by violent struggles for control of its valuable resources. After 1603 its history changed dramatically when one ruler became powerful enough to enforce his claim to kingship over all of it.

That king was James VI of Scotland, who, upon the death of his cousin, England's Queen Elizabeth I, inherited her titles to England and Ireland. He became known as James I, the first monarch to rule over all three kingdoms. But the portion of his inheritance surrounding the northern part of the Irish Sea was not a peaceful place. Ulster, populated by Gaelic-speaking Roman Catholics, was in rebellion, and both the Scottish Lowlands and northwestern England were suffering from economic distress. A clever ruler, James I believed he could solve all the problems of the region by extending a system used by earlier English colonizers in Ireland: he would "plant" Ulster by settling colonists drawn from the Lowlands and northwestern England. Those settlers, known in Ireland as Ulster Scots and later in America as the Scotch-Irish, would find opportunity in Ulster and relieve the population pressures on the Lowlands and northwest England. Because they were Protestants, mostly Presbyterians, he believed that they would be loyal in religion. They would crush Ulster's Catholic rebellion and exploit her valuable resources in the process.[4]

In fact, James's plantation scheme sowed the seeds of seemingly endless violence. The new settlers were hated by the Irish whom they displaced. And, as Presbyterians, they ironically found themselves subjected to religious discrimination as James increasingly pressured them to join the government-supported Anglican Church of Ireland. Then, in the eighteenth century, economic distress blanketed Ulster. Rapid population growth, higher rents, a succession of bad harvests, and depression in the linen industry all combined to create intense suffering. Many of the descendants of James I's plantation settlers, disillusioned by life in their new land, decided like their ancestors to migrate again. This time the promised land was America. Over the course of the century, more than a quarter of a million of these Ulster people, or Scotch-Irish, crossed the Atlantic looking for a better life.[5]

Most of them sailed from the ports of Ulster along well-established trade routes to Philadelphia where for years cargoes of flaxseed had been loaded to supply the Irish linen industry. Less-used trade routes took a few to Canada, and to Boston, New York City, and Charleston. But the majority of the eighteenth-century Ulster emigrants arrived in Pennsylvania in search of land. As the fertile soils of southeastern Pennsylvania were claimed, late arrivals pushed inland. The Allegheny Mountains, with their resistant Native Americans populations, impeded the way west. But the Shenandoah Valley opened invitingly to these pioneers, and most turned southwest to settle its gently rolling terrain. As the flow of settlers increased, latecomers had to push on. South of the James and the Dan rivers, the geography of the valley imposed a choice. Pioneers could turn to the southwest, traveling into eastern Tennessee or on to the Cumberland Gap and into Kentucky. Or they could head southeast to the piedmont area of the Carolinas. The latter route, called the Great Wagon Road and extending from Philadelphia to South Carolina, brought the majority of the Scotch-Irish who settled the southeastern backcountry.[6]

Over time, conflicting perceptions of the Scotch-Irish have led to confusion as to who and what they were. Even their name causes misunderstanding, for they were not, as the hyphen implies, the descendants of intermarriage between Scots and Irish. The name used in Ireland, Ulster Scots, accurately reflects the Scottish ancestry of the majority who planted Ulster. But it neglects the substantial minority who came from the northwest of England. The Scotch-Irish were, quite simply, those Scottish and English people who migrated to Ulster in the seventeenth and early eighteenth centuries and who developed a unique culture there, a culture partly influenced by interaction with their Gaelic Irish neighbors.

To the Gaelic Catholic natives of Ulster, the Scotch-Irish were conquerors who stole their land. In addition, their mutual religious animosity caused each faction to brand the other as heretics and enemies of the true church. The result was a persistent climate of violence, as the minority Scotch-Irish, believing themselves surrounded by enemies and in constant danger, practiced a policy of preemptive repression. Their descendants, still shaped by Ulster's culture of violence a century later, brought that siege mentality and reliance on repression with them when they in turn displaced other natives on another frontier in America. The Scotch-Irish in both Ulster and America were newcomers to lands already settled. But in both places they were powerful enough to displace the inhabitants, and in so doing they created unstable frontier environments where violence commonly was used to resolve conflict. This long tradition of frontier life on first one side of the Atlantic and then the other is reflected in the scenes of violence so frequently described by visitors to both societies.[7]

But a dependence on violence was only one piece of the cultural baggage which these Scotch-Irish migrants brought with them from their homeland and found readily adaptable to their new American one. They also brought a distinctive agricultural way of life. In Ireland most of them had practiced "mixed farming," a combination of raising livestock and cultivating grain crops. They planted crops continuously on well-manured and intensively planted "infields" near their houses but rotated the more distant "outfields" between crops and pasture grasses. In the summer they drove their animals to higher pastures on the mountainsides, where a few herdsmen living in small shed-like shelters watched over them. This lifestyle, with families living on scattered farms, was well suited to sparsely settled hilly areas with heavy clay or rocky soils, whether in Ulster or in Southern Appalachia. It contrasted sharply with the agricultural life found in the more densely populated areas of southeastern England, where farmers lived in thickly clustered villages and concentrated on labor-intensive grain crops grown on flat fertile fields.

Just as English emigrants transplanted their traditional farm villages to New England, so the Scotch-Irish brought their preference for scattered family farms to the river and creek banks of Appalachia. Towns were slow to develop and remained small in size, but it would be wrong to attribute that settlement pattern to the mistaken notion that these frontier people living in a hostile environment were nevertheless so fiercely independent that they rejected all benefits of community cooperation. Ulster's infield-outfield system was readily adapted to a region where land was plentiful and labor was scarce, although the Scotch-Irish were unfamiliar with heavily forested environments and had to learn from the Native Americans the slash-and-burn method of clearing fields. Old Country crops of wheat, oats, and barley were mostly replaced by corn and squashes, hogs capable of foraging freely were eagerly adopted, and cattle were driven to summer mountain pastures. To English and German observers accustomed to a different type of agriculture, Scotch-Irish farms may have looked slovenly, with their stump-filled fields and absence of sturdily built stock pens and outbuildings, but recent studies indicate that Scotch-Irish farms were a very productive adaptation to a sparsely populated forest region.[8] The traditional agricultural practices and settlement patterns of the Scotch-Irish in Ulster were easily adapted to the terrain and environment of Appalachia and lastingly shaped its development, as anyone who travels through the Appalachian countryside today can readily see.

The Scotch-Irish also brought religion with them to their new American home. But again, impressions can be confusing, for the Baptist version of Christianity that so strongly dominates the Southern Highlands today was not the religion that the Scotch-Irish brought. The majority of James I's colonists who settled in Ulster in the seventeenth and early eighteenth centuries were Presbyterians from the Scottish Lowlands. Their religion became the defining force in their lives. It not only sharply distinguished them from the Gaelic Catholic natives, but it also eventually alienated them from the British government, which insisted on establishing its Anglican church as the official Church of Ireland.

The earliest phase of Scotch-Irish migration to America occurred as religious revivalism—known in America as the Great Awakening—was sweeping the Western world. In Ulster, Presbyterianism was convulsed by "New Side" challengers who insisted that a personal spiritual conversion experience was necessary to obtain salvation. Their "Old Side" opponents feared this revivalist enthusiasm and hoped to control it by emphasizing the power of synods over the clergy and laity. Scotch-Irish emigrants brought this struggle to America, where many "New Side" Presbyterians decided that they felt more comfortable with Baptist and Methodist teachings about salvation and so converted.[9]

But another factor made Presbyterianism in Appalachia especially vulnerable. Because few Presbyterian ministers emigrated from Ulster to America, and because Presbyterians insisted on an educated ministry, the shortage of Presbyterian seminaries in the eighteenth century made it difficult for Scotch-Irish frontier communities to find qualified clergymen to minister to their needs. Most communities were dissatisfied with the infrequent visits of itinerant ministers, which too often led to a slow drift away from organized religious life. Instead, many Presbyterians turned to the thriving Baptist and Methodist churches which accepted the "call" from God as sufficient certification of fitness for the ministry. The Scotch-Irish brought an intense religiosity which left a strong imprint upon Appalachian culture. But its original Presbyterian form could not dominate in the unique circumstances of frontier life. Appalachia became known for its religious fundamentalism, but it was of a different kind than the harsh predestinarian creed which marked Ulster.

Language is another aspect of Appalachian culture influenced by the Scotch-Irish. Many scholars have studied the linguistic connections between Appalachia, Britain, and Ireland. Some have claimed to trace Appalachian speech patterns to sixteenth-century England, calling them a pure survival of Elizabethan speech; most scholars now believe that such efforts to portray mountaineers as speaking Chaucerian or Shakespearean English reflect insupportable romanticism. But there are several elements of Appalachian speech that can be clearly tied to Ulster.

Linguistic survivals can be traced through words, pronunciation, and grammar. The first two present difficulties because of the speed with which they change over time. Words are quickly and easily borrowed from other dialects and even languages. Pronunciation of words also changes fairly rapidly, even in isolated communities. But grammar appears to evolve more slowly and therefore should be a more reliable means of tracing linguistic ancestry. A recent study has identified forty characteristic Appalachian grammatical features in terms of their national origin. Eighteen of those forty, such as *you all, you'uns, might should, used to could, ye, they's,* and *wait on* are classified as Scotch-Irish, while another five are of uncertain origin. The author concludes that the Scotch-Irish contributed far more to Appalachian speech patterns than any other group.[10]

Finally, the music and folk tales brought to Appalachia by Scotch-Irish immigrants shaped the cultural heritage of the mountains. The work of Francis J. Child in collecting and listing five volumes of English and Scottish ballads at the end of the nineteenth century stimulated people like Olive Dame Campbell and Cecil Sharp to undertake similar projects in Appalachia a few decades later. So far, slightly over one hundred American ballads such as "Barbara Allen" and "Lord Randall" have been identified as originating across the Atlantic.[11] A more recent collector believes that thirty-three of those one hundred ballads are Scottish in origin, including "Thomas Rymer," "Mary Hamilton," and "The Gypsy Laddie." Just as the widespread historical movements of peoples within the British Isles and Ireland have made it difficult to tie specific surnames to specific localities, so too is it difficult to pinpoint the precise geographical origins of music and folk tales. Most ballads are too old, and have undergone too many alterations, for the singers to remember precise origins: "It was my mother's song . . . and she got it from her mother."[12] But it is apparent from the repertoires of modern British, Irish, and Appalachian musicians that musical links were established among them, that their influence has been significant, and that it was the Scotch-Irish who served as the primary transmitters of those musical traditions to Appalachia. As always, it is important to stress that other ethnic traditions have also influenced Appalachian music—for example, those of mainland Europe and Africa.

The Scotch-Irish also brought folk tales with them to their new home. Many were "hero" tales deriving from the Irish Finn and Cuchulain Cycles, tales of famous Irish giants and warriors whose mighty deeds were legendary throughout the island. Others were part of the Europe-wide genre of tales which scholars call *Märchen,* but which are better known in Appalachia as the "Jack Tales." In the Jack Tales, Jack is an underdog who overcomes life's obstacles, often by trickery. Similarities have been found linking these tales with Ireland and Scotland, but they have been the subject of less formal study than the ballads.[13]

Ireland, and Ulster in particular, left a profound mark on the development of Southern Appalachian culture. While it is unlikely that Scotch-Irish settlers comprised a majority of the population of the southern mountains, by acting as transmitters of culture they nevertheless shaped that society in ways that have survived to the present. While scholars are coming to realize that Appalachia has always been a culturally diverse society, and that the image of it as a pure WASP survival is only a crude stereotype, nevertheless its people's perception of its "Arsh" flavor holds true.

Notes

1. Horace Kephart, *Our Southern Highlanders* (New York: Macmillan, 1922); John C. Campbell, *The Southern Highlander and His Homeland* (Lexington: UP of Kentucky, 1969).
2. Rodger Cunningham, *Apples on the Flood: The Southern Mountain Experience* (Knoxville: U of Tennessee P, 1988); David Hackett Fischer, *Albion's Seed: Four British Folkways in America* (New York: Oxford UP, 1989); Grady McWhiney, *Cracker Culture: Celtic Ways in the Old South* (Tuscaloosa: U of Alabama P, 1988).
3. Forrest McDonald and Ellen Shapiro McDonald, "The Ethnic Origins of the American People, 1790," *William and Mary Quarterly* 3d ser., 37 (1980): 179–99; Tyler Blethen and Curtis Wood, *From Ulster to Carolina: The Migration of the Scotch-Irish to Southwestern North Carolina* (Cullowhee, NC: Western Carolina U, 1983); Thomas L.

Purvis, "The European Ancestry of the United States Population, 1790," *William and Mary Quarterly* 3d ser., 41 (1984): 98.

4. M. Perceval-Maxwell, *The Scottish Migration to Ulster in the Reign of James I* (Belfast, Northern Ireland: Ulster Historical Foundation, 1973; reprint 1990); Philip Robinson, *The Plantation of Ulster: British Settlement in an Irish Landscape, 1600–1700* (Dublin: Gill and Macmillan, 1984); Peter Roebuck, ed., *Plantation to Partition* (Belfast: Blackstaff Press, 1981).

5. R. J. Dickson, *Ulster Emigration to Colonial America, 1718–1775* (Belfast: Ulster Historical Foundation, 1966; reprint 1988).

6. Blethen and Wood, *From Ulster to Carolina.*

7. E. R. R. Green, ed., *Essays in Scotch-Irish History* (London: Routledge and Kegan Paul, 1969); J. L. McCracken, "Background to the Ulster-Scot Emigration in the Eighteenth Century," *Irish-American Review* 1 (1979): 16–23; Fischer, *Albion's Seed,* 621-39, 667-68, 765-76.

8. Maldwyn A. Jones, "The Scotch-Irish in British America," in *Strangers within the Realm: Cultural Margins of the First British Empire,* ed. Bernard Bailyn and Philip D. Morgan (Chapel Hill: U of North Carolina P, 1991), 295–302; Fischer, *Albion's Seed,* 621–39, 667–68, 765–71.

9. Kenneth W. Keller, "What Is Distinctive about the Scotch-Irish?" in *Appalachian Frontiers: Settlement, Society, and Development in the Preindustrial Era,* ed. Robert D. Mitchell (Lexington: UP of Kentucky, 1991), 79–82.

10. Michael Montgomery, "The Roots of Appalachian English: Scotch-Irish or British Southern?" *Journal of the Appalachian Studies Association* 3 (1991): 177–91; Michael Montgomery, "Exploring the Roots of Appalachian English," *Now and Then* 9 (1992): 37–38. See also Michael Ellis, "On the Use of Dialect as Evidence: *Albion's Seed* in Appalachia," *Appalachian Journal* 19 (1992): 278–97.

11. David E. Whisnant, "Thicker Than Fiddlers in Hell: Issues and Resources in Appalachian Music," *Appalachian Journal* 5 (Autumn 1977): 103–15.

12. Herschel Gower, "For Singin' and No for Readin'," *Now and Then* 9 (Summer 1992): 31.

13. Marie Campbell, *Tales from the Cloud Walking Country* (Bloomington: Indiana UP, 1958); Barbara McDermitt, "The 2 Jacks," *Now and Then* 9 (Summer 1992): 34–36.

George Scarbrough

George Scarbrough was born in Polk County, Tennessee, in 1915. He received degrees from Lincoln Memorial University (B.A.) and the University of Tennessee at Knoxville (M.A.). He worked as a newspaperman and farmer in East Tennessee from 1937 to 1943 and taught English for eighteen years in secondary schools and colleges. A southern writer, Scarbrough records locales and family traditions in a distinctive, articulate voice. Among his works are *Summer So-Called,* selected by the *New York Times* as one of the best books of 1956, and *Invitation to Kim*, which received a Pulitzer Prize nomination. His most recent publication is *A Summer Ago* (1986). Scarbrough's works also have appeared in over sixty-five magazines and periodicals, including *Atlantic Monthly* and the *New York Times*.

History

Sifted through England
On the way to Pennsylvania,
They came out of the Danelaw.
The record is set in my father's
Proud, high-prowed face.

I, English toned and tainted,
With Bucks County only a name
Like a kite at the end of a long
Thread in a cold northern sky,
Do not plan to go there.

Somewhere South through
Sweetbriar, Knox, Anderson,
Roane, to Polk, the Cherokee
Dropped in for a chat, leaving
My father such cheekbones!

They almost crowd his eyes
Shut in the old photograph (prow
Merely augmented). The Dane shows
Still in the way his head rides
His neck like a tall ship.

Scarborough (North Sea) Scarbrough,
Scarberry is the way the name goes,
Traceable on landholds: *a fortified
Place*. In the Danelaw: *Skarthi's fort,*
Ramparts apparent still

In the formidable look.
The other (Celtic) essence of me
Sounds in my mother's highland name:
McDowell: son of the dark stranger.
Sept, not clan. Perhaps

From *Invitation to Kim,* Iris Press, 1989. Reprinted by permission of the author and publisher.

Explained by the swarthy son.
Sifted through Ireland on the way
To Cape Hatteras (fleeing rejection),
They came eventually to mountains.
On the way a red-haired Dutch

Girl dropped in for a chat,
Leaving my mother her auburn hair.
It was the color of a stormcloud
Besieged by sun. In the photograph
It reddens like dawnlight.

Daughter of the wandering
Medical Scot, she crossed (at age 2)
The last western escarpment, dropping
By jolt wagon down to Tennessee,
Polk County, and my father,

Errant orphan she would later
Marry mostly from pity, she said.
But it was not a pitiful marriage,
Grim poverty notwithstanding.
She was the driving force.
Dying, he cried, "Some water,
Please," adding the word "home."
One hand under his head, with the other
She held the cup steady, returning
It full to the kitchen.

Leafing again the worn album
(Bachelor on a Sunday afternoon,
With whom avoidlessly the line stops),
Pondering the long treks they
Took to my native county,

These folks of mine,
Bringing me rich blood and certain
Not negligible gifts (acknowledged now
In far places), I am perplexed
To be the one to subvert history.

Rodger Cunningham

Rodger Cunningham, a native of West Virginia, received his Ph.D. in comparative literature at Indiana University. *Apples on the Flood* (1988), a cultural history, takes an illustrated comparative approach to Southern Appalachia and represents something of a new direction. The work has generated some controversy, as its approach to explaining the character and origins of the mountain people involves a complicated mix of Freudian and existential thought as well as historical and literary research. The result is a theory of peripheralization which places the Appalachian settlers as a link in a long chain of migrations to the edge, but not beyond the edge, of Western civilization.

To some extent, Cunningham's theorizing recalls the work of Arnold Toynbee, as he traces the movement of the mountaineers' forefathers from the Scottish lowlands through Ulster to the mountains of eastern North America and identifies the cities, particularly London and Rome, as seats of organization and order. However, Cunningham does not approach the problem of peripheralization with the same biases as his predecessor. For Cunningham, the mountaineer is a case to be studied, not a problem to be diagnosed, and his work reflects neither distaste nor dispassion, but scholarly fascination. Cunningham is on the faculty of Sue Bennett College in London, Kentucky.

The Southern Mountain Experience

In the history of Appalachians and their ancestors, I distinguish *three* regions: a metropolitan core labeling itself as "civilized" (Rome, England, the East Coast); an "outside" region labeled as "savage" or "barbarous" (the Celts, the "wild" Highlanders, the "wild" Irish, the "wild" Indians); and, all-important for my study, an intermediate region (the Scottish Lowlands, Ulster, Appalachia) that stands to the "civilized" core economically as a periphery, and politically and culturally as a frontier of expansion against the "wild" exterior. (Rogin's framework is tripartite in that he discusses England as the "mother country" but with a basically political and not economic emphasis.)

Recognizing the existence of this third zone, however, goes against the human mental tendency to perceive the world in terms of dichotomies—structural oppositions of "humanity" and "nature," "civilization" and "savagery," "order" and "chaos," and so on, all of these being versions of the primal distinction between "self" and "not-self." As a result, this intermediate peripheral zone and its inhabitants have constantly been misperceived by the "civilized" metropole—put into false positions, seen in false ways. And this

From *Apples on the Flood: Minority Discourse and Appalachia*, © 1987 by The University of Tennessee Press. Reprinted by permission of the publisher.

misperception has been committed not only by the "civilized" insider but also by the "savage" outsider. To the metropolitan, the frontiersman was essentially barbarous; to the outsider, he was the foreign intruder. In short, each of these groups has tended to see the intermediate one—the peripheral dwellers—as a version of the other, and a particularly objectionable one at that.

My basic themes, then, are two: identity, both individual and collective; and peripheralization—what it means to be looked on constantly as someone on the fringe of things. And my fundamental thesis is that, among Appalachians and their forebears, the second has had a pernicious effect on the first. Other writers have shown how the "civilized" person has created the image of the "savage" as a projection of that "civilization's" own rejected, repressed, and unsublimated infantile impulses. The result for the "savage," even when the latter has been spared physical extermination, has been psychic and sociocultural destruction. Again and again, a stable society of mature adults has been disrupted by "civilized" efforts (even, or especially, well-meaning efforts) to "raise" it from a state defined as "childish"—and these efforts have created a self-fulfilling prophecy of turmoil and dependency.

But what of the peripheral dweller? In this case—and especially if that periphery is also a frontier against "savagery"—people are subjected to a process somewhat more subtle but no less pernicious. For where a powerful "civilized" society is engaged in violence against a less powerful "savage" one, the frontier of the powerful society is identified with the unstable and violent ego-boundary of the individual, an insecure frontier which perpetuates the ego through violence. But the peripheral dwellers, the frontiersmen, are also in a weak position with regard to the metropolitan core dweller. And thus they are also vulnerable to the effects of being identified with projected parts of the core dweller's psyche. Specifically, they are identified with the unstable, violent ego-boundary. Since their whole being is identified with another's boundary, they are not seen in all their dimensions; and since they are specifically seen as something violent and unstable, they are under pressure to let violence and instability permeate their whole psyches vis-à-vis the universe. The metropole then encourages them to take out this violence on the ones next in line, the "savages." Thus they are manipulated into carrying out the metropole's genocidal program while being culturally and socially destroyed themselves. They are encouraged to see themselves as the representatives of "civilization" against "savagery," while the metropolitan in fact looks on them as little, if at all, better than savages themselves. And they are seen in this way precisely because of that violence which the metropole itself has instilled in them by undermining their sense of autonomous identity and independent self-worth. They are never themselves but always versions of another, and always in a negative sense.

In exploring this theme of impaired identity, I have not only followed Freudian and existential psychology. I have also seen connections with the writings of Joseph Campbell and other mythologists who have studied the psychological meanings of rites, and particularly of the *rite of passage* as a formal transformation of identity. Thus I have formed the thesis that a peripheralized people is the victim of (among other things) distorted rites of passage which reinforce these insecure ego-boundaries and ego-foundations. It seems to me that this interpretation is in line with, and indeed integrates and brings out hidden aspects of, the classic theories of colonial domination. Here and elsewhere my approach attempts to transcend most social critics' blanket contempt for "myth" and also most mythologists' (including Campbell's) blindness or complacency regarding the effects of socioeconomic power on myth and ritual—effects that have given myth and ritual themselves what I consider an undeservedly bad name.

I have, then, attempted to trace the themes of identity and peripheralization among the forebears of the Appalachian people not only across the spheres of life not previously linked together in this way, but also backward in time much further than has previously been attempted. Let me, then, proceed to a synopsis of my historical argument.

I begin by describing the Atlantic Zone of Europe, that distinctive though raggedly elongated "subcontinent" described so well in the works of the Irish geographer E. Estyn Evans. I briefly describe the various invasions of the area, analyzing later legendary accounts to show the psychological genesis of the dominating attitudes analyzed for modern cases by Memmi, Fanon, and their successors. While doing so, I narrow my focus first to Britain and then to the southwestern region of Scotland, the main home of what was to become the "Scotch-Irish." The Roman invasion frames a study of the Classical attitude toward Celtic and British "barbarians," and here I introduce the theme of "primitivism" as being a projection of one's own traits on the outsider. A key fact will become apparent here, and not by any means for the last time in this study: the basic identities and conflicts of the situation are not "ethnic"—at least not in any vulgar genetic sense—but *regional,* even in Europe and even at this remote date.[1]

Moving on into the early Middle Ages, I show how the Atlantic Zone in general and southwestern Scotland in particular were progressively transformed from a largely independent cultural and economic entity into a dominated periphery of mainland Europe. There follows what is in many ways the key section of the entire book—namely, a discussion of the fundamental social and cultural trauma undergone by what was to become the Scotch-Irish and Appalachian peoples. This was the forcible feudalization and anglicization of the Scottish Lowlands in the late Middle Ages by a Scottish elite of Anglo-Norman culture. The region and its population thus were transformed from an integral part of one society into a subjugated fringe of another. In this period, economic peripheralization on the unstable frontier of western Europe—unstable because there were still unsubdued lands in Scotland and Ireland—led to the development, in individuals on the periphery, of a particular type of insecure ego-boundary. This insecurity, as I have said, was wedded to a false concept of both "civilization" and "maturity," and this peripheralized personality found its natural vent in projecting the self-to-be-subdued onto the outsider, who at this time was the Scottish Highlander. A few centuries later, these themes were repeated and reinforced in the Ulster Plantation, when the frontier of European power moved outward again and Appalachians' ancestors moved along with it, continuing to be "civilization's" manipulated advance agents against the "wild" Irish, as they had been against the "wild" Highlanders.

I then outline the history of Appalachia itself from this viewpoint. First I show how, as the European periphery moved still further out, across the Atlantic, a large proportion of the Scotch-Irish moved along with it, transferring their aggression from "wild" Gaels to "wild" Indians—an old idea, but one which I explore in new ways. Then, as the Indian frontier retreated further west and the Scotch-Irish pioneers settled into the mountains, the ground was laid for the recovery of a stable, rooted identity. But this process ended up being seriously impaired.

First, in the Civil War and its aftermath, the rival lowland cultures and polities of North and South repeated the old pattern in a new way: each saw the mountaineer as a version of the other one, with effects disastrous both materially and otherwise. Then, in the late nineteenth century, when the frontier closed altogether, the mountains began to be penetrated by industrial "civilization." At this point a fundamental shift occurred in the outside perception of the mountaineer. The frontier of white against Indian having faded from consciousness, the "frontier" concept was transferred to a newly important boundary—the one between industrial society and nonindustrial. Mountaineers no longer were on the fringe—instead they were altogether on the wrong side of this "frontier." Therefore their stereotyped image now took on the essential features of their dark twins, the Indians. Like the latter, and like the Celts in ancient times, they sometimes were seen as detestable barbarians, sometimes as romantic noble savages; but these two constructs were simply versions of each other, and in neither case were the mountaineers confronted as persons. Indeed, the fact that they were seen as a version of the dominant culture—as "contemporary ancestors"—only accentuated the tendency to see them in terms of projections rather than as they were, or are. I analyze some of the results in terms which unite the psychological insights of R. D. Laing, the social analyses of Memmi and Fanon, and the observations of some modern students and natives of Appalachia.

All this may seem to make Appalachians look like passive victims in a way that is all too familiar; but I hold that this impression is an artifact of the analytical method, since analysis itself is inherently a tool for exploring the bound and not the free, necessity and not possibility, the fixed past (and the present as its result) and not the undecided future (and the present as its springboard). For the latter I conclude by returning to the realm of myth, not deconstructing it analytically as I had when exposing its distortions, but exploring it for its suggestiveness. I contend that important insights may be derived from certain "Celtic" (or Atlantic) mythic themes—insights regarding the indestructibility of authenticity and wholeness beneath the distortions of power, and regarding the necessity of translating this insight into concrete action in the world.

Note

1. A lack of understanding of this fact tends to cloud Michael Hechter's *Internal Colonialism: The Celtic Fringe and British National Development, 1536–1966* (Berkeley: U of California P, 1975), though, for those alerted to the fact, his own data point in this direction.

Bernard Stallard

Bernard (Bernie) Stallard was born in Coeburn, Virginia, in 1921 and grew up in Middlesboro, Kentucky. He later moved to northern Kentucky, where he lived until his death. He attended Lincoln Memorial University and the University of Louisville and for five years was a social worker. He taught English and speech in public schools, and he was teaching at Southwestern Ohio College at the time of his death in 1986. Stallard's first published work appeared in *Youth* magazine when he was sixteen. He was the first recipient of the Ross Carter Memorial Award, an annual creative writing award granted at Lincoln Memorial University.

Genealogy

In politics, he'd doubtful sympathies,
So Walter Stallard caught a sailing ship,
In Sixteen-forty, for the Colonies—
A costly, long, and peril-laden trip.
He landed in Virginia that May,
In Rappahannock County bought some land
And, with his wife, he settled down to stay
And at some new-ground farming try his hand.
This man who fought against his Tory foe
And then sought refuge on such savage earth—
Where only those with courage dared to go,
I like to think had principle and worth.
I sometimes wonder just where I would be
Had Walter not seen fit to disagree.

Printed by permission of Frances Stallard.

Jean Haskell Speer

Jean Haskell Speer, director of the Center for Appalachian Studies and Services and professor of anthropology and folklore at East Tennessee State University, received her Ph.D. from the University of Texas at Austin. Before assuming her appointment at ETSU in 1993, Dr. Speer was director of Appalachian studies and professor of humanities and communication studies at Virginia Polytechnic Institute and State University. Dr. Speer's teaching and research focus on the politics of culture, folk, traditions in Appalachia and elsewhere, public policy in Appalachia, and comparative studies of mountain cultures worldwide. She has done research and lectured throughout Appalachia, the United States, and Europe. She is author of *The Appalachian Photographs of Earl Palmer* (1990), coeditor of *Performance, Culture and Identity* (1992), and author of numerous book chapters, articles, and reports on Appalachian issues.

The essay which follows is extracted from a longer article, "Montani Semper Liberi: Mary Lee Settle and the Myths of Appalachia," in which Speer surveys Settle's contribution to our understanding of the Appalachian frontier.

Through the Beulah Quintet

When I read the first book of Settle's Beulah Quintet, I embarked on a journey that took me from seventeenth-century England to the frontier of Virginia before the American Revolution; from West Virginia on the eve of the Civil War to the mine wars of the Appalachian coalfields in the 1920s; and, finally, to contemporary, suburban West Virginia. As one who has spent much of my life trying to understand and teach and write about the complexities of the Appalachian region, I realized how evocative and provocative a guide Settle had been on the journey, how much more I understood of Appalachian experience, and how much I enjoyed the circuitous routes to our destination.

Circuitous indeed! The conclusion of the last of the five novels is really the beginning of the entire quintet. The final section of *The Killing Ground* (1982) is entitled "The Beginning, 1960–1980" and carries this quotation from Joseph Conrad's *Lord Jim*: "Once some potent event evokes before your eyes the invisible thing, there is no way to make yourself blind again." An admirer of Conrad, Settle confesses that her books "have always begun with questions, appearing as images, as visions."[1] Once she has seen the compelling image, the potent event, she becomes obsessed with knowing "why things happen to be the way they are."

From *Southern Women Writers: The New Generation,* ed. Tonette Bond Inge, © 1990 The University of Alabama Press. Reprinted by permission of the publisher.

The vision that spawned the Beulah Quintet was one stranger hitting another in a drunk tank on a Saturday night. In the final novel, this vision becomes
the killing of a playboy, a member of the Canona (presumably Charleston), West
Virginia, elite, by a "hillbilly," as the result of "fight night on a sweet Saturday"
(the original title of the novel). Hannah McKarkle, Settle's alter ego in the novel,
is the dead man's sister and a celebrated writer living in New York. Not satisfied with any easy explanations, she has written the Beulah novels, spanning
three centuries, to find out why her brother Johnny died and what forces led to a
seemingly casual act of violence in an Appalachian jail.

When Hannah returns to West Virginia on a final quest, her childhood
friend chides her: "What are you trying to find out, Hannah? Same old
things? Just what is it you're trying to do? Still chasing Johnny while the
world goes to hell in a handcart? You think we're disintegrating: What did
you call it once, the senility of the century?"[2]

Furiously, Hannah replies: "To hell with the century. I'm trying to find
out what lay behind one act of violence, the fist of one man hitting a man he
didn't know. You say it doesn't have anything to do with what's going on. It's
the goddamn center of it, one fist, one man, one act" (Settle, *Killing Ground* 53).

Going to the jail to confront Johnny's killer, Hannah knows what she will
find: "a shirttail hill boy, slim and mean as a rattlesnake, a Saturday-night
hell-raiser, car-roller, nigger-hater, tire-stealer . . . my feral twin from the
underbelly of the Republic, White Anglo-Saxon Protestant, Quantrill raider,
Indian killer, a Dalton Boy, a bush-whacker, agate-eyed wildcat" (235). Hannah
knows the mythology of Appalachia well. Physically, Jake Catlett does not dis-
appoint her. But as Hannah questions him about her brother's death, she un-
leashes a hatred steeped in beliefs as deeply held and keenly felt as her own.

When Hannah accuses Jake of striking out blindly at an anonymous enemy, Jake corrects her with clarity and force: "I seen him standin' before he
fell and he looked kind of surprised. Then he said, 'Thank you.' He said a
real quiet thank you, and just sighed down on the floor and hit that iron
rack. Jeez Christ, I hated him when he said that, that thank you, lording it
over a goddamn drunk tank. I never hit him hard. Just blowed off the last of
my steam. I figured he was makin' fun of the rest of us" (237). The floodgate
opened, Jake spills out for Hannah a tragic personal history of land, health,
jobs, pride, and dignity lost over the years to those of her class in West Virginia. Hannah mutters, "We didn't know" (241).

Jake reassures himself that "we're good people . . . come from upriver, up
around Lacey Creek" (239), reminding Hannah of their distant kinship and
their shared heritage of the Beulah homeplace. Shared heritage, shared family, shared land—all the ties that should bind have not been able to heal the
wounds of shared misunderstandings that have sundered them. They shout
at each other the epithets of class division. Jake accuses Hannah of "layin'
under a tree like hawgs eatin' chestnuts and never look up to see whar they
come from" (241): "They ain't a damn thing, ain't even that dress on your
back didn't come off the coal-face and don't forget it. You people puttin' on

to act high and mighty . . . " (239). Hannah yells back, "You talk about us not giving a damn. You people won't walk across the hollow. Let people ride roughshod over you and you just back a little further up your hills and whine because you haven't real guts enough . . . " (244).

Hannah stops, finally seeing herself and Jake and her brother Johnny not as strangers but inextricably and paradoxically bound to each other: "We faced each other, the razorback bone of the country, me stripped from the topsoil of training down to rock pride. If it was kinship that held me there, stark-stiff with the whole mess, the crisscross hatreds, if it was brothers, I had more of them than a dog had fleas, a whole hard valley of brothers" (244). Hannah begins to see, though darkly, that Jake and her brother Johnny and all of her other brothers in that hard valley had been willing to pay a dear price for freedom. Getting drunk for one sweet Saturday night of freedom from his troubles, Jake strikes a killing blow, also for a kind of freedom, that puts him in the prison cell where Hannah now faces him. Her brother Johnny thanks Jake quietly for a final freedom from some prisons inescapable in his life.

Writer Hannah McKarkle and writer Mary Lee Settle passionately need to know: What is the meaning and price of freedom? Must freedoms so desperately sought in acts of rebellion inevitably lead to imprisonment of one kind or other? What surged into the accumulated power of a single blow on a Saturday night in the mountains of West Virginia? How did it all go so wrong?

To find the answers, Settle originally wrote a trilogy, supported in her work by a Guggenheim Fellowship. Like Aeschylus and Sophocles, she seemed to believe that questions of individual freedom versus the collectivity of civilization, whether in Greece or Appalachia, demand a complex, cyclical treatment. Settle knew she could not answer her questions in a single, contemporary novel: "I had to go all the way back, as it turned out, to one lone woman lost in a wilderness in 1755."[3] Even her trilogy, *O Beulah Land* (1956), *Know Nothing* (1960), and *The Killing Ground* (as *Fight Night on a Sweet Saturday,* 1964) proved insufficient: "A whole part of our being as Americans was missing: our revolutionary sense.[4] In her archaeology of rebellion, Settle went digging in seventeenth-century England.

Prisons: The Prologue (1645–49)

In a manner typical of the intricate tapestry of her work, Settle found clues for *Prisons* (1973), the first book of the quintet, while writing her nonfictional account of the Scopes evolution trial. Researching the involvement of the American Civil Liberties Union (ACLU) in the trial, Settle learned that the ACLU had taken its motto from the words of John Lilburne, a seventeenth-century Puritan martyr who kept on preaching individual freedom even as he was being flogged through the streets of London. "Freeborn John" Lilburne, initially an officer in Cromwell's parliamentary army opposing Charles I, resigned in 1645 rather than subscribe to a covenant with Scotland to reform the Church of England along Presbyterian lines. From then on, Lilburne became a leader and master propagandist of the Leveler party, demanding religious liberty, the extension of suffrage to craftsmen and small property owners, and complete equality before the law. Lilburne championed natural rights over common law, insisting that

> what is done to any one may be done to everyone; besides, being all members of one body, that is, of the English Commonwealth, one man should not suffer wrongfully, but all should be sensible, and endeavour his preservation; otherwise they give way to an inlet of the sea of will and power, upon their laws and liberties, which are the boundaries to keep out tyranny and oppression; and who assists not in such cases, betrays his own rights, and is overrun, and of a free man made a slave when he thinks not of it, or regards it not, and so shunning the censure of turbulency, incurs the guilt of treachery to the present and future generations.[5]

Because of his passion for freedom, Lilburne spent most of his life in prison.

Led by Lilburne's words, Settle found the potent event necessary for the beginning of her roman-fleuve:

> Lilburne led me to a churchyard in Burford, near Oxford. I noticed that there were pockmarks on the stone wall of the church, in two lines, one at head level and the other above it. I knew at once that men had been shot against the wall and that some of the firing squad had shot over their heads. I had literally walked into my story—the story of two rebels, Johnny and Thankful, and of Oliver Cromwell, whom I use as a major character. That book was *Prisons*, the first volume of the quintet, written and published [in 1973] after the trilogy.[6]

In *Prisons* (published in England in 1974 as *The Long Road to Paradise*), young Johnny Church, a rather ordinary son of a commoner-become-gentry, makes a choice for freedom. His choice leads him, like Antigone, to inevitable doom. During his childhood, Johnny lived in awe of his wealthy cousins at Lacey House, where he often heard political arguments charged with a force he did not fully understand. Bitter words about Scots, commoners, protecting investments in the New World, the Parliament, even King Charles.

At Oxford, young Johnny is introduced to the "democratical notions" of Lilburne and others—"Twas not only newfangled notions, but words too, words that rolled and tumbled through us in a new way, as we took to the heady speech of the new dangerous men."[7] As the Civil War between Parliament and the king intensifies, Johnny is called home from Oxford by a protective father worried that the "wild-worded rabble-rousers" will "turn everyone against all the nobility and clergy and gentry in the land and destroy the monarchy itself" (48).

On the morning of Johnny's sixteenth birthday in 1645, Johnny's growing democratical notions force his hand. Charity and Lazarus, the peasant servants who had taught Johnny to see strength in the land and dignity in toil, face the dreaded "enclosure," the loss of their homes and the commonly shared land on which the crofters had lived for generations. It was these enclosures in England and Scotland that started the migration of many families who ultimately would become Appalachian settlers. Johnny says incredulously: "My father had decided to flood their village to make a lake and enclose the common up to Henlow Wood to run his deer. He had looked out one morning and found the village an offense to his eyes. There were only five squat houses in the way of his plans for a fine vista in the Italian manner" (49). In succeeding generations, the plain folk of Appalachia would continue to be "in the way of . . . plans" of others.

Shattered by his father's indifference to the common people who worked his land, Johnny chooses his first act of conscience—he refuses to show deference to his father, refuses to "doff his hat"—and in that gesture sparks a rebellious spirit that will span the generations through five novels. As Joyce Coyne Dyer observes, a central principle in Settle's historical theory is that "civil wars arise not from isolated events or decisions of kings and great men, but, rather, from anger, outrage, and tension within individuals and families."[8]

Disinherited, Johnny joins Cromwell's parliamentary army in its march against the king. He is befriended by Thankful Perkins, of the clear eyes and clear vision, and Gideon McKarkle, a Scot, enclosed off his Highland croft and now a pawn among the clashing armies of the night. Free to believe, to speak, to act, most for the first time, the ragtag army sees their hopes for freedom raised, only to be betrayed by Cromwell. As Johnny sadly observes, "The danger of the democratic way is that men are courted, instead of being honored, one by another" (Settle, *Prisons* 155). But Gideon and Thankful and Johnny have come too far, have lost too much, to turn back. Gideon and Thankful and Johnny must die or betray conscience.

Cromwell offers Johnny his freedom if he will but speak his dissent and become contrite. Like Antigone confronting Creon, Johnny's silence speaks: "There are no more words, only the turning of the wrist, the dropping of the dirt on the dead, obscene face; I did not know before how inevitable the choice, how perpetual is the taking place of the thing, the ever asking of the question, the ever turning answer" (195).

Imprisoned in Burford church, awaiting execution, the condemned men argue and sob and talk of escape to freedom in Virginia. Johnny dreams and tells Gideon McKarkle, "I dreamed that all that sets men apart from the beasts is the act without hope of reward" (206). As Johnny prepares to die, sustained by his dream, he nevertheless longs for someone to "speak a word. Hast forgot how to say no? Will no one cry cease?" (235). No one does. Johnny Church dies at twenty in the Burford churchyard where Mary Lee Settle will find him three centuries later.

In Johnny Church's search for freedom, he comes to the conclusion that "freedom's no fine thing; it is as simple as the opening of a door, or a ceasing of persuasions upon you, or a blessing. . . . To bless and grant freedom are the same. We are in prisons of other men's beliefs" (204). For the descendants of Johnny Church (through his son by the mistress of Lacey House) and Gideon McKarkle, these words will reverberate from England to Appalachia. In her statement that "we are in prisons of other men's beliefs," Settle has encapsulated a dominant issue in understanding both past and present in Appalachia.

O Beulah Land: The Promise (1754–74)

Although Johnny Church and Gideon McKarkle dreamed of freedom in Virginia, it would be left to their heirs to reach that promised land. Settle recreates the trials and tribulations of the early settlement of Appalachia in O Beulah Land, a book critics have called "extraordinary," "head and shoulders above most of its contemporaries" that have "misinterpreted American history in recent years."

In the mid-1750s, the Virginia territory in America held the promise of freedom for some, imprisoning fear for others. Some, like Jonathan Lacey, came as planters or surveyors or officers in Braddock's army to tame the wild territory. Some, like the McKarkles, enclosed off their land in the Scottish Highlands, forced into Ulster to subdue the Irish, came lusting for land to call their own. For many others, the sea crossing to America was not a matter of duty or choice or desire:

> The convicts could not imagine the hot sun, never having felt it in their London hutches of cobble and damp. They knew only that packing tobacco leaves in the fields, after the uneasy pleasures of the London streets, was in their world one of the familiar ways of dying. Virginia. The name was enough to shoot horror into the backbone of every convict aboard. Virginia, transportation to the plantations—next to death, the final punishment.[9]

Hannah Bridewell (named for St. Bride's Well prison in England) is one such "transportee," sent to America for whoring in London. Hannah, Johnny Lacey, Solomon McKarkle, and the whole polyglot of Europe and Africa pouring into America push their way into the Virginia wilderness to form improbable alliances.

The frontier has always been a liminal space, a place betwixt and between order and chaos, a threshold of expectations. The Virginia frontier, a land of wild beasts, wild savages, and endless mountains, fascinated and repulsed the early settlers. Those who still yearned for the "hairdressing, wig-combing, wit, heart, the fashion, the ton" (Settle, O Beulah Land 70) of England clung to the coast and were contemptuous of those who were compelled to go westward over the mountains. Beyond the Blue Ridge was bad enough; beyond the Alleghenies was unthinkable.

But for some, mostly those already fleeing one kind of contempt or another, the transmontane world held the promise of freedom and dignity derived from land and a chance for "democratical notions" to flourish. They were drawn to the mountains as if to paradise. Land was cheap; the price of freedom would be high.

This first Hannah (for whom Hannah McKarkle will be named in novel five) travels as servant to Braddock's army into the disastrous Battle of the Wilderness. As the army goes down to defeat, Hannah is taken captive by the Shawnee. Escaping her captors, Hannah makes her way, alone and terrified, through the mountain wilderness to the Virginia territory. *O Beulah Land* opens with the dramatic account of her flight. Near death, she is found by Jeremiah Catlett, the epitome of an early mountain man—a transportee who now lays claim to vast acres of land, an Indianized white man clad in buckskins and silence, alone in an endless wilderness sustained only by the bounty of the land and his belief in a fundamentalist New Light religion. Hannah, who seems to him a gift from God, joins Jeremiah in his solitary but sanguine existence. Jeremiah earnestly believes that "Gawd led me to this hyar valley. He meant if for me. Not that I deserve it. . . . But Gawd see fitten to watch over me. He give me this hyar green pretty valley. I call it Goshen—the Land o' Goshen" (186).

Too soon their solitude is broken by others led to the mountains by inspiration less divine. Jonathan Lacey, for his service in the French and Indian Wars, claims his bounty acreage of land and prepares to move his fashionable Tidewater family into the unknown. Aware that only a working community could stave off Indians, border ruffians, and "the war with the Elements," Lacey chooses his companions from the raggle-taggle Scots, Irish, Dutch (German or "Deutsch"), Dunkards and Quakers, American provincials and British, poised anxiously to move westward from such teeming river outposts as Brandon's Landing and Kregg's Crossing.

Lacey sizes up the possibilities with historical insight but with the consciousness of his class: the lowland Dutch and the highland Scots seem to make the best settlers, "bringing with them the self-reliance of people who are used to fending for themselves"; the Irish, poverty-ridden and too much ordered or "bossed," are useless, "like hound-dogs kept leashed too long, who turn to brainless cavorting beasts when they slip their lead"; the Protestant Irish "(they call themselves the Scotch-Irish) from the north of that island . . . are tough and self-reliant to the point of blind stubbornness" (256), carrying chips on their shoulders from religious persecution and the persecution of English law.

Lacey worries about the religious persuasions of the Scots—Presbyterianism—and of the northernmost and westerly English, "who are fine settlers, being used to small farms until forced out by so much enclosure" but who "tend to the new enthusiastic religions . . . that grow like weeds here among them" (257). Wisely, Lacey concludes that the interests of common problems "will outway religion [sic] scruple," that the great industry of these settlers "we had better to have with us than against us," and that, "in their favour, too great a class sensibility as among the English has not sapped their pride and turned it to Jealousy and Pretention" and "unbounded extravagance" (258).

Lacey populates his wilderness settlement with Carvers, Cutwrights, Catletts, Solomon McKarkle, Jarcey Pentacost (a printer), and the Lacey black slaves. (Their entwined descendants populate the remaining three novels of the quintet.) All believe the promise of Isaiah has been fulfilled: "Thou shalt no more be termed forsaken; neither shall thy land any more be termed desolate; but thou shalt be called Hepzibah, and thy land Beulah, for the Lord delighteth in thee, and thy land shall be married." So they call the Lacey settlement Beulah, and they are wedded to the land. Jarcey Pentacost tells Johnny Lacey prophetically, "Johnny, y'ought to be a proud man. . . . Ye've begun a dynasty in Beulah" (303).

But Settle reminds us of the troubles brewing in paradise. Even at their far remove, the residents of Beulah hear of the growing unrest between the colonies and the English, who treat the Virginians "with polite contempt." Closer to home, Johnny Lacey fears "some tumult," as wealthy land speculators purchase legal title to good bottom lands already claimed by sweat and toil and death, forcing "the poorer classes of settlers" into the hills. We hear in Johnny's assessment of the hill folk as "the poorer classes" grist for the mill of a mythology about Appalachia already developing in early America. But Johnny is one of the few of his class who feels sympathy for the mountaineer. "I am sorry for the people here," Johnny says, "to see the new land go in such large tracts. Some of them have waited long and patiently . . . and they seem to be poorly paid for their patience" (255). The dispossession of the centuries continues.

Even closer to home, Johnny watches with growing concern the widening gulf between the stable and "civilized" Tidewater inhabitants, the Tuckahoes of Old Virginia, and the settlers of the Appalachian frontier, the Cohees of New Virginia, seen nowhere more clearly than in his own wife, Sally Brandon. A Tidewater Tuckahoe, she chafes under the lack of decorum and deference at Beulah and insults her husband and their small wilderness community. When it becomes clear that her daughter will marry the son of Hannah and Jeremiah Catlett, Sally Brandon is defeated: "That common lanky boy with them mountain eyes. . . . All them Cohees, common as dirt. . . . To think a daughter of mine should fetch up with such dirt as that" (299). In Sally's words, the hillbilly stereotype is taking shape—the gaunt, unrefined mountaineer who is the symbolic dirt upon which the ladder of social status rests but above which it rises.

As Jonathan Lacey prepares to leave Beulah for the House of Burgesses, his neighbors remind him to "stand bluff for New Virginia again the damned Tidewater" (328). Troubled, Lacey reflects on the promise and potential of the land called Beulah: "What can we become out here? We may have brought the virtues, but we've brought a cancer, too" (233). Will "the skillful and industrious people we need . . . come to be looked down on and spurned because their ways are not ours? Back a man to a wall, with arrogance and contempt, and he strikes out blind in his roused pride" (232). Nearly two hundred years later, in the shadow of Beulah, two descendants of the whole panoply of Beulah settlers will play out Lacey's worst fears in a jail on Saturday night.

Know Nothing: *The Kingdom of Kin (1837–61)*

The cancer that Jonathan Lacey foretold has invaded the body of Beulah by 1837. The heirs have left the original homesite (now in their minds a much-mythologized "fort") and established a river plantation on the opposite side of the Kanawha River. They keep slaves for farming and Irish immigrants for operating the saltworks. The second Gideon McKarkle of this quintet, unmindful of his family's sacrifices for freedom at Burford and in taming the West Virginia wilderness, runs a small inn on the plantation, cursing the "niggers" and foreigners alike for the breath of disaster beginning to lower over Beulah Land on the eve of civil war.

Young Johnny Catlett, the third Johnny of the series and heir apparent to Beulah, is, like his predecessors, drawn to inevitable doom by the gathering storm of irreconcilable political, social, and moral forces. As he grows up in the novel, he struggles to understand his changing relationships with the black slaves he has loved and often admired; with the upstart Irish immigrants, particularly the O'Neill clan; and with the members of his own, now vastly extended, kingdom of kin.

Beulah has become an asylum. "Cousins" of all the rootbound parts of the family tree feed on Beulah like parasites—Catletts, Laceys, Brandons, Cutwrights, Crawfords, and Kreggs. Even the high and mighty Tidewater "connections," facing ruin in the economic panic of Andrew Jackson's government, grudgingly look to their Cohee cousins at Beulah for help. Sally Crawford Lacey tells her husband as they travel west to the endless mountains: "They won't let it happen . . . of course, they're plainer people than we are, and haven't had our advantages, but they're very kind . . . they are Virginians even if they are transmontane and they're your kin, too."[10]

The Beulah kin try hard not to be transmontane, but to be genteel Virginians with "connections" in an eastern Virginia contemptuous of them. Cousin Annie, a Beulah parasite, points to the source of their defensive postures: "I always say as Papa did, the farther west you get, the more people *care*. They're more Virginia than we are. . . . They have to be. That's what Papa said. Though he never dreamed his own daughter would end her days in Western Virginia. In Richmond we never knew the western counties existed" (Settle, *Know Nothing* 306).

So the women of Beulah ape the fashions and the attitudes of Tidewater civility. They "take the waters" at Egeria Springs resort (the smelly sulfur springs of old Jeremiah Catlett's first wilderness homestead), where they gossip and play brag, a ritual recital of family genealogy, so "we can keep up the standard at least. Remember who we are" (307). The gentlemen of Beulah Land look on benevolently, loose their passions on black slave women, and tell their sons, "Be good to them. Poor innocent things. I've always taught you that, ain't I . . . ? Women and niggers. They ain't fitten to look after themselves" (275).

The sons worry and marvel at the kinship and new politics that have brought together, by the 1850s, the interests of the Irish O'Neills, the eastern Kreggs, and the Beulah Catletts. Defending the platform of the Know-Nothing party,[11] Crawford Kregg argues with unrecognized irony, "The foreign menace surrounds true Americans. . . . If your ancestors and mine, Johnny, could see the hungry evil-talking scum that inherit this fair land. Our forebears came here for freedom, not because they couldn't make a living, or were the spawn of foreign jails" (272). And Dan O'Neill prophesies, "Folks here abouts are damn sick of talkin' rum and niggers. They don't want no foreigners . . . we carried the western counties: they stuck together. Our turn's a-comin. West Virginia" (272). Both Johnny and Dan wonder if the railroad can be brought into Beulah Valley to reverse their crumbling fortunes.

Johnny Catlett is troubled by alarming new attitudes he does not fully understand, attitudes suggesting that slaves enslave their masters, that one man may rule over another to his own hurt. The McKarkles, "after all these years" at Beulah, move up into the mountains for "good land and not no niggers" (184). They want, Johnny says incredulously, to "keep free of ownin niggers'—as if 'twas the whites that got freed after all" (184). The McKarkles become "strange mountaineers." Tig, Johnny's slave and boyhood friend, pities Johnny: "I feel sorry for you. It's you got the burden—women and slaves . . . you ain't got no more freedom then we got. Tears, and people leanin on you—free, white and twenty-one!" (242).

"Backwoods" Beulah will not be spared the agony, ruin, or changing values that pit friends and brothers against each other in the cataclysm of civil war. The Catlett brothers themselves divide. Lewis Catlett cloaks himself in a stern religion, emulating his Beulah ancestor Jeremiah, and defies his family by ministering to the black slaves and ultimately joining the Union army. Johnny, escaping to the Kansas territory only to discover there is no escape from the country's turmoil, loyally returns to Beulah, family, and the Confederacy to which he feels little commitment, only duty. He realizes he is among those men "fated to be the know nothings, to question, to see beyond their attitudes, but not to speak" (343). In his impotence, all that remains is what might have been the prayer of Eteocles and Polyneices, "Oh, God . . . forgive us our sins and don't let me have to kill my brother" (344). Johnny Catlett leaves no heir.

The Scapegoat: *Blood Sacrifice (1912)*

As Johnny Catlett and Dan O'Neill had hoped in *Know Nothing*, the railroad came to Beulah. So did the foreigners they feared. So did the economy of the world. Beulah had been sitting on a coal seam that was waiting to unleash its terrible energy on the land and people. Mary Lee Settle has said, "In my series, the key scene is the discovery of coal in West Virginia. That changed the entire lives of everyone living there; it became a feudal coal culture, as it were."[12]

In June of 1912, Beulah is an armed camp, with a Gatling gun on the porch of the family home and Baldwin-Felts detectives lurking in the shadows. The Lacey family's mine, Seven Stars, and most other southern West

Virginia mines, are closed; the miners are on strike. Miners are being evicted from their homes, the "transportation" (new immigrant miners) are railroaded in as hated strikebreakers, and threats of violence increase.

The Lacey branch of the family has reinherited Beulah, but Beverley Lacey is weak and dying in both body and spirit (the "cancer" his ancestor predicted). Lacey tries to protect "his miners," since they have been part of the family-owned mine operation for years (and some of them are, in fact, distant family kin). Beverley understands the miners, having worked the coal face himself on his father's orders—"no boy of mine is going to lay like a hog under a chestnut tree eating chestnuts and never looking up to see where they come from."[13] Beverley wants to negotiate, especially with his old friend and distant kinsman, Jake Catlett, a leader of the union miners. But Beverley and Beulah and the old verities prove too weak to withstand the violent changes about to occur, changes that, quite literally, will move mountains.

Divergent forces arrive at Beulah to escalate the strike and disintegrate the Lacey family fortunes. Mother Jones, eighty years old and clad in black bombazine, frilly black hat, and lacy jabot, arrives to organize "her boys" and dramatize their resistance. Corporate giants, the likes of Pratt and Pierpont and Peabody and Rockefeller, arrive to buy up the land and the mines for development. The battle lines are drawn.

Beverley Lacey and his family function more as observers than as actors in the drama unfolding all around them. Lacey says to himself, "When a man's fate has already been decided for fifty million years because his land happens to be over a seam of coal, he's licked before he starts. Coal and ideals. Goddamn both of them" (Settle, *Scapegoat* 42). His wife, waiting for her husband to die, has headaches and retreats to her "sanctum sanctorum," the cupola room of the Beulah mansion. The Lacey daughters, Mary Rose, Althea, and Lily, are in love—Mary Rose with herself, Althea with all the eligible young men, such as Dan Neill and Anderson Carver, and Lily with her liberal "movements"—women's suffrage, socialism, and improving the lot of the miners, particularly that of Eduardo Pagano, a young Italian miner.

In the end, it is only Lily who is able to act. When detective Captain Dan Neill, humiliated in the past by political and financial scandal and now by Mother Jones, seeks revenge on Eddie Pagano, Lily spirits Eddie away on a freedom train to New York. Eddie escapes to a new life; Lily escapes the confinement of social convention in West Virginia, only to die in the war in Europe. For them both, for them all, an unknown, newly arrived Italian-born miner becomes the blood sacrifice, the scapegoat.

At the novel's close, Essie Catlett, Jake's wife, miner's wife, kin to the Beulah clan, moans: "They had killed a man and nothing was ever going to be the same. She could hear the change like a creek swell, flooding nearer and nearer, and all the former things were passed away. It wouldn't never be the same, not in her lifetime, never the same, never the same, she kept saying it over and over like a prayer . . . " (298).

Essie's unfortunate prayer is answered. Settle foreshadows the coalfield violence and destruction, both human and environmental, of succeeding decades, particularly the mine wars of the 1920s. The coalfield struggles only recently have become a subject popular in writing and in media presentations about Appalachia, but Settle realized early the need to understand the radical transformation taking place in Appalachia in the early days of this century. In *The Scapegoat*, she forcefully counters the view of local colorists that Appalachia has been an unchanging, nonindustrialized, quaint culture. It has been, instead, a place of blood sacrifice.

The Killing Ground: *The End and the Beginning (1960–80)*

Hannah McKarkle believes she is more like her dead Aunt Lily than her Aunt Althea or her mother, the social climber Ann Eldridge. She, like Lily, left home for New York—left Canona, West Virginia, which has grown up and over Beulah Land. Like Lily, she has worked for causes, defending the United Mine Workers at New York dinner parties, campaigning for John F. Kennedy among the "hillbillies" of her home. Like Lily, she sees herself as Antigone, making a choice for freedom rather than security.

Like Antigone, Hannah is obsessed with a duty to her dead brother, killed in a city jail. She must find out why his life meant so little: her quest gives meaning to her own life. She has written *Prisons, O Beulah Land,* and *Know Nothing* and is working on *The Scapegoat* when she comes back to West Virginia to tie up the loose threads of the story she has so carefully pieced together. The return to West Virginia reminds her of the night of Johnny's death, of her confrontation with Jake Catlett, the mountain boy who had killed him, and of her own decision for freedom—her refusal to replace her brother in the family's neatly ordered scheme. But hers is a bittersweet victory.

"Do you want to leave?" Hannah's father asks when she refuses "to be needed at home." Hannah replies: "Whoever wants to leave home?"[14] She wants to tell him that "we were made of people who for three hundred years had left home because they had to, and who had to carry with them that sense of loss, all the way to the American soul, a black, tentative place in the spirit" (Settle, *Killing Ground* 312). She now knows this is why her brother Johnny accepted death with a "thank you"—he had no place else left to go. Imprisoned by his mother's values—her foolish pride in a family heritage that, if the truth be known, had started with a London whore, included cruel oppressors of Indians and miners, "white trash" and exploiters of land and people—Johnny tried reckless living to break his dependency. But, as Hannah observes after his death, "impotent rebellion is a form of slavery" (159).

Although Johnny McKarkle never could act for freedom in his own behalf, he urged Hannah to "run for it, get in a little convertible prairie schooner and go West" (159). His legacy to her—his desperate urging to rebel, to act, to search for the free frontier—was a legacy of the centuries that epitomizes Settle's focus in the Beulah Quintet: "The model is Antigone, for all the principle characters. The oscillation between Antigone and Creon, between the settled and the wanderer, dreams and reality, gives the movement to all the volumes. It's the essence of democracy that Antigone and Creon are locked in endless conflict. They need each other. We need them both."[14]

Hannah's story comes to an end at the funeral of her Aunt Althea. There she encounters Jake Catlett, twenty years ago her brother's killer and now a successful strip-mine operator, with a new Buick, a daughter running for the legislature, and a concern for reclaiming the despoiled mountain land. Hannah thinks, "It was so strange to be there with that dressed-up well-upholstered hillbilly in his Buick, who I had last seen caged behind bars in the county jail, desperate and skinny, that I could only take it all for granted" (326).

But Jake, "mountain conjure man, teller of tales," as Hannah calls him, tells her how it came to be that he was reclaimed from prison and from despair. At the time of Johnny's killing and Jake's arrest, Aunt Althea, an unlikely heroine, finally acknowledges the mutual dependence and long intertwined kinship between the once low but now socially elite McKarkles and the "trashy" Catletts, once one of the most aristocratic of the Beulah families.

Althea does not romanticize the Appalachian past, nor does she denigrate the culture that has produced Jake. She understands the past and the culture. This frees Althea for the potent revolutionary act of the quintet. She has the charges against Jake dismissed, she takes him from the prison herself, and she puts him to work running her mining operation. Centuries after Johnny Church, about to die in the Burford churchyard, pleaded for someone "to speak a word . . . say no . . . cry cease," Althea says, "This has gone far enough" (327). The act without hope of reward. Johnny Church's definition of our humanity.

Hannah has felt she was more like Lily than Althea until this moment of epiphany. Hannah now sees that Althea refused to mythologize the past, either of family or of place, transcended the stultifying effects of class conflict, and accepted her mountain brethren as equal shareholders in Appalachia's future. This clear vision of shared humanity is Althea's legacy to Hannah, and Settle's literary legacy to Appalachia.

As Hannah flies away from West Virginia, from Beulah, the once promised land that now is exploited ground, she looks down on the landscape and ponders the turbulent history of Appalachia: "Arrogance and lack of care toward its riches had grown into arrogance and lack of care for each other" (335). Remembering the new generation she has just seen—the melting pot children of her uncle, one clearly McKarkle, one pure Pagano, and the upwardly mobile children of Jake Catlett—Hannah hopes, "We had forgotten our frontier, the same frontier that we had always found, a frontier of indifference, whether of trees or men" (335). Hannah believes that in these children she has witnessed the only lasting result of revolution: the dream of one generation becoming the right of the next.

Moving from the external landscape below her to an interior one, Hannah reflects on what she has unearthed in her searching, "a thing deeper than land." It was stratum on stratum of connection, neither by blood nor by conviction, but by one minute, some time of refusal, whether it was Johnny Church's to doff his hat, or even Jake's fist that had struck out and carried with it all the pent-up fury against "the way things are". . . . It was the choice to choose, to be singular, burn bridges, begin again, whether in a new country or a new way of seeing or a new question, which was as ancient as the wandering itself. (336)

Hannah joins the endless wanderers—Johnny Church, the first Hannah, Jonathan Lacey, Johnny Catlett, Eduardo Pagano, Lily—all those filled with discontent, demanding the fulfillment of promises, destined to "always fail and always to win," burdened with eternal vigilance and sense of loss, unblessed—the price of freedom. But those early wanderers shared the sentiment of Johnny Church in *Prisons*: "Mostly my vision is through a glass darkly" (33). Hannah, on the other hand, is imbued with the wisdom of her own search through the past and Althea's uncompromising humanity.

Reflecting on the work that has dominated her life, Settle once said, "I had a true obsession about the subject I was dealing with in 'The Beulah Quintet.' A writer with an obsession is very lucky—like Jacob with the Angel. You don't let it go until it blesses you, until you've finished."[15]

Notes

1. Roger Shattuck, "A Talk with Mary Lee Settle," *New York Times Book Review*, 26 Oct. 1980, 43. Subsequent references will appear parenthetically in the text.
2. Mary Lee Settle, *The Killing Ground* (New York: Bantam, 1983), 52. Subsequent references will appear parenthetically in the text.
3. Shattuck, "Talk with Settle," 43.
4. Shattuck, "Talk with Settle," 43.
5. Mary Lee Settle, *The Scopes Trial: The State of Tennessee v. John Thomas Scopes* (New York: Franklin Watts, 1972), 34. Also quoted in Settle's *Prisons*, 46.
6. Shattuck, "Talk with Settle," 43.
7. Mary Lee Settle, *Prisons* (New York: Ballantine, 1981), 45. Subsequent references will appear parenthetically in the text.
8. Joyce Coyne Dyer, "Mary Lee Settle's *Prisons*: Taproots History," *Southern Literary Journal* 17 (Fall 1984): 29.
9. Mary Lee Settle, *O Beulah Land* (New York: Ballantine, 1981), 68. Subsequent references will appear parenthetically in the text.
10. Mary Lee Settle, *Know Nothing* (New York: Ballantine, 1981), 13. Subsequent references will appear parenthetically in the text.
11. The Know-Nothing party, so called because of its clandestine nature, grew in the 1850s in opposition to the political power of immigrant groups. Also called the American party, it became antislavery and flourished in the border states.
12. John F. Baker, "CA Interviews the Author [Mary Lee Settle]," in *Contemporary Authors* (89–92), ed. Frances Locher (Detroit: Gale Research, 1980), 467.

13.　Mary Lee Settle, *The Scapegoat* (New York: Ballantine, 1982), 41. Subsequent references will appear parenthetically in the text.

14.　Settle, *Killing Ground,* 312. Subsequent references will appear parenthetically in the text.

15.　Shattuck, "Talk with Settle," 46.

Jacob Carpenter

Little is known of Jacob Carpenter except that he lived at Three-Mile Creek in Avery County in Western North Carolina in the second half of the nineteenth century and the early decades of the twentieth. "Uncle Jake" kept a diary in which he recorded the name and date of the departed and his frank opinion of their way of living. On April 1, 1919, he added his own name to the ledger after he "took down sick." The ledger, according to Alberta Pierson Hannum in *Look Back with Love* (1919) "contained a rare record of the prolific vigor, the courage and self-reliance that has been in America since the beginning" (16). Carpenter's diary entries were first used as chapter headings in Hannum's book. Hannum lived for a time in Avery County, where she knew Carpenter's relatives.

These "obituaries" by Carpenter are examples of found poems, and the impulse to poetry in them—some written long after the actual deaths— may not be much different from that in *Spoon River Anthology* and other elegies.

Deaths on Three-Mile Creek: 1841–1915

Wm Davis　age 100.8　dide oc 5　1841
wars old soldier in rev ware　and got his
thie brok in last fite at Kinge's monte
he wars farmer　and made brandy
and never had Drunker in famly

Franky Davis his wife　age 87　dide Sep 10　1842
she had nirve fite wolves all nite at shogar camp
to save her caff　throde fier chonks
the camp wars half mile from home
noe she must have nirv to fite wolf all nite

From *America: A Prophecy* by Jerome Rothenberg and George Quasha, © 1973 by Jerome Rothenberg and George Quasha. Reprinted by permission of Random House, Inc.

Charley Kiney   age 72   dide may 10   1852
wars farmer live in mt on bluey rige at kiney gap
he had 4 wimmin cors maried to one
rest live on farme
all went to felde   work to mak grain
all wen to crib for ther bread
all went smok hous for there mete
he cilde bote 75 to 80 hoges every yere
and wimen never had wordes bout him
haven so many wimin
if he wod be living this times
wod be hare pulde
thar wars 42 children blong to him
they all wento preching togethern
nothing sed   des aver body go long smoth
help one nother
never had any foes
got along smoth with avery bodi
I nod him

Helen Hollingsworth

Helen Hollingsworth was born in 1930 in northwestern Alabama in a farm-house built by her grandfather. The house lay in sight of land settled in 1819 by her great-great-great grandfather, whose homestead included the utmost southern and western foothill, since named Ford's Mountain, of the Appalachian chain. Today the area retains some flavor of the frontier, no-where more evident than in the names assigned to points on the land. Mr. Irey's Bottom, Sam Sugar Cane Patch, Barn Creek, and Miss Sleetie Bridge are examples.

From the start, however, the land was more than place. By the 1930s, it and its resident owners were in tandem struggling for survival: as the land saved the people from ruin, they saved it from the utter depletion of single cropping. They brought life to the slogan: "The South will come into its own when its fields are green in Winter."

Hollingsworth is professor of English at East Tennessee State University. Editor since 1980 of the *View from the Highlands,* the newsletter of the Southern Appalachian Highlands Conservancy, she received the organization's Murray Award in 1993.

The Land of Appalachia:
From Encounter to Perception

Margaret Dickie, reviewing the *Columbia Literary History of the United States* in 1989, begins with the assertion: "The present volume is literary history as commissioned art" (89). She defends the equation by citing the editors' claim in the preface that literary histories are "'commissioned by a client who engages editors to design the basic structure and gather experts to complete assigned tasks' (xiii). Then, the 'editors and publishers cooperate to construct a book that will satisfy artistic and financial considerations and be acceptable to scholars and readers' (xiii)" (89). Such a strategy, she reasons, requires no coherent structure, no overall organization. The result is a compendium of little histories; chapters take precedence over the whole (89). Two points, each applicable to Appalachian studies, emerge here: the history of our national literature is many different stories; and the compendium approach (acceptance of diversity) is imperative if we mean to perceive the subject entire.

Appalachia has multiple faces, signs, presentations. If we fail to see all of them, we miss the givens and fall into errors of imposition and assumption such as those Henry D. Shapiro refers to in *The Encyclopedia of Southern Culture* when he says that twentieth-century interpretations have forced on Appalachia "the culture of place rather than the culture of people" (1100). Once a place—a geographical region—is identified as distinct, the assumption is that its culture must be distinct.

From among all the "little histories" of Appalachia, I have chosen the land of the Southern Highlands. The most immediate and most memorable of its features, the mountains, have been chronicled, both on and off the site, with pen and ink, stylus, brush and paint, film and camera. Overland routes, water courses, inclines, declivities, curious contours, springs—hot and mineral—all wonderful aspects have caught and continue to catch the eye and the imagination of visitor and native.

Of whatever class or kind, encounters with the land repeatedly emphasize its presence. And ours. Of course, the best and most succinct records of encounter are maps. They recall boundaries, territories, migration patterns. And they bring to mind a sense of purpose realized. The land or any of its features, seen as boundary, becomes an obstacle, something to get over, around, under, through. Directional orientation of the mountains, as shown on the maps, tells us how routes came to be: gaps, elevations, and rivers determined the main lines. Movement over a route compelled the traveler to touch the land, to experience physical, sensory, immediate contact with it. Main well-traveled roads came to be joined by paths of hunters and guides who followed game, intuition, and custom. As settlers increased in number, drovers' roads—generally north-south trade arteries for livestock—developed. The settlers, having access to the Alpine meadows, or balds, where forage was abundant and free, fell naturally into stock raising. Increasing de-

Printed by permission of the author.

mand for livestock required additional paths and trails, thus increasing the volume of traffic on the main lines. Contemporary references to the drovers' roads are frequently unflattering: cows, horses, and pigs impeded travelers because of their numbers and their droppings (Brooks 98–113).

Encounters with the land seldom result in single perceptions. For whatever "mission" the land-rover was on or whatever his method of travel, he came upon streams, rivers, waterfalls, great declivities—all obstacles. But also wonders: sources of suspense and awe, causes to expend inordinate muscular strength, reasons to struggle for maintenance of balance and equilibrium. For writer, artist, or illustrator, the more vertiginous and precarious an encounter—a crossing, an ascent, a descent—the better for the account, the record, the perception.

Perceiving the land as a source of wonder began with the colonials. William Berkeley heard in 1640 of a huge mountain with great rivers which ran into a great sea west of Jamestown. He believed it a passage to India. Ultimately, in 1670, he sent John Lederer to reconnoiter the terrain and question the "truth" of the reports. Lederer went only so far as the eastern fringe of Cherokee country, to learn that over the mountains were the Cherokees, whose land was Great Waves. His report confirmed Berkeley's belief (Blackmun 48–49). In 1670, Henry Woodward, a settler on the Ashley River, made his first journey into Indian country. Of his encounter, he wrote: "I have discovered a country so delitious, pleasant and fruitful, yt were it cultivated, doubtless it would prove a second Paradise" (Blackmun 50). By report and by immediate experience, the land is a wonder, beckoning and holding open to the explorer and settler the doors of wealth, pleasure, and fame.

For the eighteenth-century scientists André Michaux and William Bartram, the land is obstacle, source of wonder, and living laboratory. On June 1, 1781, Michaux records in a diary:

> We continued . . . we had to pass over great boulders, straddle monstrous trees fallen across the jungle of shrubbery, where one could scarcely see where to go on account of the density of the thickets. Lofty peaks towered above us, and the obscurity that a rain-dark sky produced seemed to envelope us in a somber night. This trouble and confusion was increased by the noise of waterfalls and the crashing on the rocks of the river that we had to ford up to our knees. The savages tore ahead through these streams afoot, or ran along the logs . . . there are no trails in those places except those made by bears and occasionally by Indians. I was constantly afraid of treading on snakes, but terrified when I had to ride my horse across the stream on a rotting log covered with crumbling bark and slippery vegetation that had grown upon it. (Donald C. Peattie 182)

The land is fecund, wild, noisy—rich in sensory detail and evocative of fear and terror. Civilized man, the scientist, seems distinct from nature in the raw, while the savages seem a part of it.

William Bartram, in *Travels,* claims expansion of knowledge as his purpose for recording his experiences in America during the 1770s. Yet he describes "this world as a glorious apartment of the boundless palace of the sovereign Creator . . . inexpressibly beautiful and pleasing, equally free to the inspection and enjoyment of all his creatures" (15). Bartram is ever the naturalist, but he includes observations on the topography, the lay of the land. When he gets on the high road leading toward Cherokee country, he notes a "surface undulated by ridges or chains of hills, sometimes rough with rocks and stones, yet generally productive of forests . . . [it is] an uninhabited wilderness abounding with rivers and brooks" (267). As he ascends Occonne Mountain, he records what he sees and feels: "The flaming Azaleas abound, and illuminate the hill sides. . . . " (268). Moreover,

> the mountainous wilderness . . . appearing regularly undulated as the great ocean after a tempest; the undulations perfectly regular as the squama of fish, or imbrications of tile on a roof: the nearest ground to me of a perfect full green; next more glaucous; and lastly almost blue as the ether with which the most distant curve of the horizon seemed to be blended.
>
> My imagination thus wholly engaged in the contemplation of this magnificent landscape, infinitely varied, and without bound, I was almost insensible or regardless of the charming objects more within my reach: a new species of Rhododendren foremost in the assembly of mountain beauties, next the flaming Azalea, Kalmia latifolia, incarnate Robinia . . . &c. (274)

Once arrived in Cherokee country, Bartram ascends Jore, the highest peak of all. He is transported, lifted from the world of fact to ecstasy: "I beheld with rapture and astonishment a sublimely awful scene of power and magnificence, a world of mountains piled upon mountains . . . an amazing prospect of grandeur" (293). The land and its features trigger the re-creative high moments for the scientist.

Similar perceptions are legion and continue down to the present time. A few years ago, a colleague—in a wistful, Bible-quoting mood—said to me, "It's from these hills that I gather my strength." A little further back, in 1953, Mary T. Sloop, M.D., eighty and still practicing in Crossnore, North Carolina, wrote, "For me, the calendar says I must now be entering the uncharted maze of days along the highest slope of the last mountain" (232). Dr. Sloop sees the earth and feels time, but she imagines heaven. In 1987, Annie Dillard, in the first pages of *An American Childhood*, recalls her hope that the very last memory to remain in her consciousness will be of the land as it lies "this way and that" (3). James Dickey claims in 1990 that the only drawing he has ever done is of the Blue Ridge: "Three curved marks, the spirit of the hills flowing through the line that the hand puts down . . . from this there is the illusion of a true, a spiritual connection" (44).

Horace Kephart, who credits Bartram as the discoverer of "this Eden," came to the Southern Highlands in 1904 from St. Louis "seeking a Back of Beyond."

Claiming an inborn taste for the wild and romantic, he yearned for a strange land and a people who had the charm of originality. He thought, too, that he might realize the past in the present in far Appalachia. Moreover, he says, "I wanted to enjoy a free life in the open air, the thrill of exploring new ground, the joys of the chase, and the man's game of matching my woodcraft against the forces of nature, with no help from servants or hired guides" (29–30).

Encounters with wild nature showed Kephart its unrelenting laws, which he came to perceive as shaping the settlers' "Outright Independence." He argues that the key to the highlander's character is adaptation: solitude was first forced on him, then accepted as inevitable, and finally loved for its own sake (380). Emma Bell Miles, in *The Spirit of the Mountains,* adds, "The nature of the mountaineer demands that he have solitude for the unhampered growth of his personality, wing-room for his eagle heart" (73).

This longing for space is perceived by Kephart and Miles as a permanent state of mind, a way of being. Kephart stresses that the Scotch-Irish were border people long before their arrival in the new world; consequently the quality of the soil in the highlands was of less moment than its extent. To illustrate this ranking, Kephart narrates an anecdote:

> When Arthur Lee, of Virginia, was telling Samuel Johnson, in London, of a colony of Scotch who had settled upon a particularly sterile tract in western Virginia and had expressed his wonder that they should do so, Johnson replied, "Why, sir, all barrenness is comparative: the Scotch will never know that it *is* barren." (436–37)

Kephart saw as detrimental the effects of permanent settlements. As valley lands were limited, population increases would cause all kinds of deterioration. To counter these he advised establishing vocational schools and model farms with trained native leaders. By Kephart's time, the land had for more than a century been the base for community. Just fifty years earlier, in 1862, President Lincoln had signed into law the Justin S. Morrill act creating land-grant colleges, which systematically introduced agricultural and mechanical arts into the curriculum. Within a year of Kephart's advice, the Smith-Lever act established in 1914 the Cooperative Extension Service in agriculture and home economics, thus rounding out the earlier Morrill act and echoing Kephart's vision of continuity and preservation.

Throughout the nineteenth century the land was a source of wealth: logging, mining, developing the natural wonders all figured in the profit-taking. As modes of transportation improved, industry flourished and travelers came. Salt mines and iron furnaces are examples of industry; the springs and the grand hotels brought an influx of the "afflicted" seeking the curative powers of mountain air and atmosphere and of tourists seeking uncommon sights and one another.

The highlands and their extraordinary features are constants in the history of Appalachia. We—the interpreters—are transients. The National

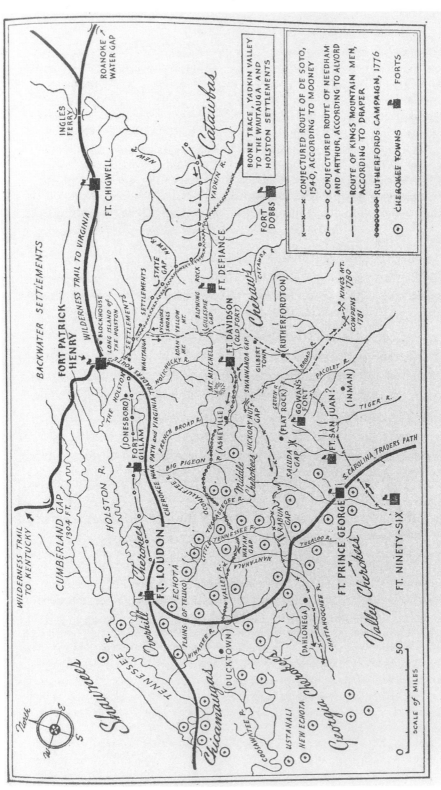

A MAP TO SHOW THE INDIAN TRIBES AND TOWNS, ROUTES OF EXPLORERS, TRADING PATHS, TRAILS, FORTS, BATTLES, AND CAMPAIGNS OF THE INDIAN AND REVOLUTIONARY WARS

Park Service, the Appalachian Trail Conference, the several land trust organizations, the Nature Conservancy, the United States Forest Service understand this truth though they don't always communicate it. The nonspecial-
ists—labeled "Eager Americans" by John C. Campbell—have views rather
more radical.

Features which drew the early traveler draw us; the differences are mainly
in the method and duration of encounter. Lederer, Woodward, Michaux,
Bartram, Kephart, and Miles physically sensed soil, water, air, and ice (if not
fire)—the cardinal elements. Their kind of encountering is advocated today by
Wendell Berry, Arthur Stupka, Ed Schell, John Ehle, and a host of our contemporaries who would have us perceive truly what is in our own backyards.

Works Cited

Bartram, William. *Travels.* Philadelphia: James and Johnson, 1791. Reprinted New York,
    NY: Dover, 1955.

Berry, Wendell. *The Unforeseen Wilderness.* Lexington : UP of Kentucky, 1969.

Blackmun, Ora. *Western North Carolina.* Boone, NC: Appalachian Consortium Press, 1977.

Brooks, Maurice. *The Appalachians.* Morgantown, WV: Seneca, 1965.

Campbell, John C. *The Southern Highlander and His Homeland.* New York: Russell Sage, 1921.

Dickey, James. "Our South in Words and Pictures." *Southern Living* 25 (Jan. 1990): 44–45.

Dickie, Margaret. Rev. of *Columbia Literary History of the United States,* ed. Emory Elliott.
    South Atlantic Review 54, no. 3 (Sept. 1989): 89–93.

Dillard, Annie. *An American Childhood.* New York: Harper and Row, 1987.

Ehle, John. *The Winter People.* New York: Harper and Row, 1982.

Kephart, Horace. *Our Southern Highlanders.* New York: Macmillan, 1913. Reprinted Knox-
    ville: U of Tennessee P, 1976, 1980.

Miles, Emma Bell. *The Spirit of the Mountains.* New York: Pott, 1905. Reprinted Knoxville:
    U of Tennessee P, 1975.

Peattie, Donald Culross. "Blue Ridge Wildflowers." *The Great Smokies and the Blue Ridge.* Ed.
    Roderick Peattie. New York: Vanguard, 1943. 172–99.

Schell, Edward. *Tennessee.* Portland, OR: Graphic Arts, 1979.

Shapiro, Henry D. "Appalachian Culture." *The Encyclopedia of Southern Culture.* Chapel Hill:
    U of North Carolina P, 1989.

Sloop, Mary T. Martin. *Miracle in the Hills.* New York: McGraw, 1953.

Stupka, Arthur. *Notes on the Birds of the Great Smoky Mountains National Park.* Knoxville: U of
    Tennessee P, 1963.

Robert Morgan

Born in Hendersonville, North Carolina, Robert Morgan graduated from the University of North Carolina at Chapel Hill and earned his M.F.A. in 1968 from the University of North Carolina at Greensboro. His awards and honors include four National Endowment for the Arts Fellowships, a Guggenheim Fellowship, and the 1991 James G. Hanes Poetry Award, presented by the Fellowship of Southern Writers. Morgan has worked as a farmer, a house painter, and a writer. Since 1971, he has taught at Cornell University, where he is currently Kappa Alpha Professor of English. Morgan's works include *Sigodlin* (1990), *Green River: New and Selected Poems* (1991), and *The Mountains Won't Remember Us and Other Stories* (1992). "The main issue of American poetry," Morgan has said, "has always been, What is self? What is America? I like the sense of discovery and spirituality in the risk of attempting definition." "The Hollow" may be considered an example of this effort.

The Hollow

First travelers to the coves of the Blue Ridge
up near the headsprings,
found no trails between
the cabin clearings. Each bit
of acreage along its branch
opened like an island inside the wilderness,
with paths to water and to the turnip patch
always stopping at the margin where
a groundhog sunned its gob of fur.
The children chewed tobacco or drank corn,
when someone picked his way
out through the thickets to obtain some.
Their best diversion of all, their most
accomplished: watching the mountain haze, the blue
haunt overhead that cooled
and lulled even the August sun
and lay out along the slopes like
a smoke of silence, an incense of their
lifelong vigil between the unstoned graves
and the wormy appletree, a screen
sent up from the oaks and hickories
to keep them hidden from disease
and god and government, and even time.

From *Groundwork,* Gnomon Press, 1979. Reprinted by permission of the publisher.

Chapter 2

Heroes and Demigods

Introduction

Certain individuals distinguish themselves from their fellows and as a result become the center of considerable attention—what Thomas Carlyle named "hero worship."

How do heroes arise, and why? The hero's nature and function are not easy to understand. But we do know that heroes are almost always a mixture of historical fact and legend. It is impossible to know the degree to which older heroes like Achilles or Odysseus have a historical basis. But in our relatively young American society we are closer to our heroes and thus better able to examine the blend of fact and fable. Our American heroes have left behind first-hand accounts, eyewitness narratives, poems, stories, and exempla which, though often inaccurate or biased, provide a starting point for examining the figure of the hero.

Appalachia has produced a striking number of heroes—not only frontiersmen like Daniel Boone and Davy Crockett, but also literary and musical geniuses, activists, educators, and missionaries. The list includes John Ross, the dignified and resourceful Cherokee chief; Sequoyah, the inventor of the Cherokee alphabet; Mother Jones, the matriarch of unionization in the coalfields; World War I hero Sergeant Alvin York; and West Virginia test pilot Chuck Yeager, who broke the sound barrier in jet flight. In the carefully researched accounts of Sergeant York by David Lee and Dixon Wecter, we can see historians attempting to separate the soldier's life from the legend. And in the case of Tom Wolfe's account of Chuck Yeager, we can see how writers may contribute to that mysterious deifying process by which heroes arise.

Parks Lanier, Jr.

Parks Lanier, Jr., has Appalachian ancestors from northern Georgia and far Western North Carolina. Born in Athens, Georgia, he is related to Sidney Lanier, whose novel *Tiger Lilies* (1867) drew early portraits of mountain people. President of the Appalachian Writers Association from 1990 to 1994, he edited *The Poetics of Appalachian Space* (1991). He enjoys writing poetry and critical essays and is professor of English at Radford College.

Sequoyah

for Marilou Awiakta

He saw the white man unfold the fragile leaf,
    Look upon its markings of the distant thoughts
        Of other men, and know.

There was magic in this knowing;
    From the leaf that spoke no words
        Came power over tribes and men and nations.
        And a spirit.

Letters he made tall like the mountain trees
    Bent like the bow that does not break
        Sharp like the arrow flying true
            Subtle as shadows on turtle's shell.

In them were chanting by the winter fire,
    Singing of women to children at night,
        Laughter of lovers, scolding of wives,
            War-lore, peace talk and prophecy.

Now his people could track their words,
    Find them tomorrow swiftly as hunters
        Who trail a deer on snow or stone,
            Bringing it down in blood,
            Praying to be forgiven.

From *Now and Then* 3, no. 3 (Autumn 1986): 23. Reprinted by permission of the author and publisher.

John Ehle

John Ehle was born December 13, 1925, in Asheville, North Carolina, and since 1957 has pursued writing as his foremost career. An alumnus of the University of North Carolina at Chapel Hill (A.B., 1949; M.A., 1952), Ehle taught at his alma mater until 1965, during which time he also served as an advisor on education to Governor Terry Sanford. Ehle has always maintained an interest in education and has served that field in a number of capacities, including membership in the National Commission for UNESCO and the National Council on the Humanities.

Ehle's writings reflect broad concerns, from frontier narratives (*The Land Breakers*, 1964), to contemporary biography (*The Free Men*, 1965), an examination of civil rights activists. *Trail of Tears* represents Ehle's historical interests, as one born on land taken from the Cherokees.

Sequoyah

Sequoyah, feeble, arthritic, in 1842 found himself buying supplies from Lewis Ross in order to travel to a portion of Mexico, now part of Texas, to look for a remnant of the Cherokee tribe that was known to live there and which he hoped might be persuaded to return to the main body. With him were his son and a few friends, all searchers, all Cherokees. They crossed the Arkansas River below Fort Gibson, passed Edwards' settlement on the Little River, and took the Leavenworth's road to Red River, arriving there fifteen days after starting.

He needed to rest for a few days. He was hungry only for bread and honey, he told his friends, and time to write. His energy was slack. One of the men found ripe, wild plums, and he ate some of them. He mentioned a pain in his chest. What in the world was he doing here? he wondered aloud. Old age gives a man dreams of conquest, but sometimes the reasoning is obscure. For him life was becoming more dream than anything else. Here he was on a journey, unsure of the details of time or place, a seeker of his people. Always the muser, the dreamer, the mender, the teacher.

After the second day of rest, the party moved on. Sequoyah endured two more weeks of pain and travel. A group of Shawnee, particularly respectful of the famous chief, gave him camp for a night. He inquired of them directions to Mexico. Six days more he traveled, arriving at a great watercourse. He and his men crossed a mountain, came to a branch, reached a bold spring where Sequoyah bathed. Bees were here in considerable number, and he asked that the group camp long enough to find honey.

From *Trail of Tears*, © 1988 by John Ehle. Used by permission of Doubleday, a division of Bantam Doubleday Dell Publishing Group, Inc.

Here the horses were stolen by a group of Tewockenees Indians. He and his men discussed returning home, but he decided to go on. They built a raft and crossed the river. Comanches came near. Because they wore caps, the Comanches thought them to be Texans and were about to kill them when they noticed the few feathers in their caps. The Comanches gave them food and listened to their explanation of needing to find the southern remnant of their people, to mend the broken pieces.

Sequoyah was too weary to go farther just now. He asked to be left alone in a cave and instructed the others to find help. They left him in this safe place, or so they believed; but the water from a river rose into the cave and he had to escape. Even though most of his provisions were lost in the water, he started toward the south, dragging his lame foot, now and again marking his trail for his companions, should they try to find him. How near death one comes in life, in old age; he reflected on that.

The others found him days later, alone. He had with him a few pages of his writings. He had honey that he had taken from a bee tree, and a bit of tobacco. He was weak. Indeed, he was close to death. Four or five days of rest did not revive him; he could scarcely move. He sent his companions on to find the Cherokees and give them the message of Sequoyah: Tell them about the great nation of Cherokee emerging to the north, where they would be welcome, where everyone was needed.

That night, alone, Sequoyah doused a bite of bread in honey and ate his supper. He read over his few pages of writings: words, words, was there no end to them? He lit his pipe. Death was quietly arriving. He knew that well enough. He noticed the stars are bright tonight.

Michael A. Lofaro

Michael A. Lofaro, a folklorist and professor of English at the University of Tennessee, was born in New York in 1948 and took degrees at Rensselaer Polytechnic Institute and the University of Maryland. Though his scholarship has focused primarily on the great frontier heroes Davy Crockett and Daniel Boone, Lofaro has also published papers on Yeats and Shakespeare, as well as on various aspects of colonial American folklore, including the War of 1812 and ballads from the era of the Revolutionary War.

The following article traces the factual life of the man who inspired so many legends.

Tracking Daniel Boone:
The Changing Frontier in American Life

In a very real sense, it is impossible to discuss the frontier without discussing Daniel Boone. Historically and imaginatively, perhaps no single individual is more central to the frontier experience.

Historically, nearly seventy of his eighty-six years were involved with the exploration and settlement of the frontier. In 1734, he was born on the western perimeter of civilization in Berks County, Pennsylvania. At the age of thirty-one, he ventured as far south as Pensacola, Florida, in search of a new home. Four years later, on June 7, 1769, after a thirty-seven-day trek that he called "a long and fatiguing journey through a mountainous wilderness," he first "saw with pleasure the beautiful level of Kentucke."[1] When he died in 1820, he was living on the western boundary of civilization in Saint Charles County, Missouri, one of the outposts for fitting out expeditions to explore the Rocky Mountains. Boone seemed constantly to place himself upon the cutting edge of civilization's advance and did so with evident relish.

Imaginatively, Daniel Boone is the prototype of the frontier hero. His life formed a general pattern that was reenacted with certain variations by the next three major heroes of the westering frontier of the nineteenth century—Davy Crockett, Kit Carson (a distant relative of Boone), and Buffalo Bill Cody. After the mastery of the physical frontier about the turn of the twentieth century, fiction became more attractive than fact, and the frontier hero became either a cowboy or a spaceman. Look closely at the characters portrayed by William S. Hart, Tom Mix, and John Wayne, or at Flash Gordon, Captain Kirk, and Luke Skywalker, and you will see reiterated the same indomitable spirit that marked the life and adventures of Daniel Boone. At the beginning of every television rerun of Star Trek, William Shatner as Captain Kirk underscores the parallel when he opens the program by dramatically intoning "Space, the final frontier," as the viewer simultaneously receives a view of the immense black and twinkling expanse of intergalactic space.

To understand fully the nature of Boone's emblematic position as the epitome of the frontier adventurer and explorer, one must also understand how the idea of an America, a "New World," a "Promised Land," shaped a new definition of the frontier. The older European concept of the frontier as a territorial limit or political boundary gave way, and the trans-Atlantic frontier instead defined a relatively unknown area that invited and even demanded exploration.

It is this same continuing desire to penetrate the unknown which links Columbus's setting sail to Captain John Smith's first walk into the forests surrounding Jamestown, to Daniel Boone's decision to leave his "family and peaceable habitation on the Yadkin River, in North Carolina, to wander

From *The Register of the Kentucky Historical Society,* Autumn 1984. Reprinted by permission of the Kentucky Historical Society.

through the wilderness of America, in quest of the country of Kentucke,"[2] and to Neil Armstrong's "giant leap for mankind," the first walk on the moon. It was no coincidence that President John F. Kennedy, an avid student of American history and heroism, chose to tie the space program closely to his "New Frontier." He recognized and sought to tap the powerful attraction of the frontier, knowing that the inherent danger and potential for conflict would again challenge and inspire Americans.

The frontier is rightly a traditional wellspring of our national spirit. It has allowed, and still allows, us to define ourselves as systemically distinct from other countries and peoples. No matter how drastically the location of the frontier changes, the spirit of the frontier remains a cultural touchstone for Americans, a source of renewal for those values that we prize most highly and praise most effusively in our heroes.

Daniel Boone is preeminent in the pantheon of frontier heroes. Like the physical frontier, he progressively moved to the west. Indeed, he and others like him were in the main responsible for the retreat of the frontier toward the setting sun. And, like the frontier, he remained an invaluable spiritual constant. Daniel Boone exemplified the American way of life, the patterns which the Revolutionary War was fought to preserve. Nationally, Boone was, and perhaps still is, the embodiment of the representative man, the ideal of frontier independence and virtue. In a country whose history has been dominated by continuing migration, the majority of early Americans believed themselves to be pioneers to some extent and, as such, identified with Boone as their hero.

In "tracking" Daniel Boone to chronicle his impact upon American life, another parallel to the frontier is apparent. Like the changing depictions of the frontier, the characterizations of "Old Dan'l" often change to suit the current beliefs or motives of the person who chooses to write or tell about him. Remember that Boone has been a highly visible "public property" for two centuries. . . . Unfortunately, [John] Filson's bombastic, ghostwritten retelling of the pioneer's "autobiographical" adventures presented the frontiersman more as a philosopher than as an Indian fighter. Yet the information gleaned from Filson's personal interviews with Boone and his companions still managed to shine through the rhetoric. Filson's Boone never captured the American public's imagination, but a quickly and rigorously edited version of his narrative did. Within a year, by means of simple editorial excision, Boone cast off his philosopher's robes and picked up his rifle.[3]

Although Daniel endorsed Filson's book as true and evidently liked to have it read to him at times, he did not hesitate to condemn another overtly rhetorical production, a book-length poem entitled *The Mountain Muse*, written by his wife's nephew, Daniel Bryan, and published in 1813.[4] It was Bryan's attempt to produce an American epic based on Boone's life and adventures and was intended to be similar in scope to Milton's *Paradise Lost*. Poetically, it was a steady disaster. Daniel sincerely regretted that Bryan was a relative, for he felt that he "could not sue him for slander." In the understated irony typical of his dry humor, he added that such works "ought to be left until the person was put in the ground."[5]

Boone's sense of humor was a facet of his character that his early biographers chose to ignore, perhaps because it turned on understatement rather than on exaggeration, the keynote of frontier humor in nineteenth-century America.[6] Two other anecdotes told about Daniel in his eighties aptly illustrate this little-known side of the pioneer. The first took place after an unfortunate political misunderstanding in which the grant of 10,000 arpents (approximately 8,500 acres) of land he was to receive for services to his country was reduced to 1,000 arpents. When that land was sold to pay his debts in May 1815, Boone came face to face with the husband of an orphan girl to whom he had generously deeded a tract of Kentucky land. As with so many of his claims, it was "shingled" or overlapped by a better claim and therefore proved worthless. The man confronted Boone with a demand that he reimburse him for the loss of the gift. Boone was seldom reported to make any ungracious remark, but in this instance he quietly told the husband "that he thought he had come a great distance to suck a bull, and he reckoned he would have to go home dry."[7]

Another relatively unknown example of Boone's wit was recorded by Chester Harding when he traveled to Missouri to paint the famous frontiersman's portrait in 1819, the year before Daniel's death. Harding stated that though Boone's "memory of passing events was much impaired, yet he would amuse me every day by his anecdotes of his earlier life. I asked him one day, just after his description of one of his long hunts, if he never got lost, having no compass. 'No,' said he, 'I can't say as ever I was lost, but I was *bewildered* once for three days.'"[8] Daniel's humor was dry to the last.

To the reader who is equally "bewildered" by the contrasting portraits of Boone, it soon becomes clear that, like John Filson and Daniel Bryan, each biographer or commentator on Boone's life consciously or unconsciously attempts to shape the pioneer's image according to his own predispositions and beliefs. In 1823, Byron includes seven verses about Boone in his long poem *Don Juan*. He uses the frontiersman as an idealized example of Rousseau's natural man to demonstrate that spiritual purity, serenity, freedom, simplicity, and good health are the results of a life lived in wilderness. Byron also promoted Boone to the rank of general.[9]

Another romantic portrayal of Boone as the natural man resulted from that now-famous meeting with John James Audubon in Kentucky about 1810. Audubon's description of his stay with Boone unmistakably reveals the strong influence that the backwoodsman's presence exerted on his mind. Audubon stated:

> The stature and general appearance of this wanderer of the western forests approached the gigantic. His chest was broad and prominent; his muscular power displayed themselves in every limb; his countenance gave indication of his great courage, enterprise and perseverance; and

when he spoke, the very motion of his lips brought the impression that whatever he uttered could not be otherwise than strictly true. I undressed, whilst he merely took off his hunting shirt, and arranged a few folds of blankets on the floor, choosing rather to lie there, as he observed, than on the softest bed.[10]

Although he is here not mythologizing the meeting which had occurred twenty years earlier, since the passage is a transcription of his original description of the frontiersman entered in his journal,[11] Audubon nonetheless chooses to retain his original, highly romanticized conception of Boone which literally defines a hero who is larger than life. While there is no reason to impugn the accuracy of Audubon's personal impressions of Boone's character, there is substantial evidence that Boone's "stature and general appearance" did not approach the "gigantic."[12]

Timothy Flint continued and expanded the treatment of Boone as the natural man in his full-length, best-selling *Biographical Memoir of Daniel Boone.* First published in 1833, it went through fourteen editions by 1868. However, Flint saw Daniel's life in the wilderness as only an initial stage in the working-out of a grand Providential plan which culminated in the triumph of civilization and civilized life. Flint stated flatly that "in the order of things, . . . it was necessary, that men like Finley and Boone, and their companions, should precede in the wilderness, to prepare the way for the multitudes who would soon follow."[13] Boone the hunter and Boone the pioneer were characterizations that were subsumed within Flint's main theme of the advance of civilization.

The changes in the character of Daniel Boone as a result of literary license go on and on. William Gilmore Simms presented a Boone who was a "knight errant," a heroic exemplar of the virtues of the southern aristocracy. Yet this noble lover of natural beauty also paralleled James Fenimore Cooper's Hawkeye as a man who could out-Indian the Indians and who, as Simms said, "was a hunter of men too, upon occasion."[14]

This more savage side of the pioneer was given full voice in John A. McClung's *Sketches of Western Adventure,* published in 1832, thirteen years before Simms's sketch. McClung, a devotee of "the only good Indian is a dead Indian" school of thought, gave his readers a Boone who pined away for the "thrilling excitement of savage warfare" after Kentucky had become too thickly settled.[15] This Boone also made a single appearance in the Crockett almanacs. Termed "The Great Lion and Father of Adventures of the Back Woods," Boone defeated an Indian attack upon his cabin by decapitating two Indians with his sword, which he then used to sever his daughter's hair in such a way that the remaining braves who were trying to drag her away "fell full length into the fire."[16]

The violent Boone of the first half of the nineteenth century did make his way into a small number of dime novels, although his adventures, like those of Davy Crockett and Kit Carson, were vastly outnumbered by the hundreds of cheap publications devoted to the exploits of Buffalo Bill. One brief example should suffice. Part of Burke Brentford's *The Thunderbolt of the Border; or, Daniel Boone on the Warpath* is based upon the actual event of Boone's rescuing both his daughter and the daughter of Colonel Callaway from the Indians. (Historically, two, not one, of Callaway's daughters were taken.) Brentford, however, heightens the rescue by creating a hand-to-hand combat scene between Boone and an Indian lookout: "One of Boone's hands grasped the redskin's windpipe with a grip of iron before a sound issued from it, the other dashed the uplifted tomahawk aside, and the next instant the knife of the hunter passed through the man's heart, cleaving downward from the shoulder blade."[17] Perhaps Audubon was right about Boone's "gigantic" size.

These various depictions of Boone do not demonstrate all the changes in his portrayals over the span of two hundred years but do give a sense of their variety. Mention should be made also of the pamphlet published in 1823 by C. Wilder which cast Boone in the role of a white Indian or racial turncoat by plagiarizing large sections from a book entitled *An Account of the Remarkable Occurrences in the Life and Travels of Col. James Smith* (Lexington, 1799) and attributing them out of context to Boone.[18] He did so to flesh out the pioneer's life after 1782, the cutoff date of Filson's narrative. Also worthy of note, as likely the most idiosyncratic biography of the frontiersman, was that penned by John Mason Peck, who presented Boone not as the hunter or pioneer, but rather as the ideal Christian, family man, and farmer, and as a pious teetotaler.[19] Peck was an itinerant Baptist minister.

With all the material already mentioned, the twentieth century remains untouched. The modern biographies, the silent and talking pictures, five television seasons of Fess Parker starring as Daniel Boone, and, more recently, a feature-length cartoon of considerable historical accuracy, all continue the tradition according to which writers see in Daniel Boone what they believe typifies the best of the American spirit at a particular point in history. In tracking Daniel Boone, one thing becomes very sure: Boone's malleability insures his stability as our greatest frontier hero.

But let him speak for himself. The following letter written by Daniel Boone was located only in April 1984, at the Huntington Library in San Marino, California. Dated September 11, 1782, at Lexington and addressed to Governor Benjamin Harrison, it concerns the aftermath of the Battle of Blue Licks. It does not have the urgency or mass of detail of Boone's famous August 30 letter to the governor on the battle, but instead focuses on the practical matter of resupplying the nearly exhausted stores of the county.

From a Late R[etur]n of the Publick Stores of this County, [I fear?] they are almost exhausted [.] The no less Dangerous, than Precarious Situation of our County Requires An Immediate supply of Ammunition & Salt—for which purpose I Rely on your Excellency Goodness in furnishing Mr. And.ʷ Steele with Two Hund,ᵈ Weight of Powder & Lead in Proportion a small Quantity of Gun flints & some writing Paper, &

as he has hitherto had the Conducting of [such?] [s]tores in this County I hope your Excellency will Confirm his Appointme[nt. He] seems well Calculated for such pub[lic t]rust—

As the Dry Beef [in our?] store is of an unsound Quality & not [suit?]able & It may be necessary to Lay up a [new store?] this fall for Emergencie[.] [For this pur?]pose I would Request Twenty [one word missing] [bus]hels of salt as our store is Indebt by the Late fatal Excurtion of the savages—

It is [not for me to?] [give?] you a Detail of [that?] [3 or 4 words missing] as I Expect you have already Rec.[d] a perfect account[.] I would only Inform y[r] your [*sic.*] Excellen[y], that Sixty six of our Brave Kanetuckians fell the Matchless Massecraed victoms of their Unprecedented Crueltie, Y[r] Excellency, Compliance with the above Request will Oblige Your Assured f[r]iend & Hb.[e] Sev[r]

Daniel Boone[20]

This letter allows us to fix Boone in history and view him as a concerned military leader. However, track Daniel Boone through his other varied careers of explorer, adventurer, wagoner, husband, father, farmer, surveyor, land speculator, conservationist, hunter, spy, scout, sheriff, coroner,[21] tavern proprietor, elected representative, and Spanish magistrate, and you can see a series of categories which tell little of the essential unity of the man, his legend, and his legacy. View him through the vantage point of the changing frontier, see him as a vital evolving part of the "spirit of America" through his many depictions, and realize that, as long as Americans venture forth into the unknown in any field or endeavor, we need only look up ahead to see the trail "Old Dan'l" is still blazing for us.

Notes

1. "The Adventures of Col. Daniel Boon," in John Filson, *The Discovery, Settlement and Present State of Kentucke* . . . (Wilmington, DE: James Adams, 1784), 51.

2. "Adventures of Col. Daniel Boon," 50–51.

3. For a detailed treatment of this issue, see Michael A. Lofaro, "The Eighteenth Century 'Autobiographies' of Daniel Boone," *Register of the Kentucky Historical Society* 76 (1978): 85–97. New information kindly provided by Louis R. Boone of St. Louis, Missouri, a descendant of the pioneer, has allowed an earlier dating of the condensed "autobiography" than that which was stated in my article.

4. Filson, *Kentucke,* 3; Lyman C. Draper Manuscript Collection, 7C 43 (1), State Historical Society of Wisconsin, Madison; John A. McClung, *Sketches of Western Adventure* . . . (Maysville, KY: Collins, 1832), 92; William H. Bogart, *Daniel Boone and the Hunters of Kentucky* (1854; Auburn, NY: Miller, Orton, and Co., 1857), 51; Daniel Bryan, *The Mountain Muse: Comprising the Adventures of Daniel Boone and the Powers of Virtuous and Refined Beauty* (Harrisonburg, VA: Davidson and Bourne, 1813).

5. Draper MSS, 7C 43 (1).

6. For more information, see Michael A. Lofaro, "From Boone to Crockett: The Beginnings of Frontier Humor," *Mississippi Folklore Register* 14 (1980): 57–74.

7. Draper MSS, 6S 252.

8. Chester Harding, *My Egotistigraphy* (Cambridge, MA: John Wilson, 1866), 36.

9. Lord George Gordon Byron, *Byron's Don Juan: A Variorum Edition,* ed. Truman G. Steffan and Willis W. Pratt, (4 vols., Austin: U of Texas P, 1957), 3: 143–45. Byron's "error" was corrected in those American works that reprinted the verses as a separate eulogy.

10. John James Audubon, *Ornithological Biography* (5 vols., Edinburgh: Adams and Charles Black, 1831), 1: 503.

11. Maria R. Audubon, *Audubon and His Journals* (2 vols., 1897; Freeport, NY: Books for Libraries Press, 1972), 2: 241.

12. See, e.g., John Bakeless, *Daniel Boone: Master of the Wilderness* (1939; Harrisburg, PA: Stackpole Co., 1965), 338–39, and John Bakeless, "Daniel Boone—James Mosely," in William Gilmore Simms's *Southern and Western Magazine* 2 (Aug. 1845): 131–32.

13. Timothy Flint, *Biographical Memoir of Daniel Boone,* ed. James K. Folsom (1833; New Haven, CT: College and UP, 1967), 46.

14. William Gilmore Simms, "Daniel Boone—The First Hunter of Kentucky," in *Views and Reviews in American Literature, History and Fiction* (1845; Cambridge, MA: Belknap P, 1962), 149–51. The article first appeared earlier that year in Simms's *Southern and Western Magazine* 1 (Apr. 1845): 225–42.

15. McClung, *Sketches of Western Adventure,* 91.

16. *Crockett Almanac* (Philadelphia, 1852), [5].

17. Burke Brentford, *The Thunderbolt of the Border, or, Daniel Boone on the Warpath* (New York, 6 Aug. 1891), 3. This issue is #125 of Street and Smith's Log Cabin Library.

18. Daniel Boone, *Life and Adventures of Colonel Daniel Boone . . .* (Brooklyn, NY, 1823); rpt. by Henry Trumbull in 1824 and as #17 of Heartman's Historical Series (New York, 1916).

19. John Mason Peck, *Life of Daniel Boone, the Pioneer of Kentucky,* in *The Library of American Biography,* 2d ser., vol. 13, ed. Jared Sparks (Boston, 1847). At present, no comprehensive and competent treatment of all the biographical portrayals of Daniel Boone is available. Henry Nash Smith's perceptive chapter on the pioneer in his *Virgin Land: The American West as Symbol and Myth* (1950; Cambridge, MA: Harvard UP, 1970) merely touches on the tradition. The only extensive examination of the Boone biographies is contained in Richard Slotkin's *Regeneration Through Violence: The Mythology of the American Frontier, 1600–1860* (Middletown, CT: Wesleyan UP, 1973). Slotkin's analysis of the biographies as part of the American frontier mythology, which advances the argument that Boone's portrayals are modeled closely on the divine king myth described in Sir James Frazer's *The Golden Bough,* is provocative but unconvincing. For example, his discussion of distinct regional depictions of Boone in the first half of the nineteenth century in the West, East, and South (403, 440, 461) is genuinely informative but ignores readily identifiable cross-sectional influences. In my opinion, Slotkin unfairly subordinates the biographies to his heavily thesis-oriented analysis of the alleged mythological unity in frontier writings spanning 260 years.

20. This letter (HM 39952) is edited and reproduced by permission of the Huntington

Library, San Marino, CA. The letter is in poor condition and occupies both sides of a single sheet of paper. It may, in fact, be the conclusion of a longer letter. Another problem occurs with the *dating* of the letter. The statement "Lexington Sb.ʳ 11th 17[?]" appears to conclude Boone's message. When the item was cataloged separately, the date was read as "Fb.ʸ 11th [1780?]." The [1780?] date is incorrect since Boone is describing the country's situation after the Battle of Blue Licks (19 Aug. 1782). The difference of opinion regarding the abbreviation of the month is due to Boone's orthography. Only the letter "b" is absolutely clear. My choice of Sept. rather than Feb. rests on three premises: the proximity to the date of the battle; Boone's penchant for irregular spelling; and the fact that Andrew Steele, the man mentioned in Boone's letter, also used the phrase "the matchless massacraed victims of their unprecedented Cruelty" to refer to those killed at Blue Licks in his letter dated 26 Aug. 1782, and sent to Gov. Harrison. Steele used the phrase again in writing the governor on 12 Sept. 1782, the day after I believe Boone wrote his letter, to describe the 860 casualties that had occurred since 1776 (*Calendar of Virginia State Papers . . . ,* vol. 3 [Richmond, 1883]: 270, 303). The manuscript staff of the Huntington Library, upon reviewing the document, agrees with my dating of the letter. If I am incorrect, the letter is then likely dated 11 Feb. 1783, since the peace treaty was signed on 19 Apr. 1783.

21.   I only recently discovered that Boone was appointed coroner of Fayette County on 7 Apr. 1781 (*Journals of the Council of the State of Virginia* [Richmond, 1932], 2: 329).

George Gordon, Lord Byron

Born in London in 1788, Lord Byron is well known as a British Romantic poet. Although he was lame from birth, he attended school and was educated at Harrow School and Trinity College, Cambridge, where he read much, swam, boxed, and led a dissipated life. In 1809 he set out on a grand tour of Europe, which he later used as the source for *Childe Harold's Pilgrimage* (1812). Other works followed in quick succession: *Giaour* (1813), *Lara* (1814), *The Bride of Corinth* (1815), and the last canto of *Childe Harold* (1817). His literary success and his intriguing love affairs made him the darling of London society. A staunch champion of personal and political freedom, he gave help to Italian revolutionaries, and with Leigh Hunt founded the short-lived journal *The Liberal*. In 1823 he joined the Greek cause against the Turks and died at Missolonghi. His love of liberty and the romantic idealization of nature is nowhere more evident than in canto 8 of *Don Juan,* which celebrates the free, adventurous spirit of Daniel Boone.

Daniel Boone

LXI

Of all men, saving Sylla the man-slayer,
    Who passes for in life and death most lucky,
Of the great names which in our faces stare,
    The General Boon, back-woodsman of Kentucky,
Was happiest amongst mortals anywhere;
    For killing nothing but a bear or buck, he
Enjoy'd the lonely, vigorous, harmless days
Of his old age in wilds of deepest maze.

LXII

Crime came not near him—she is not the child
    Of solitude; Health shrank not from him—for
Her home is in the rarely trodden wild,
    Where if men seek her not, and death be more
Their choice than life, forgive them, as beguiled
    By habit to what their own hearts abhor—
In cities caged. The present case in point I
Cite is, that Boon lived hunting up to ninety;

LXIII

And what's still stranger, left behind a name
    For which men vainly decimate the throng,
Not only famous, but of that *good* fame,
    Without which glory's but a tavern song—
Simple, serene, the antipodes of shame,
    Which hate nor envy e'er could tinge with wrong;
An active hermit, even in age the child
Of Nature, or the man of Ross run wild.

LXIV

'Tis true he shrank from men even of his nation,
    When they built up unto his darling trees,—
He moved some hundred miles off, for a station
    Where there were fewer houses and more ease;
The inconvenience of civilisation
    Is, that you neither can be pleased nor please;
But where he met the individual man,
He show'd himself as kind as mortal can.

Michael A. Lofaro

See volume 1, chapter 2, for biography.

From David to Davy:
The Growth of the Legendary Crockett

> In the following pages I have endeavoured to give the reader
> a plain, honest, homespun account of my state in life, and
> some few of the difficulties which have attended me along
> its journey, down to this time. . . . I know that, obscure as
> I am, my name is making considerable deal of fuss in the
> world. I can't tell why it is, nor in what it is to end. Go
> where I will, everybody seems anxious to get a peep at me.
> . . . But just read for yourself, and my ears for a heel tap
> [the bit of liquor left in a glass after drinking], if before
> you get through you don't say, with many a good-natured
> smile and hearty laugh, "This is truly the very thing itself—
> the exact image of its Author, DAVID CROCKETT."
>
> From *A Narrative of the Life of David Crockett*
> *of the State of Tennessee*[1]

The famous frontiersman turned politician revealed a good deal about himself and his era in these brief excerpts from the preface to his autobiography.
He presented himself to his readers as a truthful, "down-home" country boy
who was modestly bemused at his fame and who simultaneously recognized
the political appeal of portraying the events in his life with a thoroughly
engaging and genial sense of humor. The publication of this bestseller in
1834 also marked Crockett's first major attempt to separate himself from his
growing legend, a legend that would literally engulf "the exact image of its
Author" within a few years.

Timing is often a crucial factor in the creation of a historical or legendary
hero. David Crockett at least inherently sensed that the "considerable deal of
fuss in the world" that he now made gave him a rare opportunity for true
historical greatness. His *Narrative* was in part a corrective to what he called
the "catchpenny errors," "outlandish" language, and "false notions" of the
"autobiographical" work published under his name by Mathew St. Clair
Clarke a year earlier in 1833 and was in part a campaign biography designed

From Introduction to *David Crockett: The Man and the Legend,* ed. John B. Shackford (Univer-
    sity of North Carolina Press, 1986). Substantial portions of this article are reprinted
    here by permission of the publisher.

to pave the way for a presidential bid in the election of 1836, when Andrew Jackson was to step down from office.[2] Crockett's dilemma was that he had to deny the "outlandish" Crockett in order to succeed as a serious candidate, yet could not totally divorce himself from the same backwoods image that was the source of much of his political appeal.

Crockett arrived at this dramatic juncture in his career through his own efforts, but also because of the era in which he lived. Born in 1786, fifty-two years after the birth of Daniel Boone and only ten years after the Declaration of Independence, Crockett matured with the new nation. By the time that Boone's *Biographical Memoir* and Crockett's *Sketches and Eccentricities,* the first full-length biography of each of the two men, appeared in 1833, it was clear that the role of the frontier hero had been redefined and had exerted considerable influence upon American politics—as witnessed by Jackson's election and the age ushered in by his presidency.[3] The American ideal of the dedicated and noble pioneer of the eighteenth century had given way to the brash and cocky backwoodsman of the nineteenth century, just as the centers of political power had begun to move from the drawing room to the tavern, from the control of the upper class to within reach of the common man.

Ironically termed the "gentleman from the cane," Crockett early in his career was viewed by some of his fellow members of the Tennessee legislature as an unsophisticated and unrefined politician. They thought that he had stepped directly from the wild recesses of a West Tennessee canebreak onto the floor of the House. Crockett turned their mockery to his advantage by pinning to his shirt a fancy cambric ruffle of the same cut as that of his main antagonist, a Mr. James C. Mitchell. When he rose to speak after one of Mitchell's particularly informative addresses, David's newly affected finery stood out on his backwoodsman's shirt in such a ridiculous fashion that the members of the House burst into a prolonged tide of laughter that forced an embarrassed Mitchell from the chamber.[4]

Crockett was no fool. He knew his image and continued to manipulate it to his political advantage, especially in his early campaigns.[5] His run against Dr. William E. Butler in the state elections of 1823 provided some of the best examples of this same type of wit. Crockett played up his "gentleman from the cane" image and labeled Butler an aristocrat. When visiting his opponent's house and noting the expensive furnishings, he refused to walk upon a particularly handsome rug and subsequently incorporated a telling comparison as a high point in his speeches: "Fellow citizens, my aristocratic competitor has a fine carpet, and every day he *walks* on truck finer than any gowns your wife or your daughters, in all their lives, ever *wore!*" He told Butler that he would have a buckskin hunting shirt made with two pockets large enough to hold a big twist of chewing tobacco and a bottle of liquor. After a prospective voter took a taste of "the *creature,*" Crockett said that he would immediately hand him a replacement for the "chaw" he had to discard to take the drink and thus "he would not be worse off than when I found him; and I would be sure to leave him in a first-rate good humour." Crockett once even memorized Butler's standard campaign speech and delivered it word for word just before it was Butler's turn to speak.[6] The two men fortunately remained on good terms, and Butler often enjoyed Crockett's brand of entertainment as much as the rest of their audiences.

David Crockett's sense of humor was one of the reasons that he was perhaps more emblematic of the spirit of Jacksonian democracy than Jackson himself. Never achieving the heights of Jackson's great successes in the military and political arenas, he was never removed from a realm deemed approachable by the average citizen. His humor and, somewhat ironically, his lack of extraordinary success and achievement, may well have kept Crockett a more attainable and attractive ideal in the popular mind during his public career. Again, timing was critical. Had he not opposed Jackson so vehemently, had he not taken time from his congressional duties to tour the northern and eastern states as a possible presidential candidate, he might not have lost his bid for reelection to the House in 1835 to Adam Huntsman, a peglegged lawyer supported by Jackson and Governor Carroll of Tennessee, by 252 votes.[7] It was because of this defeat that he decided to explore Texas or, as Crockett himself put it: "Since you have chosen to elect a man with a timber toe to succeed me, you may all go to hell and I will go to Texas."[8] At this point, he had no intention of joining the fight for Texas independence. His last surviving letters, however, show that Texas changed his plans. Crockett literally rejoiced at the opportunities before him and spoke confidently of the fact that Texas would allow him to rejuvenate his political career and to acquire the wealth that had eluded him all his life by becoming the land agent for the new territory.[9] He clearly felt that he was in the right place at the right time; he might well have succeeded if he had not become a participant in the Battle of the Alamo.

The motives behind his allegiance to Texas almost always are obscured by the controversy over the much-disputed facts surrounding Crockett's death at the Alamo. Based on the best evidence available to him, James A. Shackford, Crockett's scholarly biographer, built a case supporting the oral eyewitness accounts of Madam Candelaria, who testified that David was one of the first defenders killed and that he died unarmed. Shackford was not totally convinced on the matter and rightly asserted that "too much has been made over the details of *how* David died at the Alamo."[10] New information has come to light that surprisingly indicates that the story as given in the "fictional" *Col. Crockett's Exploits and Adventures in Texas* is substantially correct. The two key works on which this view is based are *With Santa Anna in Texas: A Personal Narrative of the Revolution,* the eyewitness diary of Lieutenant José Enrique de la Peña, and a study of it and several corroborating accounts by Dan Kilgore in *How Did Davy Die?* Lieutenant de la Peña identified Crockett as one of the six or seven survivors who were captured when Mexican troops took the Alamo about six o'clock in the morning. The captives were taken before Santa Anna under the protection of General Manuel Fernández Castrillón, who hoped to have them spared, despite Santa Anna's orders to take no prisoners. Angered by Castrillón's insubordination, the general ordered them executed immediately. Although, according to de la Peña, the battle-proven Mexican "commanders and officers were outraged at this action and did not support the order, hoping that once the fury of the moment had blown over these men would be spared." Several officers, who had not fought and who evidently were hoping to win Santa Anna's favor, carried out his wishes. It was likely that the entire episode, from capture to execution, took place within only a few minutes.[11]

While the death of the historical *David* Crockett at the Battle of the Alamo on March 6, 1836, assured that he would replace Daniel Boone as the then-preeminent hero of the American frontier, it also loosed the floodgates for the unrestrained expansion of the image of the legendary *Davy* Crockett in the popular media of his day and ours.

David in fact already had become Davy to a certain extent. The *Sketches and Eccentricities,* his *Narrative, An Account of Colonel Crockett's Tour to the North and Down East* (the Whig account of his three-week campaign swing in 1835, probably written by William Clark),[12] and the posthumously published *Col. Crockett's Exploits and Adventures in Texas* contained a number of tales that had taken root in fertile soil. As part of the vanguard of what was later termed the "humor of the old Southwest," these stories were reprinted in a series of very popular Crockett Almanacs that were published from 1835 to 1856.[13] The early fictional Davy was not yet a full-blown "ring-tailed roarer" in the first almanac, but, building upon the historical David's ability to give vent to a humorous boast, Davy became a screamer who could "run faster,—jump higher,—squat lower,—dive deeper,—stay under longer,—and come out drier, than any man in the whole country." The ante escalated rapidly in the hands of the Boston literary hacks who created tall tales for the next six almanacs of the "Nashville" series. In the 1836 issue, for example, Davy had an epic underwater battle with the twelve-foot long "monstratious great Cat-Fish," and in the next volume, he saved the United States from destruction by wringing the tail off Halley's comet. Davy, however, wanted nothing more to do with "see-less-tial bodies" after this experience for, as he explained,

> I was appointed by the President to stand on the Allegheny Mountains and wring the Comet's tail off. I did so, but got my hands most shockingly burnt, and the hair singed off my head, so that I was as bald as a trencher. I div right down into the Waybosh river, and thus saved my best stone blue coat and grass green small clothes. With the help of Bear's grease, I have brought out a new crop, but the hair grows in bights and tufts, like hussuck grass in a meadow, and it keeps in such a snarl, that all the teeth will instantly snap out of an ivory comb when brought within ten feet of it.[14]

This adventure was but a mild warm-up for America's first comic superman. In later almanacs, Crockett convinced his pet alligator to bite its tail and churn like a paddle wheel so he could ride up Niagara Falls; he also became a Promethean figure who saved the solar system by unfreezing the "airth" and sun that had "friz fast" to their axes with hot bear "ile" and then "walked home, introducin' the people to fresh daylight with a piece of sunrise in my pocket. . . ." But there was as well a darker side to Davy's "comedy" which proved a less flattering mirror of America's cultural past. His creators made him an ardent warrior in the cause of territorial expansionism, with Mexico and Oregon only the nearest of his targets. And perhaps most distasteful to modern sensibilities, Davy was the "humanitarian" who killed and boiled an Indian to make a tonic to help cure his pet bear's stomach disorder.[15] Blacks and other "sub-humans" fared no better.

The violent, jingoistic, and racist Davy of the almanacs competed with, and was eventually subsumed by, a far more enduring tradition of Davy as the hero of romantic melodrama. From Nimrod Wildfire, James Kirke Paulding's Crockettesque character in his play *The Lion of the West* (1831), to Frank Mayo as the co-author and leading man in the long-running *Davy Crockett; Or, Be Sure You're Right Then Go Ahead*, the heritage was passed on through a series of silent and modern films that culminated in the Davys played by Fess Parker and John Wayne, who were equally at home in movie theaters or in rerun after rerun on television screens. Nineteenth-century drama and twentieth-century film always presented a heroic Crockett in the kindest light.[16] Courageous, dashing, and true blue, this nobleman of nature protected with equal fervor his country and all those who were helpless.

The Walt Disney–Fess Parker–inspired Crockett craze of the mid-1950s was without question the height of the impact of this legendary Crockett. A media-generated event, it occurred at the point when television began to reach a mass market and as Walt Disney entered that fledgling medium with his innovative premise that children were a constantly changing and renewable audience. Disney had no idea of how powerful a force he had tapped by reintroducing Crockett through television. Grosset and Dunlap's *The Story of Davy Crockett* sold ten thousand copies a year before 1955; during the craze, sales increased to thirty times that figure. The youth of America clamored for coonskin caps and fringed deerskin jackets and pants, department stores set up special Crockett sections to sell clothes and other Crockett paraphernalia (such as records, lunch boxes, towels, wallets, athletic equipment, baby shoes, and even women's panties), and the total Crockett industry realized sales of approximately $300 million.[17]

Although Davy's perennial bestseller status meant that economic motives were behind the creation of many of the different Crocketts, that fact need not tarnish our enjoyment of them. Davy, in whatever guise he appears and for whatever reason, almost always gives his audiences more than their money's worth. Neither should the Gordian tangle of man and myth obscure the essential unity of Crockett. He is congressman, speculator, superman, blazing patriot, boisterous braggart, and backwoods trickster, but all these roles are smoothly dissolved by a broad, puckish, good humor and recast into a single fun-loving, dominant presence. The characterization is not fragmented or contradictory but whole. Like Whitman in "Song of Myself," Crockett is large; he contains multitudes. Invested in him, man and myth, are the hopes and beliefs, the virtues and values, and the shortcomings and triumphs of each generation that takes him up as their hero. Ultimately, it is the inseparability of the historical and fictional components of the legend in the popular mind that generates and guarantees the great effect Crockett has on American thought and culture. He is a character no longer bound by the achievements of mortal man, but only by desire and the imagination of those who seek him out; a culture hero whose adventures both parallel those of Old World heroic narratives and who, at the same time, is truly a "gen-u-ine original."

Notes

1. An earlier version of this work appeared as the introduction to the revised 1986 edition of *David Crockett: The Man and the Legend,* ed. James A. Shackford (1956; Chapel Hill: U of North Carolina P, 1986). I gratefully acknowledge the kindness of the press in allowing use of this material. David Crockett, *A Narrative of the Life of David Crockett of the State of Tennessee,* ed. James A. Shackford and Stanley J. Folmsbee (1834; rpt. in an annotated facsimile ed., Knoxville: U of Tennessee P, 1973), 6, 7, 10–11.

2. Crockett, *Narrative,* 3, 4, 5. [Mathew St. Clair Clarke], *The Life and Adventures of Colonel David Crockett of West Tennessee* (Cincinnati, OH: Published for the proprietor, 1833). The latter work will subsequently be cited by its best known title, under which it was reissued that same year: *Sketches and Eccentricities of Col. David Crockett, of West Tennessee* (New York: J.& J. Harper, 1833). Although Crockett pleaded ignorance as to the identity of the author, it was surely he who provided the bulk of the biographical information to his friend Clarke (see Crockett, *Narrative,* p. 3, n. 3).

3. Timothy Flint, *Biographical Memoir of Daniel Boone* (Cincinnati, OH: N. & G. Guilford, 1833).

4. [Clarke], *Sketches and Eccentricities,* 57–59; Shackford, *David Crockett,* 52–53.

5. Crockett did not seem to exercise the same control over his image in the national arena. When he first came to Congress in 1827, the Jacksonians applauded his backwoods virtues (in part as a means of exerting some sway over his vote), and the Whigs just as vigorously ridiculed him as a bumpkin and a fool. When Jackson was elected to a second term as president in 1832, the Whigs exploited Crockett's growing animosity toward Jackson, courted him as an anti-Jackson candidate for the presidential election of 1836, and reversed their portrayal of him. Quite naturally, the supporters of Jackson then took up the old Whig depictions. Crockett's increased prominence made him a valuable tool for others to manipulate and correspondingly decreased his own ability to shape his image.

6. Shackford, *David Crockett,* 64–65; Crockett, *Narrative,* 168–70.

7. Shackford, *David Crockett,* 203–5; Crockett, *Narrative,* 211, n. 18. The official returns were Huntsman, 4,652 and Crockett, 4,400.

8. [Richard Penn Smith], *Col. Crockett's Exploits and Adventures in Texas . . . Written by*

Himself (Philadelphia: T. K. & P. G. Collins [Carey & Hart], 1836), 31; Shackford, *David Crockett,* 212.

9. Shackford, *David Crockett,* 214–16.

10. Shackford, *David Crockett,* 229–35, 238.

11. José Enrique de la Peña, *With Santa Anna in Texas: A Personal Narrative of the Revolution,* trans. and ed. Carmen Perry (College Station: Texas A&M UP, 1975), 53; Dan Kilgore, *How Did Davy Die?* (College Station: Texas A&M UP, 1978); see also Richard Boyd Hauck, *Crockett: A Bio-Bibliography* (Westport, CT: Greenwood, 1982), 50–54.

12. [William Clark?], *An Account of Colonel Crockett's Tour to the North and Down East* (Philadelphia: Carey & Hart, 1835). The other of Crockett's Whig books is not included in this list because it consists mainly of artless invective rather than tales. See [Augustin Smith Clayton], *The Life of Martin Van Buren, Heir-Apparent to the "Government," and appointed Successor of General Andrew Jackson* (Philadelphia: R. Wright [Carey & Hart], 1835).

13. For a brief summary of the history of the Crockett Almanacs, see Michael A. Lofaro, "The Hidden 'Hero' of the Nashville Crockett Almanacs," in Michael A. Lofaro, ed., *Davy Crockett: The Man, The Legend, The Legacy (1786–1986)* (Knoxville: U of Tennessee P, 1985), 46–49. John Seelye first proved the Boston origins of the "Nashville" Almanacs. See his "A Well-Wrought Crockett: Or, How the Fakelorists Passed through the Credibility Gap and Discovered Kentucky," in Lofaro, *Davy Crockett,* 21–   45.

14. Lofaro, "Hidden Hero," 51–57.

15. Richard M. Dorson, *Davy Crockett: American Comic Legend* (New York: Spiral Press for Rockland Editions, 1939), 10–12, 16–17, 157–58, 138–39, 152.

16. For the best survey of the range of this material and its significance, see Richard Boyd Hauck, "Making It All Up: Davy Crockett in the Theater," in Lofaro, *Davy Crockett,* 102–23. In the same volume, see 125–36 for an example of the legendary Davy in a 1916 silent film.

17. Margaret J. King, "The Recycled Hero: Walt Disney's Davy Crockett," in Lofaro, *Davy Crockett,* 148, 143; for information on the music of the craze, see Charles K. Wolfe, "Davy Crockett Songs: Minstrels to Disney," in Lofaro, *Davy Crockett,* 177–87.

The Legend of John Henry

The historical John Henry is now all but lost to the historian, but his true identity and deeds are of little importance. The John Henry of legend embodies the struggle of the common man to retain his place or at least his pride in the face of industrialization and mechanization. A populist favorite for decades, John Henry is a man who gave his life to establish the primacy of humanity over machinery, illustrating an important theme in the ongoing history of industry in the Appalachians. There is a monument to this hero at Marlington, West Virginia. For further information on this hero, see "Presentations of the Legends of John Henry," Blacks in Appalachia, ed. William H. Turner and Edward J. Cabbell (1985), 269–70. The following is only one of many versions of this celebrated myth.

When John Henry was a little baby, sitting on his papa's knee,
Well he picked up a hammer and little piece of steel,
Said "hammer's gonna be the death of me, Lord, Lord;
Hammer's gonna be the death of me."

The captain said to John Henry,
"I'm gonna bring that steam drill around,
I'm gonna bring that steam drill out on the job,
I'm gonna whup that steel on down."
(Lord, Lord!)

John Henry told his captain,
"Lord, a man ain't nothing but a man,
But before I'd let your steam drill beat me down,
I'd die with a hammer in my hand!"
(Lord, Lord!)

John Henry said to his shaker,
"Shaker, why don't you sing?
Because I'm swinging thirty pounds from my hips on down,
Just listen to that cold steel ring."
(Lord, Lord!)

Now the captain said to John Henry,
"I believe that mountain's caving in."
John Henry said right back to the captain,
"Ain't nothing but my hammer sucking wind."
(Lord, Lord!)

Now the man that invented the steam drill,
He thought he was mighty fine;
But John Henry drove fifteen feet,
The steam drill only made nine.
(Lord, Lord!)

John Henry hammered in the mountains,
His hammer was striking fire,
But he worked so hard, it broke his poor heart
And he laid down his hammer and he died.
(Lord, Lord!)

Now John Henry had a little woman,
Her name was Polly Anne,
John Henry took sick and had to go to bed,
Polly Anne drove steel like a man.
(Lord, Lord!)

John Henry had a little baby,
You could hold him in the palm of your hand;
And the last words I heard that poor boy say,
"My daddy was a steel driving man."
(Lord, Lord!)

So every Monday morning
When the blue birds begin to sing,
You can hear John Henry a mile or more;
You can hear John Henry's hammer ring.
(Lord, Lord!)

Booker T. Washington

Booker T. Washington was among the first activists campaigning to improve the standard of living for blacks in America. Born a slave in 1858 in Hale's Ford, Virginia, following the Civil War, Washington and his family moved to West Virginia, where he spent his childhood in the mines and salt furnaces. He emerged from the Appalachians, however, to attend Hampton Institute in Hampton, Virginia, and he taught there as well. Washington's outspoken style and intellect won him an appointment to found an academy for blacks in Tuskegee, Alabama; thus was born the Tuskegee Normal and Industrial Institute, Washington's great life work. Tuskegee became the most successful and prestigious school of its kind in the country. Its reputation reflected Washington's own, as he became one of the best-known and most respected individuals in the country, serving as an advisor on racial and social matters to President Theodore Roosevelt and President William Howard Taft. *Up From Slavery*, Washington's autobiography, from which "Boyhood Days" is excerpted, documents not only his deeds but also the self-reliant philosophy that fueled them. Washington died in Tuskegee in 1915.

Boyhood Days

This experience of a whole race beginning to go to school for the first time, presents one of the most interesting studies that has ever occurred in connection with the development of any race. Few people who were not right in the midst of the scenes can form any exact idea of the intense desire which the people of my race showed for an education. As I have stated, it was a whole race trying to go to school. Few were too young, and none too old, to make the attempt to learn. As fast as any kind of teachers could be secured, not only were day-schools filled, but night-schools as well. The great ambition of the older people was to try to learn to read the Bible before they died. With this end in view, men and women who were fifty or seventy-five years old would often be found in the night-school. Sunday-schools were formed soon after freedom, but the principal book studied in the Sunday-school was the spelling-book. Day-school, night-school, Sunday-school, were always crowded, and often many had to be turned away for want of room.

The opening of the school in the Kanawha Valley, however, brought to me one of the keenest disappointments that I ever experienced. I had been working in a salt-furnace for several months, and my stepfather had discovered that I had a financial value, and so, when the school opened, he decided that he could not spare me from my work. This decision seemed to cloud my every ambition. The disappointment was made all the more severe by reason of the fact that my place of work was where I could see the happy children passing to and from school, mornings and afternoons. Despite this disappointment, however, I determined that I would learn something, anyway. I applied myself with greater earnestness than ever to the mastering of what was in the "blue-back" speller.

My mother sympathized with me in my disappointment, and sought to comfort me in all the ways she could, and to help me find a way to learn. After a while I succeeded in making arrangements with the teacher to give me some lessons at night, after the day's work was done. These night lessons were so welcome that I think I learned more at night than the other children did during the day. My own experiences in the night-school gave me faith in the night-school idea, with which, in after years, I had to do both at Hampton and Tuskegee. But my boyish heart was still set upon going to day-school, and I let no opportunity slip to push my case. Finally I won, and was permitted to go to the school in the day for a few months, with the understanding that I was to rise early in the morning and work in the furnace till nine o'clock, and return immediately after school closed in the afternoon for at least two more hours of work.

The schoolhouse was some distance from the furnace, and as I had to work till nine o'clock, and the school opened at nine, I found myself in a difficulty. School would always be begun before I reached it, and sometimes my

From *Up from Slavery,* Doubleday, Page, and Co., 1901.

class had recited. To get around this difficulty, I yielded to a temptation for which most people, I suppose, will condemn me; but since it is a fact, I might as well state it. I have great faith in the power and influence of facts. It is seldom that anything is permanently gained by holding back a fact. There was a large clock in a little office in the furnace. This clock, of course, all the hundred or more workmen depended upon to regulate their hours of beginning and ending the day's work. I got the idea that the way for me to reach school on time was to move the clock hands from half-past eight up to the nine o'clock mark. This I found myself doing morning after morning, till the furnace "boss" discovered that something was wrong, and locked the clock in a case. I did not mean to inconvenience anybody. I simply meant to reach that schoolhouse in time.

When, however, I found myself at the school for the first time, I also found myself confronted with two other difficulties. In the first place, I found that all of the other children wore hats or caps on their heads, and I had neither hat nor cap. In fact, I do not remember that up to the time of going to school I had ever worn any kind of covering upon my head, nor do I recall that either I or anybody else had even thought anything about the need of covering for my head. But, of course, when I saw how all the other boys were dressed, I began to feel quite uncomfortable. As usual, I put the case before my mother, and she explained to me that she had no money with which to buy a "store hat," which was a rather new institution at that time among the members of my race and was considered quite the thing for young and old to own, but that she would find a way to help me out of the difficulty. She accordingly got two pieces of "homespun" (jeans) and sewed them together, and I was soon the proud possessor of my first cap.

The lesson that my mother taught me in this has always remained with me, and I have tried as best I could to teach it to others. I have always felt proud, whenever I think of the incident, that my mother had strength of character enough not to be led into the temptation of seeming to be that which she was not—of trying to impress my schoolmates and others with the fact that she was able to buy me a "store hat" when she was not. I have always felt proud that she refused to go into debt for that which she did not have the money to pay for. Since that time I have owned many kinds of caps and hats, but never one of which I have felt so proud of as the cap made of the two pieces of cloth sewed together by my mother. I have noted the fact, but without satisfaction, I need not add, that several of the boys who began their careers with "store hats" and who were my schoolmates and used to join in the sport that was made of me because I had only a "homespun" cap, have ended their careers in the penitentiary, while others are not able now to buy any kind of hat.

My second difficulty was with regard to my name, or rather *a* name. From the time when I could remember anything, I had been called simply "Booker." Before going to school it had never occurred to me that it was needful and appropriate to have an additional name. When I heard the school-roll called, I noticed that all of the children had at least two names, and some of them indulged in what seemed to me the extravagance of having three. I was in deep perplexity, because I knew that the teacher would demand of me at least two names, and I had only one. By the time the occasion came for the enrolling of my name, an idea occurred to me which I thought would make me equal to the situation; and so, when the teacher asked me what my full name was, I calmly told him "Booker Washington," as if I had been called by that name all my life; and by that name I have since been known. Later in my life I found that my mother had given me the name of "Booker Taliaferro" soon after I was born, but in some way that part of my name seemed to disappear and for a long while was forgotten, but as soon as I found out about it I revived it, and made my full name "Booker Taliaferro Washington." I think there are not many men in our country who have had the privilege of naming themselves in the way that I have.

More than once I have tried to picture myself in the position of a boy or man with an honoured and distinguished ancestry which I could trace back through a period of hundreds of years, and who had not only inherited a name, but fortune and a proud family homestead; and yet I have sometimes had the feeling that if I had inherited these, and had been a member of a more popular race, I should have been inclined to yield to the temptation of depending upon my ancestry and my colour to do that for me which I should do for myself. Years ago I resolved that because I had no ancestry myself I would leave a record of which my children would be proud, and which might encourage them to still higher effort.

The world should not pass judgment upon the Negro, and especially the Negro youth, too quickly or too harshly. The Negro boy has obstacles, discouragements, and temptations to battle with that are little known to those not situated as he is. When a white boy undertakes a task, it is taken for granted that he will succeed. On the other hand, people are usually surprised if the Negro boy does not fail. In a word, the Negro youth starts out with the presumption against him.

The influence of ancestry, however, is important in helping forward any individual or race, if too much reliance is not placed upon it. Those who constantly direct attention to the Negro youth's moral weaknesses, and compare his advancement with that of white youths, do not consider the influence of the memories which cling about the old family homesteads. I have no idea, as I have stated elsewhere, who my grandmother was. I have, or have had, uncles and aunts and cousins, but I have no knowledge as to where most of them are. My case will illustrate that of hundreds of thousands of black people in every part of our country. The very fact that the white boy is conscious that, if he fails in life, he will disgrace the whole family record, extending back through many generations, is of tremendous value in helping him to resist temptations. The fact that the individual has behind and surrounding him proud family history and connection serves as a stimulus to help him to overcome obstacles when striving for success.

The time that I was permitted to attend school during the day was short, and my attendance was irregular. It was not long before I had to stop attending day-school altogether, and devote all of my time again to work. I resorted to the night-school again. In fact, the greater part of the education I secured in my boyhood was gathered through the night-school after my day's work was done. I had difficulty often in securing a satisfactory teacher. Sometimes, after I had secured someone to teach me at night, I would find, much to my disappointment, that the teacher knew but little more than I did. Often I would have to walk several miles at night in order to recite my night-school lessons. There was never a time in my youth, no matter how dark and discouraging the days might be, when one resolve did not continually remain with me, and that was a determination to secure an education at any cost.

Soon after we moved to West Virginia, my mother adopted into our family, notwithstanding our poverty, an orphan boy, to whom afterward we gave the name of James B. Washington. He has ever since remained a member of the family.

After I had worked in the salt-furnace for some time, work was secured for me in a coal-mine which was operated mainly for the purpose of securing fuel for the salt-furnace. Work in the coal-mine I always dreaded. One reason for this was that anyone who worked in a coal-mine was always unclean, at least while at work, and it was a very hard job to get one's skin clean after the day's work was over. Then it was fully a mile from the opening of the coal-mine to the face of the coal, and all, of course, was in the blackest darkness. I do not believe that one ever experiences anywhere else such darkness as he does in a coal-mine. The mine was divided into a large number of different "rooms" or departments, and, as I never was able to learn the location of all these "rooms," I many times found myself lost in the mine. To add to the horror of being lost, sometimes my light would go out, and then, if I did not happen to have a match, I would wander about in the darkness until by chance I found someone to give me a light. The work was not only hard, but it was dangerous. There was always the danger of being blown to pieces by a premature explosion of powder, or of being crushed by falling slate. Accidents from one or the other of these causes were frequently occurring, and this kept me in constant fear. Many children of the tenderest years were compelled then, as is now true, I fear, in most coal-mining districts, to spend a large part of their lives in these coal-mines, with little opportunity to get an education; and, what is worse, I have often noted that, as a rule, young boys who begin life in a coal-mine are often physically and mentally dwarfed. They soon lose ambition to do anything else than to continue as a coal-miner.

In those days, and later as a young man, I used to try to picture in my imagination the feelings and ambitions of a white boy with absolutely no limit placed upon his aspirations and activities. I used to envy the white boy who had no obstacles placed in the way of his becoming a Congressman, Governor, Bishop, or President by reason of the accident of his birth or race. I used to picture the way that I would act under such circumstances; how I would begin at the bottom and keep rising until I reached the highest round of success.

In later years, I confess that I do not envy the white boy as I once did. I have learned that success is to be measured not so much by the position that one has reached in life as by the obstacles which he has overcome while trying to succeed. Looked at from this standpoint, I almost reach the conclusion that often the Negro boy's birth and connection with an unpopular race is an advantage, so far as real life is concerned. With few exceptions, the Negro youth must work harder and must perform his tasks even better than a white youth in order to secure recognition. But out of the hard and unusual struggle through which he is compelled to pass, he gets a strength, a confidence, that one misses whose pathway is comparatively smooth by reason of birth and race.

From any point of view, I had rather be what I am, a member of the Negro race, than be able to claim membership with the most favoured of any other race. I have always been made sad when I have heard members of any race claiming rights and privileges, or certain badges of distinction, on the ground simply that they were members of this or that race, regardless of their own individual worth or attainments. I have been made to feel sad for such persons because I am conscious of the fact that mere connection with what is known as a superior race will not permanently carry an individual forward unless he has individual worth, and mere connection with what is regarded as an inferior race will not finally hold an individual back if he possesses intrinsic, individual merit. Every persecuted individual and race should get much consolation out of the great human law, which is universal and eternal, that merit, no matter under what skin found, is, in the long run, recognized and rewarded. This I have said here, not to call attention to myself as an individual, but to the race to which I am proud to belong.

Mary "Mother" Jones

Mary "Mother" Jones remains today one of the great icons of the American labor movement, her name synonymous with radical activism. Born in Cork, Ireland, in 1830, she emigrated to America with her family in 1835 and traveled about the nation seeking work. Misfortune, however, pursued her, as her husband, an ironworker, and her children were killed in a yellow fever epidemic in Memphis in 1867, and four years later she lost all her possessions in the great Chicago fire. From her brooding over these tragedies came Mother Jones's sense of social justice. She joined the fledgling Knights of Labor and, as she did in all other labor organizations with which she was involved, soon became one of its foremost leaders.

Thus began a career of labor agitation that would continue to the end of Mother Jones's life and include most of the major strikes and insurrections of her time, among them the Haymarket (1877) and Pittsburgh (1886) riots and the Birmingham railroad strike (1894). By the late nineteenth century, most of her activities were focused on the coalfield wars in the Appalachian mountains, where she quickly garnered a reputation as a fearless and eloquent fighter, unafraid of arrest or violence. This long campaign is documented in her *Autobiography*, which serves mostly to confirm and propagate Mother Jones as a figure of legendary stature. Its wild tales capture the spirit, if not always the facts, of the woman who, even beyond her death in 1930, was perceived as "the most dangerous woman in America." The following selection from the *Autobiography* reveals much of her relentless spirit.

How the Women Mopped Up Coaldale

In Lonaconia, Maryland, there was a strike. I was there. In Hazelton, Pennsylvania, a convention was called to discuss the anthracite strike. I was there when they issued the strike call. One hundred and fifty thousand men responded. The men of Scranton and Shamokin and Coaldale and Panther Creek and Valley Battle. And I was there.

In Shamokin I met Miles Daugherty, an organizer. When he quit work and drew his pay, he gave one-half of his pay envelope to his wife, and the other half he kept to rent halls and pay for lights for the union. Organizers did not draw much salary in those days, and they did heroic, unselfish work.

Not far from Shamokin, in a little mountain town, the priest was holding a meeting when I went in. He was speaking in the church. I spoke in an open field. The priest told the men to go back and obey their masters and their reward would be in Heaven. He denounced the strikers as children of darkness. The miners left the church in a body and marched over to my meeting.

"Boys," I said, "this strike is called in order that you and your wives and your little ones may get a bit of Heaven before you die."

We organized the entire camp.

The fight went on. In Coaldale, in the Hazelton district, the miners were not permitted to assemble in any hall. It was necessary to win the strike in that district that the Coaldale miners be organized.

I went to a nearby mining town that was thoroughly organized and asked the women if they would help me get the Coaldale men out. This was in McAdoo. I told them to leave their men at home to take care of the family. I asked them to put on their kitchen clothes and bring mops and brooms with them and a couple of tin pans. We marched over the mountains fifteen miles, beating on the tin pans as if they were cymbals. At three o'clock in the morn-

From *The Autobiography of Mother Jones*, Charles H. Kerr Publishing Co, 1969. Reprinted by permission of the publisher.

ing we met the Crack Thirteen of the militia, patrolling the roads to Coaldale. The colonel of the regiment said "Halt! Move back!"

I said, "Colonel, the working men of America will not halt nor will they ever go back. The working man is going forward!"

"I'll charge bayonets," said he.

"On whom?"

"On your people."

"We are not enemies," said I. "We are just a band of working women whose brothers and husbands are in a battle for bread. We want our brothers in Coaldale to join us in our fight. We are here on the mountain road for our children's sake, for the nation's sake. We are not going to hurt anyone and surely you would not hurt us."

They kept us there till daybreak, and when they saw the army of women in kitchen aprons, with dishpans and mops, they laughed and let us pass. An army of strong mining women makes a wonderfully spectacular picture.

Well, when the miners in the Coaldale camp started to go to work, they were met by the McAdoo women who were beating on their pans and shouting, "Join the union! Join the union!"

They joined, every last man of them, and we got so enthusiastic that we organized the streetcar men who promised to haul no scabs for the coal companies. As there were no other groups to organize we marched over the mountains home, beating our pans and singing patriotic songs.

Meanwhile, President Mitchell and all his organizers were sleeping in the Valley Hotel over in Hazelton. They knew nothing of our march onto Coaldale until the newspaper men telephoned to him that "Mother Jones was raising hell up in the mountains with a bunch of wild women!"

He, of course, got nervous. He might have gotten more nervous if he had known how we made the mine bosses go home and how we told their wives to clean them up and make decent American citizens out of them. How we went around to the kitchen of the hotel where the militia were quartered and ate the breakfast that was on the table for the soldiers.

When I got back to Hazelton, Mitchell looked at me with surprise. I was worn out. Coaldale had been a strenuous night and morning and its thirty-mile tramp. I assured Mitchell that no one had been hurt and no property injured. The military had acted like human beings. They took the matter as a joke. They enjoyed the morning's fun. I told him how scared the sheriff had been. He had been talking to me without knowing who I was.

"Oh Lord," he said, "that Mother Jones is sure a dangerous woman."

"Why don't you arrest her?" I asked him.

"Oh Lord, I couldn't. I'd have that mob of women with their mops and brooms after me and the jail ain't big enough to hold them all. They'd mop the life out of a fellow!"

Mr. Mitchell said, "My God, Mother, did you get home safe? What did you do?"

"I got five thousand men out and organized them. We had time left over so we organized the streetcar men and they will not haul any scabs into camp."

"Did you get hurt, Mother?"

"No, we did the hurting."

"Didn't the superintendents' bosses get after you?"

"No, we got after them. Their wives and our women were yelling around like cats. It was a great fight."

David Lee

David Lee, a professor of history at Western Kentucky University, was born August 5, 1948, in Cincinnati, Ohio. Lee received his B.A. from Miami University of Ohio in 1970, and his M.A. (1971) and Ph.D. (1975) from Ohio State University. His scholarship centers on the Appalachian region, particularly Tennessee, whose political and social life he has examined in a series of books and articles.

Lee's biography, *Sergeant York: An American Hero* (1985), draws on extensive research into the words of the man himself as well as the prolific, and frequently quite distorted, media attention that focused on York following his distinguished, distinctive combat feats. This portrait of York highlights not only the individual, but also the region which gave rise to him.

In the Service of the Lord

York's first weeks in the army were among the most miserable of his life. He had never been away from the mountains before and noted disconsolately that his training site, Camp Gordon, Georgia, was "pretty flat country." He also found himself "throwed in with a lot of Greeks and Italians" and other kinds of people he had never encountered before. The product of a very homogeneous area, York had had little contact with people who were not white Anglo-Saxon Protestants and felt an enormous cultural gap between himself and his fellow inductees—a feeling the "Greeks and Italians" also felt toward this product of the mountain South.

His discomfort was compounded by the army's way of doing things, a process that York, like millions of other new soldiers, considered puzzling and ridiculous. For example, his first morning at Camp Gordon was spent picking up cigarette butts in the company area, an assignment York consid-

From *Sergeant York,* University Press of Kentucky, 1978. Reprinted by permission of the publisher.

ered odd for any soldier but especially for one who did not smoke. Later, he was genuinely appalled by his first encounter with an army rifle. Raised with guns, he always took good care of them. The weapon the government issued him was full of dirt and grease. Nevertheless, the recruit promptly set about cleaning and mastering the rifle—probably a 1917 Enfield—and soon declared that he and his weapon were "good friends." It was an accurate rifle, York admitted, but he proudly insisted that up to a hundred yards it was no more accurate than the muzzle-loaders used back in Fentress County. Perhaps his most alarming experience came when "them there Greeks and Italians and even some of our own city boys" took those rifles on the firing line where, unaccustomed to guns, they "missed everything, everything except the sky." York himself discovered that army targets were much larger than the heads of turkeys, and he "generally made a tolebly good score."

At the root of York's unhappiness lay his lingering doubts about the morality of war, although he told his superiors nothing about his convictions until he was assigned to Company G, 328th Infantry, Eighty-second Division, a combat unit that seemed destined for front-line service. Then he went to see his company commander, Captain Edward Danforth, a Harvard-educated Georgian who quickly recognized the private's sincerity and took him to Major George Edward Buxton, the battalion commander and a devout New Englander who so impressed York that he later named a son for him. Buxton and York spent a long night discussing the Bible's teachings concerning war. The major began by quoting Christ's admonition, "He that hath no sword, let him sell his cloak and buy one" (Luke 22:36), and asked York if the Christ who drove the moneychangers from the temple would ignore German "war crimes" in Belgium. He pointed out that Jesus had told his followers, "For my kingdom is not of this world; but if my kingdom were of this world, then would my servants fight" (John 18:36). Buxton argued that the United States was an earthly government due the "things that are Caesar's" and therefore the Christian servants of that government should fight for its preservation. He ended by reading a long passage from Ezekiel (33:1–6) that suggested that the Lord expected his people to defend themselves.

The conversation introduced York to many new ideas and left him more confused than ever. The strange camp setting with its endless activity unsettled him still more, so Buxton and Danforth gave him a ten-day pass to go home and collect his thoughts. He arrived in Pall Mall on March 21, 1918, having walked the last twelve miles over the mountains lugging his suitcase. Although Buxton had assured him of a noncombat assignment if he requested it, York's honesty forced him to analyze the major's ideas even though his mother, Pastor Pile, and the congregation all urged him to accept Buxton's offer. Finally he fled again to the mountains where he spent all of one day, that night, and part of the next day praying for divine guidance.

That night on the mountain, York experienced, in effect, a second conversion, returning home convinced that God wanted him to fight and would preserve him unharmed in battle. As he put the issue to a disappointed fellow church member, "If some feller was to come along and bust into your house and mistreat your wife and murder your children, maybe, you'd just stand for it? You wouldn't fight?" Just as his first conversion to religion had made him an active Christian, now York plunged into military life with tremendous zeal. When Pastor Pile invited him to come to the church to say good-bye to the congregation, York pointedly refused, insisting that he would be home safely very soon. Throughout the rest of his military career his officers remarked on his calm, self-assured manner both in and out of combat. Highlighting York's new demeanor was an aggressiveness tinged with fatalism. To survive in battle, he advised, "Get determined to get the other fellow before he gets you, keep on thinking about it and with that determination you'll come through." Set against this feeling was York's realization that fate often determined survival in war. A few months after he left Pall Mall, he wrote that whatever soldiers might do, shells would still burst in trenches, rain would still flood them, and lights would still silhouette doughboys as they went "over the top," so "what is the use of worrying if you can't alter things. Just ask God to help you; and accept them; and make the best of them by the help of God." With God, a man could make the best of his trials, but if he faced them alone, they would destroy his peace of mind.

York's second conversion points up some significant aspects of his personality. First of all, he was something of a plunger who committed himself recklessly to whatever project won his loyalty. Perhaps out of an innate need for excitement, York seemed incapable of moderate or temperate methods. When he became a Christian, he had thrown himself into a severe, fundamentalist church and had given of his personal and material resources unstintingly. Now he experienced the same sort of emotional commitment to the war against Germany. Second, York had a taste for violence that he controlled only with difficulty. He had turned against his "hog wild" days, embraced the church, and insisted that he never "backslid" because he realized how easily he could fall back into his old ways. Thus, when patriotism offered him a legitimate release for his violent impulses, he grasped the opportunity with the enthusiasm of a religious warrior.

Unfortunately, Buxton's judicious handling of York was not typical of how most military authorities handled such dissenters in 1917 and 1918. To his credit, Buxton displayed an unusual degree of compassion in the matter. Local draft boards were very reluctant to honor pleas for conscientious objector status, and even those who received this exemption were sent to regular army training camps to await War Department instructions about alternative service. Although regulations called for these men to be treated with "kindly consideration," they were often harassed by recruits bound for combat assignments. Of some twenty thousand men granted conscientious objector status by the selective service system, approximately sixteen thousand ultimately yielded to this pressure and decided to take up arms. Members of well-established pacifist churches usually encountered few problems from the camp officers, but men like York who belonged to more obscure denominations faced a board of inquiry whose members often derided claimants for their convictions. It was York's good fortune to be under the command of a superior who respected his sincerity and handled his case with integrity.

The last step in York's coming to terms with the war came after he had returned to duty. On April 19, his unit moved to Camp Upton, New York, to prepare for immediate embarcation for France. With the war closer than ever, York began to realize that he had no clear concept of why it was being fought, so he once again visited Captain Danforth to ask for an explanation. Just as Buxton had stressed German "war crimes" in his earlier conversation with York, Danforth now portrayed the Germans as a barbaric people governed by reckless warlords bent on overrunning the world. For York, the explanation dovetailed nicely with the words of Jesus, "Blessed are the peacemakers . . .," and on May 1, he grimly sailed for France convinced that "we were to be peacemakers. . . . That was we-uns. We were to help make peace, the only way the Germans would understand."

Robert Morgan

See volume 1, chapter 1, for biography.

Uncle Robert

M Sgt. Robert G. Levi 1915–1943
Serial No. 34119284
813th Bomb Sqdn.
482nd Bombardment Group
Eighth Air Force

In the little opening in the woods
your cot springs were a crisp red wool
on the moss. While we raked leaves
for the cowstall Grandma told me how
you came up here on summer afternoons
to read and paint and sleep after
working the hootowl shift at the cottonmill.

From *At the Edge of the Orchard Country*, © 1987 by Robert Morgan. Reprinted by permission of Wesleyan University Press.

You must have meant to return to leave
your couch on the innerspring moss
on the mountainside.

                              The metalwork you did
in the CCC—toolbox, a vase, buckets
thick as stoves—was scattered through house
and barn. I lost your flies and tackle
in the weeds above the garden, and stuck
your chevron patches to my flannel shirt.
In the messkit returned from England
I fried sand like snow, and found
the picture of your fiancée in the cedarchest.

It was hinted I was "marked" somehow,
not only by your name, but in some way
unexplained was actually you. Aunts and cousins
claimed we favored and I spoke with your stammer.
Your paintings watched me
from the bedroom wall and mantel
and your poem clipped from the paper
yellowed among the rationbooks. I inherited
your Testament with its boards of carved cedar,
and the box of arrowheads you picked
from the dust of bottomlands on Sunday afternoons
like seeds and teeth of giants.

No one opened the steel coffin sent back
to see what bone splinters or rags
had been found where the B-17 novaed
above East Anglia. I touched the ribbons
and medals in the bureau, the gold buttons.
Your canoe lay in the barnloft for years
between the cornpile and the wall, heavy
with dust as the boat in a pyramid
and tracked by mice and swallows. The paint
and canvas curled away from the cedar slats.
I meant to use it someday but never dared:
it was not creekworthy without new skin
and too heavy for one to carry. I turned
it over and looked into the belly
and sat on the webbed seat, rocking
on the corn-bearinged floor. Once hornets
built in the prow what I imagined
was a skull with honey brains. On snowy days

I sat there and paddled across the wilderness
of loft dark. The summer before you left
you portaged to the river and back,
then carried the canoe up there.
Something was always scary about the craft:
each time I turned it over fearing to see
a body inside. It lay among the shucks
and fodder as though washed up by a flood
and stranded forever.

                              One day I found your bugle
in the attic, velveted with dust and lint.
The brass felt damp with corrosion,
the bell dented and dark as leather.
I took it out behind the house and,
facing west, blew into the cold mouthpiece
a hopeful syllable. The metal trembled
and blared like a sick steer, went quiet.
I poured all my body heat into the barrel
and a sour flatulence shook out and echoed
off the mountains. I made half-musical
squeaks and bursts till dizzy, aiming vowels
like watermelon seeds into the tube.
When the groans returned from Buzzard Rock
I thought they must be wails from the cove
for someone dead, and nothing I had sent,
or the ghost of a train lost in the valley
and relayed like an aural mirage from
the past still with us and talking back.

The flag that draped your casket was kept
folded in the trunk. They said
I had the high-arched "Levi foot"
like you, and your quick laugh. I was told
you made your own marbles as a boy
by rolling branch clay into balls and baking
in the oven. Mama liked to take out
of cloth a clay statue of a naked man
face down in the dirt which you once
modeled and called "The Dying Warrior."
I marveled at the cunning work of leg
and tiny arm and spilling hair, and touched
your fingerprints still clear on the base.

Elizabeth Hunter

A native of Boston, Elizabeth Hunter, after spending part of her youth in New Hampshire, entered Radcliffe College, where she graduated in 1967. Heading south, she earned a master's degree in teaching at East Tennessee State University, but she never taught. "I couldn't get a job teaching," she jokes, "because I wasn't related to anybody." After working for a number of newspapers in the mountains, Hunter in 1981 became a freelance writer. In addition to writing for magazines, she contributes to several local papers, but on her own time and on subjects she chooses. Among her credits are *The State, Blue Ridge Country,* and *North Carolina Homes and Gardens.* In her house overlooking the Toe River, she sometimes hears at night her three favorite sounds: rain on a roof, a train passing, and a cat purring. Then she knows she is "ideally situated."

"Farmer Bob"

To the politicians in Washington, D.C., he was a power to be reckoned with. But to residents of his native Alleghany County in the North Carolina high country, he was just "Farmer Bob."

Robert Lee Doughton—landowner, farmer, livestock producer, and country store proprietor, whose feet required a size fifteen shoe and whose palate required apples at every meal—didn't arrive in the nation's capital until he was nearly fifty years old.

But once elected to represent rural northwestern North Carolina's Ninth District in the U.S. House of Representatives in 1910, he spent the next forty-three years there, eighteen of them as chairman of the powerful House Ways and Means Committee, before retiring from a distinguished career of public service at the ripe old age of ninety.

During that period he shepherded the Social Security Act into being and played a crucial role in the creation of the Blue Ridge Parkway—a role that earned him the title of "Father of the Parkway." The 470-mile pleasure road links the Shenandoah National Park in Virginia to the Great Smoky Mountains National Park on the Tennessee–North Carolina line.

While Doughton may be no more than a name to most parkway visitors (six-thousand-acre Doughton Park, located close to the midpoint of the parkway, was renamed in his honor in 1951), Farmer Bob is still recalled with affection by Alleghany County residents who remember the big, down-

From "Father of Blue Ridge Parkway is Still 'Farmer Bob' in Sparta," a feature story prepared for *North Carolina High Country Host,* Boone, in the late 1980s. Reprinted by permission of the author.

to-earth man who never "rose above his raising" despite the respect he commanded in Washington.

Even in his old age, Doughton had "a powerful presence you could feel when he came into a room," his granddaughter Betsy Dillon recalls. Dillon, now an Alleghany County high school teacher, remembers a summer she spent "taking care" of Doughton at his Laurel Springs home:

> No matter how early I got up, I never managed to rise before he did. He was still farming then, though a tenant farmer did most of the actual work. He went to bed at 7 P.M. every night; there was no TV in the house, just an old radio that only half worked. He was in his eighties then; his hearing was going, but it seemed he could turn it on and off at will, depending on what was being discussed.

"Even though he became a legend to the people around him, my grandfather had a very practical sense of humor about himself," Dillon said.

"He wasn't the wheeling-dealing kind of politician we have now; just a down-to-earth, hard-working man. We didn't really think of him as being as influential as he was at that time," said Pauline Jolly, Alleghany County librarian and vice-president of the county historical society. Jolly remembers Doughton well, from the days when she worked in the town telephone office, which occupied quarters over a store across the street from the office the congressman maintained in Sparta when he wasn't in Washington. At the time, there were only two long-distance lines out of town, and Doughton waited in line to use them, just like everyone else.

"He'd come over to the telephone office when he needed to make a call. I used to call Mr. (President Harry) Truman at the White House for him. After he'd talked to the President, he'd stop and talk to me awhile before going back to his office," Jolly said.

A tireless worker who generally reached his congressional office in Washington by 6 A.M., Doughton vowed he'd quit running the first time anyone opposed him in the Democratic primary, Dillon said. But that never happened, and while he frequently faced Republican opposition in the general election, voters returned him to office for twenty-one terms before he retired in January of 1953.

Doughton found retirement more difficult than work. "This doing nothing's the hardest thing I've ever done," he told a reporter a few weeks before his death on Oct. 1, 1954. To the end he was a familiar figure in the county, walking to the post office in the morning to pick up his mail, stopping for a chat with folks at the general store.

During his years as a congressman, he was an ardent supporter of improving postal service, rural electrification, establishment of the Tennessee Valley Authority, veterans' affairs, and labor. A powerful Democrat, Doughton surrendered the chairmanship of the House Ways and Means Committee only once from 1933–35, when the Republicans enjoyed a two-year stint as the majority party. The Blue Ridge Parkway was a pet project from the time of its conception in the early 1930s until his death.

His was a strong voice on the side of the victors when a long, heated battle raged between Tennessee and North Carolina over the parkway's route; and it was his legislative finesse that ultimately engineered passage—despite fierce opposition—of a thrice-defeated house resolution that permanently placed parkway maintenance and administration under the Department of the Interior.

Though a three-man board appointed by Franklin Roosevelt's Secretary of the Interior Harold Ickes initially recommended that the parkway follow a route through East Tennessee rather than North Carolina, Doughton and other North Carolinians persuaded Ickes to overrule his board's findings on grounds that North Carolina's scenery was superior and that Tennessee was already receiving Depression-era relief through development of the Tennessee Valley Authority.

That battle won, Doughton was forced to wage yet another on behalf of his beloved project, when a host of fellow congressmen (including some still-disgruntled members of the Tennessee delegation) opposed his resolution to place the parkway's future administration and maintenance under the National Park Service's aegis.

Opponents, who thought the parkway ought to be treated like any other road project after construction was completed, would have succeeded in blocking the measure, had they "been dealing with an ordinary legislator," according to parkway historian Harley Jolley. But Doughton saw the bill through to passage after four defeats, assuring the Blue Ridge Parkway's permanent status as a national treasure.

Chapter 3

War and Revolution

Introduction

Because the culture of Southern Appalachia was born in violence, it is not surprising that the region would gain a reputation for its fighters. In the mountains numerous battles played themselves out: between invaders and natives in the tangled wilds of the early frontier, between Revolutionaries and Tories at King's Mountain, South Carolina in the Revolution, and between Union troops and Confederates at Chicamauga, northern Georgia and Lookout Mountain, Tennessee in the Civil War, for example. In foreign wars Appalachians have frequently distinguished themselves, especially Sergeant Alvin C. York and "The Sergeant York of World War Two," Sergeant James I. Spurrier, Jr., a farmer from Bluefield, West Virginia, also called "A One-Man Army." Characteristic of many military heroes of the region, York and Spurrier were reluctant to discuss their exploits.

It seems fitting that much of the work on the atomic bomb, the consequences of which James Agee describes, was done in this region whose people frequently have embodied a combination of warlike finesse and sheer brute force. In fact, the region continues to produce much of the hardware of war at a number of munitions plants. The greatest impact and sacrifice reside in the fact that the Southern Appalachians have supplied the nation with some of its most effective and deadliest weapons.

Alexander Withers

Born a Virginian long before the Civil War, Withers lived most of his life in the mountains near the border of what would later become the state of West Virginia. His genteel background provided him extensive education, first at Washington College (now Washington and Lee University) and then at William and Mary School of Law. He was a barrister and gentleman farmer by vocation, but scholarly work always held an important place in his life. His *Chronicles of Border Warfare* (1831) are the fruits of this latter effort. He died in Parkersburg, West Virginia, on January 23, 1865.

Alexander Withers was one of the earliest historians to undertake a systematic documentation of the struggle between the settlers of the Appalachian region and the Native Americans they displaced. Although they evince the prejudices of the day, Withers's *Chronicles* are an important history, based in part on the first-hand accounts of the fighters themselves. Although Withers' book seems biased against the Indians, he does remark, with insight unusual for the time, that the two great evils of the colonization were the practice of slavery and the treatment of the natives.

Border Warfare and Captivity

In the summer of 1761, about sixty Shawanee warriors penetrated the settlements on James river. To avoid the fort at the mouth of Looney's creek, on this river, they passed through Bowen's gap in Purgatory mountain, in the night; and ascending Purgatory creek, killed Thomas Perry, Joseph Dennis, and his child and made prisoner his wife, Hannah Dennis. They then proceeded to the house of Robert Renix, where they captured Mrs. Renix (a daughter of Sampson Archer) and her five children, William, Robert, Thomas, Joshua, and Betsy—Mr. Renix not being at home. They then went to the house of Thomas Smith, where Renix was; and shot and scalped him and Smith; and took with them, Mrs. Smith and Sally Jew, a white servant girl.[1]

In Boquet's treaty with the Ohio Indians, it was stipulated that the whites detained by them in captivity were to be brought in and redeemed. In compliance with this stipulation, Mrs. Renix was brought to Staunton in 1767 and ransomed, together with two of her sons, William, the late Col. Renix of Greenbrier, and Robert, also of Greenbrier—Betsy, her daughter, had died on the Miami. Thomas returned in 1783, but soon after removed and settled, on the Scioto, near Chilicothe. Joshua never came back; he took an Indian wife and became a chief among the Miamis—he amassed a considerable fortune and died near Detroit in 1810.

Hannah Dennis was separated from the other captives, and allotted to live at the Chilicothe towns.[2] She learned their language; painted herself as they do; and in many respects conformed to their manners and customs. She was attentive to sick persons and was highly esteemed by the Indians, as one well skilled in the art of curing diseases. Finding them very superstitious and believers in necromancy, she professed witchcraft, and affected to be a prophetess. In this manner she conducted herself, 'till she became so great a favorite with them, that they gave her full liberty and honored her as a queen. Not-

From *Chronicles of Border Warfare*, Arno Press, 1971, © 1895.

withstanding this, Mrs. Dennis was always determined to effect her escape, when a favorable opportunity should occur; and having remained so long with them, apparently well satisfied, they ceased to entertain any suspicions of such a design.

In June 1763, she left the Chilicothe towns, *ostensibly* to procure herbs for medicinal purposes (as she had before frequently done), but *really* to attempt an escape. As she did not return that night, her intention became suspected; and in the morning, some warriors were sent in pursuit of her. In order to leave as little trail as possible, she had crossed the Scioto river three times, and was just getting over the fourth time 40 miles below the towns, when she was discovered by her pursuers. They fired at her across the river without effect; but in endeavoring to make a rapid flight, she had one of her feet severely cut by a sharp stone.

The Indians then rushed across the river to overtake and catch her, but she eluded them by crawling into the hollow limb of a fallen sycamore. They searched around for her some time, frequently stepping on the log which concealed her; and encamped near it that night. On the next day they went on to the Ohio river, but finding no trace of her, they returned home.

Mrs. Dennis remained at that place three days, doctoring her wound, and then set off for home. She crossed the Ohio river, at the mouth of Great Kenhawa, on a log of driftwood, traveling only during the night, for fear of discovery—She subsisted on roots, herbs, green grapes, wild cherries, and river muscles—and entirely exhausted by fatigue and hunger, sat down by the side of Greenbrier river, with no expectation of ever proceeding farther. In this situation she was found by Thomas Athol and three others from Clendennin's settlement, which she had passed without knowing it. She had been then upwards of twenty days on her disconsolate journey, alone, on foot—but 'till then, cheered with the hope of again being with her friends.

She was taken back to Clendennin's, where they kindly ministered to her, 'till she became so far invigorated, as to travel on horseback with an escort, to Fort Young on Jackson's river, from whence she was carried home to her relations.

In the course of a few days after Hannah Dennis had gone from Clendennin's, a party of about sixty warriors came to the settlement on Muddy creek, in the county of Greenbrier. That region of country then contained no inhabitants, but those on Muddy creek, and in the Levels; and these are believed to have consisted of at least one hundred souls. The Indians came apparently as friends, and the French war having been terminated by the treaty of the preceding spring, the whites did not for an instant doubt their sincerity. They were entertained in small parties at different houses, and every civility and act of kindness, which the new settlers could proffer, were extended to them. In a moment of the most perfect confidence in the innocence of their intentions, the Indians rose on them and tomahawked and scalped all, save a few women and children of whom they made prisoners.

After the perpetration of this most barbarous and bloody outrage, the Indians (excepting some few who took charge of the prisoners) proceeded to the settlement in the Levels. Here, as at Muddy creek, they disguised their horrid purpose, and wearing the mask of friendship, were kindly received at the house of Mr. Clendennin. This gentleman had just returned from a successful hunt, and brought home three fine elks—these and the novelty of being with *friendly Indians,* soon drew the whole settlement to his house. Here too the Indians were well entertained and feasted on the fruit of Clendennin's hunt, and every other article of provision which was there, and could minister to their gratification. An old woman, who was of the party, having a very sore leg and having understood that Indians could perform a cure of any ulcer, showed it to one near her; and asked if he could heal it—The inhuman monster raised his tomahawk and buried it in her head. This seemed to be the signal of a general massacre and promptly was it obeyed—nearly every man of the settlement was killed and the women and children taken captive.

While this tragedy was acting, a negro woman, who was endeavoring to escape, was followed by her crying child.—To save it from savage butchery, she turned round and murdered it herself.

Mrs. Clendennin, driven to despair by the cruel and unprovoked murder of her husband and friends, and the spoliation and destruction of all their property, boldly charged the Indians with perfidy and treachery; and alleged that cowards only could act with such duplicity. The bloody scalp of her husband was thrown in her face—the tomahawk was raised over her head; but she did not cease to revile them. In going over Keeny's knot on the next day, the prisoners being in the centre, and the Indians in the front and rear, she gave her infant child to one of the women to hold for a while.—She then stepped into the thicket unperceived, and made her escape. The crying of the infant soon led to a discovery of her flight—one of the Indians observed that he could "bring the cow to her calf," and taking the child by the heels, beat out its brains against a tree.

Mrs. Clendennin returned that night to her home, a distance of ten miles; and covering the body of her husband with rails and trash, retired into an adjoining cornfield, lest she might be pursued and again taken prisoner. While in the cornfield, her mind was much agitated by contending emotions; and the prospect of effecting an escape to the settlements, seemed to her dreary and hopeless. In a moment of despondency, she thought she beheld a man, with the aspect of a murderer, standing near her; and she became overwhelmed with fear. It was but the creature of a sickly and terrified imagination; and when her mind regained its proper tone, she resumed her flight and reached the settlement in safety.[3]

These melancholy events occurring so immediately after the escape of Hannah Dennis; and the unwillingness of the Indians that she should be separated from them, has induced the supposition that the party committing those dreadful outrages were in pursuit of her. If such were the fact, dearly were others made to pay the penalty of her deliverance.

Notes

1. The name is Renick. Robert Renick, who was killed on the occasion referred to, was a man of character and influence in his day. His name appears on Capt. John Smith's company roll of Augusta militia as early as 1742; four years later, he was lieutenant of a mounted company of Augusta militia. Instead of 1761, the captivity of the Renick family occurred July 25, 1757, as shown by the Preston Register, which states that Renick and another were killed on that day, while Mrs. Renick and seven children, and a Mrs. Dennis, were captured; and the same day, at Craig's Creek, one man was killed and two wounded. The Renick traditions state that Mrs. Renick had only five children when taken; and one born after reaching the Indian towns; and corrects some other statements not properly related in Withers's narrative of the affair.
2. In 1763–65, the great Shawnee village just below the mouth of the Scioto (site of Alexandria, Ohio), was destroyed by floods. Some of the tribesmen rebuilt their town on a higher bottom just above the mouth (site of Portsmouth, Ohio), while others ascended the Scioto and built, successively, Old and New Chillicothe.
3. Further particulars of this captivity are in Anne Newport Royall's *Sketches of History, Life, and Manners in U.S.* (New Haven, CT: privately printed, 1826), 60–66.

Theodore Roosevelt

Theodore Roosevelt easily ranks among the most colorful characters of American history. He is best known as the outspoken twenty-sixth president of the United States, the author of the doctrine of gunboat diplomacy, the force behind the Panama Canal, the populist "trust buster," the hero of San Juan Hill in the Spanish-American War, and the man who would "speak softly and carry a big stick." He was also a Harvard-educated historian, and in that capacity he produced many scholarly works, beginning with *The Naval War of 1812,* which remains authoritative today. The four-volume *Winning of the West* (1889–96) forms an account of the conflicts by which America expanded its borders in fulfillment of its "Manifest Destiny." His comprehensive documentation of the Battle of King's Mountain evinces obvious admiration for the mountaineers who contributed greatly to that crucial Revolutionary War victory, but Roosevelt tempers that sentiment with scholarly impartiality and factual precision.

King's Mountain

The mountain men had done a most notable deed. They had shown in per-
fection the best qualities of horse-riflemen. Their hardihood and persever-
ance had enabled them to bear up well under fatigue, exposure, and scanty
food. Their long, swift ride, and the suddenness of the attack, took their foes
completely by surprise. Then, leaving their horses, they had shown in the
actual battle such courage, marksmanship, and skill in woodland fighting,
that they had not only defeated but captured an equal number of well-armed,
well-led, resolute men, in a strong position. The victory was of far-reaching
importance and ranks among the decisive battles of the Revolution. It was
the first great success of the Americans in the South, the turning-point in
the southern campaign, and it brought cheer to the patriots throughout the
Union. The loyalists of the Carolinas were utterly cast down, and never recovered from the blow; and its immediate effect was to cause Cornwallis to
retreat from North Carolina, abandoning his first invasion of that state.

The expedition offered a striking example of the individual initiative so
characteristic of the backwoodsmen. It was not ordered by any one authority;
it was not even sanctioned by the central or state governments. Shelby and
Sevier were the two prime movers in getting it up, Campbell exercised the
chief command, and the various other leaders, with their men, simply joined
the mountaineers, as they happened to hear of them and come across their
path. The ties of discipline were of the slightest. The commanders elected
their own chief without regard to rank or seniority; in fact, the officer who
was by rank entitled to the place was hardly given any share in the conduct
of the campaign. The authority of the commandant over the other officers, and
of the various colonels over their troops, resembled rather the control exercised
by Indian chiefs over their warriors than the discipline obtained in the regular
army. But the men were splendid individual fighters, who liked and trusted
their leaders; and the latter were bold, resolute, energetic, and intelligent.

Cornwallis feared that the mountain men would push on and attack his
flank; but there was no such danger. By themselves they were as little likely
to assail him in force in the open as Andreas Hofer's Tyrolese—with whom they
had many points in common—were to threaten Napoleon on the Danubian
plains. Had they been Continental troops, the British would have had to deal
with a permanent army. But they were only militia[1] after all, however formidable from their patriotic purpose and personal prowess. The backwoods
armies were not unlike the armies of the Scotch Highlanders; tumultuous
gatherings of hardy and warlike men, greatly to be dreaded under certain
circumstances, but incapable of a long campaign and almost as much demor-
alized by a victory as by a defeat. Individually, or in small groups, they were
perhaps even more formidable than the Highlanders; but in one important
respect they were inferior, for they totally lacked the regimental organization which the clan system gave the Scotch Celts.

_____

The mountaineers had come out to do a certain thing—to kill Ferguson and scatter his troops. They had done it, and now they wished to go home. The little log-huts in which their families lived were in daily danger of Indian attack; and it was absolutely necessary that they should be on hand to protect them. They were, for the most part, very poor men, whose sole sources of livelihood were the stock they kept beyond the mountains. They loved their country greatly, and had shown the sincerity of their patriotism by the spontaneous way in which they risked their lives on this expedition. They had no hope of reward; for they neither expected nor received any pay except in liquidated certificates, worth two cents on the dollar. Shelby's share of these, for his services as colonel throughout '80 and '81, was sold by him for "six yards of middling broadcloth"; so it can be readily imagined how little each private got for the King's Mountain expedition.[2]

The day after the battle the Americans fell back towards the mountains, fearing lest, while cumbered by prisoners and wounded, they should be struck by Tarleton or perhaps Cruger. The prisoners were marched along on foot, each carrying one or two muskets, for twelve hundred stands of arms had been captured. The Americans had little to eat, and were very tired; but the plight of the prisoners was pitiable. Hungry, footsore, and heartbroken, they were hurried along by the fierce and boastful victors, who gloried in the vengeance they had taken, and recked little of such a virtue as magnanimity to the fallen. The only surgeon in either force was Ferguson's. He did what he could for the wounded; but that was little enough, for, of course, there were no medical stores whatever. The Americans buried their dead in graves, and carried their wounded along on horse-litters. The wounded loyalists were left on the field, to be cared for by the neighboring people. The conquerors showed neither respect nor sympathy for the leader who had so gallantly fought them.[3] His body and the bodies of his slain followers were cast into two shallow trenches, and loosely covered with stones and earth. The wolves, coming to the carnage, speedily dug up the carcasses, and grew so bold from feasting at will on the dead that they no longer feared the living. For months afterward, King's Mountain was a favorite resort for wolf-hunters.

Notes

1. The striking nature of the victory and its important consequences must not blind us to the manifold shortcomings of the Revolutionary militia. The mountaineers did well in spite of being militia; but they would have done far better under another system. The numerous failures of the militia as a whole must be balanced against the few successes of a portion of them. If the states had possessed wisdom enough to back Washington with Continentals, or with volunteers such as those who fought in the Civil War, the Revolutionary contest would have been over in three years. The trust in militia was a perfect curse. Many of the backwoods leaders knew this. The old Indian fighter, Andrew Lewis, about this time wrote to Gates (see Gates MSS., 30 Sept. 1780 [in Houghton Library at Harvard University and Perkins Library at Duke University]),

speaking of the "dastardly conduct of the militia," calling them "a set of poltroons," and longing for Continentals.

2. Among these privates was the father of Davy Crockett.

3. But the accounts of indignity being shown him are not corroborated by Allaire and Ryerson, the two contemporary British authorities, and are probably untrue.

Edward Francisco

Edward Francisco is a poet, novelist, and professor of English. His poems have appeared in more than a hundred magazines and journals, including *Appalachian Heritage, Southern Review, Kansas Quarterly,* and *William and Mary Review.* Francisco was a finalist in the 1990 Yale Younger Poets competition. He was also chosen as a Voices and Visions Poet-Scholar for the National Endowment for the Humanities and the American Library Association. Francisco currently lives in Strawberry Plains, Tennessee.

Abraham Lincoln
Contemplates Jefferson Davis
Located Somewhere Out of Sight

When I was a boy I sat on our
knotted stoop, waiting for my father
to bring a seven-cent wagon from Louisville.
He draped the surprise under sackcloth,
his being the singular vision of a man
perpetually bent on a joke. I stood
like a plank, trying not to sob on
the apple in my throat, knowing that
large for my years, I would appear
even sillier than boys of lesser
stature. Now I stare out on the
dull glass of the Potomac, bellying
laughter one minute, scalding eyes
and surprising myself the next.
Is there no end to this joking?

Printed by permission of the author.

Mostly I think about him and what
he must be thinking about me.
Jeff, did I wake up on your dark
side this morning? Did you glance
around the room with your one
good eye and see all that I saw,
razor poised at the line of my throat,
staring back? Did you shake the
curtains for signs of me, restless,
ready to knot your sheets, pranking
in ways you would probably fail
to appreciate. Jeff, I have pity for
you as only a Southerner can—I
who am surrounded by firebrands
and their theories, each a dangling
predicament ready to loop my
throat with only enough slack
as to allow me to do what they
hoped I'd do all along.
Is it like that for you, Jeff?

Do you stand each morning with your
back facing the mirror, waging campaigns
on both fronts at once? Macbeth,
you'll recall, lost his head for refusing
to believe his eyes too late. What
are we going to do now, Jeff?
How will we climb out of this
intact? Of all the men I know,
you are even less qualified than
I to run a country. Look there.

A cloud hangs now at eye-level just
over the spot where it comforts
me to know you're probably sitting
head cocked at an angle best
suited for reflecting the light.

Does that mean you can see
your way clear to see it my
way, Jeff?

Does a single eye offend
you in the least?

Straining, can you see
as I seem to see all that is withheld temporarily
from view?

Do you see you as I

  do
  you see
   you
  do you
   see

Jeff?

Martha Crowe

Martha Butcher Crowe has lived in East Tennessee all of her life. She is a graduate of King College in Bristol and East Tennessee State University in Johnson
City. She attended the University of Tennessee at Knoxville and currently
teaches in the Department of English at East Tennessee State University.
Among her teaching and research interests are American poetry and satire.
For at least ten years, she has concentrated her efforts on preserving and tran-
scribing manuscripts connected with the DeVault family and the ancestral
home, the DeVault Tavern, important in the history of East Tennessee. She
has presented papers at the Popular Culture Association, the Tennessee Philo-
logical Association, and the Appalachian Studies Conference on the town of
Leesburg, the DeVault Tavern, and the epistolary love of Mary Jane DeVault
and Edward Owings Guerrant. She continues work on the manuscript, *Sunny
Side and the Kentucky Soldier,* from which the following letters are extracted.

Sunny Side and the Kentucky Soldier

A Letter always feels to me like immortality because it is
the mind alone without corporeal friend. Indebted in our
talk to attitude and accent, there seems a spectral power in
the thought that walks alone.
                    —Emily Dickinson, 1869

Printed by permission of the author.

In the nineteenth century, letter writing held a position of respect as a special means of communicating the writer's truest thoughts, a lasting record of his education, good taste, and character. It was considered an art. Mary Jane DeVault of Leesburg, Tennessee, and Edward Owings Guerrant of Sharpsburg, Kentucky, shared this view. Their 193 letters, dating from August 1864 to May 1868, reflect a growing awareness of the importance of their correspondence, especially since it was their only communication after several brief meetings and eventually became their only means of courtship. The four-year separation allows us to follow their epistolary romance as it endured the Civil War and Reconstruction. Today we treasure such letters because they can provide the specificity—the real story from real people in real places—that the history books cannot do, giving us a breadth of experience that offers much more than the generalizations and stereotypes about Appalachia or even the picture of Scarlett grubbing for turnips in the dirt at Tara. We can see how the "thought that walks alone" can span thousands of miles and years of separation as two young people try to find their personal identities after the loss of their national lives.

The story begins in the tiny community of Leesburg in war-torn East Tennessee. Leesburg is an excellent example of a region within a region. Located less than five miles from Jonesborough, it is a part of the South. The general perception is that East Tennessee was entirely pro-Union; the picture is much more complex, however. Within this region within a region, there was much division; the situation was about as uniform and predictable as a ten-day weather forecast in East Tennessee in March. Although the majority may have been pro-Union, there was a significant number of Confederate supporters, and they were fierce in their loyalties. During the war many were tolerant of the loyalties of others. For example, there is a story of two families in Jonesborough, the Masons and the Dillworths—one southern, the other Union—who lived in one house. When the Yankees came, both families moved to the "Yankee" side; when the Confederates came, both moved "south." Mary told of a slave, Old Uncle Abe, who hid in their cellar the one horse the Yankees had not taken; it was the only means "both Southern and Union women" had for carrying water and hauling flour from the mill. The bitterness came later when, after the war, Mary saw her nice carriages and wagons pass with "awful" people in them (Letter to Grace). In East Tennessee, the so-called reconciliation period was the time of the most bitterness and violence for the civilians, as Union supporters sought revenge and—more dangerous—as bushwhackers, in the name of righteous reprisal, practiced nothing less than out-and-out meanness.

One spring day in 1863, a captain in the Confederate army stopped with "the pitiful remnant of Giltner's Brigade" before a spring house near the DeVault home—"Sunny Side"—which was known as a haven for Rebel soldiers. The Union army was in close pursuit, and the Kentucky soldier feared that he would not have time to dismount and drink. He was delighted to see a diminutive, blue-eyed "mountain maid" or "Tennessee bushwhacker," as he later called her, offering a tray of honey and pumpkin pie. As he rode away, she heard him tell a friend, "Bart, I'd like to steal all of that old man's honey" (Letter to Grace). He later confided to a fellow officer, "I'm going to come back and get that little girl when the war is over" (McAllister and Guerrant 46). He visited several times, and, before he left to join Morgan's ill-fated command in Greeneville, he asked permission to write. Mary DeVault hesitated, but, at the urging of her mother, agreed to correspond. This love-at-first-sight meeting becomes a romantic tale of unfulfilled love. Long after the war's end, Edward Guerrant could not come to the Union stronghold of East Tennessee since, as adjutant general to Marshall, his signature appeared on orders for arrests of Union soldiers and civilians, as well as on orders for raids in the area. Mary could not join him, since she had promised her dying mother that she would take care of her father and five younger brothers.

What is remarkable about the letters is the way these two gifted writers made their personalities come alive.

Mary Jane DeVault (1844–1937), the "Sunny Side" of the letters, was the only daughter and eldest child of John and Amanda Jane Russell DeVault. An ardent Rebel, she proved her loyalty in the face of danger. She hid a wounded soldier in a secret room in the attic of the DeVault Tavern, her ancestral home located across from Sunny Side. She slipped to the attic to nurse him despite the fact that Union supporters were living in the house at the time. The soldier recovered to rejoin his troop and years later returned to thank her (Butcher). She observed a skirmish on the road and saw a Rebel struck from his horse. She took him to her home and sent for the doctor. Too afraid to come, the doctor sent directions for the soldier's care, but a woman reported his presence and Mary was forced to give him up after threats that her home would be burned if she did not. She never knew if he recovered (Letter to Grace). She protected her dying mother from marauding Union soldiers, putting up such a fight that the commander took pity on her and ordered his men to leave. Upon learning that the officer had been punished for disobeying orders, Mary commented that there were some good Yankees, after all. Mary, though tiny—only four feet, eleven inches tall—was spunky, with a temper to match her red hair. She spiced her letters with epithets such as "Yankee like" and "enough brass to mold a cannon." Although her hatred and despair were certainly genuine, sometimes there is a barely perceptible trace of humor in her recital of Yankee crassness.

Edward Owings Guerrant (1835–1916), who signed himself "Kentucky Soldier," was the son of Henry Ellis and Mary Beaufort Howe Owings Guerrant. Edward distinguished himself in school, excelling in athletics as well as academics. He graduated from Centre College at Danville, Kentucky, in 1859 and gained a reputation as "an excellent student, speaker and powerful debater." Edward joined General Humphrey Marshall's Kentucky forces, which meant he would serve in southwestern Virginia and East Tennessee protecting the railroad and the salt and lead mines for the Confederacy. Because of his education and writing skills, he was given a position on Marshall's personal staff and was later appointed to assistant adjutant general in 1862 and promoted that same year. He participated in Bragg's campaign in Kentucky in 1862, and in Marshall's and Morgan's in 1864 (McAllister and Guerrant 29–41).

Edward kept a "War Journal"; one of the first entries describes leaving home to join General Marshall's forces across the mountains, arriving in Powell County "almost frozen," and receiving "uncommonly common accommodations":

> After breakfast—about 10 A.M. we again took up our line of march. Crossed over the mts, and fell upon the head of Indian Creek—which we followed to its mouth into Red River, over 12 miles of as bad road as my eyes had ever been pained with the sight of—hogs, stumps, trees, quicksand—holes—footpaths—nobody knows what except passengers up or down Indian Creek— . . . Arrived at Red River, we followed up its muddy and swollen current some 3 or 4 miles over terrible ways— once blockaded by a great tree which compelled us to scale a mt where nothing but birds and rattle snakes had ever intruded upon the solitude of Nature and took up our quarters for the night . . . on Chimney Top Fork of Red River. . . .
>
> I hate to appear Epicurean in mentioning our fare so minutely—but cannot forbear to record the fact that our fare since home has consisted mainly of Sour Kraut, and Cabbage, and Sorghum Molasses—. (January 17, 1861)

He soon became disillusioned with camp life, "waiting for orders, tired of the endless rain," tired of constantly fighting nausea which was treated with "Calomel and rhubarb (about 10 grams each)." Senna tea every morning helped "relieve" him as well as bitters of "mean" whiskey, rhubarb, and gentian. He was disgusted with the habits of gambling and drinking in camp, but he described them with grim humor and tolerance, since he understood the boredom:

> "John Barleycorn" spent a merry evening in camp . . . I am tired! tired! tired! Tired waiting on the slow motion of our army in going to this land and the people I love. Tired of the dread ennui of August days and nothing to do or read (Wed. Aug 13, 1861)
>
> . . . Jno Heckley and John Barleycorn had difficulty riding the same horse last evening. (August 17, 1861)

Edward faithfully recorded entries almost every day, no matter how rushed, but he took the time to observe each holiday and to record his feelings on that special day.

His commemoration of Washington's Birthday is typical of his eloquent prose and of the southern soldier's idealism early in the war:

> Strange day—Strange sight! What thoughts of mingled amazement and sorrow crowd our minds and burden our memories, as we reflect upon the

past and the present: upon the labors of Washington and our Revolutionary sires—and their rich and glorious results now overthrown or to be preserved in an ark floated upon a sea of hero blood—Alack! Alack!! Alack!! . . .

Today another poor soldier died in town: far away from home—from father and mother and sisters and brothers—and all the comforts—the endearments and consolations of home. He died. I know not who he was. Sufficient to know he was a man—a soldier—A Southerner. He paid the highest sacrifice of a patriot upon the altar of his country.

Ah! how we should prize our liberties if ever gained—when they are bought at such a price! Everyday witnesses the sacrifice of tens and hundreds of bloody victims laid upon the bloody altar of Freedom's Cause. In the coldest of weather—in snow and hail and rain—I have seen these heroic men without a tent or covering but the black, angry looking cloud that poured its furious torrents upon them—encamped in the forest and cheerfully endeavoring to fan the spark of life into a little flame—to draw out a little longer for their country's cause the threads of existence—which only holds its tenure at her will and disposal. Such men as these can never be conquered—They may be slaughtered but not conquered.

This day Jefferson Davis is inaugurated President of the Confederate States of America—despite the efforts of Lincoln to prevent a partner in his office and a division of his domain. Today the Government of the Confederate States —ceases to be "Provisional" and becomes Constitutional and I hope, stable and perpetual. . . .

Oh! *Mighty Washington!* Would thy presence were again our safety and our shield to victory. (February 22, 1862)

The growing disillusionment with the war is recorded in a Christmas journal entry:

If any one had said "Xmas Gift!" to me this A.M., I guess I would have given my last corn dodger to him. . . .
We washed our faces in snow, ate our breakfast off a piece of cold corn beef—and waited for . . . the war to close. . . . That's all we have to wait for in this country. The boys made Christmas fires and gathered hog's heads from the Yankees' camp and made a jubilee over the feast! (December 25, 1864)

The first letter from Mary to Edward shows her growing fears about the war:

I know you think I do not intend answering your kind letter but it would be ungrateful not to recognize this favor of a Kentucky soldier, one that has denied himself the pleasures of home society, endured the many privations that cannot be avoided for our Sunny South. But you have made a strange selection, some novelty exist[s]. I feel my incompetency, and feel as if it would be impossible for me to interest you, but when noticed, will do . . . the best I can, and perhaps will relieve the monotony of camp life for a few minutes.

I understand your insinuations pretty well—(but soldier-like, you *do not mean them*) and I will not misconstrue them.

All have passed, not a creature to be seen, all look gay, but me. I feel lonely and sad. You will think I am a strange rebel, to feel sad, when prospects are so bright, but sympathy, and an amount of selfishness rule, and prevent my rejoicing when I would. But how can any one be glad to see so many brave and noble men, preparing to meet the enemy? Who will survive? How many fail? I do know I am a good rebel, but a dark picture engages me, for the first time since the war. I am impatient for the long looked for time when we are to be a free and independent people.

You will not wonder at my impatience when I tell you that last evening I heard of the fall of three cousins in the last fight before Atlanta, among them my favorite, "Vollie Devault." He seemed almost as near as a brother, always pleasant and seeking to please others. Just to think of dying away from home and friends. What tidings for a widowed Mother! But such things must be borne with fortitude, and all try to encourage the living. My influence being very limited, fear few will be encouraged by my sayings.

I saw Genl. J. H. Morgan pass a few minutes ago. Hope the Yankees will hear of his approach and run too fast for you to catch them, unless you can capture without fighting. (August 17, 1864)

In a letter to Mary, Edward describes the "overthrow and surrender" of Lee's army:

We were struck dumb! with grief! and astonishment! It came like midnight at midday. We never thought or dreamed of such a thing.

In fond but faint hopes it might be a mistake, we moved on East and the night after leaving Christiansburg we camped on the head of the Roanoke River. That night some 2000 men deserted Echoe's Army, but *not one* from Giltner's Brigade!

The next day Gen. Echoe, having lost all hope and courage, disbanded his forces and sent them home in all directions. Col. Giltner refused to disband his brigade, but led it to Ky.—with the intention of surrendering here if necessary, or of going thro' Southern Ky. to West Tenn., and Trandsilus's; if any hope was left us of doing good thereby. . . .

Although the Yankees treated us with the utmost kindness and the very greatest consideration, still, the pain, the sorrow, and the mortification of that moment was awful beyond description. It's black raven shadows will long bury the joys of being at home and among my old friends and relatives.

I found all my people well and rejoiced to see me. . . . I have every want and wish gratified, but I am very unhappy. "Freedom—the noblest aspiration of generous souls" no more has a dwelling place in my heart, and it has left a void "the world can never fill." When I think of the past I am miserable.

But over all these beautiful skies and matchless carpets of green grass and gently rolling hills, a heavy pall as of darkness and death rests, like a fearful judgment of Heaven. The spirit of her glory and her greatness has fled. Her historic renown here perished, and her ancestral honors are faded and fallen, like a meteor from the firmament. This pall oppresses my soul and I sigh for the free air and almost desolate plains of Tennessee! . . . Alack! Alack! Alack! (June 27, 1865)

Edward imagined Mary's as the "kind, sweet clarion voice" from Sunny Side, likening it to the bell on the wrecked steamer *The Arctic,* that "lone wave-shaken bell" which "tolled its sad requiem over those who went down to sleep in the coral caves of the great sea. . . . For all I possess of that happy, halcyon past is the voice and smile of 'Sunny Side'" (October 11, 1865).

The situation in Kentucky was much better than in East Tennessee. Edward was able to teach school and then to travel to Philadelphia and to New York the next year to study medicine. He excelled in his studies and passed his examinations, although the professors quizzed him more about politics than medicine. He wrote to Mary that he had heard of "the lawless proceeding of your enemies to deprive you of property, of home and country and even life" and lamented "insults unresented, wrongs unrevenged, virtue despised and innocence outraged" (October 22, 1865).

Mary described the bitterness in Tennessee under Brownlow's administration.

Do you want to know something of this wicked land?
. . . Union people are seemingly happy. Rebels are miserable beyond utterance. There's no help for us, since some are void of conscience. . . .
Mr. Barding, a well known Southern man . . . was shot through the neck while sitting in the family circle, by an unknown person, was permitted to live two weeks, when a party of his nearest neighbors went to his bed-side and in the presence of his wife and children, pierced his breast with eight balls, killing him instantly, then bayoneted his lifeless body. Mrs. Brading [spelled two ways in original] knew the men, reported them for which she was whipped, robbed, driven from home. . . . A few nights ago the same band was at Uncle R. A. Thompsons. Did not succeed in breaking his doors, shot at the house several times. . . . Last night another cousin . . . was whipped, her husband beaten with thorn bushes. . . . A great many have been beaten with thorn bushes, the most severe punishment that can be inflicted. . . . You say you would flee such a country. . . . I would do so if I could . . . , but my poor sick mother and our home cannot be moved. (November 17, 1865)

Mary repeated stories of robberies and violence and complained of a government that condoned such, denying rebels the right to own property and allowing "negroes and radicals" to vote. "What does Brownlow mean to do with us?" she asked on April 2, 1866. On April 20, she told of more troubles in East Tennessee: "They have begun anew, more whipping than ever. Mr Campbell was taken from his house by ten or fifteen men two nights ago, so badly beaten that his recovery [is] doubted." On the same night, Morrow's Mill two miles away was burned. "The guilty go unpunished, only Rebels injured." She described armed Union men and blacks (and "black white men") who stood at voting places and kept the Confederates from entering (October 16, 1866). During another election, "Negroes and radicals had a good time here today voting . . . the negroes armed—to keep the Rebels away—they were shooting near the house all evening. . . . A negro judge and negroes stood at the door with their rifles . . ." (July 31, 1867).

As late as 1867 there were reports of exiled Confederates shot while returning home. Mary reported a conversation between her father and another southern sympathizer: "Have not heard so many treasonable remarks in some time. Neither could say anything half bad enough, so they ended by chaining Brownlow near a large fire, forcing Negroes to cut his flesh and cook [it], then make him eat it until he ate himself up" (January 18, 1867).

What was hardest for Mary to forgive was that her own neighbors have been "our worst enemies, and their mothers and sisters encouraging them in their meanness." A neighbor led a band that "stripped the house of every single mouthful of provision . . . not sparing my mother's medicines and cursing her for pay" (March 12, 1865). Though Mary could not forget, many in East Tennessee were able to; she was incensed that there had been "no less than a dozen marriages near here . . . and almost all without a particle of reason. Rebel girls and Yankee soldiers, cousins, and old maids and young boys, and little girls and old widowers" (October 16, 1867).

Finally it was safe for Edward to come to East Tennessee, and, since Mary's father had remarried, she was free to go home with her Kentucky soldier. The letters show the growing anticipation as their wedding day, "blessed by and by," approaches. A few weeks before their wedding she sent Edward this diet:

> Take one spoonful of cin. oil before breakfast. Eat nothing but pork, cornbread and dried apples—not more than three cups of strong coffee. Your dinner equally as light. For supper—a dozen hard-boiled eggs and twenty-four walnuts. Then take one teaspoon of paregoric. That should keep you healthy until you come to me. (April 10, 1868)

Either because of or in spite of the diet, he did come and they were married on May 12, 1868. They moved to Kentucky, where Edward practiced medicine until he decided to enter the ministry. After several years as pastor in Lexington and Louisville, Edward became a missionary to the Southern Highlands and is credited with having established many schools and missions. Because of the years he spent in the Appalachians and his devotion to the little "mountain maid," Edward fought the myth of Appalachia as "a strange land and a peculiar people." With the help and love of "Sunny Side," who provided the "light for his shady side," Edward wrote three books on his mission in the mountains: *The Soul Winner, The Galax Gatherers,* and *The Gospel of the Lilies.*

Works Cited

DeVault, Mary Jane. Letter to Grace Owings Guerrant, 11 Dec. 1929. Courtesy of Mary DeVault Butcher of Leesburg, TN.

DeVault, Mary Jane, and Edward Owings Guerrant. Letters from 1864 to 1868. Courtesy of Edward Owings Guerrant, Altadena, CA.

Guerrant, Edward Owings. War Journal. One copy in possession of Martha Crowe, quoted courtesy of Edward Owings Guerrant. Original in Archives, Wilson Library, U of North Carolina at Chapel Hill. Quoted courtesy of Edward Owings Guerrant.

McAllister, J. Gray, and Grace Owings Guerrant. *Edward O. Guerrant: Apostle to the Southern Highlanders.* Richmond, VA: Richmond Press, 1950.

Albert Stewart

An East Kentuckian, Albert Stewart is the founding editor of *Appalachian Heritage* and the founder of the Appalachian Writers Workshop at the Hindman Settlement School. Students of Appalachia everywhere owe Albert Stewart a debt of gratitude for the contributions he has made as a poet, teacher, editor, and student of the region. His major collection is *The Untoward Hills* (1962).

Men on Morgans

Under bronze beeches a ragged outfit came,
Reining tense Morgans, limned by skies
As wistful as a Morgan's soft, absorbent eyes.
Down to dusk they rode by ways of flame.

So dusty: it was hard to say
Whether their garb was blue or grey.
Hands languid: yet ready for the pistol locks,
They studied the camp site in the rocks.

From *The Untoward Hills,* Morehead State College Press, © 1962, renewed 1987. Reprinted by permission of the author.

And pitched their tents and set up guard
By streams that lipped the grey beech roots.
They sat on lichened stones as hard
As Indian flint and took off their boots.

I saw the fear writ in their eyes
And fear hang on them like a blame.
They stood beneath all dying skies
Alone, both hunter and hunted: the same.

I saw them lead tired Morgans to the stream
And pause to pat a nose or rub a flank
And watch patiently the antique dream
As each drank, lifted head to gaze, and drank.

No matter what I heard them say;
Nor why men come or go away.
No matter: the charge of Blue or Grey,
Or what they thought they thought that autumn day.

They came on Morgans to the end of day
And hovered to a central flame
That nursed them down an awkward way.
No need to name a magic name,

Dull master key that turns all locks:
These words can only tell,
And they must even be at pains to tell,
How men retrieved their living in these rocks.

Richard Marius

Richard Marius, a historian and student of the Renaissance, was born in 1933 in Martel, Tennessee. He was educated at the University of Tennessee (B.S.), the Southern Baptist Theological Seminary (B.D.), and Yale (M.A. and Ph.D.). As an undergraduate, Marius worked as a newspaper reporter, and, after completing his doctorate, he taught at Gettysburg College. He then taught history at the University of Tennessee before taking his current position as director of expository writing at Harvard University.

Marius's works include three novels, beginning with *The Coming of Rain*

(1969), which was designated best novel of 1969 by Friends of American Writers. He is also the author of *Luther: A Biography* (1974) and *Thomas More: A Biography,* which was nominated in 1984 for the American Book Award in nonfiction. Of particular interest to him is the American Civil War, which provides the background for *The Coming of Rain,* from which the following selection is taken. He writes, "I taught two years at Gettysburg College where I vividly remember the wintry mists swirling over the battlefield and the ghostly monuments when I drove up from the farmhouse where I lived south of the city."

Brian Ledbetter

Virgil lapsed into thought. His sandy hair flopped gently with the motion of his mule. The sweat streaked his face and neck, droplets of sweat quivering and shaking and shining in the blistering sun. He asked with even more delicate caution: "Why'd you do that? Why'd you go and fight for them?"

Brian came out of his own hot reveries and looked frowning at the boy. For a while he didn't say anything but looked away again, into the trembling heat waves on the road. "It was one of those things," he said laconically.

"Was it for the niggers? Was you a niggerlover? Did you want to make the niggers free?"

"Well," Brian frowned uncomfortably, "in a manner of speaking. I mean it wasn't *right* that niggers was slaves. But I guess that didn't matter much to me. I didn't see no sense in fighting for somebody else's niggers. I don't give a damn one way or another about niggers lessen it's. . . . Well, I just don't give a damn." He was about to say he didn't give a damn about any niggers except for the pleasures of nigger whores, and he was on the point of giving Virgil a lecture on the joys of nigger whoredom. But he decided in midsentence that the subject wasn't delicate. Not on this day.

"Mamma says the Yankees wanted all our money, and that's why we had the War."

Brian fought manfully with his first impulse. But the effort of choking down what he wanted to say was so great that he couldn't say anything.

"Mamma says if we'd of won, we'd all be rich now, and we wouldn't have all this trouble we're having in the world."

"Virgil, let me tell you something. If you folks had of won, you'd be living like a nigger right this minute. You'd have yourself a little shack, and it wouldn't even be yours. And some big-assed rich man would be hollering 'Boy' at you all the time, and you couldn't do nothing but say 'Yessir!' You'd live on the weedy ass of some rich feller's place, and that's all you'd get out of life. The ass end of everything."

From *The Coming of Rain,* Knopf, 1969. Reprinted by permission of the author.

"Mamma says we'd of all been rich, and we'd have lots of parties, and we'd all have us a horse to ride."

"You'd be poorer than a church mouse."

"Mamma says if we'd of won, we'd all have a slave. Only . . . " He hesitated in some confusion.

"Only *what?*"

"Only she says she's glad we don't have a lot of slaves around the house." He brightened suddenly, an innocent, sure cognizance breaking over his tanned face. "But if we'd of won, we'd have us *good* slaves. We wouldn't have no *bad* slaves—the kind that steals and does sinful things. And we wouldn't have a lot of other things." This last he said with such bold insinuation that Brian's dander was raised.

"What, for instance?"

"Gambling and drinking for instance. Card playing and . . . And folks like you not going to church on Sunday morning. Mamma says our side was awful strong on church. If we'd won, we'd make everybody go."

Brian sighed in profound contempt. "Jesus H. Christ! I reckon you think the whole Rebel Army was one big floating Sunday School."

"Mamma says Stonewall Jackson prayed ever time he drunk a glass of water. You can't show me no *Yankee* general that done that."

"Jackson was crazy," Brian said darkly. His words were a subdued muttering, an uncomfortable reflection over a horror. "He loved to kill, that man did. If the War hadn't come along, that man would of ended up just like Simson yesterday. He was a fanatic, one of the worst men that ever was." He uttered a malicious laugh. "I wish he'd seen the end. Lord God, I sure as hell wish he'd knowed he was whipped."

"What makes you say such things?" Virgil asked in a hurt tone. "You done all the awful things you done, and you ain't even sorry!"

Brian guffawed with deliberate cruelty, shaking the notes of laughter out like a whip over a raw back. He looked at Virgil with a sneer. But again something walled in his words. *He don't even know.* The amazing thought jumped into his brain. Again the something thoughtful and terribly serious came back. "Virgil, I'm going to tell you why I done the things I done and why I say the things I say. I remember sometimes that it wasn't yesterday. Time's getting away so fast. So *damned* fast.

"I was in town the day we heard about Sumter. I remember what it done to people that ought to of knowed better. Sumter was like a big drunk. It made a lot of folks foolish. Maybe the whole goddam country got drunk on Sumter.

"A feller named Condon was the telegrapher. You don't remember him. He's been dead for many a year. But I remember just the way his voice sounded. Like yesterday. I remember him singing out the news all day long, and I remember the way the news shot out into the country and made people come into town. And they come! Lord God, they come! Everybody was pushed in around it and listening to the news, and it was *some*thing.

"It was spring. And I'll tell you something. You'd be surprised how I remember the way things smelled on that day. And I seen J. W. Campbell that day. That's something else I won't ever forget. Him and me wasn't good friends back then. He was a lot older than me. I guess I knowed his boy better than I knowed him. His boy was four or five years younger than me. His boy was a quiet sort. Not like J. W. It was a strange thing when I think on it. J. W. can always be so calm about things. You figure he's got everything under control. His boy wasn't like that at all. His boy was always sitting around and watching his daddy and listening, but the only time he'd say anything was when you spoke to him, and then he wouldn't say much. He'd grin and shake his head, and he had a big, loud laugh. He was always breaking out in that big, loud laugh. Only it wasn't *funny* laughing. He wasn't laughing because he thought things was *funny.* It was sad to hear him laugh thataway. Oh, I can't explain it."

"You was talking about the way the War begun," Virgil said.

"I know it, damn it. I know it. I was just thinking about things. Well, J. W. was standing on his porch with his hands folded behind his back, and his boy was sitting on the porch with his feet hanging off the edge. Neither one of them was saying anything, but they looked like grim death! So *still.* All that noise and commotion, and them two was so *still.* J. W., he look at me. His eyes caught on me for just a second and then moved on, and he looked off like he didn't want to talk. So *still.* But I could tell what the look meant, and I went off and thought about it.

"And you know the next time I seen J. W. Campbell? It was way up in Virginia. Out in the middle of nowhere before Cold Harbor where I got my foot shot off. He come in to where I was, sitting at a fire, and it was raining. Well, we seen each other, and we stood by the fire with the rain spitting in it, and we talked for five, ten minutes. He asked me right then if I'd heard anything from his boy. Course I hadn't, and hell, his boy wasn't going to write *me,* and if he had, I couldn't *read* it. So when I said I hadn't heard a word, he lost interest and went off. Next time I seen him was back here, after the War, when it was all over.

"But that day, the day of Sumter, all them fools like your grandpaw was standing there yelling and cheering and slapping hands when they heard Old Man Condon sing out the news. We was all standing around there, and everything smelled like the daffodils, and it wasn't like blood at all. But we was making up our minds which side we'd kill for. They was a lot that made up their minds about dying that afternoon.

"J. W., he taken his boy up to Knoxville that very same night. And ever time the folks around the telegraph yelled, it made me make up my mind just a little bit more. I can't explain it now. But after a while I knowed I had to haul my ass out of here before it got too late.

"I went on home. Didn't say nothing to nobody in town. I just went home, and I told my mammy and my daddy what I was going to do. My mammy didn't say nothing. She didn't cry, didn't give me no argument. I never seen her again after that day. I always used to think about her dying and me crying by her bed and all that, but she died before I got home. My daddy said she cried ever night for a week after I got gone, and she went down to her death worrying about me. She didn't say a thing that night, except she asked me what I wanted to take.

"My daddy said he guessed I'd need a horse. I said I didn't want to take none of the horses. I knowed stock'd be hard to come by in the War, but he said the place was mine as much as it was his, and he said he'd be damned if he'd let a boy of his'n go off to war without a horse.

"We was sitting around talking all of a sudden like I'd growed up that afternoon. Lord God, I was twenty year old! We was most all children that foughten that war. Oh, they was folks like J. W. and lots of others that was older, but most of us was children. We was the kind of boys that you expect to stay home and watch their short hairs curl except on Saturday night. But we was the very ones that went off and foughten the goddammedest war that *anybody* ever fought! It's a wonderful thing when you think on it. War's so big you think it ought to be fought by bankers and presidents and senators and railroad men and preachers and school teachers. But it ain't. It's fought by a bunch of poor dogs like me. And we was all just children back then, and we didn't know to say excuse me when we farted. We was the ones that foughten that war! I tell you, it makes you think!"

They rode along, and Brian reveled for a few moments in the grand thought of what he'd done, an expression of full wonder and satisfaction on his beaming face.

"Get on with it," Virgil said. "Go on and tell me about it."

"Well, I was pretty well packed up, ready to get when it got dark, and my daddy was fixing to run me up a horse when up in the afternoon Matthew Crittendon came riding into my yard. Right where you rode this morning. You never did know Matthew Crittendon, that son of a bitch!"

"Mamma says he was one of the biggest heroes that ever was!" Virgil was hurt and anxious.

"Matthew Crittendon was one of the biggest sons of bitches that ever was! He was the kind that would of run this country if you folks had of won. He had him a uniform on already when he come to see me, and you know something! It was *white!* He looked like a goddam admiral of the ocean sea! He rode up with a bunch of young piss-ants, little bastards willing to eat his shit so's they be near to that *white uniform!* He had long greasy yellow hair, Matthew did. It was all the way down to his shoulders. He was getting a troop up to fight the Yankees, he said. They'd elected him captain, and they was out looking for more men.

"I tell you what's true. He wanted to kill me right then. He smelled like whiskey, and he was mean. He run me off his place once. I tracked a deer onto his land and killed it, and he come when he heard the gun and cussed me out and run me off his place. Wouldn't even let me take the deer. Said I was a trespasser, and I eat beans that night instead of deer meat. I ain't never forgot the taste of them beans to this day. I think he wanted me to say I was going Union, and he was going to kill me and maybe my folks, too. I can't prove it. He's dead now. But I got my thoughts on it. It was the look in his eye. He was all set to see blood. And there he was with them friends of his, and they wanted to start the War with me.

"Damned if it don't make me laugh yet! I pitched a fit. I talked about Abe Lincoln like he was a dog. I said I'd had my doubts, but this was too much, too damned much! I had wanted the Union, I said, but I didn't want no killing of brave Southern men, and by damn now I'd made up my mind, and I was going to give them Yanks hell, and I'd be honored to fight with Captain Matthew Crittendon. I said him and me had had our differences, but now I'd be right proud to shake his hand, and we done it. We done it, and we swore brotherhood forever.

"Matthew Crittendon didn't know what the hell was going on. He had a lot of sense, that boy did! Like a burned stump. Like my wood leg. *God,* was he dumb! And he was real surprised and pleased. He smiled. The kind of smile you see on a idjit's face when you rub his back. I said them mean old Yanks wasn't going to come down here and rape *my* poor old mammy, and I put my arms around her and give her a big hug. Lord, Virgil, you ought to of seen it! My mammy, she nodded her head like she was scared to death of being raped, and my daddy took it from me and got cussing mad at the Yanks and the Republicans and Abe Lincoln. I said that if Captain Crittendon would let me stay this one more night with my dear mammy and daddy, I'd be out to meet him first thing in the morning. So him and his shitty friends went off, and he was smiling all the time, and we must of shook hands ten times before he got going. Matthew and me was about the same age, but I called him 'Captain' most ever other word, and it tickled his ass. He couldn't hardly sit on his saddle his ass was tickled so much.

"But I tell you the truth; we was scared. I didn't know what he'd do to my mammy and daddy when he found out the truth. But I had to do it. I had to do what I done, and it worked out all right. Even Matthew Crittendon couldn't go round killing old folks. Not if they was *white.* We waited till it got good and dark, and then my daddy run me up a horse, and I lit out. I went north, to Kentucky, and that's how I went to the War. And I'm glad I done it." Brian sighed heavily and wistfully for something lost and shook his head in ponderous wonder.

"I was scared shitless. When I rode out of here, I had a knot in my chest. I could almost put my hand on it and feel it. It was so big I thought it'd stop me breathing. And I'll tell you something, Virgil. On the road to Knoxville that night, I cried. Oh, you needn't look at me that way. Men cries sometimes. On the road that night, out under the sky with the air smelling fresh and clean. I cried. I never had even been away from home for a night in my whole life, and I was twenty years old and going to fight a war, and you try to do that without crying! But I'd do it again. I'd do it all just like I done it if I was young and the War was to come again. I can't tell you why exactly, but I'd do it. I made history when I was twenty years old, and I'll never forget it. No, I'll never forget it." He shook his head again with that profound, blissful, nostalgic wonder.

"So you was a Yankee horse soldier," Virgil said.

"Hell, boy! I wore my poor old horse out on that trip. I rode him all the way up into Kentuck, and he was lame when I got there, and they put me on a train and hauled me to Washington City, and I was in First Manassas. We got cut up pretty bad then, and after that they stuck me in the Sixty-Ninth Pennsylvania Infantry. It was a Irish outfit, and with a name like Brian Ledbetter they thought I was a goddamn Irishman and belonged with them." He chuckled in reminiscence, and his fleshy face glowed with pleasure in the dark shade of his hat brim. "That was what they call the fortune of war. I fought out the whole shebang with a bunch of men that couldn't even talk right. Yep, Virgil, it was a great thing. I'd do it again. Damned if I wouldn't, if I was young."

"You really had it," Virgil said in admiration. Then his voice dropped and became abruptly mournful. "I ain't never going to have nothing like you had. We ain't never going to have no more wars. It's all over for me. All over before I even begun."

Brian burst out laughing. "Shit," he said.

"If you'd only fought on the right side," Virgil said with a flat note of condescension.

"I *did* fight on the right side," Brian said.

Virgil looked pugnaciously at him. "Mamma says you knowed better than you done. She says that's why God taken your leg off."

Brian pulled violently back on the reins of his horse and stopped the animal dead in the road. "She *what!* She said *what!*"

Virgil stopped too and looked alarmed. But he held on bravely to his original utterance. "She said you knowed better than you done. And God punished you for it by taking off your leg."

"Well, I'll be a goddam son of a mongrel bitch in a nigger whorehouse," Brian said.

"You're mad," Virgil wailed. "I've made you mad!"

Brian's face went from purple to a hideously enraged vermilion the color of sick wine. He expressed himself for a great while with boiling, swelling eloquence. He called up words he had not used since the War. He invented words never before heard by man. He juggled words which never in history had been thrown into the same fantastic sentence together. It could not last. The high intensity of the moment burned him out. Suddenly—quite suddenly, in fact—Brian Elisha Ledbetter toppled backward and, flailing silently, fell into the deep of exhausted quiet. He glared speechlessly at Virgil. After a long time he spoke with a calm as frozen as the Arctic void: "I done what I done, and I'm glad!"

Virgil snicked with his tongue to his mule. The animal flicked his ears back in the way of mules and went plodding on ahead. The boy looked

around at Brian as if peering remotely at some remarkably bizarre object cast
suddenly down from the sky. But he spoke as he passed by, saying, "That's
why Mamma says God taken off your leg."

Brian closed his eyes tightly and put a hand over his tortured face. His
features were contorted in a fearful grimace. The crushing sunlight was on
his head. And he was hungry. Good Lord, he was hungry! Helplessly he
kicked at his horse and went on behind Virgil toward breakfast.

Garry Barker

Garry Barker is another Appalachian author who lived the mountain life of
which he writes. One of nine children, Barker was born and raised in the
northeastern Kentucky community of Bald Hill. He displayed a talent for
writing early on and has received numerous awards, including the Catholic
Press Association's "Best Short Story" prize. A 1965 graduate of Berea College, Barker remains there as director of the Student Crafts Program and
has served as executive secretary of the Appalachian Writer's Association,
advisory editor to *Appalachian Heritage*, and a member of the National
Book Critics Circle.

"Kaiser," from the *Mountain Passage* collection, documents the difficult
and sometimes tragic circumstances of readjustment to civilian life for the
Appalachian soldier.

Kaiser

When Webster Watts finally came home from The War To End All Wars,
he never stopped wearing his high-topped cavalry boots and trooper's hat,
never stopped carrying the little .32 Smith & Wesson revolver he took from
the body of a fallen comrade.

Webster did hang his Enfield rifle on pegs over the fireplace, beside his
ribbons and medals and the German bayonet he pulled from his thigh and
used to kill the Hun infantryman who overran the trenches during a battle
in a French hayfield. And somehow Webster came back to Caney Creek with a
regulation U.S. Army saddle and saddle blanket, bridle, and clanking spurs, and
the second week home swapped Mack Ward Harper's two heifers and a pair of
German field glasses for the highstepping roan stallion named, now, "Kaiser."

From *Mountain Passage,* Kentucke Imprints, 1986. Reprinted by permission of the author
    and publisher.

Eight-year-old Harper, who'd raised the heifers from calves, hated the big stallion. He watched quietly as Webster gave most of the barn to the new horse, daily brushed and currycombed the roan, waxed the saddle and polished the silvery hardware.

Weary Rose Watts, by now over her surge of happiness at Webster's return, tried to comfort Harper. "Your daddy had a hard time of it," she told the boy. "It'll take a while for him to settle down, after all the killing."

"But he liked the fighting," Harper said suddenly. "He'd druther have stayed over there. All he's gonna do now is drink moonshine and mess with that ugly old horse."

"He ort not to have swapped off your heifers," Rose said tiredly. "But, Harper, he's your daddy. He can do what he wants."

"I wish he hadn't of come home," blurted Harper.

"Don't you ever let me hear you say such as that again," snapped Rose. "I'll take a stick of kindling to your behind."

Harper walked stiffly away, grumbling. "Walks like a little old man," Rose said softly. "That boy had to grow up too fast, with his daddy gone." She turned as Webster and Kaiser clattered up the path from the barn, sparks flying from the big roan's feet, Webster swaying in the saddle. He reined the snorting stallion to a stop by the picket fence.

Webster grinned. "Harper still crying over them two old cows?" he asked. "We'll get him some more, come spring." Kaiser skittered sideways and Webster sawed the reins. "Whoa, you devil!" he ordered. "Mack said this old horse was as mean as me." He reached to rub Kaiser's ears. "Some hoss," Webster said admiringly.

"Where are you going?" asked Rose. "You said you'd get firewood laid in, and finish cutting the corn."

"All in good time, woman," grinned Webster. "First I got to go see a man about a horse." He chuckled. "Let Harper start chopping that wood. Boy needs something to get his mind off of them cows."

Webster reined Kaiser around and spurred the big horse. He clung to the saddle and sent the big roan headfirst toward the rail fence. Kaiser didn't hesitate but didn't jump. He plowed through the rotted rails. Webster hung on, yelling happily, as Kaiser regained his footing and galloped on up the muddy wagon path.

Webster, blessedly free from the cabin, children, cornpatch, and woodpile, spurred Kaiser up the mountainside. Webster, six and a half feet tall and too big for most horses, rode easily on the big stallion. He let Kaiser slow to a walk at the top of the ridge, and pulled a bottle from his coat pocket. Webster drained the last of the moonshine, broke the bottle against a flinty rock, and sent Kaiser across the ridge at a gallop. He reined in the big muddy roan at Ches MacFarland's barn, swung down and marched inside. "Break out the playing cards, Ches," roared Webster. "And get us a bottle or two of that hundred proof."

Ches MacFarland gravely inspected Webster. "Got any cash?" he finally asked.

Webster chuckled and dug out a roll of bills. "I'm still living good off of Uncle Sam," he said. "I drawed six months pay just before I come home."

"Then you'd best buy them youngens some shoes," grunted Ches. "You with no crop, you'd best start worrying about making it through the winter."

"Hell," spat Webster, "Rose and the boy, they growed two acres of burley. We ain't hurting, Ches. I'll take care of me and mine. Where's the boys?"

"In by the stove," growled Ches. "Whiskey's two dollars a bottle."

"Here's you ten," grinned Webster. "Let me know when it's used up and I'll get you some more." He carried two pint bottles into the warm tobacco stripping room. "Howdy, Eck," said Webster. "Nelson. Good to see you, Alonzo. When did you get back?"

"Week ago," said Alonzo Cox. "They finally let me out of the hospital in Lexington."

"Rose said you got gassed," said Webster. "Hell, boy, you're lucky to be alive."

"Guess so," said Alonzo. "But I wisht I could grow me back some hair." He cut a chew and stared at Webster. "They tell me you got hit twict, and cut on the leg."

"Yeah," grinned Webster, "but the Hun that done it to me got worse. I got his bayonet hanging on the wall at the house, and his brains got blowed all over a hayfield in France." He uncorked a pint bottle, took a long pull, and passed it around.

"Did you get to Paris, Alonzo?" he asked. "Lordy, what them French women won't do for a man."

"Never got nowheres but them damn trenches," grunted Alonzo. "All I seen was mud, blood, and hospital beds."

"I had me one hell of a time," grinned Webster. "Tell you the truth, I kind of hated to see her end. I could have spent five more years over yonder and loved ever minute of it."

"You always was crazy," Alonzo said softly. "Always went looking for a fight, ain't you?"

Webster shrugged, "I sure ain't never run from one." He shuffled a deck of playing cards. "You fellers got any loose money you'd like to give me?"

Harper was still awake, staring out at the gray dawn, when Webster rode down the path loudly singing "Over There." "Drunk old fool," whispered Harper. He watched as Webster slid off the saddle and sat on the ground to watch the big roan trot off toward the barn.

Webster finally stood and staggered toward the house. Harper listened, tiny fists clenched, to Webster's roaring curses and Rose's futile protests, to the sounds of sharp blows and his mother's whimpers.

"I'll kill him," swore Harper. "I'll kill him dead."

 è

By early winter Rose was pregnant again, Webster had drunk up the cash he'd brought home from the Army, and young Harper Watts was living a tortured existence. Pushed, ridiculed, and punished, Harper bore the brunt of his father's frustrations, Webster's resentment of being so tied to eighty hillside acres and three children.

Harper, in Webster's eyes, could do no right. Harper rode his end of the crosscut saw and caused it to bind. Harper's clumsiness was the reason Webster—half-drunk on moonshine whiskey—dropped the gutted shoat into the mud during the Thanksgiving Day butchering. It was somehow Harper's fault that the tobacco crop stripped out light and discolored. Harper's carelessness caused the hammers to rust on the old .12 gauge shotgun. Harper's inattention to the fire caused the still to malfunction. But in this case, Harper noted, Webster drank the stuff anyhow.

The stallion Kaiser was, to young Harper Watts, the symbol of Webster's evil. Snorting, kicking, yellow teeth bared when anyone but Webster dared to approach him, the big roan tortured the other animals and the Watts children. The stallion particularly delighted in chasing chickens, Rose's dominecker hens, much to Webster's drunken pleasure.

In the saddle, Webster Watts lost his heavy awkwardness and gloomy outlook. He rode with a natural ease, one with the horse, always smiling, a graceful cavalryman in total command as he wheeled and charged and practiced with his old .32 revolver. From horseback, riding full tilt, Webster Watts could put six shots square in his target, a bouncing lard can. With his tobacco stick lance, Webster impaled the terrified rooster, and rode laughing across the hayfield with his quarry lifted high.

"My granddaddy," Webster announced proudly, "rode with Mosby in the valley. Went over from Kentucky to join up, just so he could ride with the best. Wasn't but sixteen, but grandpap run the Yankees up and down that valley for three year. Hell, he was with Morgan when he wasn't but fourteen, then went to Virginny when he heard about Mosby. Had a big gray named Abe, packed a pair of Colt .44s and a Bowie knife, and they say he sent many a Yank soldier to hell."

Harper didn't comment.

"Well, hell, boy," chuckled Webster. "Don't you want to learn how to ride and shoot?"

"Nope," grunted Harper. But, with his little .22, the boy learned to shoot. With never a wasted bullet, Harper bagged squirrels and rabbits for the table.

"Regular little Dan'l Boone," chuckled Webster. He grinned. "I reckon you'll make a foot soldier. Hell, somebody's got to wade through the mud and do the dirty work. Me, I'd druther set in a saddle and let the horse do the walking."

"They don't use horses no more," Harper pointed out.

"How would you know?" asked Webster. "Was you there?"

A dozen times, hidden in the scrub brush, Harper centered the shiny sights of his rifle on Webster's laughing face. And, often, he sat with his gun and glared at Kaiser, wondering if a properly placed .22 shell would fell a prancing stallion.

ƀ

On Christmas Eve, Webster sold the milk cow to buy a gallon of Alonzo's moonshine and a box of .32 cartridges. He rode jauntily across the ridge, spurs jingling, pistol barking, scattering hens and hounds with rebel yells, blistering gunfire, and thundering cavalry charges.

Whipping snowflakes and a bitter north wind finally took their toll, and Webster spurred Kaiser up the path to Willie Ward's store. He tied the lathered stallion away from the wind, reloaded his pistol, and stomped up the steps. Inside, huddled around the stove in flickering lamplight, he found Willie, Ches MacFarland, and Alonzo Cox.

"Ain't this one hell of a Christmas?" roared Webster. "I keep trying to celebrate, but everbody else just wants to set by the fire." He kicked snow from his high-topped boots and slapped his hands together. "Doggone, Alonzo," he laughed. "Ain't you at least got a jug?"

"Looks to me like you've done had a plenty," Alonzo said softly. "Ain't it about time you bought some peppermint for the youngens and went on home?"

"Home, hell," chuckled Webster. "Ain't a thing there but a bigbellied woman and three snotnosed youngens. I'm out to raise me some cain, boys."

"You've done raised a plenty," grunted Willie. "Ever dog and chicken on the ridge has got a bullet in him. Go home, Webster."

"Get me a bottle, Ches," ordered Webster.

"You got money?" Ches asked warily.

"I'm good for it," snapped Webster. "By God, Ches, have I ever shorted you?"

"Nope," said Ches. "And you ain't going to, neither."

"Well, hell," grinned Webster. "Let's swap."

"Swap what?" asked Ches.

Webster shrugged. "What do you want?"

"Them spurs." Ches studied. "Maybe that big old red horse."

Webster laughed. "My horse can't be had, boys. Kaiser, and this here old pistol, ain't for sale."

"You'd be better off," said Alonzo, "with a team of mules and a double bitted axe. Go on home now."

"Who the hell are you to tell me what to do?" demanded Webster. "Willie, what have you and Ches got to say about that?"

Willie stared at the floor. "You've had too much to drink, Web," muttered Ches. "Go on home."

"I'll just be damned." Webster grinned, toyed with his .32, and chuckled. "Old maids. Three old women." He cocked the revolver and smiled at Alonzo. "Let me see you dance, old woman."

"Put the pistol away, Webster," Ches said quietly.

"Put it away? Damn, it's Christmas." Webster stood up. "Time to raise cain." He laughed, and waved the pistol. "I said for you to dance, Alonzo."

"Go home, Web," said Willie Cox. "I'm closing up the store."

"I ain't going nowheres," grinned Webster. He waved his revolver. "I aim to have me some fun." He fired suddenly onto the floor at Alonzo's feet, then shot out a lamp.

"It's getting dark, Willie," cackled Webster.

Alonzo crawled out from behind the counter with Willie's old .44 Colt.

Webster blasted another lamp.

Alonzo took aim and fired twice. His first slug spun Webster Watts sideways, and the second tore out his throat.

❧

Harper heard the horses in the yard even before heavy footsteps pounded across the porch. He crawled to the window. He saw shadowy shapes, four horses, one with a limp bundle tied across the saddle. The horse snorted and pranced sideways, and Harper recognized Kaiser.

"So drunk he can't even ride," whispered Harper.

Somebody banged at the door.

Through the cracks in the loft floor Harper saw lantern light. "I'm coming," said Rose. Harper scrambled to the top of the ladder to watch. Rose opened the door and three men came in.

Ches MacFarland took off his hat. Willie Ward and Alonzo Cox shuffled nervously to the fireplace.

"It's Webster," Ches said suddenly.

"Drunk?" asked Rose.

"Worser, this time," Ches said glumly. "He's dead, Rose."

Harper froze.

Alonzo turned to face Rose. "I shot him," he said.

"Lonzo had to," added Willie. "Webster shot the store all to hell."

Rose clutched a chair arm for support. "Where is he?" she asked hoarsely.

"Outside," Ches said stiffly. "We brung him home."

"I'm sorry, Rose," whispered Alonzo.

Rose stood erect. "So am I, Alonzo. But you just did what you thought had to be done. Would youens bring him in?"

"I'll put the horse away," Alonzo offered.

"No!" Rose said sharply. "Let it freeze to death."

Alonzo backed away, put on his hat and went to help carry Webster's body. Rose carried a lantern to the big, cold back room, and watched as the men wrestled Webster's body onto the cot. "I'll go for Aunt Gracie," offered Ches, "to help lay him out, and all."

"I thank you," said Rose. "And could one of you tell Moses Ward I'll be needing a box? Him and his boys, they make the finest ones."

Back before the fireplace Willie dug into his coat pocket. "Here's Web's gun," he said.

"Lay it on the mantle," Rose said wearily.

Alonzo rubbed his hands together. "I reckon Sheriff Barker, he'll be by tomorrow. I sent word."

"Webster was drunk, Rose," Ches said softly. "Spoiling for a fight. He shot at Alonzo three times."

"He never meant to kill Alonzo," said Rose, "or it'd be him laid out." She sighed. "But I reckon you didn't have no way of knowing that."

Ches hesitated at the door. "Let me put the horse in the barn," he offered.

"No!" shrieked Rose. "No." She stared out at the snowstorm. "You all go on now." She watched until the three riders were gone then latched the door. She turned, and saw Harper crouched by the fireplace. "You was watching all the time?" she asked.

Harper nodded.

"Go on back to bed," ordered Rose. "And don't wake up the little ones."

"What about Daddy?" Harper finally asked.

"I reckon," Rose said coolly, "that Alonzo Cox has done saved you the trouble of killing him." She met Harper's dull stare. "Go on to bed."

Harper crept up the ladder, and stopped at the top to stare back down. Rose added logs to the fire, stuck her irons up close, and fetched Webster's Army dress uniform from the trunk. When Harper finally drifted back off to sleep, Rose was pressing wrinkles from the brown wool trousers.

Harper woke up with a start, three hours later. Rose was asleep in the rocking chair, covered with a quilt. Harper pulled on his boots and shirt and crept down the ladder. He laid three hickory logs on the fire, took Webster's pistol down off the mantle, found his coat and cap and slipped outside.

Kaiser, humped backwards against the howling wind, was covered with snow and ice. Harper broke ice from the reins. "Come on, horse," he said softly. In the barn Harper lit a lantern and stripped the saddle off the trembling stallion. He rubbed briskly with a dry saddle blanket, and for once Kaiser did not offer to bite or kick. Harper draped a ragged old quilt over the stallion's back and led him to the stall. He broke ice and dipped water, and brought four ears of corn. The grateful stallion snorted softly.

"Wasn't your fault, horse," said Harper. "You never killed him." Harper dragged the saddle to a sawhorse, and hung the bridle on a peg. Kaiser nickered.

"It's Christmas Eve," remembered Harper. "Horses and cows is supposed to talk tonight." But Kaiser only gnawed noisily at the corn. Harper hung over the rail and watched him for a long time. "I guess you're my horse now," he finally decided.

Kaiser snorted.

"You and this gun," said Harper. He held Webster's revolver up to study it in the lamplight. "Both mine now." His tiny chest swelled. "Yeah." Harper grinned. "Got me a pocket gun and a saddle horse."

He slipped quietly back into the house, but Rose was awake. "I put the horse in the barn," explained Harper. "He was about froze."

Rose stared dully. "I would have thought you'd be glad to see that old horse dead," she said. "Much as you've carried on." She saw the bulge in Harper's coat pocket. "That your daddy's gun?"

Harper nodded. "I want to keep it."

"Why?" Rose asked bitterly. "You hated him."

"I didn't hate Daddy," whispered Harper. "I just wanted him to stop hurting you."

"He got crazy from the War," said Rose. "Harper, your daddy wasn't like that before he went off. They done it to him in the War."

"Yeah," Harper said softly. "That's what it was."

❧

For three days relatives and neighbors carried food to Rose Watts and her children, sat up with them and Webster's body, and finally helped lower the oak casket into the earth.

The house was finally still.

Rose and Harper sat in ladderback chairs beside the fire, relieved that it was all over but suddenly aware of the emptiness. Rose sighed. "Didn't Brother Skaggs preach just fine, Harper? The way he talked about your daddy, what a fulsome and goodhearted man he was, how he never had an unkind word to say to anybody. Just too full of life, that's how Brother Skaggs said it. That's how he was, Harper."

Harper didn't comment.

Rose bent to poke at the fire. "You're the man now," she said. "You got to help me take care of the youngens, farm, and maybe hire out some for cash money."

"Won't we get a Army pension?" asked Harper.

"I don't know," said Rose. "Maybe. But if we do it'll be a while coming." She sat back, rigid and tightlipped. "That's how come I sold the horse."

"Kaiser?" Harper stiffened.

"Back to Mack Ward, for fifty dollars."

"Daddy's saddle, and everthing?"

"Ever bit," said Rose. "Spurs too."

Harper stared at the snapping ashes.

"You got his gun, and the railroad watch," said Rose.

"I'd druther have the horse," whispered Harper.

"I won't have that red devil around this place," Rose said fiercely.

"But I got him tame now," protested Harper. "He ain't so mean, if you pet him and give him sugar."

"It's done," said Rose. "Mack is coming for the horse in the morning."

Mack Ward came through the snow with a team of high-stepping grays hitched to a sled, tied Kaiser on behind, and stopped at the house. He declined hot coffee, counted out $50 from a worn leather pouch, and buttoned his coat to go back out.

Harper blocked his way.

"What are you going to do with him?" the boy asked.

"The horse?" Mack grinned. "Try to get my money back out of him, in the spring. Or maybe just keep him. That's some hoss."

"His name is Kaiser now," said Harper. "Daddy changed it to that."

"That so?" Mack grinned. "Suits me. He's Kaiser."

"He likes sugar," said Harper. "And he likes to have his belly scratched."

"Dang, boy," chuckled Mack, "you make him sound like a puppy dog. I thought I had me a war horse." He smiled. "Any time you want to, Harper, you can come and see him." Mack pulled on his wool cap. "I got to be going."

Harper watched until the horses and sled vanished into the snow, then walked stiffly back to warm himself by the fire.

"I had to do it, son," Rose said softly.

"I know." Harper drew himself up tall and spat into the fire. "We can't be wasting feed on a horse that don't work. We ain't got money to keep a saddle horse."

"It won't be easy," said Rose, "but we'll make it through somehow, Harper."

"I got to go take care of the pigs," mumbled Harper. He pulled on his coat and stumbled to the barn. He sat on the wagon tongue for a long time, then started practicing what he'd tell them when he went back to school.

"My daddy," whispered Harper, "he whupped the Germans bad, killed over five hunderd of 'em all by hisself. And my great-granddaddy, he rode with Mosby in Virginia and killed more Yankees than anybody. Daddy, he had this big old horse named Kaiser, meanest thing they ever was, wouldn't let nobody but me or Daddy close to him. Me and my daddy, we . . . " Harper blinked back tears. "Me and my daddy, we went everwhere together."

Don Johnson

Don Johnson, a professor of English at East Tennessee State University, graduated from the University of Hawaii (B.A., 1964; M.A., 1966), where he also worked for one year as an instructor. He brings an interesting perspective to writing about Appalachia in his poetry, which focuses on moments and individual personalities that take on symbolic or metaphorical importance when transformed into verse. Johnson is also the author of *Watauga Drawdown,* a collection of verse, and numerous scholarly articles on topics ranging from Joseph Addison to "Hawaii Five-O." He serves as editor of *Aethlon,* a journal of sports literature. His poem "The Sergeant" (from his first volume of poetry, *The Importance of Visible Scars*) examines the permanent marks that experiencing the barbarities of war leaves on the individual.

The Sergeant

When others mustered out in '46, you soldiered
on, commanding a squad that buried box
after narrow box the Army sent home from abroad.

For a year the wind off the Kasserine,
peasants mudded to their knees on Mindanao
and oceans being oceans all over the world
kept turning up dead West Virginians.

You brought all the known soldiers home,
to Coal Fork, Seth, Clendinin,
to the smudged daguerreotypes of company shacks
that lay beyond slick rivers without bridges.

Your honor guard traveled the state that year
making heroes.
                    You and your men were heroes—
the War ceremonially perfect—
in hills the newsreels never reached.

Sometimes twice a day you stiffened
against the world's first standing order:
assigning remains to the last slit trenches
they would hold, awarding the widows flags
they would bundle away under cedar
or hang on the wall of the child
conceived a month before Pearl Harbor.

                                  ❧

You were occupied with death
                              and mother ironed
ten uniforms a week to keep you creased
and properly rigid. Starch drifted
like dry snow in parlor corners where I etched
stick figures in the dust—
              my own command.
And I learned to fold the flags
into tight blue parcels of stars, to execute
the manual of arms with the snap
of a garrison corporal.
                    But you never said
"Death" or took me along to the hills.

From *The Importance of Visible Scars,* Wampeter Press, 1984. Reprinted by permission of the author.

Coming in to the warm laundry smells of your room,
I'd find you silently polishing brass or trying to coax
from your boots the last bright sheen the leather
remembered. And I knew I would rise the next morning
in darkness, roused by the small-bore crack
of your clothes—your limbs forcing open shined khaki—
to watch you go quietly off to your men.

                                          ❧

One summer night you had the neighbors in the yard
for home-made peach ice cream and army films
projected on the flaking wall of the hen-house.

G.I.s bridged the Rhine at Remagen; Jap bodies
spilled like sun-struck worms from a pill box,
their faces scaled like snakes in the old wall's
peeling paint.
                And I wondered who buried them
but lay in the sweet summer grass unafraid
until the black-and-white war was done. Barrages
stopped. Helmeted winners of medals marched home.

Still the film reeled on, to Buchenwald, Dachau,
where bulldozers shoved gray bones into pits
without ritual, where the living were mute
fluoroscopic ghosts you called D.P.s, real stick people
crushed into huts like our mildewed sheds.

Out of your sight, in the dark, I cried
for them all, and for the man with a child
thinner than any mountain stray. His face,
framed in a single paint chip, leaned into the yard
and, with the eyes like the half-blind bank mules'
at the mines, he seemed to stare at the light
from my bedroom window.

                    After the films
had run out, while your friends were gathering plates
or whispering good-night, I sat by your polished
brown shoes, wanting to say,
                            "The man . . . ,"

that he held that child in his coat-hanger arms
then shoved him through the warp in the lapped boards
covering our coop. That the boy was in there
huddled in the dung and feathers, waiting.

But you never knew how he clung
to those humid walls with the hens
or how the flung door's slicing trapezoid of light
cornered him in shadow.

You were occupied with death,
while every day I trooped the darkened rows of nests,
gathering the still-warm eggs with held breath.

James Agee

James Rufus Agee, poet, journalist, film critic, screen writer, and novelist, was born in Knoxville, Tennessee, on November 7, 1909. A graduate of Phillips Exeter Academy and Harvard University, Agee has earned recognition as one of the great writers of twentieth-century America. Agee's diversity of talent outweighs his relatively small volume of work; he adapted what critic Archibald MacLeish called his "poetic gift" to a wide variety of endeavors. He began with a volume of poetry, *Permit Me Voyage* (1934), but turned to journalism immediately thereafter, joining the staff of *Fortune* as a contributing editor and submitting freelance work to a variety of publications. His essay on Alabama sharecroppers, accompanied by photographs by Walker Evans, won wide praise when published in book form under the title *Let Us Now Praise Famous Men* (1941). Agee was also a noted film critic and screen writer. As a novelist, he created *A Death in the Family*, which ironically was left unfinished at Agee's own death of a heart attack in 1955. The story of the emotional impact of untimely death on the immediate family won Agee a posthumous Pulitzer Prize.

Agee's *Time* essay on the development of the atomic bomb strikes close to home, literally, as Agee was born only a few miles from Oak Ridge, where research and assembly of the weapon helped to usher in the Atomic Age, opening a new chapter in the Appalachian heritage.

The Bomb

The greatest and most terrible of wars ended, this week, in the echoes of an enormous event—an event so much more enormous that, relative to it, the war itself shrank to minor significance. The knowledge of victory was as charged with sorrow and doubt as with joy and gratitude. More fearful responsibilities, more crucial liabilities rested on the victors even than on the vanquished.

© 1945 Time Inc. Reprinted by permission.

In what they said and did, men were still, as in the aftershock of a great wound, bemused and only semi-articulate, whether they were soldiers or scientists, or great statesmen, or the simplest of men. But in the dark depths of their minds and hearts, huge forms moved and silently betrayed themselves: Titans, arranging out of the chaos an age in which victory was already only the shout of a child in the street.

With the controlled splitting of the atom, humanity, already profoundly perplexed and disunified, was brought inescapably into a new age in which all thoughts and things were split—and far from controlled. As most men realized, the first atomic bomb was a merely pregnant threat, a merely infinitesimal promise.

All thoughts and things were split. The sudden achievement of victory was a mercy, to the Japanese no less than to the United Nations, but mercy born of a ruthless force beyond anything in human chronicle. The race had been won, the weapon had been used by those on whom civilization could best hope to depend; but the demonstration of power against living creatures instead of dead matter created a bottomless wound in the living conscience of the race. The rational mind had won the most Promethean of its conquests over nature, and had put into the hands of common man the fire and force of the sun itself.

Was man equal to the challenge? In an instant, without warning, the present had become the unthinkable future. Was there hope in that future, and if so, where did hope lie?

Even as men saluted the greatest and most grimly Pyrrhic of victories in all the gratitude and good spirit they could muster, they recognized that the discovery which had done most to end the worst of wars might also, quite conceivably, end all wars—if only man could learn its control and use.

The promise of good and of evil bordered alike on the infinite—with this further, terrible split in the fact: that upon a people already so nearly drowned in materialism even in peacetime, the good uses of this power might easily bring disaster as prodigious as the evil. The bomb rendered all decisions made so far, at Yalta and at Potsdam, mere trivial dams across tributary rivulets. When the bomb split open the universe and revealed the prospect of the infinitely extraordinary, it also revealed the oldest, simplest, commonest, most neglected, and most important of facts: that each man is eternally and above all else responsible for his own soul, and, in the terrible words of the Psalmist, that no man may deliver his brother, nor make agreement unto God for him.

Man's fate has forever been shaped between the hands of reason and spirit, now in collaboration, again in conflict. Now reason and spirit meet on final ground. If either or anything is to survive, they must find a way to create an indissoluble partnership.

Marilou Awiakta

Marilou Awiakta was born in Knoxville, Tennessee. In 1945, at the age of nine, she moved to nearby Oak Ridge. A graduate of the University of Tennessee at Knoxville, Awiakta combines her Cherokee-Appalachian heritage with her experience of growing up on the "atomic frontier" of Oak Ridge to infuse her writing with a respect for her region's history and a concern for humanity's ability to cope with life in the high-tech age. Her first volume of poetry, *Abiding Appalachia: Where Mountain and Atom Meet* (1978; 8th ed., 1994), questions humanity's reverence for life in the face of nuclear technology. Her second book, *Rising Fawn and the Fire Mystery* (1983), is a story of the Choctaw Removal in 1833. Her third book, *Selu: Seeking the Corn-Mother's Wisdom* (1993), applies Cherokee traditional teachings to contemporary issues. Awiakta was the recipient of the 1989 Distinguished Tennessee Writers Award and the 1991 Award for Outstanding Contribution to Appalachian Literature. She is profiled in the *Oxford Companion to Women's Writing in the United States*.

"Genesis" deals with two of Awiakta's most famous Themes—atomic folklore and history.

Genesis

Settlers sowed their seed.
Then their sons took the plow and in their turn grew old.
And the mountains abided, steeped in mist.
But in the deep was a quickening of light, a freshening of wind. . . .
And in 1942, as fall leaves embered down toward winter,
new ground was turned near Black Oak Ridge.
The natives pricked their ears.
These descendants of old pioneers
lifted their heads to scent the wind—
A frontier was a-borning.
Many had to pack up hearth and home and go.
But others joined the energy that flowed toward Black Oak Ridge
as to a great magnetic power:
Thousands of people streamed in.
Bulldozers scraped and moved the earth.
Factories rose in valleys like Bear Creek
and houses in droves sprang up among the trees
and strung out in the lees of ridges.

From *Abiding Appalachia: Where Mountain and Atom Meet,* 8th ed. (Bell Buckle, TN: Iris Press, 1994). Reprinted by permission of the author.

A great city soon lay concealed among the hills.
Why it had come no one knew.
But its energy was a strong and constant hum,
a new vibration, changing rhythms everywhere. . . .
It charged the air in Knoxville, where we lived
and when I saw my parents lift their heads,
I lifted my head too, for even at seven
I knew something was stirring in our blood,
something that for years had drawn the family along frontiers
from Virginia to West Virginia, on to Kentucky and Tennessee.
And now, a few miles away, we had a new frontier.
Daddy went first, in '43—leaving at dawn, coming home at dark
and saying nothing of his work except,
"It's at Y-12, in Bear Creek Valley."
The mystery deepened.
The hum grew stronger.
And I longed to go.
Oak Ridge had a magic sound—
They said bulldozers could take down a hill before your eyes
and houses sized by alphabet came precut and boxed, like blocks,
so builders could put up hundreds at a time.
And they made walks of boards and streets of dirt (mud, if it rained)
and a chain-link fence around it all to keep the secret.
But the woods sounded best to me.
My mind went to them right away . . .
to wade in creeks and rest in cool deep shadows,
watching light sift through the trees
and hoping Little Deer might come.
In the Smokies I'd often felt him near
and I knew he'd roam the foothills too.
Woods were best. And if the frontier grew too strange
my mountains would abide unchanged,
old and wise and comforting.

So I kept listening to the hum, and longing. . . .
Mother said we'd go someday, in the fullness of time.
And when I was nine the fullness came,
exploding in a mushroom cloud that shook the earth.

Dan Crowe

Dan Crowe, a native of Carter County, Tennessee, is a graduate of East Tennessee State University and a retired teacher of political science and track coach at Dobyns-Bennett High School in Kingsport, Tennessee. He is the author of *The Horse Shoe People* (1976), a history of a mountain community in Carter County, Tennessee; and of *Old Butler and Watauga Academy* (1983), a history of the Watauga River Valley in East Tennessee before the coming of the Watauga Dam. Crowe's passion for historical accuracy is reflected in his quiet outrage at the manipulation of casualty figures in war, as seen in "Song of the Body Count." The poem "Conversation with a Chinese Soldier" is based on Crowe's experience as a soldier in the Korean War.

Conversation with a Chinese Soldier

Green skirmish lines . . . bent, broken
Inching up some hill
    Say 513.

Those who make it
Mop-up
    The top of 513.

A Chinese fellow . . .
I remember frozen blood,
    Tennis shoes charred.

Rats running away
Months-full of rice rations,
    A quilted uniform, torn.

What do you say to the enemy
On the occasion of his death?
    First, you don't remove your helmet.

How are things in
    Kweichow?
        Or some other province?

"Conversation with a Chinese Soldier" first appeared on envelopes postmarked Washington, DC, July 1985, the first day of the issue of the stamp honoring the veterans of Korea. Reprinted by permission of the author. The "V.C.G.I." portion of "Song of the Body Count" appeared in *Now and Then* 4.3 (Fall 1987) and is reprinted by permission of the author and *Now and Then*.

Greetings to Mao Tse-Tung.
Merry Christmas,
Harry Truman.

Shrapnel marks your face.
We could have been friends
Another time, another place.

Song of the Body Count

Bodies sprawled.
Bodies stacked.
Ghastly bodies, gangrened,
Whole bodies, dismembered bodies.

Six here
Seven there
Slowly they total up.
Should a child count one-
half?

Use a computer.
Use an abacus.
Inflate estimations.
Include outlying hamlets.

Ten by gun-ship
Ten by napalm
Two by punji stick
The brass wants to know.

Four white
Four black
Four yellow
Friend . . . foe.

V.C.
G.I.

All blood is red.
All the killed are dead.

Mostly soldiers
Mostly Oriental
An old man
Mostly young men.

Issue to each
A pine box
And rubber bag shroud . . .
The dead ain't proud.

Emphasize kill ratio.
Count those still dying.
Speculate on those yet to die . . .
Mothers, subtract your sons.

Norman Eugene Eades

Norman Eugene Eades was born in Bristol, Virginia, in 1948. Son of a veteran of World War II and a descendant of Alvin York, he served in Vietnam in 1970–71. A two-year odyssey across the United States, from Maine to California, followed. He has worked as a carpenter, farmer, and bartender. He is a 1993 graduate of East Tennessee State University.

The Owl, My Father, and the German Officer

The white house I was born in,
My father built with his own hands,
The garden in the back,
ran down to the creek bottom.
    Whooo? The owl asked from the darkness.
Rages of alcohol and war,
Kept the family fractured and weak,
Sanity hanging by a slender thread.
A dead German officer's ghost appeared,
Tormenting, taunting, day and night.
    Whooo? Was his name?
Shocks of electricity did no good.
Medicines only made it worse, when
mixed with the rage of alcohol.
Conversations with esteemed doctors,
was just talk.
    Whooo? Was responsible for this?
A good-looking, hard-working man
could have no life, because

Printed by permission of the author.

of a dead German officer.
Shot in the head, for refusing
to order his captive men to move.
    Whooo? The owl wants to know.
They lie buried in Susong cemetery,
My father and the German officer.
Bound together in eternity.
Brothers now.
    Whooo, goes to war now?
                        · Their son.

David Huddle

A native of Ivanhoe, Virginia, and a Vietnam veteran, David Huddle has lived and taught in Vermont since 1971. He is a faculty member of the Bread Loaf School of English and a professor of English at the University of Vermont. His work has appeared in *Esquire, Harper's, Hudson Review, Yankee, Field, Virginia Quarterly Review, New York Times Magazine,* and many other journals; his books include *Paper Boy* (1979), *Stopping by Home* (1988), and *Only the Little Bone* (1986).

Work

I am a white, Episcopal-raised, almost
college-educated, North American male.
Sergeant Tri, my interpreter, is engrossed
in questioning our detainee, a small,
bad-smelling man in rags who claims to be
a farmer. I am filling in the blanks
of a form, writing down what Sergeant Tri
tells me. This is dull. Suddenly Tri yanks

our detainee to his feet, slaps him twice
across the bridge of his nose. The farmer
whimpers. Tri says the farmer has lied and waits
for orders. Where I grew up my father
waits at the door while my mother finishes
packing his lunch. I must tell Tri what next.

"Work" and "Cousin" from *Stopping by Home,* Gibbs Smith, Publisher, © 1988 by the author. Reprinted by permission of the author.

Cousin

for John H. Kent, Jr., 1919–1982

I grew up staring at the picture of him:
oak leaves on his shoulders, crossed rifles
on his lapels, and down his chest so many medals
the camera lost them. He wore gold-rimmed
glasses, smiled, joked about fear. He told true
stories that were like movies on our front porch:
he'd fought a German hand to hand. The word
courage meant Uncle Jack in World War Two.

Ten years from my war, thirty from his, we
hit a summer visit together; again
the stories came. He remembered names of his men,
little French towns, a line of trees. I could see
his better than mine. He'd known Hemingway!
I tried hard but couldn't find a thing to say.

Terry McCoy

Terry McCoy is a native of Oakdale, Tennessee. During 1967–68, he was
wounded twice while serving with the 9th Infantry Division in Vietnam, an
experience which has been the inspiration for many of his poems. Later he
earned an M.A. degree at Tennessee Technological University, where he
also taught for several years. He currently teaches English at Pamlico Community College in North Carolina.

The Goat Post

I am tied to the war in Vietnam
Like a goat to a post.
Passing years that tangle and shorten my rope
Always pull me back and ever closer
To the things I thought to escape.
Twenty years are just long enough
To strip away yellowed flesh

"The Goat Post," "Rotating Home, 1968," and "Requiem" printed by permission of the
author.

From bodies I left fresh and bleeding
And to leave bones dry and loose-fit
Like tinkling bamboo sticks
Swinging in time's wind chime.

Rotating Home, 1968

I waited at the airstrip listening
for the sound of a helicopter in the wind,
holding a roach til it singed my fingers,
trying for a buzz to float me like reefer smoke
over body bags strewn like big watermelon seeds
and waiting with me for a lift to Saigon and the world.

Requiem

I can barely remember Shriver's face,
A memory from the war twenty years before,
Now lodged in time like a kite
Hung on telephone wires
String broken—fabric tattered and faded.

Chapter 4

Labor, Wealth, and Commonwealth

Introduction

In the Deep South cotton was king, but in the highlands the reigning monarch has traditionally been King Coal. Thus any discussion of labor in Appalachia inevitably focuses on mining. The coal industry arrived in the region in force in the early twentieth century and has never departed, though its grip on the region has been lessened somewhat.

The struggle between coal management and labor has made Appalachia the scene of some of the most intense, bitter, and violent strikes the country has experienced. Repeatedly throughout the century, the coal industry has made Appalachia the site of national controversies having to do with workers' rights and social justice. Labor-management conflicts have given rise to populist heroes such as Don West and Myles Horton, founder of the Highlander School. Coalfield troubles have also drawn the attention of poets such as John Beecher and reformers such as Mother Jones.

As the Tennessee state motto "Agriculture and Commerce" suggests, in Appalachia industry has always existed within a predominantly agrarian region. Recent years have brought a greater variety of commerce and industry, causing some scholars to argue that the increasing industrialization erodes the distinctive character of the region. What is certain is that the industrial movement and its effects have become a part of the region's character, reflecting the turbulence that has always been a part of life on the frontier. The nature of this conflict has changed from man-against-nature to man-against-machine, but the play of forces upon the region's inhabitants has remained basically unchanged. While the foe changed, the Appalachian people remained suspended between the push and pull of different worlds, and the violence and sometimes the nobility of this situation help stamp the mountains and their people with a distinctive personality.

John Beecher

The long and varied career of John Beecher defies easy summary. Born January 22, 1904, to upper-middle-class parents in New York City, Beecher originally set out to be a chemist and metallurgist for U.S. Steel. Somewhere in the process, however, Beecher became less concerned with the product and more concerned with the producers. Having this interest, he was the fitting inheritor of a family tradition of activism going back to his great-great-uncle and -aunt, Henry Ward Beecher and Harriet Beecher Stowe. As Beecher put it, "Spontaneously, I started to write . . . I hadn't even heard of Marx or Lenin, but violent and revolutionary poems started coming out."

Thus began the career that would result in Beecher being hailed by William Carlos Williams as "an authentic American folk hero." That career was marked by fighting all the way—against the Ku Klux Klan, against corporations, against McCarthyism, against all forms of oppression in favor of true democracy. Beecher's poetry is characterized by a balance between stark realism in its depiction of the life of the poor and an idealism that almost pleads for such noble virtues as courage, honesty, dignity, and love, values that Beecher believed in and strove for up to his death in San Francisco in 1980.

The Seed of Fire

For Highlander Folk School

The celluloid is old. It snaps and must
be spliced. The worn-out sound-track garbles words.
But here they are, the marching union men,
the girls with banners. Pitiful! A torrent
of mountain water plunging from the rocks
to lose itself downstream in stagnant sloughs,
mud-clogged meanderings and stinking pools.
The nation rots. What we were once looks out
of this old film with shining eyes. Where did
we miss our way? New men rise up with skins
dark-hued to take the vanguard place of those
grown compromised and well content to rake
fat winnings from the gamble of death. Dark too
those women who indomitably face
plantation lords and teach sea-island folk,
disfranchised all their voiceless lives, to stand
and vote. Here is the continuity,
the precious seed of fire in these sad ashes.

From *Hear the Wind Blow!* International, 1968. Reprinted by permission of the publisher.

Don West

Don West, like his colleague Myles Horton, participated in a wide variety of activities related to life in Appalachia, and particularly to the struggle for social justice. A union organizer in eastern Kentucky during the 1930s, West also has served as a preacher and a teacher in both college and secondary school, in addition to working daily as a poet and a farmer. Myles Horton once described West as a "mountain socialist," and this particular brand of populism informs all his activities. Langston Hughes described this force at work in his poetry: "Don West marshals words into poetry to sing for democracy and decency, to picture and plead, to startle and shock." West's work has the immediacy of experience and the honesty of an unsubtle desire for equality and equity. West's unsophisticated style belies the loftiness of the ideals he preserves and defends in his combative verse.

Kentucky Miners

Folksongs rise from the people's feeling of the true and the good, or the false and the bad. Whenever a great tragedy comes, either to one or a lot of folk, it usually has its ballad or folksong. The song tells a story—maybe of hurt or of hope, or it may be of joy or sorrow or anger. The source of this song is the plight of the ex–Appalachian miners.

> Way down in Kentucky
> Where the mountains are steep
> There is want and starvation
> To cause you to weep
> Little children go hungry
> All the days through
> Their fathers are jobless
> With nothing to do.
>
> Miners of Kentucky
> Who used to dig coal
> Went under the mountains
> Until they were old
> Made riches for owners
> In some far-off place
> Now see families hungry
> With sad pinched face.
>
> Come all you good people
> Wherever you be

From *O Mountaineers!* 1974. Reprinted by permission of Ann West Williams.

Can this be the home of
The brave and the free
Where children go hungry
Each night to their bed
With mothers heart-broken
Wishing they were dead?
In this land of great riches
Now called U.S.A.
Where Negroes are murdered
American way
You who love freedom
Get on the right track
Join hands now my brothers
Poor white and poor black!

Harlan Portraits

I've seen beauty in Harlan,
In the trailing arbutus,
The dogfennel and pennyroyal
In the fence corners,
The forests dressed
In a foliage of
Rattleweed and ditney.
I've seen beauty when
Gray winter strokes his beard
With bony-white fingers,
And trees are skeletons
Of summer's glory . . .

But beauty
Never visits the coal diggers.
They live in the coal camps—
Dirty shanties,
Stinking privies,
Grunting pigs,
And slop buckets . . .

Gaunt-eyed women
With dull hopeless faces
Cook soggy wheat biscuits.

Tall gaunt men
Eat soggy bread

From *Clods of Southern Earth*, 1946. Reprinted by permission of Ann West Williams.

And fat meat,
Gulp down black coffee,
Work all day—
Digging, digging,
Everlastingly digging.
Grime and dirt
And digging.
In their dreams they dig
And smell unpleasant
Odors.

For beauty
Is a stranger
To the coal camps . . .

Ronald D Eller

Originally from southern West Virginia, Ronald D Eller has spent the last quarter of a century writing and teaching about the Appalachian region. A descendant of eight generations of families in the southern mountains, Dr. Eller currently serves as director of the Appalachian Center at the University of Kentucky. There he coordinates research and service programs on a wide range of Appalachian policy issues, including education, health care, economic development, civic leadership, and the environment. He is in demand as a speaker on Appalachian issues at colleges, conferences, and community forums throughout the nation; and he serves as a frequent consultant to civic organizations and the national media. A former Rockefeller Foundation scholar, Dr. Eller holds the Ph.D. from the University of North Carolina at Chapel Hill and is widely known as a scholar of Appalachian history and the study of rural economic development and social change. He has published more than thirty articles and reports but is most well known for his award-winning book *Miners, Millhands, and Mountaineers: The Industrialization of the Appalachian South* (1982).

The Miner's Work

For the rural whites, blacks, and immigrants who came to work in the mountain coal mines, the greatest adjustments in their lives came not so much

From *Miners, Millhands and Mountaineers: Industrialization of the Appalachian South, 1880–1930,*
© 1982 by The University of Tennessee Press. Reprinted by permission of the publisher.

from the nature of their work as from the industrial organization and the feudal living conditions which accompanied that work. Mining, unlike factory employment, continued to provide contact with the land. It required some skill, but primarily physical energy, and in the early years the miner enjoyed a high level of independence on the job. The work was dirty and usually tiring, much like that with which they were accustomed on the farm. Yet the work routines, job discipline, safety conditions, and environment of the company towns provided a marked contrast to traditional agricultural life. To a degree, coal mining reinforced old cultural patterns, while it introduced new social attitudes, behaviors, and problems.

The most striking aspect of the miner's job in the early years of the coal industry was that almost all of the work was done by hand. Mechanical undercutting machines which helped to loosen the coal from the seam were invented as early as the 1870s, but they were slow to gain acceptance in the nation's coal mines. By 1900 only 25 percent of American coal was mined by machines. In 1915 that figure reached 55 percent, but as late as 1930, 20 percent of the U.S. coal production was still being mined by hand.[1] Many of the smaller mines, of which there were hundreds in the southern mountains, did not begin to mechanize until after World War II. The loading of the coal into mining cars, which was the most time-consuming part of the miner's job, continued to be done by hand throughout the period from 1880 to 1930. While mules and later locomotives were used to haul the loaded cars to the mouth of the mine, the most arduous and dangerous part of the production process was done at the face of the coal seam by the miner himself.

Most Southern Appalachian mines were of the drift mine variety which allowed for easy entry and minimized the need for expensive ventilation and transportation equipment. The coal seam of a drift mine was located on a hillside above the valley floor, and the workers entered the mine laterally rather than through the vertical shafts which characterized other American coalfields. The drift mine drained well and was less gaseous; further, because it required little machinery, its operations could be undertaken with very little initial investment. This latter fact contributed significantly to the rapid overexpansion of the industry in the mountains, as well as to the heavy reliance on cheap human labor. During the early years, moreover, the ease of entrance into a drift mine resulted in considerable freedom for miners to leave their work place as they pleased, but as the mines penetrated deeper into the hillside and as company discipline hardened, this advantage was lost to the miners of the region.[2]

Once the coal seam had been penetrated, the miners set to work cutting and loading the coal. The mining process was relatively simple. Generally pairs of miners worked in small rooms off the main entry tunnel. The rooms were separated from each other by pillars of coal left standing to support the roof, and a system of trackage was extended into each of the rooms from the main haulageway. After the coal was removed from the seam and loaded into a coal car, it was pushed to the room entrance, where mules or locomotives gathered the cars and transported them to the loading tipple outside. When all of the rooms in a section had been mined, the pillars were carefully removed as the men retreated toward the main shaft. "Pillar drawing" was extremely dangerous, as it often resulted in the collapse of the overburden in the room, but it was a necessary part of the operation. Proper pillar removal could reduce the amount of coal left in the mine and hence lost to production.[3]

The miner's day started long before daylight and often ended well after dark. In the early morning hours, the miners would set out for the mines carrying their lunch pails and water bottles and wearing lard oil lamps to light their way. The procession, "like fireflies all around the mountain," disappeared into the mine about 6 A.M., none knowing who or how many would come out alive.[4] At the coal face, the miner and his helper or loader began work by undercutting the coal seam. This he accomplished by making a horizontal or wedge-shaped slit with his pick at the bottom of the seam, so that the coal would fall when blasted from above. Most of this undercutting had to be done lying on his side and swinging a short-handled pick into the coal seam. The miner had to be constantly aware of the condition of the coal he was mining, since there was always danger of coal falling from the face onto the worker below.[5] After taking two or three hours to make an undercut, the miner then drilled holes in the coal, loaded the holes with black powder, and fired them, bringing down the undercut coal. When the dust settled, the men pushed empty mining cars into the room and began loading the coal, being sure to separate out the pieces of rock and slate to prevent being "docked" for loading dirty coal. Several hours after the process began, the miners pushed their loaded cars to the room entrance to be hauled away. Near the bottom of the car, the workers placed a brass check bearing the laborers' payroll number. The check was removed by the "check man" at the tipple and the tonnage credited to the proper man.[6]

The miner's job, however, was not finished when the car was removed from the work place. Wasted rock and debris had to be removed from the room and steel track laid from the main entry to the new facing. In most mines, the miners themselves were responsible for setting their own timber safety props in place to support the roof from falling on the workmen. It often required hours to carry and install these posts, and the procedure was done entirely at the miner's expense, since he was paid by the ton of coal loaded, not by the time spent on the job. After these preparations were made, the cycle would begin again with undercutting, drilling, blasting, and loading. In mines where drainage was a problem, the miner's clothes often got wet with the first undercutting, and he had to work the remainder of the day in damp clothing.[7] The end of the shift usually came about sundown, and the wet, dust-blackened miners trudged home to a tub of water and a few hours of rest before the next day's work began.

Under these conditions, the average pick miner could earn about two dollars a day at the turn of the century, and an exceptionally hard-working miner might earn as much as three dollars.[8] Wages varied greatly from time to time and from area to area in the mountain coalfields. During the 1920s some coal operators in Southern Appalachia paid wages higher than the national average in an attempt to squelch unionization, but, on the whole, the region lagged behind national wage averages. In order to compete with northern coal companies, mine owners in the mountains sought to reduce the price of their coal by cutting miners' wages and other expenses. A pick miner in southern West Virginia, for example, was paid an average of 38.5 cents per ton in 1912 for run of the mine coal, while the statewide average was 48 cents. In the coalfields of Ohio, Indiana, Illinois, and Pennsylvania, miners' wages ranged from 57 cents to $1.27 per ton. Rates in the southern fields, moreover, were based on "long tons" of 2,240 lbs., but those of the Northern fields were figured on "short tons" of 2000 pounds, "hence the wage differential was even greater than it appears."[9] In addition to the marked difference in net wages, a higher percentage of miners in Southern Appalachia lived in company towns, and thus a larger share of their wages was returned to the coal company for housing, tools, education, food, and other expenses. The gradual introduction of cutting machines in the years before World War I dramatically increased coal production in the mines, but the miners themselves received a disproportionately low share of the gains from increased efficiency.[10]

While wages remained comparatively low in the coalfields, coal mining continued to rank as one of the most dangerous occupations in the United States. In fact, the introduction of machines and electricity actually added to the perils of the mine. Mechanical haulage systems and low-hanging electrical wires became major factors in mine safety, and the higher levels of dust raised by the new cutting machines created new explosive dangers and health hazards.[11] Despite the passage of "progressive" mine safety laws in the first two decades of the twentieth century, the rate of mine fatalities per thousand in the coal industry actually increased steadily after 1906. Over the next thirty years, mine workers lost their lives in underground accidents at the rate of about 1,600 per year.[12]

The most feared and best publicized mine accidents were the dramatic explosions which sometimes killed dozens or even hundreds of men. Although most of the Southern Appalachian drift mines were relatively free of natural gases, the accumulation of explosive methane gas and coal dust were an unavoidable byproduct of coal mining. The gas could be removed from the mine by adequate ventilation, and the coal dust could be rendered nonexplosive by treatment with water or rock dust. But in the hectic days of the coal boom, many companies were unwilling to spend additional money on mine safety, and many of the miners were too pressured by the demands of production to spend time on safety precautions. As a result, mine disasters increased sharply in the mountains after 1900.

Prior to the turn of the century, there had been only two major explosions in the mountain coalfields. The most tragic occurred at Pocahontas, Virginia, only a year after the railroad reached the mines of the Southwest Virginia Improvement Company. On March 13, 1884, coal dust in the Pocahontas Laurel mine exploded, killing the entire night shift of 114 men. An investigation determined that the disaster probably had been caused by an open miner's lamp igniting a small quantity of fire-damp (methane), which in turn set off a large quantity of coal dust.[13] The second disaster occurred in 1895, when a gas explosion ripped through the Nelson Mine at Dayton, Tennessee, killing 28 miners.[14]

As mechanization and production took off in the next decades, major disasters occurred with shocking frequency. In 1900 the Red Ash Colliery in Fayette County, West Virginia, exploded, killing 57 men and boys; and two years later, 184 miners were killed at the Frateville mine in Coal Creek, Tennessee.[15] Between 1902 and 1927 there were serious mine explosions in the region almost every year and major disasters at Stuart (1907), Switchback (1908 and 1909), Jed (1912), Eccles (1914), Layland (1915), Beckley (1923), Yukon (1924), and Everettsville (1927) in West Virginia; again at Pocahontas, Virginia (1906); at Browder (1910) and Happy (1923) in Kentucky; and at Briceville (1911), Catoosa (1917), and Rockwood (1926) in Tennessee.[16] The causes of most of the mine explosions were widely known, generally the accumulation of gas and/or coal dust, but coroner's juries impaneled to determine the causes of the disasters almost never ruled against the companies. According to Howard B. Lee, who served as West Virginia's attorney general during the 1920s, out of eleven mine explosions in that state, "in no case was the coal company even censured for its willful neglect or refusal to take necessary safety precautions to prevent the slaughter."[18] Most of the juries ruled that the deaths of the men were "accidental." For example, after the mine at Eccles, West Virginia, exploded twice in 1914, killing 183 miners, the coroner's jury found that the explosion had been caused by a "short circuit of air" which had allowed gas to collect in the mine. "This short circuit," the jury ruled, "was caused without the knowledge or consent of the company or any of its operating staff, and . . . the company is in no way to blame for the disaster."[19] Another jury ruled in a similar case that the victims had met their deaths as the result of "an Act of God."[20]

State and federal governments at this time did little more than the coroner's juries to hold the coal companies responsible for mine safety. The U.S. Bureau of Mines was created in 1910, but it served only in an advisory capacity and until 1941 did not have the power to enter upon the property of a mine owner without his consent.[21] Between 1879 and 1912, mine safety laws were passed in all of the coal mining states, establishing mining codes and creating mine inspection to enforce the codes.[22] The political influence of the coal operators, however, assured that the codes remained weak and ineffective. "Apparently," wrote Howard B. Lee, "their only purpose was to protect the coal operators—the miners were forgotten."[23] The laws generally placed the sole responsibility for mine safety on the miners, and the mining codes simply established regulations for individual work patterns. The codes emphasized one general rule—"Be Careful." Enforcement was almost nonexistent. It was not until the mid-1920s that state and federal mine bureaus began to place any responsibility for mine safety on management, and even then the coal operators were protected from most liability.[24]

Although most of the public outrage which resulted in the passage of mine safety legislation was stirred by the sudden rise in mine explosions, such disasters claimed only a fraction of the total number of miners killed and injured each year. Of the nearly 48,000 fatal mine accidents in the United States from 1906 to 1935, only 16 percent were killed by gas and dust explosions, while over 71 percent died from roof falls or haulage accidents. Unlike the more highly publicized explosions which killed many miners at once, roof falls and other accidents were solitary killers, and they went unnoticed by the public.[25] Roof falls alone accounted for the majority of mine deaths, claiming an average of about three miners a day.[26] As with other aspects of safety, the responsibility to secure the roof of the work place with posts was placed upon the miner, and any injury resulting from the failure to "post" was considered to be a product of his own "carelessness." During periods of low wages and management pressure for increased production, miners often waited until the last possible moment to break off from their work to begin posting. If the miner waited too long, weak shale roofs and inadequate supports might bring tons of rock down on the men, crushing them instantly. Each year roof falls claimed the lives of hundreds of inexperienced and young miners, but large numbers of veteran laborers were also victims of falling coal and slate.

Low wages and poor health and safety conditions on the job were not the only tribulations of the miner's life, however. After the turn of the century, coal operators increasingly required their employees to live in the company towns. In many communities there was no alternative to company housing, since the coal and land companies owned all of the land for miles around. The company towns, moreover, were directly related to coal production, in that the mine managers often used forms of off-the-job control to maintain profits and enforce company discipline.

Notes

1. Keith Dix, *Work Relations in the Coal Industry: The Hand Loading Era, 1880–1930* (Morgantown, WV: Institute for Labor Studies, 1977), table 2, p. 20.

2. Dix, *Work Relations*, 1–3; and W. R. Thomas, *Life Among the Hills and Mountains of Kentucky* (Louisville, KY: Standard Printing, 1926), 210.

3. Dix, *Work Relations*, 4–7.

4. Florence Reece, "They Say Them Child Brides Don't Last," quoted in Kathy Kahn, *Hillbilly Women* (New York: Doubleday, 1973), 4.

5. John Brophy, *A Miner's Life* (Madison: U of Wisconsin P, 1964), 43; and Dix, *Work Relations*, 8.

6. William Purviance Tams, Jr., *The Smokeless Coal Fields of West Virginia: A Brief History* (Morgantown: West Virginia U Library, 1963), 35–36; Dix, *Work Relations*, 8–10.

7. Dix, *Work Relations*, 11–12.

8. Tams, *Smokeless Coal Fields*, 41.

9. Edwin Albert Cubby, "The Transformation of the Tug and Guyandot Valleys: Economic Development and Social Change in West Virginia, 1888–1921," Ph.D. diss., Syracuse U, 1962, 261–62.

10. Thomas, *Life Among the Hills,* 202.

11. Dix, *Work Relations,* 25.

12. Dix, *Work Relations,* 67; see also Thomas, *Life Among the Hills,* table 7A, "Mine Fatalities in West Virginia," 230.

13. J. N. Bramwell et al., "The Pocahontas Mine Explosion," American Institute of Mining Engineers, *Transactions* 13 (1884–85): 237–49, 247–48.

14. Hiram Brown Humphrey, *Historical Summary of Coal Mine Explosions in the United States, 1810–1958,* U.S. Bureau of Mines Bulletin No. 586 (Washington, D.C., 1960), 20.

15. William Nelson Page, "The Explosion at the Red Ash Colliery, Fayette County, West Virginia," American Institute of Mining Engineers, *Transactions* 30 (1900): 854–63; and Humphrey, *Historical Summary,* 24.

16. Humphrey, *Historical Summary,* 24–110. On 6 Dec. 1907, the largest mine disaster in the U.S. up to that time occurred in northern West Virginia at Monagah, killing 358 men.

17. Based on Humphrey, *Historical Summary,* 24–110.

18. Howard B. Lee, *Bloodletting in Appalachia: A Story of West Virginia's Four Major Mine Wars and Other Thrilling Incidents of Its Coal Fields* (Morgantown: West Virginia U, 1969), 83.

19. R. Dawson Hall, "The Explosion at Eccles, West Virginia," *Coal Age* 5 (23 May 1914): 846–50, 850.

20. Lee, *Bloodletting in Appalachia,* 83.

21. Dix, *Work Relations,* 80.

22. Humphrey, *Historical Summary,* 15.

23. Lee, *Bloodletting in Appalachia,* 103.

24. Dix, *Work Relations,* 80–93.

25. Dix, *Work Relations,* table 3, p. 72; and 71.

26. Based upon statistics provided in Dix, *Work Relations,* table 3, p. 72.

James Still

A native of LaFayette, Alabama, James Still graduated from Lincoln Memorial University and completed his master's degree in 1930 at Vanderbilt University. Still has worked as a librarian and as a freelance writer. For several years he was an associate professor of English at Morehead State University. Skilled in several genres, Still is among the best known and most respected of Appalachian writers. His first volume of poems, *Hounds on the Mountain* (1937), displays a sense of authenticity which has continued to characterize his work. The short story "Bat Flight" won the O. Henry Memorial Prize in

1939. Still's best-known work, *River of Earth* (1940), which won the Southern Authors Award, has been compared to *The Grapes of Wrath* for its accuracy in chronicling the demoralizing years of the Great Depression. Like his contemporaries Jesse Stuart and Harriette Simpson Arnow, Still continues to receive praise for his depiction of Appalachian life in prose and poetry.

Earth-Bread

Under stars cool as the copperhead's eyes,
Under hill-horizons cut clean and deft with wind,
Beneath this surface night, below earth and rock,
The picks strike into veins of coal, oily and rich
And centuries-damp.

They dig with short heavy strokes, straining shoulders
Practiced and bulging with labor,
Crumbling the marrow between the shelving slate,
Breaking the hard, slow-yielding seams.
Bent into flesh-knots the miners dig this earth-bread,
This stone-meat, these fruited bones.

This is the eight-hour death, the daily burial
In a dark harvest lost as any dead.

Mountain Coal Town

These stark houses hung upon the hills,
The ragged slopes and interstices of the barren rock
Are havens for miners in an upper world.
Here is their pool of daylight and their stars
Waiting after darkness in the gutted cave
Emersed in coal and slate and flickering gleam.
A sweeter dampness rises from the river's flowing
Than leaks from the black caverns of the earth,
and the ear here turns to man's firm laughter
And the long clear whistle of the cardinal singing.

Night in the Coal Camps

Cold yellow windows to the night, the trees
Frozen with dark, and eyes sleepless
Along rutted streets. Clear the sparrow words

"Earth-Bread," "Mountain Coal Town," and "Night in the Coal Camps," from *The Wolfpen Poems*, Berea College, 1986. Reprinted by permission of the author and publisher.

Pierce thumb-latched doors; blowing they pass
Like field larks dustily through seeding grass.

Drawn faces on pillows, mouths hollowed in breathing
The unquiet air; and the million-tongued night tremulous
With crickets' rasping thighs, with sharp cluckings
Of fowls under drafty floors. In the caverns deep
The picks strike into coal and slate. They do not sleep.

Marat Moore

Marat Moore grew up in Johnson City, Tennessee, and has lived in North Carolina, West Virginia, and Washington, D.C. She has worked as a coal miner, journalist, and oral historian, and as a labor organizer during the Pittston coal strike. Her photographs have appeared in *Business Week, U.S. News & World Report,* and the *Chicago Tribune.* She has won awards for investigative reporting, essay writing, and photography, and is completing a book of oral history on women coal miners in the United States. She spent nearly a decade on the staff of the United Mine Workers of America. Her story "Because the Earth Is Dark and Deep" portrays the everyday reality of an underground mine with the detail and feeling of first-hand experience.

Because the Earth Is Dark and Deep

On my window ledge sits a slab of gray slate, the size of a dinner plate and several inches thick, covered with the dark lace of fossil ferns. In an imprint of coal, the fronds overlap, sealing the moment more than 250 million years ago when a swamp forest sank and plant became stone.

Ferns, an old miner I worked with once told me, are the flowers of darkness. They are what blooms in the underground. Afterwards, I foraged through roof falls like a child searching out shells on a beach, hunting for signs of towering horsehair ferns or knobby trilobytes, a relic of Paleozoic seas.

My finger traces the serrated edge of a fern leaf caught forever in the act of dying. This piece of earth-memory, unlike our own, is exact in its detail. But what kind of power would crush massive life and sustain the frivolous curl of a fern?

&

Five A.M. Day shift. I woke before dawn and padded to the kitchen, still in darkness. The day was still too raw to recognize. The teapot shrieked, and I packed the round-bottomed dinner bucket with heartburn-free food: no ba-

From *The American Voice* 22 (Spring 1991): 73–88. Reprinted by permission of the author.

nanas, hot peppers, or sardines. Today's menu was a cheese sandwich, Fritos, and Juicy Fruit to ward off the choking dust. And a few Tampax, just in case.

As a day-shift miner, I rose before the sun in order to move beyond it. It was a strange, backward journey, a sudden leaping from day into night and back again that skewed the body's rhythms. After only a month underground, the blisters had hardened, the skin had paled, and the eyes flinched at sudden light.

Stepping out on the front porch of my rented house, I breathed in the sweet air and wondered again why I had sought this job, far from the middle-class suburbs of my youth. Newspaper work first drew my interest to mining, but a stronger force drew me underground, some compulsion I did not understand.

One by one, lights blinked on in houses that lined the hollow. A pair of headlights turned up the road and paused at the deeper ruts. I glanced at my watch. Willie was never late. Other women had told me I was lucky to have found a ride, but Willie was single, a rare thing at #20 mine. Married men refused rides to women miners, claiming their wives would never allow it, even with others along.

"Mornin'." Willie's eyes, blue beneath dark lashes, were grave. He turned on the radio and picked up Merle Haggard through the static. The shadowy valley opened and closed before us as we swayed into each curve of West Virginia Route 49 through Merrimac, past Sprigg and Hatfield Bottom and by the huge coal silo at Lobata, spiraled with lights.

Willie was quiet. It was too early for talk, and there were problems at the mine. Yesterday a major roof fall had blocked the mainline track where crews traveled every shift. August was a killer month. Moisture-laden air condensing in the cracks of the mine roof could bring whole sections down without warning.

The gravel parking lot was packed with pickup trucks and a few dusty sedans that belonged to the midnight or "hoot owl" crew that was younger and statistically at greater risk than miners on day or evening shift.

Willie's face eased as he climbed out of the truck. "You look a sight." He grinned at my red hardhat, the sign of a new hire. "I'll give you one more week in a mudhole." He turned toward the men's bathhouse, set in a sprawl of pre-fab buildings. Through an open door, bosses crowded around a wall-sized mine map. Two men smoking cigarettes by the door fell silent and stared.

In the women's bathhouse, I sat on a wooden bench and pulled on steel-toed rubber boots, then took a round caplight and battery pack, attached by its black rubber cord, off a wall rack. The leather mining belt sagged with the weight.

The bathhouse was cramped. A row of lockers, a toilet, shower stalls stained red from acid water, a bench, and a wooden table piled with hardhats filled the small space. Every surface—walls, table, mirror, toilet seat—was layered with a fine gray talcum of coal dust. Grease and muck obscured the cracked linoleum. In contrast, the men's bathhouse was huge, with a concrete floor, twenty-foot ceiling, and wire baskets strung overhead to deposit wet work clothes for drying. We stuffed our wet clothes into damp lockers and kept close track of the mildew. Still, the bathhouse was a welcome place to be, to get a cup of coffee and a few minutes away from the eyes of the men before the shift began.

The door flew open. Annie stalked in, her arms loaded with flannel shirts. Small, lean, and hard-muscled, she was hired five years ago when a divorce left her with a three-year-old daughter. With the support of her father, one of the oldest miners there, she was among the first women hired in the mid-1970s, and one of the few who stayed.

"Morning," I offered. Annie was known for her sense of humor, but today she looked haggard.

"It ain't a good one, Red," she said. Balancing a burning cigarette on the bench, she pulled on a faded pink sweatshirt and began tucking bobby pins into her brass-blonde hair.

The door opened again. "Are we late yet?" Ellie called out. She was plump and cheerful, but seeing Annie's face, she fell silent.

"The doctor called me last night. My baby might have cancer. They won't know until next week." Annie sank down on the bench.

Ellie looked at me, then at Annie. "Why don't you go on home?" she said. "You don't need to be on that roof bolt machine with that on your mind."

Annie shook her head. "I got to save my time for taking her to the doctor," she said bitterly, grinding her cigarette into the floor. She looked up, her jaw set, "and if we don't get the hell out of here, they'll send us all down the road."

Several yards from where the mine mouth gaped, the day-shift crew gathered, about forty men and three women. The group fidgeted, eager to get away from the bosses and back into the cool dark of the mountain. Once underground, the power shifted. Union miners, not bosses, ran the coal.

"Well," Fletcher said behind me on the bleachers, waggling a finger through a hole in the crotch of his coveralls, "won't you just look at that."

Next to him, Boss Hog eyed Fletcher. "Must be a lot of fun for the old lady."

"If you ain't got the real thing, I guess you gotta play with something," drawled Ellie, tossing a smoldering cigarette.

Shift boss Ray Gene, a bearlike man in his early thirties, strode in front of the crew. "Listen up, boys. Safety talk," he announced. The crew groaned. He waved a clipboard for silence.

"Now boys, we had a fatality in Pennsylvania. That man had three kids. You know his wife is gonna have a hard time making it. You gotta remember to stay back from that roof and set those jacks." He spit an arc of tobacco juice into the ground for emphasis.

"Yeah," Boss Hog muttered, "to hear them inside, we don't have time to set jacks, just get that coal."

The loudspeaker rasped with static, carrying the message from underground: "FIRST NORTH TO THE OUTSIDE, FIRST NORTH TO THE OUTSIDE." Rail cars clattered out of the hole, and black-faced miners piled out and half-sprinted toward the bathhouse.

"All right, boys, let's run some COAL!" yelped Ray Gene. We scattered, grabbing dinner buckets, and moved toward the portal.

❧

In the mountain the darkness waits, watchful as a close friend, patient as death. Seamless, impenetrable, the blackness is absolute, the aura of the coal. With time, it becomes a sheltering silence, a buffer between the miner and the cares of the outside world. With time, the darkness soaks down into the blood, becoming a warm dark river calling you home.

"No room—NO ROOM!" came a voice from inside the mantrip, one of the low-slung rail cars that carried crews in and out of the mine. Inside the enclosed car, three men lay folded close as matchbooks.

"Aw, let the woman in here, Buzzard."

Buzzard climbed out and unfolded his thin frame, scowling. "I need the outside seat. Gotta spit," he said around a bulge in his cheek. I crawled into the tight dark space and swallowed a sudden urge to flee. Except for one open side, there was no seeing out. Hardened chewing gum jammed the cracks, and obscenities sprawled across the peeling yellow paint.

"'Scuse me." Next to me, his chin jammed into his chest, Boss Hog loomed like an impending mud slide. He let out a huge sigh.

On my other side, young Baby Face punched my elbow. "Don't let him get fresh with you, Red. Boss Hog's big with the women here."

Buzzard snorted. "Women, hell. Hog's just plain damn BIG," he said.

"Huh. It's the kid you better watch." Boss Hog retorted. "Hasn't had time to get used to his old lady, already he's wanting more."

The mantrip jerked. We were on our way into the mountain.

Shooting into the dark, we dozed, lulled by the communal warmth and by the drummed, atonal sound of the rails. Caplights were shut off in the mantrip dark. The rail car dipped, then climbed, as it followed the coal seam the mine was built to accommodate. The air cooled as tunnel intersections, called breaks, blinked by. The coal walls, or ribs, were powdered with gray limestone dust, a safety measure that reduced the risk of a deadly methane fireball.

Grinding, ringing steel upon steel, the mantrip moved through the darkness toward the coal face, the dead end of the mountain where crews prepared every shift for the ripping of the seam.

We screeched to a stop halfway to First South section, just over a mile inside. It could have been ten. We lost daylight, it seemed, hours ago.

"Your stop, Hung Low," the driver called to Pete Lau, a South Vietnamese refugee. "Watch out for your redhat. You stick with her ALL the time. Got that?"

"Yeah boss," shrilled Pete with a high-pitched giggle. My face burned. With no toilets underground, miners were left to their own resources. A law enforcing the buddy system for new miners complicated the situation for women.

With a clatter, the mantrip moved off, gathering speed. The headlights disappeared around a bend. It was quiet and, except for the twin beams of our caplight, completely dark. From the next entry came the deep thrumming of the conveyor belt. Our job was to shovel out the coal spillage beneath it.

Pete lifted the metal door that led into the belt entry. I stumbled through and grabbed my hardhat as the door slammed with a massive, echoing boom. Before us stretched the beltline, the aorta of the mine that carried coal to the preparation plant near the portal, where it was loaded on rail cars to travel to the Virginia docks, and then floated to auto factories in Japan. Pete picked up a wide-mouthed shovel. With a twist, he slid it under a layer of muck, pulled it up and, grunting, heaved it onto the belt. I took the other shovel and moved on down the beltline. With each step, mud sucked at my boots and I yanked them free.

The air wrapped around us, heavy and warm. To reduce the fire risk, ventilation was restricted in the belt entry, which made breathing difficult. I hoisted a shovelful of cement-like muck and heaved it onto the belt, passing at shoulder height.

Gradually my muscles relaxed as the rhythm settled in. My hands were slippery with black mud, and I smiled, thinking of my childhood, which was clean and orderly. We lived in a midsized town in East Tennessee where my father cared for many of the town's teeth. On his work table lay crowns and bridges, gold inlay and porcelain, all perfect and shining and white. I don't remember the needles and drills and blood. He had a talent for not inflicting pain in the dental chair.

Since his fatal heart attack a year before, the fabric of our home had been torn. My mother had let loose her widow's tears, but my grief hit like a drought. I felt as hard as parched earth.

Coal dust floated around us, glittering in the path of our caplights. Bending, lifting, sweating in the dark, we worked our way down the beltline. After two hours of steady labor, my glasses were fogged, but the mine floor was scraped clean. I wiped my forehead with a dusty bandana.

Pete made a circling motion with his caplight, a miner's signal. "Take a break," he said. His pale face was mottled with grime. "You work too hard, you get hurt. You get hurt, I lose my helper." He grinned and his teeth flashed white against coal-smeared skin. I glanced upward.

"What, you scared of the roof?" His caplight played over my face, then up to the roof above, seamed with cracks of stress.

"Just respectful, Pete."

He nodded. "It's good to watch. Me, I'm a great chicken. A chicken in the war. Now a chicken digging in a hole." He laughed softly and pulled out a battered thermos. Steam hung in the air as he poured. His fingers, like the features of his face, were delicate as a child's.

He stood up, looking at the belt's dark burden. "It's good here. No bosses. Quiet. You can sing if you want. Like in Saigon before the war. We always sang in Mass." He closed the thermos, and we moved farther down the beltline.

As I shoveled, I heard a soft sound over the steady rumbling. Muted and sad, the notes of Pete's song rose above the river of coal. He was in Mass, in a French Saigon.

Beyond his bent figure, a caplight bobbed in the darkness. We kept shoveling. It could be the belt boss making his rounds. Instead it was Mac, who ran supplies to the working sections.

"You're coming with me," he said. "First Right needs a redhat."

Pete smiled sadly. "They give, and they take away." The beam of his caplight brushed my eyes. "You come back, girl. I treat you right."

On the mainline track, I climbed into the open cab of the supply car, which was hooked to three flatcars loaded with sacks of rock dust.

"GRAPEVINE TO FIRST RIGHT. GRAPEVINE TO FIRST RIGHT," Mac's voice brayed on the mine phone. "Yeah buddy, I got the redhat." He switched on the headlights and the supply car jerked.

Dank air pushed past my face as we gained speed. The roof stretched like a piebald hide, showing dark patches where chunks of slate had fallen out since the last rock dusting. We passed stacks of wooden timbers and metal rollers used to anchor the conveyor belt. The vehicle shuddered to a stop and Mac handed me my dinner bucket.

"Be careful," he said as a matter of course. "They're up about five breaks. Watch out for the buggies. Flag them down or they'll run right over you." As the headlights disappeared, the tracks fell away: streaks of silver deadending into the blackness just beyond my faint circle of caplight.

Five breaks up. Not a bad walk. Ahead, I could hear the muffled roar of production. But away from the storm of noise and dust on the section, there was a strange peace to the underground. Water dripped from a rusted roof bolt into a pool of ground water. Alone, I drew close to the mountain, as helpless within its body as an undeveloped child.

Suddenly my caplight flickered, then dimmed. The clean-edged spear of light dissolved into a muddy smudge. My stomach jumped. I was going blind.

Run. No—stop. Cut if off. Let it recharge. The instructions ran through my head, but my feet were moving. Run. Faster. Four more breaks. Can't stop. Going blind. Lights ahead. Buggies will run right over you.

Blackness fell and I pitched forward into cool dirt. My dinner bucket clattered. I crawled toward the rib, but touched cold steel, the mainline track. Somewhere above it hung the "trolley wire," a bare copper wire carrying four hundred volts. I crawled in the other direction until my fingers touched the damp cushion of rock dust on the other rib.

The darkness pressed in like a vise. My hand, warm before my face, was annihilated. For night-dark is nothing like the mountain's black. The deepest moonless night yields a subtle play of shadow, a hint of color the pupil can widen to distinguish. Even stars spread a sprinkling of light. But the gut of the mountain casts no shadow.

A rustling wrinkled the stillness, followed by a faint click of metal. My muscles tensed. A rat, made bold by the dark, had found my dinner. I felt for a piece of rock and threw it blindly. A swift scurrying, then silence. The gnawing resumed. Panicked, I hurled a handful of small rocks and waited. He was gone.

I groped for the caplight switch on my hardhat. Turning it off, I counted slowly to fifty and tried again. The beam faltered, then brightened. I snatched my bucket and rushed toward the section.

Three breaks up, shuttlecar headlights jounced around a corner. I avoided the path of the vehicle and approached a cluster of caplights.

"You get lost, Red?" asked Donnie, a ventilation man. My caplight beam wobbled. He flicked his light across my eyes. "Better watch out if that light goes out," he said, teasing.

"She's a redhat. She don't know what that means," said Fletcher, beside him.

Donnie looked at me. Coal rimmed his blue eyes like thick eyeliner. "It means some woman's making time with your old man while you're slaving in this hole."

"She's welcome to him, whoever he is."

Donnie chuckled. A shuttlecar roared by, trailing thick electrical cable. He grabbed my arm. "That buggy cable can break your leg if you ain't careful."

We turned up to the coal face. Ahead the big-daddy of the mine's machines, the continuous miner, loomed out of the darkness. It dwarfed the working space. At the front end was the ripperhead, a cylindrical drum fitted with steel teeth that spun into the seam to cut the coal. In the giant's belly, mechanical claws pushed the coal onto an internal conveyor that pushed it onto a boom, which dumped the load into the five-ton bed of a waiting shuttlecar.

The continuous miner roared to power, lurching forward as the ripperhead slowly gored the face. Shock waves rode through my body. Billowing dust shrank our caplight beams to thin cones and nearly obscured the figure of the miner-helper, who stood close to the big machine. Unlike the miner operator, whose cab was roofed with a steel canopy, the miner-helper worked unprotected near the face, in the zone of the greatest danger. With his caplight, he searched for signs of impending collapse; a thin trickle of dust from the roof, or small pieces of rock falling. He monitored the machine's trailing cable, which was the size of a man's arm. If the cable was severed, a fire could release deadly vinyl chloride fumes.

After several cuts, the machine backed out on its caterpillar-tread to move to an adjacent room. Leroy, the section boss, stood back and checked his watch, then marked the tonnage on a grimy notepad. As the continuous miner moved out, two roof-bolt operators maneuvered the roof-bolting machine into place. One was Annie. She and her partner stood on opposite sides of the dual-head bolter, drilling to insert five-foot steel bolts into the roof. They worked methodically, installing the bolts in rows until they reached the coal face. Donnie and I followed, fastening a heavy drape of waterproof canvas near the tunnel wall to help direct air flow after it had swept the face.

We worked a half hour when Leroy stomped over from the next room. "Miner's down again. Might as well eat," he said with a grimace. We set our tools down and followed Boss Hog and Fletcher to the dinner hole, a makeshift table with a timber at each corner for roof support. A sickly-sweet smell hung in the air. Donnie picked up a plastic milk jug filled with water and splashed it over his blackened hands, then wiped them carefully with white paper napkins. He glanced at Fletcher's open dinner bucket. Inside, a Baggie bulged with plastic pill bottles.

Donnie whistled softly. "You're a damn drug store, buddy." Fletcher laid down his sandwich, leaving black fingerprints on the white bread.

"Doctor's orders," he said. "I got nerve pills, heart pills, blood pressure pills, stomach pills, breathing pills, and pills to help me with the old lady."

"I'll take care of your old lady. You can forget them horny pills," said Boss Hog, winking at Donnie.

Fletcher shrugged. "It's a damn shame when a forty-year-old man can't do nothin'." He rummaged through his lunch. "She's mad all right," he said. "All I got is beanie-weenies."

"You got more than Red here," Donnie said. "Looking at you musta made her lose her appetite."

"I lost my light and a rat got my lunch," I said. Donnie reached into his bucket and passed me a sandwich and a can of Pepsi. A pile began to grow: sandwiches, Doritos, candy bars, and snack cakes. I laughed and pushed it away.

"Girl, you can't work with no fuel in the tank," Donnie warned. "You never know what's gonna happen down here."

Annie walked up with Johnny, an older miner with a beaked nose. Leroy was close behind.

"Hog, we need you over on that miner," Leroy said, wiping his gaunt face.

"Fine, boss. But we got a contract that says if dinner gets interrupted, we get an extra half-hour." He tucked a chew of tobacco in his cheek.

"This damn miner keeps going down and you'll have a permanent vacation," Leroy shot back. "And Johnny, since we ain't running any coal, you can take the redhat over to timber in the returns." He looked at Annie eating in silence.

"What's your problem? You on the rag?"

"None of your damn business." She glared at him.

"Hey Leroy, why don't you get off her back for once," Donnie said.

"I'd be on it, if she'd let me," Leroy leered.

Annie slammed down her thermos. "I ain't listening to your garbage," she said. "Us ladies are going to the powder room, and we don't want to be disturbed." She shut the lid of her lunch box, and I followed her across the main entry and past the beltline. We lifted the metal door to the return entry, which was used as an escapeway, a dumpsite for mine waste, and a bathroom. Pieces of fallen slate littered the mine bottom and rotten timbers lay in pools of black water.

Annie scouted around with her caplight.

"You gotta watch around here. One time, a scoop operator came up on me right in the middle of things. He was more tore up about it than I was."

She handed me a fistful of yellow Kleenex. "Men have it so damn easy," she went on. "They just whip it out and they don't even have to take off their light."

"Does Leroy always go after you like that?"

"He's like the rest of them. The bosses get their pick of the women assigned to their section. Once you've got seniority, you can sign another job. Leroy's no problem. I'm just not half right today, thinking about Susie."

I paused. "Do you trust that doctor, telling you something like that over the phone?"

"It was a pretty damn dirty thing to do." She stood silent for a moment. "But I tell you one thing. I ain't gonna sit back and watch my baby die. If God takes her, she won't go alone." She turned and walked toward a darkened corner of the tunnel.

I moved behind a five-foot pile of gob and shone my light on the roof. It all looked "raggedy," as the older miners called it. I removed my hardhat and unstrapped the heavy belt and set it aside. I squatted in the darkness. I felt vulnerable without my light and protective gear.

In a tourist town by the ocean, I had watched my father die. My parents had rented a hotel room with a brown-and-gold sofa and a kitchenette; my brother had stayed home. That night we watched a movie rerun on TV, and I fell asleep very late. Hours later I was awakened by a loud noise. At first I thought it was snoring. But it was deeper, a rattling noise. It didn't sound human. Then my mother cried out his name.

"You ready?" Annie walked up and I blinked. We went back across the beltline and the mainline track, where Johnny sat on his haunches, waiting.

He rose stiffly and watched Annie trudge back toward the section.

"I never thought I'd live to see you little girls in this hole," he said, cocking his head to look at me with bright black eyes. "I worked with that one's daddy back in the handloading days. Got a dollar a day," he said.

Headlights swung around a curve and we climbed onto the cab with Mac. "Another fall on Foundation section," he told us. "The whole intersection came in. But they were eating lunch, so nobody got hurt." As we rode down the tracks, I closed my eyes and tried not to think about the fractured roof above us.

The brakes screeched. "That's one bad-ass place," Mac said. "Watch yourself." Johnny moved off in the miner's posture: back bent, hands clasped together behind his back, his caplight moving from mine roof to floor. Where the roof dipped, we ducked our heads. But we were lucky. Some miners worked in "low coal" seams less than a yard high where they shoveled, ran equipment, and ate while kneeling or lying on the mine floor.

Johnny stopped and sucked for air. I studied his red flannel shirt, now gray with dust. Color did not survive the underground. The brief blaze of a scarlet bandana, the bright-yellow machine paint, even the delicate pinks of human lungs—all fell victim to the coal dust and were muted finally to gray.

Several breaks down we heard a thud, then an echo. "Little piece down by the belt." Johnny paused. "You listen to the mountain, Red, and it'll talk to you."

"How?" I was instantly curious.

"Used to be, before these machines came in, you could always hear the top a-workin. You'd hear it creak like it was groaning. Then it would crack, or pop like popcorn, and you'd know to get your ass out of there." He spat on the mine floor. "But sometimes you don't hear nothin' and the mountain just sits down."

We tramped past heaps of rock dust, bundles of wooden wedges and stacks of squared-off timbers. In front of a waterhole bridged by narrow boards, he stopped abruptly and shone his light into the dark pool. We heard a faint scurry and a tiny splash.

"Rat," he said.

I stepped across the sagging boards. Timbers set at the pool's edge were streaked with rot. The air was close and stagnant, like the inside of a stop-pered bottle.

A caplight bobbed toward us. "Miner down again?" Goat, a boss with sandy hair and a drooping mustache, squinted at Johnny, who nodded.

Goat's light flicked over me. "A woman. I never do get the right tool for the job," he waved us toward the crew. The other redhat, Charles, was young, blonde, and stocky. Next to him, Buzzard leaned against a timber, mopped the sweat off his forehead, and wheezed. I glanced his way and was startled by a silvery flash from his hardhat; two strips of reflective tape in the form of a cross.

I half-ran to keep up with Charles. "Buzzard looks bad," I said, panting.

"Two years on the miner on First Left. They didn't ventilate worth a shit. So now he's down with black lung. He ain't no old man, either. Thirty-four."

"Can't he get benefits and get out of here?"

"He doesn't have enough years, and the company's fighting it," Charles said. "So they put him down here, out of the dust, but he doesn't have the strength to pack a timber. So guess who does the work." He laughed sourly and hoisted a six-foot oak timber onto his shoulder. He staggered off. I lifted the end of another and gasped, then dragged it off. Johnny followed us with bundles of wooden wedges.

After several trips, I spotted a board tacked to the roof lettered in chalk: "DANGER—KEEP OUT." Beyond, sheared-off pieces of slate hung from roof bolts like huge smoked hams. Six-foot-high tunnel walls were squeezed to mere inches. Splintered timbers protruded from fallen slabs like human limbs. Farther back, the mountain had caved in completely.

Quickly, I looked around. No one in sight. I stepped carefully through the debris and under the danger board. The roof above gaped open with a crevice nearly a foot wide. I crouched on a hunk of slate, shining my caplight into the black hole. The fissure was deeper than my light could penetrate.

That's when I see him. The death rattle claims him. No hands. No eyes. A jerking thing. I leap on the bed, clasp my hands in a fist and try to smash my father's heart. Crack it open. Wake it up! I suck air and push it into the drooping mouth. My breath comes back empty. His eyes are broken bowls. I wasn't trained to save him. How could I? He was already gone.

"What the hell are you DOING?" Johnny flashed his light furiously back and forth at me. Shaking, I scrambled over the slippery rock and under the danger board. He stared hard at me.

"You sneeze in there, the whole place could come in," he said tersely. "Listen, Red. I'm gonna do you a favor. I'm not gonna tell Goat where I found you, 'cause if I did, you might not have a job."

I shook my head.

"You can't wander off down here, girl. Too much happens." He handed me a bundle of wedges and we made our way back to the crew.

Goat stomped up to us. "We ain't got all day. Get that rock busted up for a walkway," he said, pointing to a pile of rock pieces broad as car hoods.

I hefted the sledgehammer and brought it down with a satisfying CRACK. As the rock split, I worked harder and faster, gasping as tears flooded my eyes. CRACK! My glasses fogged. I felt like a dam had burst. I kept smashing rock slabs, and dragging them off the roadway until I was breathless and perspiring. In the rubble of broken rock, one small piece caught my attention. I wiped my eyes and dusted it off.

"Seems like the worse the place is, the prettier them fossils are," said Johnny, coming up behind me. "Didn't know there were flowers down here, did you?"

He propped up his sledgehammer. "Looks like it's quit time, little sister." We trudged in single file toward the main entry. I wedged the fossil tightly beneath my arm.

In the cab of the mantrip, Donnie called outside. "FIRST LEFT TO THE OUTSIDE. This train's headed for GLORY!"

From within the mantrip, we couldn't see the pinpoint of light that grew to the size of a dime, then bigger. Minutes later, we spilled into dazzling sunlight. Dazed, I took a deep breath of fresh air and staggered a few steps until the sky steadied into blue.

Mike Yarrow

Mike Yarrow, professor of sociology at Ithaca College, came to the West Virginia–eastern Kentucky–southwestern Virginia area during the coal strikes of 1978 to interview the miners and their spouses. His study, conducted jointly with his wife Ruth, in many cases took on a poetic air. Their story in verse, extracted below, illustrates how the combined forces of mechanization and foreign competition are eroding, perhaps forever, the effectiveness of the miners. These "found poems" are for the most part laments, or elegies, at the decline of a people and their way of life.

Miners' Wisdom

Disabled Miner
In the Mines Thirty-Three Years

The coal companies didn't want a highly educated man as a miner.
They didn't want you to be enlightened.
The man in that day with the money got education too,
  and still kept you down, made you have these inferior feelings.
Even if you knew the boss was wrong,
he could treat you any kind of way
because you didn't feel like you had any worth, you know.

So John L. Lewis came along and he knew people.
He knew what the miner needed,
and he knowed how to make them feel good about themselves.
He told them, "The operators are treating you wrong and robbing you."
The miner loved him.
You didn't say nothing to no coal miner agin him, buddy,
if you didn't want a fight.
Because he was a man that *really* stood up for the miner.

I used to be a man that felt these great inferior feelings myself.
If you had come to my house, you couldn't a bit more gotten me
to come and sit down on the couch and talk to you.
'Course, it's hard to believe now, as much as I talk.
I felt inferior to my wife.
She's pretty well educated and she's got a good mind.
I depended completely on her.
Her family were fighters in the school system.
For me, a little loud voice or something would push me back.
It would close me right up.

I committed my life to Christ 30 years ago.
He set me free, showed me what a man really is,
what God thinks about a man.
Like John L. Lewis come along and told them miners what they
    really were
and how somebody cheated them
and they began to lose the inferior feelings.
My testimony as a Christian is a man can get in touch with God
and God can do wonderful things,

From *Appalachian Journal* 15.2 (Winter 1988), © *Appalachian Journal*/Appalachian State University. Used with permission.

but first He has got to make a man out of him.
It don't make an overbearing person,
or a person that will hurt somebody,
but it will make a person that *stands*.

A lot of the Christians think that you just go through the world
    and let
them trample on you, do everything that's wrong,
and you don't do *nothing,* you know.
That's the picture the world gets of Christianity.
That's the wrong picture.

Laid-Off Miner
In the Mines Ten Years
Laid Off Ten Months

My father was a miner.
Going underground and digging coal had real meaning,
continuance of life, one generation to the next.
Once I got in the mines, I loved it, I really felt at home.
I enjoyed learning that skill.
When you go in the mines you turn that light on
and it's a whole different world, the danger of it,
the intimacy, everybody dependent on everybody else.
It brought back feelings I had in the war.
All that camaraderie.

I was working six days a week, sometimes 10 and 12 hours a day
and I made about $35,000.
Sounds like a lot—a lot of Saturdays, a lot of overtime.
I was able to save, but I wasn't prepared to be laid off.
They shut her down in November.
They give you a kick in the ass,
then they give you this letter about how great it's been
you served us but because of this or that
we are closing this mine permanently, writing it off the books.
It shocked me.

I took all my savings and paid off every bill I had,
Master Charge, car, and put away $2,000.
My wife went to graduate school on that.
We plan to get through to the end of August.
By that time I'll find a job.
I've been to 7-11 stores, I've been to every hotel,
everything conceivable I've applied for.

I ended up mowing grass.
When you don't have nothing, $10 is a lot of money.

Looking for work is a forty-hour job.
Takes three months to learn how to do it.
And it's expensive—résumés, gasoline,
driving to Charleston to take Civil Service tests.
I know one miner who lost his phone.
Now he's too poor to get a job.

I lost any sense of direction.
I got so I lacked confidence in myself.
January and February, thousands of others were looking, too.
You have a better chance going out and
buying a lottery ticket once a week.

March and April was my major depression,
rejection after rejection after rejection.
On the American Slicky-Slide.
You see yourself sliding down.
You don't know where you're going to land.
A lot of people land at the welfare office.

We started cutting corners everywhere we could.
I put up a clothesline
because the drier used too much electricity.

One time I was off for nine months and unemployment ran out.
I was going to graduate school, and I got called back to work.
I had to quit school, but I was so happy,
the feeling of going back.
I remember getting the first paycheck,
going to the store, buying food, coming home, and crying
because I was happy I could buy food.
All the other people at the store were on food stamps.
I was watching how they weighed their decisions
to buy this or that with their stamps,
decisions I was making just a week before—
could I buy a popsicle or not for my kid?—
and I filled my cart up with steaks, with pop for the mines.

You get that paycheck, it insulates you from poverty.
The more you deal with problems at work,
the less and less you notice the poverty around you.

Statisticians are people without tears.
People don't know what unemployment is.

Working conditions now are so severe
I couldn't tolerate the stress,
not reading a book to my son at night.
Seeing him maybe on Sunday? Nooo!
You hear older miners talk how miners came home,
set their lunch buckets down, fell asleep beside the fire,
got up and went back to work, dirty and just so tired.
That history is repeating itself.
People working now in these hell holes—
I don't know how they handle it, be a father,
hold their lives together.
I couldn't.

Mingo County, McDowell, even Raleigh County
are as much a part of the Third World as the Third World is itself.
The "global economy" gives you peasants next door.
They disperse the steel mills to Mexico, capitalist enterprise
to keep them from communist aspirations.
Capitalism can come to them,
but the price is we have to become part of the Third World.

When you're so poor, existence is a war.
These goddamn hard times!
That's the hardest thing, finding the hope.
All I know is just carry on every individual day with love and
caring.
Just see what you can learn from that.

Woman Miner
In the Mines Ten Years

I've had some good times,
think I've done the job, done it really well.
The problem wasn't the work.
My biggest problem was height (four feet eleven).
Because I can carry about anything the guys can carry,
run most any of the equipment or do anything.
And I get along real good with them.

For a long time I was the only woman they'd let run the equipment.
You have to prove you can handle it,
that you're not going to cry if you mash a finger
or get a little dirt on you.

At first they didn't like the idea of us women being in there,
but one crew I worked on, a couple of them came to me one night,

told me they were glad I was there.

One day I was cleaning the dinner hole
and this big timber was in my way—I mean *it was big*—
so I just picked up one end and slung it out of the way.

The boss told the guys, "Connie picked that up.
After she left, I tried to pick it up too, and I couldn't."
I'm 38 now, and I've lost some of my strength.
When I was younger, I could pick up a refrigerator.
I was in that kind of shape.

When we were kids, we didn't have water in the house,
had a well back up the hill and I'd carry water for Mom,
a washtub full at a time instead of a couple of buckets.

The guys, after they get to know you, tell you about their kids
and their wives and how they met and what they're getting her
for her birthday. I wouldn't trade that for anything.
Some of them aren't worth a dern,
but most of them are.

At Christmas I cooked dinner for the crew,
had the dinner hole fixed up nice for them,
tablecloth, Christmas stockings hung, a tape player,
and we had Christmas dinner.
One Christmas they took up a collection, bought me a camera.
It tickled me to death.

Once we were working section Eight South.
It was dinnertime, everybody laying down, and Bill says,
"Give me that cushion."
I said, "No, you can't have my cushion."
He says, "Well, won't you let me lay my head in your lap?"
I was the only woman down there among seven or eight.
So I said, "Okay, Bill, I'll let you lay your head in my lap,
but you gotta lay *face down.*"
He hasn't spoken to me since.
I humiliated him in front of all those men.

We got this one guy aggravates me *to death* all the time.
One night he put his hand down on top my head,
pushed so hard I dropped to the ground.
I throwed my hands out to catch myself,
so he stepped on my hands, just goofing off, you know.
He's not doing it to hurt me.

The minute he lets go of me he knows he's in for it.
I come straight off the ground against him,
shove him plum back against the wall, get a neck hold on him,
and he tries to get away so we're both rolling on the ground.
One minute I got him down, the next he's got me.
When we get up our hands are scratched all to pieces.
It's just goofing off.
The boss said, "Them guys know not to touch you.
You'll beat the shit out of them."
Some of the married guys, they'll want to go out with you,
sit there, tell you all the problems they have with their wives.
They'll act like it's their wives' fault.
At work they'll sit around and talk about women all night long,
how many they went out with over the weekend, how easy they was.
After a while you get sick of listening to stuff like that.
To them you're the same thing.
I don't pay much attention because if I did
I'd probably chop a few heads off.
I try to keep it all a joke.

After a while you don't feel like the person you were.
I think it caused a lot of problems between me and Wesley.
Rumors went around: I was sleeping with this one and that one,
going out with the bosses,
and he got to the point where everybody was telling him this stuff
and he didn't want to take my word for it
and I got tired of arguing with him:
"If you want to believe it, believe it.
If you don't, don't."

I tried going out after the divorce,
but nobody wants you as a person.
I guess I've lost a lot of my trust in men.
If they say anything I pass it off as a joke.
I told them I wasn't anything they'd want to take home to their mothers.
They call me a lady,
and I say, "Ugh!
You don't know anything about me."

It didn't bother me at first as much as it does now.
The guys call me one of the guys, and I am rough.
Basically I've got bad manners just like one of them.
I don't care if I never dress up,
and I don't wear much jewelry or anything.

Sometimes I think, "Well, what in the world am I doing here?
I should be at home taking care of the house,
taking care of my daughter, acting like other women do."
I've tried to be like nice women,
going to parties, baby showers,
but when they start playing all these little ignorant games,
it just drives me up a wall.

Sometimes I'd like to get out and quit,
but what in the world would I do?
I've got so used to being in there, working with those guys.
When I was sick and off-work for two or three days,
one of the guys came by, brought me one rose.
And they're always doing something for you.
I guess it's just what you get used to.

Section Boss
In the Mines Nineteen Years
Foreman for Three Years

"The guys will tell you in a minute,
if you don't do it fast enough,
or don't do it at all,
They'll say, 'You ain't been Sheldenized, Son.'"

I worked at Affinity Mines for sixteen years.
I didn't take no shit for sixteen years.
Pardon the french.
I didn't let Affinity run *nothing* down my throat.
But in three years I have took more off of Shelden
than I ever thought of taking off of Affinity.

"Kissing hindend to hold a job."
I've worked so sick I couldn't hold my head up.
If I'm off two or three days and *not* over in the hospital,
I don't have no job.
They tell you what you have to do to survive.
They'll tell you either do it or else.
They'll tell you in a heartbeat there's ten thousand men out there
waiting for your job.
And never bat an eye when they say it.

I've heard the guy that is president of Shelden Coal
say *he* wouldn't work for Shelden.

Used to be you had 100,000 coal miners.
Down to nothing now.
Ones that's working is barely holding on.
They're not going to say nothing to jeopardize their job.

At one time I liked mining coal, liked going to work.
The men stayed "up" all the time, joke, carry on.
I hate to even go to work now.
At Shelden everybody is as serious as a heartbeat.

Firebossing always fascinated me.
I was trying to protect my buddies.
If I didn't do my job right they could be in trouble.
I was supposed to report any dangerous conditions.
I knowed what my job was then.

All right
I go fireboss at Shelden,
I got to run like a crazy man,
not get to do my job,
just go through the formality,
don't write up no serious violations,
sign the book,
put my neck out on the block.
We were running without proper air
and that's a gassy mine.
Blowed up in 1982 and killed seven or eight people.
When I was a union fireboss I could do my job.
Shelden buffaloed me.
Being Sheldenized is you give them your life.

My buddy Dan's not Sheldenized. He gives me
a lot of crap for letting them do it to me.
But if it came down to it, Dan would get Sheldenized right quick.

Boss told us to put "I'VE BEEN SHELDENIZED"
bumperstickers on our cars.
Yeah, I got one on the back window.
I didn't stick it on the bumper.

I have worked seven days a week for three years.
I had a sixteen-year-old boy before he passed away.
He said, "Hey dad, take me hunting.
Hey dad, do this with me."
"No, son, I've got to work."

There was no stronger union man than me.
They took all of my self-esteem away, you know, everything.
You're just like a robot to them.
Sometimes you have to eat crow to survive.

Myles Horton

Bill Moyers

Myles Horton's career as an activist spanned over five decades, and his dedication marked him as one of Appalachia's most significant voices of reform. Born in Savannah, Tennessee, in 1905, Horton graduated from Cumberland College in Lebanon, Tennessee, and studied at Union Theological Seminary in New York City and the University of Chicago. In 1932, following a tour of Scandinavian folk schools, Horton returned to the mountains with a mind to establish a similar movement in the Appalachians. The result was the Highlander School, originally based among the depressed communities in the hills west of Chattanooga. Highlander attempted to use education as a tool for social change, beginning with workshops designed to enable poor workers of all races to pass the literacy examinations then required for voter registration. Horton involved Highlander in union organization, helping found chapters of the CIO among the mountain workers. He later distinguished himself as an ardent supporter of racial equality, and Highlander played host throughout the fifties and sixties to some of the civil rights movement's most famous (or, in those days, infamous) activists—not only Martin Luther King, Jr., but also Stokely Carmichael, Rosa Parks, and Andrew Young. The school maintained a policy of integration from the outset, even in the face of threats (and realities) of harassment and violence.

Stepping down from the directorship of Highlander in the late 1960s, Myles Horton nonetheless remained an outspoken voice in liberal reform until his death from cancer in 1990. His story, told through a series of interviews with noted journalist and editorialist Bill Moyers (excerpted here), is that of a die-hard populist, a man who believed in the essential dignity of all humans and was willing to push for that dignity against any forces marshaled against him.

Born in 1934 in Hugo, Oklahoma, Bill Moyers received the B.J. degree from the University of Texas at Austin and the B.D. degree from Southwestern Theological Seminary in Fort Worth, Texas. He also attended the University of Edinburgh. He began his long association with public television in 1970. He is the author of Listening to America: A Traveler Rediscovers His Coun-

try (1971) and *A World of Ideas: Conversations with Thoughtful Men and Women about American Life Today and the Ideas Shaping Our Future* (1989). Among his television documentary series are "Joseph Campbell and the Power of Myth" (1987) and "Moyers: The Power of the Word" (1989).

Bill Moyers Interviews Myles Horton

MOYERS: Myles, you've upset a lot of people down here over the years. *The Mill Owner* said that Highlander was about the boldest and most insulting thing in an Anglo-Saxon South that has yet been done; one Georgia governor said that you were a cancerous group spreading throughout the South; the state of Tennessee closed you down, confiscated your property, sold it at auction; the Ku Klux Klan beat up your staff and burned your buildings; a United States senator had you ejected from his hearings. Now what's a nice man like you doing upsetting all those people?

HORTON: Well, I don't try to upset people. I try to help people grow and be creative, and fulfill themselves as people. And in the process of doing that, they upset a lot of people.

MOYERS: How do you mean?

HORTON: Well, they start doing things, asserting their rights, for example, working people asserting their rights to have a union, asserting their rights to be treated decently, people in the mountains asserting their rights to be left alone to live their own way if they want to, without having the absentee landowners run them out of their holdings, their heritage. And we try to help people, you know, stand up against this kind of thing. We try to help people become empowered so they themselves can do things, and that's very irritating. One of the reasons they confiscated Highlander was because the charge was made by the governor of Georgia that this cancerous growth was spreading over the South and that the civil rights movement came out of Highlander. And only a racist white person could make that assumption that some white people had to be doing that kind of thing. So they assumed that since a lot of the blacks had been at Highlander long before the civil rights movement and during the civil rights movement—blacks couldn't do anything themselves, so it had to be some white people. So they got four or five of the governors together and closed Highlander. And it was only after they closed it they found out that they, you know, didn't have anything to do with the civil rights movement, the blacks were doing the civil rights movement.

MOYERS: I think that's what really upset a lot of people.

HORTON: And they got upset, I think, when they found out they couldn't stop it by confiscating Highlander. When they first came, they came and

From *Appalachian Journal* 9.4 (Summer 1982), © *Appalachian Journal*/Appalachian State University. Used with permission.

padlocked the building, and some of the news reporters that were there, said "What are you laughing about?" I was standing outside laughing, and they took a picture of me standing there laughing. And the sheriff padlocked the building. I said, "My friend here, you know, he thinks he's padlocking Highlander," but I said, you know, "Highlander is an idea—you can't padlock an idea."

MOYERS: You say Highlander is an idea. What's the idea?

HORTON: Well, we have a philosophy, that we know, that we can identify. We believe in people. Our loyalty is to people, not institutions, structures. And we try to translate that belief and trust in people's ability to learn into facilitating peoples' learning. Now you don't teach people things, since they're adults; you help them learn. And insofar as you learn how people learn, you can help. And that's a powerful dynamic force, when you realize that people themselves in these hollows and these factories and these mines, you know, can take much more control of their lives than they themselves realize.

MOYERS: How does it work, I mean, how do you teach—how do you help people learn something like that?

HORTON: Well, first thing you have to clarify is that—you have to understand, you have to know that people—working people, common people, the uncommon common people—they're the most uncommon people in the world, the common people—have mainly a past, they're adults. Unlike children in the regular school system, who have practically no past and are told by the schools that their present isn't worth anything, they are taught about the future, they're prepared for the future. Adults come out of the past with their experiences. So you run a program at Highlander based on their experiences, their experience in learning—from which they may not have learned very much, because they haven't learned how to analyze it, but it's there, the grist for the mill is there. And our job is to help them understand that they can analyze their experiences and build on those experiences, and maybe transform those experiences, even. Then they have a power that they're comfortable with. See people—first I should tell you that not only are people adults with a past, with experiences, but they are leaders in their communities. I don't mean official leaders, but grassroots leaders.

MOYERS: You mean, not bankers and—

HORTON: No, they are the people in the people's organizations, like labor unions or community organizations of various kinds. Well, those people come and we say, "Okay, what are your experiences that relate to this topic—not all your experiences, but your experiences that relate to this topic?" Now they hadn't considered those experiences too important—they hadn't thought of them being very important. We say, this is very important because that's the curriculum, that's the building stones that we're going to use here. And it's something you can take back with you, because you, you know, brought it here. So we start out—

MOYERS: They didn't know it, when they got there.

HORTON: They don't—they hadn't learned to analyze those experiences so they could learn from them. You know, people say you learn from experiences—you only learn from experiences that you learn from, you know. That's not all experiences. And we try to help them learn from their experiences in such a way that when they go back they'll continue to learn. But we have to also learn from our experiences. And one of the things we have to do in addition to what they have to do, is to learn how to relate our experiences to theirs. And you do that by analogy, you know, you do it by storytelling. You don't get up and say, "Look here are some facts we want to dump on you." We say, "Well, you might consider this. Now this happened to somebody kind of like you in a different situation." So we get them doing the same thing with each other. You get peer teaching going, where everybody that's in the circle is part of a peer teaching group.

MOYERS: What's radical about that? What was radical about that back in 1930?

HORTON: Well, it's terribly radical, because it goes against what education is supposed—Education is supposed to prepare people to live in whatever system the educational school system is about. Like in our system it's to prepare people to live under capitalism and be—you know, fit into that system. In the Soviet Union, it's to prepare people to live in that system, and fit in that system. And that's what education, official education, is all about, to prepare people to fit into the system, and support the system.

MOYERS: And Highlander?

HORTON: Really, it's to turn them into nuts and bolts to keep the system together, you see, whatever kind of system it is. Highlander says, No. You can't use people that way. People are, you know, creative, you've got to allow them to do a lot of things that don't fit any kind of systems, and you've got to have a lot of deviations, to have a lot of pluralism. We believe in people keeping a lot of their old customs, and adding new ones. And we said, that's what enriches life. So we're going to focus on that, and there's a lot of dynamics and a lot of power in that, that scares people. When people in the South, before the civil rights were started, began to feel that they could do something, in spite of the laws, in spite of tradition, and started doing it, then you know, all hell broke loose. We had that experience earlier, in the thirties. We started back in the Depression, in the pre-industrial union movement in this country, before the CIO was started. And many of our students who had been at Highlander before, you know, became leaders in the unions in the early days when it was rough. When we first started organizing, it was illegal to have a picket line, and a lot of our activities were illegal. Highlander itself was illegal up until about four years ago. We defied the state law on segregation in private schools, which stayed on the books long after the public schools were integrated. You know, we had to work that way to live up to our principles. So, to get off the subject a little bit, but the people have all this power, but it's suppressed by the public school system and by the institutions. We, having loyalty to the people and not the institutions, you know, always try to throw our weight on the side of the people, and help them do things that are right. Now you can't get people to do something they think is wrong. You know, you can't—you know, people say Highlander is a propaganda nest, you get all these ideas in people's heads and they go out and do things they learned at Highlander, well, you know, that's not the way things are.

MOYERS: They were in their minds.

HORTON: They were in their minds, they're seeds. What you do, you develop those seeds. They're crusted over, you know, with all kinds of things and the people don't even know they're there. We know they're there, we dig for them, and we cultivate those seeds. We help prepare the ground for them to grow, and we help people learn, they can learn from each other, that they're stronger. Individualism is enhanced by being part of a group, you know, individuality, I guess, would be a better way of saying it, is enhanced by being part of a group, instead of telling people they should go it alone, they should be competitive, they should, you know, compete with their fellow man. We say, work together, and you'll be a better person.

MOYERS: What started you thinking radical thoughts a long time ago?

HORTON: Well, Bill, I was asked that question by a priest back in the CIO days when there were a lot of efforts to have labor schools. And Highlander was—we were officially designated as *the* CIO school of the South. And we had more programs than anybody else. So they had communist-sponsored labor schools, Catholic-sponsored labor schools, and some independent schools like Highlander. And a priest in Nashville, who was trying to start a Catholic school, kept coming to Highlander, and he says, "I did—I go back, I do everything I learned at Highlander, I go back and I just imitate everything I learned. It doesn't work, doesn't work." And he said, "It doesn't do—it's no good just to look at it, but it's something I don't understand. Maybe I can get at it by asking you what books influenced your life most. Because I got to understand this," he said. And I said, "Well, I can tell you, but it won't help you any, because, you know, like all people I got my own track of development, and my own background is a part of it." And I said, "I grew up in a religious family, like most people in the South," and I said, "undoubtedly the first book that influenced my life was the Bible, there's no question about that. All my early influences came from the Bible and things like that, you know, not an ultrareligious family, but a conventionally religious family, and that was the values in little country towns, you know. You went to church and you went to school. There wasn't anything else to do." So I said, "There's no question, and I still, the values of the Bible I still hold dear," I said, and he said, "Well, what in particular?" And I said, "Well, okay, there's two—there's the New Testament and the Old Testament. In the New Testament we learned about love," and I said, "You can't be a revolutionary, you can't want to change society if you don't love people, there's no point to it. So you know, love people, that's right out of the Bible. And another thing is, the Old Testament tells primarily about the Creation. God was a creator. If you're going to be with people, born in God's image, then you've got to be creators, you can't be followers, you know, or puppets, you've got to be creators. So from the Bible, I guess, people ought to be creative, or love people, people ought to be creative." Well, he thought that was rather skimpy theological background, but anyway, I was trying to tell him the things that affected me, and then I said, I got so discouraged by seeing the people in the church and politicians and all being hypocritical, that well, I almost got very cynical about society. And the way I knew this because I used to work in a store and I used to do things where I knew people, when I was growing up. And I just found that the leaders, you know, were all hypocrites. So, I said, that's the way people are. So I was getting very cynical, and I decided, well, you know, what's it all about, the business of loving people and sharing with people in this cynical world. So at that time, I always loved poetry, I always read a lot of poetry. And I ran into Shelley.

MOYERS: Shelley?

HORTON: Shelley. And, he said the same thing. He said, "Shelley!" like you did. [*laughs*]

MOYERS: It's been a long time since I read any.

HORTON: He said, "What has Shelley got to do?" Well, Shelley was a young rebel, he died young, same age Christ died. But he wrote some wonderful poems, about, you know, defying all authority if it's wrong to obey authority, and living your own life. And you do things without fear of punishment or for rewards, you know, and somehow I—

MOYERS: You do it for the good—

HORTON: You do it because they're right. And Shelley just hit me at the right time, he gave me a feeling that I wasn't going to get cynical, I was going to live my own life. And it made me think independently and say, well, I'm going to create my own life, I'm not going to play the games of other people if I don't believe in them. I'm going to find a way to survive and live my own life. Shelley did that for me. Then I realized that what's good for me is not—if I just want to live my own life, you see, I've got to think everybody should have the same rights I have, a universality of rights. If they're right for me, then I've got to work for them to be right for everybody else, or they're not—I have no right to them.

MOYERS: You do believe there are certain truths and rights self-evident?

HORTON: Yes, and those have to be shared. It can't be for me—I can't have something that isn't for you, or for the poorest person, you know, in the world. And I believe that, and I believe you've got to work for that. Well, I had nothing in my background that prepared me to work for things like that. You know, I didn't have any understanding, I'd gone to a little liberal Presbyterian college, and I had only the kind of academic background that anybody would have—so there's nothing in my schooling that would help me on that, nothing in my background, nothing in the Bible, nothing in Shelley. And it was then that I discovered about Marxism and analysis of society on a class basis. I discovered that first, not by knowing about Marx, but by the *Federalist Papers,* when Hamilton talked about classes, that's when I first got to understand classes, from Alexander Hamilton, when he said that the, you know, workers would vote their interests, the farmers their interests, and the merchants their interests. That was the first insight I had, and then I found Marx said the same thing, a little more elaborately. So I found out from Marx I could get tools, not blueprints, tools that I could use for analyzing society. That helped me analyze. Then I had to get a synthesis of my religious background and my understanding of economic forces. And then I started trying to work on a synthesis. And those are the things that helped kind of get me to think and gave me some kind of guidance. Now I've never been a doctrinaire, you know, religious person, or a doctrinaire Shelley advocate, or a doctrinaire Marxist, but you know I got from all those things—ideas—that helped me.

MOYERS: I thought you might have become a Christian-poet-activist.

HORTON: Well, I did a lot of poetry in life. I think that somebody said, you know, Highlander is a myth. And I said, well, you know, it's a poem, too, it's a picture. It's because it's not anything that any of us here have done, but the people have come here have made a mosaic out of Highlander. And it's a—poetry's a beautiful thing, you know.

MOYERS: The segregationists, and the Klanners, and the politicians were fond, in the old days, of calling Highlander communistic, and calling you a communist. Were you ever a communist?

HORTON: I was never a member of the Communist Party, and I was invited to be member of the Communist Party, and then I was told two years later that I couldn't be a member of the Communist Party by the head of the Communist Party.

MOYERS: Why?

HORTON: Well, I asked him the same question. And he said, well when we first wanted you to be a member of the Communist Party, you know, you were a radical activist—I was active in college—and we thought, you know, you'd be a good Communist, but you started Highlander and began to get ideas of your own, you know, you wouldn't be trustworthy. Because you'd want to do things, you wouldn't follow discipline. . . .

MOYERS: Can you describe for me what conditions were like for the workers in this part of the country in those days?

HORTON: Well, they tried to organize Elizabethton up here, where my ancestors came from, Watauga settlement, and that was in the late '20s, and they brought troops there to break the strike and run people back into the hills until they behaved themselves, and all they were doing was trying to have cut down on the twelve-hour work day and get more than eight dollars a week for working. And you know, they beat them into submission.

MOYERS: They?

HORTON: I mean, the company, it was the first multinational, it was—it came here in the '20s.

MOYERS: What was it?

HORTON: It was a Bemberg rayon plant. It was a multinational plant—of course, we didn't know that then. But that's what it was that I'm talking about—

MOYERS: And the workers tried to organize?

HORTON: They tried to organize. And that plant was built on the land that one of my ancestors got, the first land grant in Tennessee, that's where that plant was built, right on that spot. And—but those people were just being pushed around. Now those people had a background like my background, they came out of a good tradition and so on.

MOYERS: Mountain people are supposed to be pretty tough, pretty independent, they could take care of themselves.

HORTON: Well, tough, till you know you bring these troops in, tough, you don't stand up against hard gun thugs, and police, and troops.

MOYERS: Well, given that reality, why did you think that a bunch of teachers at a seclusive place like this could identify with men in circumstances as painful as those?

HORTON: Okay, now, I believe that it had to be done. And I was determined to try to do it. And I was determined to identify, to be—have these people perceive that I had solidarity with them. I knew that had to be.

Jeff Daniel Marion

Jeff Daniel Marion is a poet as well as a teacher, farmer, and printer. Marion took both undergraduate and master's degrees at the University of Tennessee at Knoxville. A resident of New Market, Tennessee, since 1966, Marion has taught English and creative writing at Carson-Newman College. In addition, he edited *The Small Farm*, an independent journal of poetry, from 1975 to 1980 and since 1983 has edited Mill Springs Press, a handprinting venture devoted to publishing Appalachian poets. His poetry has been widely praised and anthologized, and Marion has authored three books of verse, including *Out in the Country, Back Home* (1976), *Tight Lines* (1981), *Vigils: Selected Poems* (1990), and *Hello, Crow* (1992), a book for children.

Razing the Well House

wooden shingles lie scattered
like the scales of a life
shed

parched tongues that burn
speaking

"Razing the Well House" and "The Farm Wife's Aubade" from *Vigils: Selected Poems,* Appalachian Consortium Press, 1990. Reprinted by permission of the publisher.

the loss of a labor
with froe & mallet
this August air perfects a silence
to sing the departure,

but the pump will not leave
the willow's roots entwined

this wedlock in earth
tapping
hidden springs

The Farm Wife's Aubade

Let this land's corduroy,
an apron of brown
plowed fields & green rows,
always wear its colors
in blessed light.

Whenever darkness falls,
let it be sown with moon & stars,
a zodiac to guide
the labor of these hands.

Let the rooms that house my labors
be sweet with a lingering incense:
yeast of daily bread,
cinnamon
& the hint of hickory smoke.

Let my song be a kitchen window,
dipper & water bucket on the sill,
filling with the world outside.

Let my life pour
across these days in honeyed light
slow & rich as the dawn of May.

"Mrs. Grundy"

Something of the legend of engineers on mountain railroads is captured in *Mrs. Grundy*, which was the name of the Tracy City, Tennessee, newspaper prior to 1934, in an obituary for Matt Cope, dated March 15, 1917. Cope had also been a fireman on "the Mountain Goat," a short-line railroad at Sewanee, Tennessee, noted for the engineering marvels of long tunnels and steep grades. The obituary was noted by J. W. Arbuckle and Alan C. Shook, railroad historians, and reprinted in their book, *The Mountain Goat* (1992).

Matt Cope Dead

Matt Cope, aged 55, a veteran engineer of the N. C. & St. L. Ry., died at his home in this city Friday afternoon, March 9th, at 12:50 o'clock, surrounded by the members of his immediate family. His death came after a lingering illness of many months and was from a complication of diseases involving stomach and intestines.

Mr. Cope was born in the Oak Grove neighborhood, three miles east of Tracy City, May 8, 1861. He spent his early childhood days there but at the early age of 17, came to this place and commenced his railroad career as fireman, on a switch engine, under Supt. E. O. Nathurst, for the old T. C. I. & R. R. Oo. [*sic*], which at that time, operated the railroad from East Fork to Cowan. Promotion came to him rapidly, however, on account of his efficiency and adaptability to the work, and while still little more than a boy, he became an engineer. When the T. C. I. & R. R. Co. sold out to the N. C. & St. L. Ry., Mr. Cope continued in the service and was one of most trusted and competent men in the employ of that company until the end of his working life, which was on March 14, 1916, when, on account of declining health, he [was] forced to leave his post. He was placed on the retired list January 1st, 1917.

During his long tenure of service as an Engineer, Mr. Cope witnessed the passing of many of the old-timers of the Tracy City Branch, some of whom died peacefully in their beds, others of whom were killed in the course of duty. Geo. Colyar, who died in 1908, was for many years his conductor; William Bolton, killed at the Depot platform, March 1, 1897, was a lifelong friend and co-worker with Mr. Cope, as were also James Rust, Ben Finch, Elisha Hardin, Jim Wilson, John Sansom and many others of the older railroad men who have gone before. During his long career as an engineer, Mr. Cope had numerous close calls for his life but was never seriously injured, and it is a matter of note among the few survivors of the early days that, no

From *Mrs. Grundy* (Tracy City, Tennessee), vol. 31, no. 1 (Mar. 15, 1917). Reprinted in *The Mountain Goat* by J. W. Arbuckle and Alan C. Shook., Overmountain Press, 1992. Used here by permission of J. W. Arbuckle.

matter what the emergency, he always stuck to his cab. And through it all, he was modest and unassuming, kindly and genial and "on the square" with everyone and these are some of characteristics which endeared him to the hearts of all. He will be sadly missed by his family and his friends all along the Tracy City Branch, but it is a sweet solace to know that he was a Christian, did his life's work well, and was ready to go:

> And his soul is mounting higher
> To the home where 'twill abide,
> Like an engine, surely, strongly,
> Going up the mountain side.

In the faraway days of his early experiences, the life of a railroad man on the Tracy City Branch was full of an eminent and ever-present peril. The rails were of iron and easy to break. The engines, small unstable affairs, caricatures of the huge, finely equipped moguls of today, were prone to the eccentric tricks of jumping the track, turning over, and any other unexpected thing. Air, as applied to cars, was unknown then, and the safety of the trains on the precipitous grades of Cumberland Mountain depended solely upon the use of steam and the hand brakes. The cars, of less than half the capacity of those in use now, were coupled together with link and pin. One dark, rainy winter night, a train of coal cars left the Tracy City yard with Mr. Cope in the cab of Engine number 93. The train proceeded to a point beyond Sewanee without mishap, where a wreck occurred. The train was pieced together and the downward journey resumed. The brake rigging had been stripped, and the engine was held closely to the train to ease it down the heavy grades. Four brakemen, helpless with broken brakes, were scattered over the train. The conductor, John Simpson, and fireman, Levi Sitz, were in the cab of the engine with Matt Cope. The descent was being made smoothly, it seemed, when some member of the crew discovered the head car of the train was about three car lengths from the engine. Mr. Cope tried to regain his position against the train, and the engine received a jolt which loosened everything that was not already loose. The engineer realized then that their only hope was to beat the train down the mountain. He put on all steam. Rushing, roaring behind him was that mass of iron and wood and coal. There was certain death behind, if overtaken, and ahead of him there was—he knew not what. But it was a chance and he took it. There were moments when he could have slowed for an instant and jumped to safety but jumping was the one thing, probably, of which he did not think. There were lives in his hands and company property, so he gripped the throttle and stuck. The engine reached the valley and the flat track a little in advance of the persuing [sic] train. There might have been some luck mixed in with the adventure; certainly there was a large element of nerve, and maybe a Being greater than all was watching the race from out of the darkness above. In any event, several old-timers in Cowan recollect that the little old "No. 93" went through that station, chased by its own train, at a rate of speed never dared by No's 98 or 99. Mr. Cope did not stop at the depot, as was customary. He did not even hesitate. But at a point a mile or so beyond, out on the main line toward Decherd, he stopped, backed up on the now mollified train and pushed it into Cowan. This instance is only typical of many such escapes experienced and lived through by Mr. Cope.

He was married about 1885 to Mrs. Mollie Heffner. To this union two daughters were born. The home life was ideal. He was ever a loving and generous husband and father. The home he built for them, set in a magnificent grove, is a thing of beauty.

Mr. Cope was a member of the Episcopal Church, and the funeral ceremony was conducted by Rev. Dubose of Sewanee and Rev. Boyd, Rector of the Tracy City Episcopal Church. The brief and impressive burial service of that church was said at home and the grave Sunday afternoon. The floral offerings were profuse and splendid. Beautiful wreaths of all-white flowers literally covered the grave. These were given by railroad men, the lodges of which he was a member, and friends. A design from the Brotherhood of railroaders, bore the initials "B.L.E." in gold.

The deceased was an honored member of various lodges. He belonged to the B.L.E., R.A., I.O.O.F., and K. of P.

A special train was run up from Cowan Sunday in his honor, and it was crowded to its full capacity. The active pallbearers at the funeral were six locomotive engineers. They were: Messers I. J. and S. C. Kinningham and J. A. Porter (retired) of Cowan, and Messers T. J. Crick, G. B. Marler, and W. H. Eller, of Tracy City. Those Honorary were selected from different Lodges of which he was a member. They were: Messers Louie Hassler, Henry Schild, T. B. Roddy, Ed. Robertson, Dallas Hargis and Thos. Weaver.

Mr. Cope is survived by his widow and two daughters; Miss Wilcie, of Tracy City and Mrs. Murray Bradley, of Brewton, Ala.; a grandson, Raymond Bobo, and brother, Amos, of this place and one brother, Harris Cope, of Sequatchie Valley.

A floral offering in the form of an engine driving wheel, emblematic of his trade, and tendered by the Nashville Brotherhood of Locomotive Engineers, was withheld on account of a flaw in the design, a spoke being broken. This will be placed upon the grave later.

Nan Arbuckle

Nan Arbuckle, born in Middle Tennessee, lived on both the east and west sides of that state's defining river. With her father from the Cumberlands ("The Mountains" in her poetry), she grew up knowing the hills and plateaus. While her first published work focused on the century-old cemetery with generations of her family, the poetic centrality of the southern roots did not appear until the poem "Flatlands and Hill People" won the Oklahoma Student Poetry Award during her doctoral work at the University of Oklahoma. Now the title poem of a volume nearing completion, its theme of exile still holds for Arbuckle, an assistant professor of English at Ohio State University at Lima. Just as being from Tennessee while living in the North influences much of her poetry, having been severely disabled with rheumatoid arthritis for thirty-five years has become both a creative and critical topic for her newer work, promising new directions.

Grandfather's Song

The Osage family moved slowly to the beat,
circling the drum with sons and daughters,
grandchildren and great-grandchildren.
Friends joined behind and beside.
We outside the dance stood quiet,
solemn as the dancers in tribute.
To have a song with Grandfather's name,
a tribute for a whole tribe to know,
respect for those now our memories—
we should learn from this pride.

My grandfather's song will have the rhythm
of train wheels on tracks, slow
regular, climbing long slopes.
It will dip and cry like the whistle
of steam rising over the valley,
sharp as red leaves on a mountainside.
Word sounds will jumble and roll
like the voices of many children calling,
playing homemade games of older days.
And in the end it will settle soft,
with the screaking click of a rocker
on a wood porch and tall hemlocks sighing, quiet
as the slow breath of an old man, remembering.

Let us, too, make songs of honor so our old men
are never quite gone.

Printed by permission of the author.

Ambrose N. Manning

Ambrose N. Manning is a native of North Carolina and a graduate of Atlantic Christian College, Wilson, North Carolina, and of the University of North Carolina at Chapel Hill. He holds the Ed.S. (specialist) degree from Peabody College in folklore. The coeditor (with Robert J. Higgs) of *Voices from the Hills* and several books of folklore with Thomas Burton, he also is author of several articles on folklore and a well-known collector of songs and lore. The Burton-Manning Archives at East Tennessee State University are named in honor of him and Tom Burton. He and Burton have received the Laurel Leaves Award for their contributions to the Southern Appalachian region. Manning, a past president of the Tennessee Folklore Society and the Appalachian Consortium, is professor emeritus at ETSU, which conferred upon him its Distinguished Professor Award.

Railroad Lore: The Songs of the Gandy Dancers

There are folk songs dealing with railroad heroes ("John Henry"), "brave engineers" ("Casey Jones"), and tragic accidents ("Wreck of Old 97" among many others). Overlooked, however, except for the mythical John Henry, are the men who laid the rail lines and kept them repaired. Along with the disappearance of these "gandy dancers" (because of the mechanization of laying rails and the maintenance of them) one finds, naturally, the disappearance of their work chants.

In 1965 Professor Thomas Burton and I, after a great deal of searching, finally located two former railroad workers who had helped to lay and repair the lines on the Southern Railway through the mountains of East Tennessee between Bristol and Knoxville. Mr. Ab Miller and Mr. W. H. Carter, both blacks, were living in the southern part of Washington County, Tennessee.

As they explained, the lead singer of the work crew did nothing but direct the chants, while the others laid and aligned the tracks of steel. The purpose of the singing and chanting was not only to relieve the tedium and boredom of the hard work and to soothe the men's feelings, but they were also used to keep the laborers in unison; for, in this kind of work, without the rhythmic pace, someone could have been seriously injured.

The leader would usually walk backward so that he could direct not only the chanting but also the straightening of the sections of rail. Without interrupting his singing, and with only a slight motion of his hand or arm that almost always carried a stick, he could communicate to the crew what needed to be corrected before tamping down the spikes which held the line to the cross ties.

He would chant a few lines (usually two); and then, at the ends of the

Used by permission of the author.

next four lines, the entire crew would chime in. The assigning of six lines to the "stanza" is arbitrary on our part, for the length varied; but generally they were six-line "stanzas." (The workers would not have thought in poetic or musical terms such as "stanzas"; thus I have put it in quotation marks.)

As Mr. Miller and Mr. Carter chanted for us, they used pliers to hit upon coal tongs to try to duplicate the noise of hitting steel on steel as they did while they worked.

Following are some of the chants we recorded:

(An' you see, 'e just walked along there, n' whenever a foreman 'd stop me right there, well, I'd stop, well I'd say, "Boys, are you right?" They'd say, "Right here, right here." Well, they put the bars under the rail; well, I'd start out):

> Well, work all summer n' a half the fall,
> Had to take Christmas in our over/*h*/alls;
> Oh boys, you got to move it (yeah);
> Oh boys, you got to line (now);
> Oh boys, you got to pick it up (yeah);
> Oh, boys, you got to line (yeah).
>
> Well, look over yonder, whut'd I see?
> Brand new mule comin' after me.
> Oh boys, you got to line (yeah);
> Oh boys, you got to pick it up (shake it);
> Oh, boys, you got to line (yeah, mmm).
>
> Boys, are you right? Right, right.
> Oh, captin, captin, cain't you see
> This here boy's killin' me?
> Captin, captin, (got the line)
> Cain't you see (mm mm)
> This here boy's (mm mm) killin' me? (mm mm)
> Boys let's (grunt) (mm mm);
> Boys let's (grunt) (mm mm);
> Boys let's (grunt) (mm mm)—ho!
>
> Gonna chew my 'baccer; gonna spit my juice;
> Would tell a lie, but it ain't no use;
> Ay, you got to line it (yeah);
> Boys, you got to shake it (yeah);
> Boys, you got to pick it up (yeah);
> Boys, you got to line (yeah).
>
> Well, shoot my pistol; have my fun;
> Run like hell when the poleece come;

Oh, boys, you got to line it (shake it);
Boys, you got to line (mmm);
Boys, you got to line (mm mm);
Boys, you got to line (mmm).

Old Ant Dinah dead n' and gone;
Left me here to sing this song;
Yea, you got to line (yeah);
Boys, you got to pick it up (yeah);
Boys, you got to shake (yeah);
Boys, you got to line.

Well, *I* don't know but believe I will,
Make my home in Jacksonville; uh;
Got to shake it; uh;
Believe I will (mm mm);
Make my home (mm mm)
Jacksonville.

Oh, I woke up this morning an a half past four;
Crawfish passin' out around my door;
Yea, you got to line (yeah);
Boys, you got to shake it (yeah);
Boys, you got to pick it up (yeah);
Boys, you got to line; mmm.

Oh, you got right, boys (got right again);
Are you right, boys? (mmm ready now);
Oh, you need no mule
You don't need no jack,
Tightenin' on the bar an' let's line this track;
Oh boys, ya got to move it (yeah);
Oh boys, got to shake it (yeah);
Oh boys, ya got to pick it up (yeah);
Boys, you got to line.

Oh, he's 'bout lined this track,
Quarter 'head and halfway back.
Oh, you got to shake it;
Line the track;
Quarter 'head;
Halfway back (yeah!).

'Druther be in the bottom with the whuppoorwhill,
Be here rollin' for a dollar bill.

Oh, boys, you got to shake it (yeah);
Oh, boys, you got to pick it up (ah);
Oh, boys, you got to line (mmm);
Oh, boys, you got to shake.

George Scarbrough

See volume 1, chapter 1, for biography.

Tenantry

Always in transit
we were always temporarily
in exile,
each new place seeming
after awhile
and for awhile
our home.

Because no matter
how far we traveled
on the edge of strangeness
in a small county,
the earth ran before us
down red clay roads
blurred with summer dust,
banked with winter mud.
It was the measurable
pleasurable earth
that was home.
Nobody who loved it
could ever be really alien.
Its tough clay, deep loam,
hill rocks, small flowers
were always the signs
of a home-coming.

From *Invitation to Kim*, Iris Press, 1989. Reprinted by permission of the author and publisher.

We wound down through them
to them,
and the house we came to,
whispering with dead hollyhocks
or once in spring
sill-high in daisies,
was unimportant.
Wherever it stood,
it stood in earth,
and the earth welcomed us,
open, gateless,
one place as another.

And each place seemed
after awhile
and for awhile
our home:
because the county
was only a mansion
kind of dwelling
in which there were many
rooms.
We only moved from one
room to another,
getting acquainted
with the whole house.

And always the earth
was the new floor under us,
the blue pinewoods the walls
rising around us,
the windows the openings
in the blue trees
through which we glimpsed,
always farther on,
sometimes beyond the river,
the real wall of the mountain,

in whose shadow
for a little while
we assumed ourselves safe,
secure and comfortable
as happy animals
in an unvisited lair:

which is why perhaps
no house we ever lived in
stood behind a fence,
no door we ever opened
had a key.

It was beautiful like that.
For a little while

Patricia D. Beaver

Patricia D. Beaver was born and raised in Asheville, North Carolina, and earned her B.A. and Ph.D. degrees from Duke University. She is currently professor of anthropology at Appalachian State University, Boone, North Carolina, where she has served as director of Appalachian studies and director of Asian studies. With scholarly interests in gender issues, social and economic change, family and community, and narrative ethnography, she divides her time between teaching and research on Appalachia and the American South, and on northeastern China.

Work and Worth

"Worth" is a term rarely used in a positive sense; the negative condition "worthlessness" is frequently expressed.[1] For example, "He ain't worth the bullet it'd take to kill him, or he'd a been dead years ago"; "that worthless old woman"; "he ain't worth shit"; and "he ain't worth a pinch of dried owl shit."[2] "Most folks," or people of worth, are responsible for their actions, are rational in their decisions, and have common sense. Common sense is an important quality that, if developed and used by the individual, motivates the individual to rational action. Worth is thus assumed to exist in people because they are people. Worth is a natural quality of adults, both male and female.

Young children have worth, and, though they may act foolishly, irrationally, or in a worthless manner, it is not because of their own lack of worth but because of their parents' irresponsibility. Parents are responsible for the actions of their children; children must be taught self-control and responsibility if they are to "act right." Parents therefore may have indirect effects on the worth or lack of worth of adults. Worthless parents may produce chil-

From *Rural Community in the Appalachian South*, © 1986. Reissued 1992 by Waveland Press, Inc., Prospect Heights, Illinois. Reprinted by permission of the publisher.

dren who become worthless adults who "don't know no better." However, children of worthless parents are not automatically categorized as worthless. All children, legitimate or not, or born of worthless parents or not, have the potential for worth and are not excluded by virtue of birth status or parentage. Each person demonstrates his or her own worth or lack thereof, and worthless parents may produce children of worth. The worthless "whoring" woman in the community who had illegitimate children of different men produced children of worth.

Although common sense is an important quality of worth, one may act as if one had "no sense" or "no common sense" and not by that fact alone be considered worthless. Lacking common sense, one is considered foolish or simply a fool. T. R. Campbell has no common sense. T. R. and his wife, Sally, and their two small children live on part of T. R.'s parents' 135 acres. T. R. and Sally are both college-educated, and Sally is a social services employee. T. R. has tried farming, dairying, and storekeeping but mostly likes to hunt. T. R. always hires neighbors to help him work his tobacco; although hiring neighbors is not unusual, T. R. and his hastily assembled crew are always harried because T. R.'s tobacco is always late and is among the last to get to market after Christmas. T. R. likes farming less than devising ways to make farm work easier. T. R. designed and built a tomato wagon to make picking tomatoes easier. While his wife and friends worked the tomatoes, T. R. worked on the wagon. When it was finally ready, it failed on the first day's efforts because the brakes proved faulty. The people and tomatoes almost fell off the wagon when it went careening down the hill. Neighbors laughed for the next year about the retired wagon and wondered what T. R. would devise next. T. R. tried dairying but, unfortunately, didn't like to milk regularly. At last report, he was running a small store and enjoying the conversations afforded him by his customers. T. R. said that during deer season he was going to close up, and, if anybody wanted him, they'd know where to find him.

Although T. R. is the butt of much humor and has little common sense, he is respected and well liked in the community. T. R. and Sally have worked hard in the church, particularly in organizing activities for the children. T. R. was the first person to hire Larry Douthit. Larry initially was ostracized by some residents as a "hippie," but because T. R. opened the door to him, others followed suit. T. R. is an "educated fool" who has "no common sense." He is admired for his generosity, sense of humor, and humility and is respected for his efforts, though they are often misdirected. T. R. is a man of worth.

Worth is assumed until demonstrations of worthlessness prove otherwise. Worth is not easily lost and need not be guarded with excessive diligence. Rather than being a value that must be achieved and perpetually reachieved, worth is assumed until severe transgressions prove its nonexistence.

The most common way of becoming worthless is not to work. One may also become worthless by drinking too much; yet here, again, the distinction depends on work. If a drunkard works hard on a regular basis, he is not necessarily worthless. One man drinks almost every afternoon and continues during most evenings. When drinking, he usually associates with male friends, playing cards or just gossiping in his garage. He works hard during the mornings and afternoons and supports his family, thus fulfilling his economic responsibilities to his children. Furthermore, some people feel that he drinks so much because his wife and her parents disapprove so heartily of his drinking. Because of this, and also because he doesn't cause any trouble when drunk, he is not considered worthless (except by his parents-in-law).

One who is disruptive to community harmony or is a "troublemaker" may also be considered worthless. Lloyd Miller is a self-ordained preacher and a part-time deputy sheriff and considers himself to be guardian of community morality. Lloyd is a meddler. He is quite visible in the community and, because he prowls around in the mountains, is frequently suspected of spying on his neighbors. Lloyd found the marijuana growing in the woods and took the sheriff to it. When the Presnell boy was sent to prison for shooting his friend during a poker game, Lloyd tried unsuccessfully to organize a petition "to get the Presnells thrown off the creek." Lloyd supposedly stole some money from coworkers when working in the mines. Lloyd shot one of J. B.'s hunting dogs one night. When his tomatoes got the blight, Lloyd is rumored to have walked in his neighbors' tomatoes so that theirs would blight too (one man finally put up a "No Trespassing" sign to try to keep him out). When T. R.'s cows got out because T. R. didn't get around to mending his fences, Lloyd put up a sign reading "All Trespassing Animals Will Be Shot." Lloyd is always seen in the company of his "poor" wife and daughter "so nobody will shoot him." Lloyd is "not worth shooting, or he'd a been dead already." Lloyd works hard to make a living and supports his family, but he seems perpetually to stir up trouble. Lloyd is a troublemaker, a meddler who cannot be trusted; he is "worthless."

A person of worth has the common sense to know when not to interfere, when to leave well enough alone. According to the "high sheriff" (as distinguished from the deputies), "Folks 'round here are the nicest you'd want to meet anywhere. Sometimes trouble gets started, but you can usually avoid problems by using your common sense." The high sheriff is respected for leaving well enough alone much of the time. The highway patrol "boys," however, over whom the county has little control, "don't know when to leave things alone" and, accordingly, are resented.

Demonstrations of worth depend primarily on work. Claude Phillips, who resides with his family at the bottom of the creek, spends many of his waking hours reclining on a couch on the porch. Claude is "only renting"; he is "no kin" to any of the Phillipses in the community and is "on welfare 'cause he's too lazy to work." Claude is worthless and ignored. Thus, from an endemic point of view, a large category of "worthwhile" people exists in the community, some of whom have had more success at manipulating the environment and the economy than others, and a minuscule group of worthless individuals, who are normally discussed only when outsiders pry into their existence. For most purposes, this small group does not exist. When kinship is queried, they seem to be kin to no one, even though their family names may be the same as those of community members. For residential analysis they are forgotten, and when the question is pursued, they are "only renting." They are temporary residents, not really part of the community. Further probing reveals that "they're on welfare 'cause they're too lazy to work." Thus, although another family may be as poor as the worthless family, if they work, they are included in the large category of "community" because persons of worth work. The poor family of worth will be defended to the outsider, and instances of individual achievement in spite of hardship will be told and retold. This distinction between worthless and worthwhile seems to depend on whether the individual in question makes some effort at coping with subsistence.

"Work" and "public work" have different meanings in rural Appalachia. Public work includes any job that entails working under someone else's authority for a regular salary, normally with no return from the job other than the wage earned and possible fringe benefits. Work in industry, education, or government would be included in this category. The broader category of "work" includes any economic activity that contributes to subsistence or maintenance, with the specific exclusion of "public work." Public work most commonly results in wages; work may or may not result in wages. Work thus includes gardening, child rearing, housekeeping, farming, timbering, and mining for personal or private profit and not in industry, and a tremendous variety of other, often daily, activities of this nature. Thus, although I was never asked, "Do you work?" I was frequently asked, "Do you do public work?"—the assumption being that I, like most people, work. Thus, when an individual is considered worthless because he won't work, he is being criticized not for not getting a job (that is, a public job) but for not making at least some effort at coping with basic subsistence problems. Furthermore, although public assistance is not a very "worthwhile" source of subsistence, families receiving public assistance are not by that fact alone classed as worthless. Thus, some families are part of the "most folks" category who are in fact receiving assistance in the form of welfare or food stamps, although this is an undesirable alternative.

Worth is not a limited good, nor is it in limited supply, since every individual potentially has an equal and personal amount.[3] Through the individual's personal decision to act in a worthless manner, he is viewed as lacking worth. Thus the worthlessness of one individual in no way increases the worth of another. In fact, in certain situations such as marriage, an individual's worthlessness may place an unusual and undeserved burden on another, which may, theoretically, cause the latter person to lose worth. Jane Presnell is a hard-working woman who is married to a worthless man. Cicero Presnell is worthless because he stays drunk most of the time and is "too lazy to work." Jane runs her household, takes care of the children, and works for people in the community. Jane is respected for her efforts and is a woman of worth.

Theoretically, Jane could give up trying to defy Cicero's behavior and would become worthless too. Likewise, her children could follow in their father's footsteps and become worthless.

Although worth may be lost, it may also be regained through changing behavior. T. R. Campbell went through a worthless period for several years after marriage and became a carousing drunk. T. R. had a serious automobile accident and "hasn't touched a drop since." Another "worthless drunk" underwent a religious conversion during a revival in a local church and since has been a hard-working, religious, responsible supporter of his family. Rebecca Phillips's young daughter-in-law is worthless because she "lays around all the time and won't do nothing." Although her parents are worthless "'cause they're on welfare and Darlene never learned to do nothing," there is a good possibility that Darlene will not stay worthless. Although she is a married woman and therefore a responsible adult, Darlene is only fifteen and, through the help of her affines, probably will learn to do the things that women are supposed to do.

Community evaluation of work, and thus of the worth of an individual, is the major factor in determining integration or social interaction with newcomers. Although initial social interaction is avoided, the newcomer is closely observed. After several weeks, residents are able to determine whether or not the newcomers seem to be working in some way, and they will then initiate interaction. The cultivation of closer personal relationships depends on numerous other factors such as value orientations, personality, and religious philosophy. But in terms of basic acceptance, which in the rural mountain community has a great deal to do with determining a comfortable existence even for those who are not dependent on agriculture, the criterion of work, and thus worth, is foremost.

As defined, worth is assumed to exist in people and is innate intelligence or common sense that motivates rational judgment. Men and women possess worth in the same way, although, because of the division of labor by sex, it is manifest in different ways. Community ideas of worth assume an ideal self-sufficiency and independence of the individual, although the individual of worth recognizes the rational limitations of such individualism and the value of cooperative action in specific circumstances. There are only a few worthless individuals in each community. Thus egalitarianism as a conceptual system applies only to community members, the "most folks" category, and excludes the few worthless individuals.

Notes

1. "Worth" as used in this context is in some ways comparable to Mediterranean notions of "honor" as described by J. K. Campbell (*Honour, Family, and Patronage* [Oxford: Clarendon Press, 1964]); Julian Pitt-Rivers ("Honor," in *International Encyclopedia of the Social Sciences,* ed. David L. Sells [New York: Macmillan and Free Press, 1968], 6:

503–11.); and J. G. Persistiany (*Honour and Shame* [Chicago: U of Chicago P, 1966); and of "brains" as described by Ernestine Friedl in *Vasilika: A Village in Modern Greece* (New York: Holt, Rinehart and Winston, 1962). With respect to the latter concept, Friedl writes: "The villagers assume that intelligence and self-control are basic human qualities which differentiate men from animals. The villagers are in many ways committed humanists and assume that once these traits are developed each man will have the strength to face life and its vasana (trials and pains)" (77). "Worth" is likewise comparable to "honor" in the sense that it refers to "a sign of the recognition of the excellence or worth of a person . . . [and] expresses the worth, whether this is an economic value in a market, or social worth evaluated in a complex of competing groups and individuals" (Campbell 268).

2. According to Cratis Williams, this graphic and poetic phrase was a favorite of his father's.

3. Greek honor has, according to Campbell's qualification, features of a "limited good" in the sense that Foster describes certain qualities that "exist in finite quantity and are always in short supply" (John M. Foster, "Peasant Society and the Image of the Limited Good," *American Anthropologist* 67 [1965]: 296).

Bettie Sellers

Bettie Sellers is a native of Tampa, Florida. After receiving degrees from La Grange College, La Grange, Georgia, and the University of Georgia, she taught English at Young Harris College, Young Harris, Georgia, and later became chair of the Division of Humanities there. Her first volume of poetry, *Westward from Bald Mountain* (1974), was followed by *Spring Onions and Cornbread* (1977). In these same years she was the recipient of awards for her poetry. In "Liza's Monday," the title poem for another volume of Sellers's verse, the poet reminds us that labor in Appalachia takes many forms other than mining and railroading.

Liza's Monday

She has left her tubs and boiling sheets, fled
north across the woodlot, heard no grumble
from the pigs as she passed, the chicken shed
where eggs wait to be gathered, felt

From *Liza's Monday and Other Poems*, Appalachian Consortium Press, 1986. Reprinted by permission of the publisher.

no pain as December's harsh wind dried
lye soap on her arms, reddened hands held
stiff by her sides, palms forward as to catch
the gusts that sweep the slopes of Double Knob.

Inside the cabin: Ethan's shirt to patch,
the fire to mend, small Isaac sleeping
in his crib, soon to wake for nursing.
These and other chores are in her keeping,

but she hurries up the mountainside
as on an April day to search for mint
and cress, to find first violets that hide
in white and purple patches by Corn Creek.

The ridge is steep and rocky, sharp with briars.
Raked inside by gales howling bleak
as northern winds around the cabin whine,
she does not feel the laurel tug her dress,

the briars pricking dark red beads that shine
on bare arms. All winter afternoon she climbs
until she gains the highest rocks, the knobs
where one can look out, trace the spines

of distant mountains, scan the valley floor—
black dots for shed and cabin, smoke only wisps
blown by the wind. Liza sees no more:
not broken stones underfoot, not heavy sky

holding snow. She sits on Double Knob, back
against the ledge, and watches night come by
to close the valley, wipe her clearing out
as though it has never been. Snow clouds

roil around Liza's head, wrap cold arms about
bent shoulders, fill her aproned lap, open hands.
Below, the wash-fire has burned down to embers;
Ethan long begun the search across his lands.

John Gaventa,

Barbara Ellen Smith,

and Alex Willingham

As these authors note, the labor scene in Appalachia and the South has changed considerably in recent years, but the challenge to labor, management, and local communities remains the same: how to dignify labor in a democratic manner.

John Gaventa accepted the task of succeeding Myles Horton as director of the Highlander Research and Education Center, New Market, Tennessee. While the Horton legacy looms large, Gaventa is an individual unique unto himself. Raised for the most part in Nigeria, Gaventa returned to the United States with an outsider's perspective, until, as a college student in 1971, he traveled to Appalachia, where his family had its roots. There, much reminded him of his former African home, as he saw a rural culture being exploited to some extent by outside forces, resources hauled away, and benefits slow to appear. He began a scholarly investigation of the state of the region. What Gaventa found only reinforced his sense of injustice and abuse; he turned his findings into a dissertation in political sociology, which became his book *Power and Powerlessness: Quiescence and Rebellion in an Appalachian Valley* (1980).

A Rhodes Scholar and recipient of a MacArthur Fellowship, Gaventa continues to pursue scholarship as a sociology professor at the University of Tennessee at Knoxville, having undertaken projects ranging from landownership surveys to public health projects. He continues his active participation at Highlander as a staff member of the Research and Education Center.

Barbara Ellen Smith is former research and education director of the Southeast Women's Employment Coalition. She is the author of *Digging Our Own Graves: Coal Miners and the Struggle Over Black Lung Disease* (1987); *Women of the Rural South: Economic Status and Prospects* (1986); and numerous articles on labor and women's issues in the South.

Alex Willingham is a professor of political science at Williams College, Williams, Massachusetts. He was formerly research director at the Southern Regional Council and a consultant on voting rights issues in the South. He is editor of the *Voting Rights Review* and has written on voting rights and black political participation for a number of journals, including *Southern Changes, Social Science Quarterly*, and *Urban League Review*.

Toward New Strategies

The struggles for alternative development, for protecting old jobs and communities, and for organizing the new are at one level diverse and separate. But at another level, the efforts are interconnected: they all speak to the common concern of creating spaces in which grassroots communities act and participate in defining their own economic futures. The questions, they suggest, are not only about substituting one set of policies for another. Rather, they are about who shall participate in shaping the policies in the first place, and how success will be defined. They ask not only "Development for whose interests?" but also "Development by whom? toward what end?" They reflect demands not only for economic development but also for economic democracy, not only for growth but also for quality and dignity.

The process of broadening the definition of who participates in the development debate leads, of course, to different definitions of what constitutes success. As strategies to take charge rebuild the link between "community" and "economy," it becomes artificial to separate the economy as a single issue from other concerns. At the local level, "the economy" is part of a broad web of relationships which includes the relationship not only to a job or employer but also to the land and environment, as we saw in the struggle by citizens in Robeson County to protect the Lumbee River or in the efforts in Kentucky against strip mining the mountains. Economic concerns become more holistic, more than just a paycheck. They also involve personal relationships to family, community, and culture.

Within that web, just as demands for development cannot be separated from demands for participation, neither can they be separated from concerns of dignity and equity, be they based on class, race, or gender. The mutual struggles for development and for dignity mean crossing barriers that traditionally have divided social groups in the South and elsewhere. Throughout these studies we have seen hopeful ways in which diverse movements are interacting and supporting one another. The movement for women's employment in the mines worked patiently, and in the end successfully, to link up with the traditional, predominantly male union. The building of cooperatives in Alabama and Georgia grew from and strengthened the demands for black political participation. The creative new organization of workers in South Carolina, the Workers' Rights Project, prides itself on the leadership that women and blacks are giving to it.

Similarly, other newly formed efforts are bringing together unions, civil rights organizations, and community groups to link their common concerns. In November 1987, more than five thousand people marched in Nashville as part of the Jobs with Justice campaign, one of the largest demonstrations in the region since the civil rights movement. Later coal miners and other union members joined the leaders of the Southern Christian Leadership Con-

From *Communities in Economic Crisis: Appalachia and the South,* Temple University Press, 1990, © 1990 by Temple University. Reprinted by permission of Temple University Press.

ference for a symbolic march across the South, representing a new unity across race and region that was not present twenty years ago.

At the same time, there is much to be done if these local efforts are to translate themselves into a movement. More steps and strategies are needed to link and expand the emerging community-based activity.

First, the new participation in the economy implies the need for economic education. Education, in this sense, is not for the purpose of adapting to new jobs in an economic model over which people have no control, but is for helping people recognize the validity of their own knowledge of their economy and begin to create new definitions of development that would be successful in their terms. It is a process of gaining the economic literacy needed to act and participate in economic decision making and economic change.

Second, the movement for economic justice must begin to translate its increased awareness and activism about economic matters into new, more democratic economic policy. In many ways, the failure of the traditional state and local economic policies based on the industrial recruitment model has created a policy vacuum which is ripe for new ideas that could be supported by diverse and broad constituencies. Federal legislative and policy interventions were crucial to the growth of the civil rights movement in the South. In the same way, the movement around economic issues must involve governmental participation if local action is to be sustained. And, given trends in the federal government that favor devolving many policies for economic well-being back to the states, the local level takes on new significance as a building block for policy change.

Indeed, there are examples of the political process's being effectively used to address economic concerns. In Kentucky, the successful public referendum against the broad-form deed represented a citizens' victory against the historic economic power of the coal industry. In South Carolina, the Workers' Rights Project has also been successful in gaining new policies on worker compensation. In West Virginia, Pennsylvania, and Ohio, the Tri-State Conference on Steel has proposed a public Steel Valley Authority, which would involve local governments, unions, and community groups in economic planning for the area. In West Virginia, a conservative governor, Arch Moore, challenged traditional business prerogatives by suing Newell Company for $615 million after it decided to close its Anchor Hocking Glass plant, which had previously been subsidized by low-interest state loans.[1] In Arkansas, a state-supported Rural Development Bank is exploring ways of using state pension funds for local development. All these are only examples of ways the state and local arena is becoming an arena for new policies for a more democratic economy—a process that must continue.

While emphasizing local grassroots action, we have argued at the same time here that the regional economic crisis is part and parcel of a national and international crisis as well. Just as constituencies and issues must be linked within the region, so, too, must locally based movements make links with those concerned about change in the larger arena. To do so involves building horizontal links with other regions and groups in the country whose own futures are being played off against our own. We must recognize that, while important gains have been made in our region, they have often been achieved with the help of broader structures—progressive churches, unions, foundations, some government agencies—which now often battle for their own survival at the national level. We must also tie local efforts to national ones, remembering that the linkage needs to be a two-way process, one that mandates national groups to hear and include the voice of the grassroots and the grassroots to join movements for a more progressive agenda nationally.

Finally, the nature of the current crisis challenges us to link local and international concerns. Often, in our movements for social change, domestic concerns have been seen as separate from international issues. The movement of capital and industries from home to abroad and the playing off of workers and communities across national boundaries link local and international concerns in a new way. In recent years, many groups in the region have begun to respond to the new conditions by developing their own grassroots interchanges with groups affected by similar issues elsewhere. The Africa Peace Tour sponsored in 1987 by church and community groups linked economic and political concerns in southern Africa to those in the Deep South. A tour of health and safety activists from India following the Bhopal disaster linked groups questioning the location of hazardous industries, which occurs in poor communities here as well as abroad.[2] Similar exchanges have brought together leaders of cooperatives in Nicaragua and Alabama and of rank-and-file democratic unions in Mexico and Tennessee.

While national and international restructuring serves on the one hand to deepen inequities in the South and to challenge traditional models of economic development and social change, so, too, has it spawned the seeds of a new movement. At the moment, the movement is at the grassroots, relatively invisible to the national eye. To grow, it will need broader economic education, coalition building, policy development, and national and international linkages. But as the new participation builds, it has the possibility of transforming contemporary economic restructuring into a new model of development, one that links matters of the economy to matters of democracy and dignity—at the local level as well as in the broader arena.

Notes

1. "Corporate Shutdowns Draw Fire," *Knoxville Journal,* 29 June 1988.
2. See, for example, Anil Agarwal, Juliet Merrifield, and Rajesh Tandon, *No Place to Run: Local Realities and Global Issues of the Bhopal Disaster* (New Market, TN: Highlander Research and Education Center, 1985).

Chapter 5

Nature and Progress

Introduction

As industrialism has gradually emerged as a force in the Southern Appalachian region, the lives of the people and the face of the land itself have changed radically. Perhaps because the region is a relatively new frontier for industry, older residents can still recall a different way of life and remember the land in a more pristine state. Poets have lamented the passing of the old ways, and environmentalists have called for reform.

But the simple desire to earn a living is—and always has been—at odds with nostalgia and environmental concerns. Appalachian people must weigh their love of natural beauty against the need to make a living. This dilemma cuts to the heart of the Appalachian crisis and clearly illustrates that the forces at work in Southern Appalachia arise neither solely inside nor outside the region. While the economic dilemma historically has been exploited by outside interests, Appalachian people themselves have been culpable—in the harvest of virtually all the virgin timber on the Blue Ridge and in the sale of mineral rights. Businesses and corporations headquartered elsewhere—even the federal government—have altered Appalachian life and the face of the land, but all the region's problems cannot be attributed to "outsiders." Understanding Appalachian life means recognizing that the relation between land and people has always involved conflict as well as harmony and appreciation of natural beauty. The tension between progress and nature is yet another facet of the profoundly complicated Appalachian condition.

Robert Morgan

See volume 1, chapter 1, for biography.

Passenger Pigeons

Remembering the descriptions by Wilson
and Bartram, and Audubon and other
early travelers to the interior, of the sky
clouded with the movements of winged pilgrims
wide as the Mississippi, wide as the Gulf
Stream, hundred-mile epics of equidistant wings
horizon to horizon, how their dropping
splashed the lakes and rivers, how
where they roosted whole forests broke down
worse than from ice storms, and the woods floor
was paved with their lime, how the settlers
got them with ax and gun and broom
for hogs, how when a hawk attacked
the endless stream bulged away
and kept the shift long after
the raptor was gone, and having read how
the skies of America became silent, the fletched
oceans forgotten, how can I replace
the hosts of the sky, the warm-blooded jetstreams?
To echo the birdstorms of those early
sunsets, what high river of electron, cell and star?

From *At the Edge of the Orchard Country,* © 1987 by Robert Morgan. Reprinted by permission of Wesleyan University Press and the author.

Barbara Smith

Like Jesse Stuart, Barbara Smith reminds us of the regenerative power of spring and the constant threat to nature's resources. Chair of the Division of the Humanities at Alderson-Broaddus College, Philippi, West Virginia, she is active in several projects to improve the quality of life in Southern Appalachia. She is the editor of the literary journal *Grab-a-Nickel*.

Appalachian April

Clinging to clay caught
    in mountainside crevices,
    bluets finger spring.

Red bud transplanted
    dies fast as a man without
    memories of mountains.

The lilac tower
    of fair-haired Rapunzels
    not letting down hair.

Lawn-eating chickweed,
    ditch-damning silence:
    orchids under glass.

Amid chattering
    daisies a pregnant silence
    offers the rosebud.

But for a sporty
    crimson caught, mere purple would
    be purple poppies.

Legends of dogwood
    cover scars on coal-bleeding
    Appalachia.

Printed by permission of the author.

John Muir

John Muir (1838–1914) is one of America's original and premier naturalists. Born in 1838 in Scotland, he immigrated to the United States with his father while still a boy. His early education was self-administered but sufficient to win him admission to the University of Wisconsin. In 1863 Muir decided to leave the university to travel on foot throughout the Midwest and eventually down the Mississippi to the Gulf of Mexico, an experience that later became the core of his memoir, *A Thousand Mile Walk to the Gulf* (1916).

Muir eventually moved west and dedicated the remainder of his life to securing the safety of the wilderness against the encroachment of humanity. It was Muir's influence on President Theodore Roosevelt that resulted in the establishment of the first national parks. Muir also found time to write, combining philosophical musings heavily influenced by Christianity, Shakespeare, Carlyle, and Thoreau with keen observations of the physical world. The genial and unconventional conservationist and adventurer died in 1914 in Los Angeles. An avid admirer of Henry David Thoreau, Muir convinced Theodore Roosevelt to set aside 148 million acres for forest reserves, thus contributing greatly to a magnificent heritage for all Americans.

Crossing the Cumberland Mountains

Toward the top of the Cumberland grade, about two hours before sundown I came to a log house, and as I had been warned that all the broad plateau of the range for forty or fifty miles was desolate, I began thus early to seek a lodging for the night. Knocking at the door, a motherly old lady replied to my request for supper and bed and breakfast, that I was welcome to the best she had, provided that I had the necessary change to pay my bill. When I told her that unfortunately I had nothing smaller than a five-dollar greenback, she said, "Well, I'm sorry, but I cannot afford to keep you. Not long ago ten soldiers came across from North Carolina, and in the morning they offered a greenback that I couldn't change, and so I got nothing for keeping them, which I was ill able to afford."

"Very well," I said, "I'm glad you spoke of this beforehand, for I would rather go hungry than impose on your hospitality."

As I turned to leave, after bidding her good-bye, she, evidently pitying me for my tired looks, called me back and asked me if I would like a drink of

From *A Thousand-Mile Walk to the Gulf,* © 1916 by Houghton Mifflin Co., © renewed 1944 by Ellen Muir Funk. Reprinted by permission of Houghton Mifflin Co. All rights reserved.

milk. This I gladly accepted, thinking that perhaps I might not be successful in getting any other nourishment for a day or two. Then I inquired
whether there were any more houses on the road, nearer than North Carolina, forty or fifty miles away. "Yes," she said, "it's only two miles to the
next house, but beyond that there are no houses that I know of except empty
ones whose owners have been killed or driven away during the [Civil] war."

Arriving at the last house, my knock at the door was answered by a
bright, good-natured, good-looking little woman, who in reply to my request for a night's lodging and food, said, "Oh, I guess so. I think you can
stay. Come in and I'll call my husband." "But I must first warn you," I said,
"that I have nothing smaller to offer you than a five-dollar bill for my entertainment. I don't want you to think that I am trying to impose on your hospitality."

She then called her husband, a blacksmith, who was at work at his forge.
He came out, hammer in hand, bare-breasted, sweaty, begrimed, and covered with shaggy black hair. In reply to his wife's statement, that this young
man wished to stop over night, he quickly replied, "That's all right; tell him
to go into the house." He was turning to go back to his shop, when his wife
added, "But he says he hasn't any change to pay. He has nothing smaller
than a five-dollar bill." Hesitating only a moment, he turned on his heel and
said, "Tell him to go into the house. A man that comes right out like that
beforehand is welcome to eat my bread."

When he came in after his hard day's work and sat down to dinner, he
solemnly asked a blessing on the frugal meal, consisting solely of corn bread
and bacon. Then, looking across the table at me, he said, "Young man, what
are you doing down here?" I replied that I was looking at plants. "Plants?
What kind of plants?" I said, "Oh, all kinds; grass, weeds, flowers, trees,
mosses, ferns,—almost everything that grows is interesting to me."

"Well, young man," he queried, "you mean to say that you are not employed
by the Government on some private business?" "No," I said, "I am not employed
by any one except just myself. I love all kinds of plants, and I came down here to
these Southern States to get acquainted with as many of them as possible."

"You look like a strong-minded man," he replied, "and surely you are able to
do something better than wander over the country and look at weeds and blossoms. These are hard times, and real work is required of every man that is able.
Picking up blossoms doesn't seem to be a man's work at all in any kind of times."

To this I replied, "You are a believer in the Bible, are you not?" "Oh,
yes." "Well, you know Solomon was a strong-minded man, and he is generally believed to have been the very wisest man the world ever saw, and yet he
considered it was worth while to study plants; not only to go and pick them
up as I am doing, but to study them; and you know we are told that he
wrote a book about plants, not only of the great cedars of Lebanon, but of
little bits of things growing in the cracks of the walls.[1]

"Therefore, you see that Solomon differed very much more from you than
from me in this matter. I'll warrant you he had many a long ramble in the
mountains of Judea, and had he been a Yankee he would likely have visited

every weed in the land. And again, do you not remember that Christ told his disciples to 'consider the lilies how they grow,' and compared their beauty with Solomon in all his glory? Now, whose advice am I to take, yours or Christ's? Christ says, 'Consider the lilies.' You say, 'Don't consider them. It isn't worth while for any strong-minded man.'"

This evidently satisfied him, and he acknowledged that he had never thought of blossoms in that way before. He repeated again and again that I must be a very strong-minded man, and admitted that no doubt I was fully justified in picking up blossoms. He then told me that although the war was over, walking across the Cumberland Mountains still was far from safe on account of small bands of guerrillas who were in hiding along the roads, and earnestly entreated me to turn back and not to think of walking so far as the Gulf of Mexico until the country became quiet and orderly once more.

I replied that I had no fear, that I had but very little to lose, and that nobody was likely to think it worth while to rob me; that, anyhow, I always had good luck. In the morning he repeated the warning and entreated me to turn back, which never for a moment interfered with my resolution to pursue my glorious walk.

September 11 [1867]. Long stretch of level sandstone plateau, lightly furrowed and dimpled with shallow groove-like valleys and hills. The trees are mostly oaks, planted wide apart like those in the Wisconsin woods. A good many pine trees here and there, forty to eighty feet high, and most of the ground is covered with showy flowers. Polygalas [milkworts], solidagoes [goldenrods], and asters were especially abundant. I came to a cool clear brook every half mile or so, the banks planted with *Osmunda regalis, Osmunda cinnamomea*, and handsome sedges. The few larger streams were fringed with laurels and azaleas. Large areas beneath the trees are covered with formidable green briers and brambles, armed with hooked claws, and almost impenetrable. Houses are far apart and uninhabited, orchards and fences in ruins— sad marks of war.

About noon my road became dim and at last vanished among desolate fields. Lost and hungry, I knew my direction but could not keep it on account of the briers. My path was indeed strewn with flowers, but as thorny, also, as mortal ever trod. In trying to force a way through these cat-plants one is not simply clawed and pricked through all one's clothing, but caught and held fast. The toothed arching branches come down over and above you like cruel living arms, and the more you struggle the more desperately you are entangled, and your wounds deepened and multiplied. The South has plant fly-catchers. It also has plant man-catchers.

Note

1. The previously mentioned copy of Wood's *Botany,* used by John Muir, quotes on the title page I Kings 4:33: "He spake of trees, from the cedar of Lebanon even unto the hyssop that springeth out of the wall."

Bob Henry Baber

Bob Henry Baber's Appalachian work has focused primarily on the coalfields, where he has worked at Appalshop, the multimedia center; at Southeast Community College, Harlan County, Kentucky; and, more recently, as director of the Bonner Scholars program at Concord College, Athens, West Virginia. His poems "The Stripping of Cold Knob" and "Cold Knob Reclaimed" testify to his concern for the devastation of the coalfields.

The Stripping of Cold Knob

Earth is alive. The soil is her flesh, the rocks are her bones,
the wind is her breath, trees and grass are her hair. She lives
spread out, and we live on her. When she moves, we have
an earthquake.
                              —From an Okanogan Legend.

God's Renegade? Contemporary Neanderthal? Satan's Blood Brother?
What kind of a man were you, Maust?
How great was the audacity or ignorance
that compelled you to gut Cold Knob—
God's jewel, the beauty, third highest peak in the state?
What crossed your mind
when your blade turned the first rib up to air,
when the coal, exposed at last, lay in a heap at your feet?
And when you looked out over your legacy
to the Greenbrier Valley and Virginia
did you feel almost akin to the creator
knowing you had the brute power to wreck in one short year
what eternity had wrought?
Maust, did the coal light Cleveland for eleven minutes?
Did you turn a handsome profit on the hunchback of grief?
Did the boy from Scarsdale laugh all the way to a Florida bank
when he told the Great State of West Virginia
where it could stick its $50 an acre Reclamation Bond?
And did your heart ever know guilt or remorse, Maust—
the pang of a man who has Mother Fucked nature?
Or did you roar off to town

"The Stripping of Cold Knob" and "Cold Knob, Reclaimed" from *Appalachian Journal* 13, no. 3 (Spring 1986): 285–86. "The Stripping of Cold Knob" reprinted by permission of the author and publisher. "Cold Knob, Reclaimed" reprinted by permission of the author.

tightening your swashbuckling pants
and bragging of your exploits
all over what was still left of creation
till drunken sleep reclaimed you?

Maust
did the spirits of trees come then
to haunt your fitful dreams?
Maust
did a chorus of ancient rocks
curse you in the dead of night?
Maust
did bulldozers strip the skin from your flesh?
Maust
did men with green eyes rip black guts
from your breast and leave you to die
unattended and Canadian cold on the side of the knob
your pathetic demise frozen in the eyes of stoic deers and
black bears?

If there is justice in the world Maust   they did so

they did so

Cold Knob, Reclaimed

(Putting lipstick on a corpse)

From scalped rim the blue ridge stretch
violet mist draped towards Trout Valley
from Kennison Mountain and Bushy Ridge
designated by rustic timber company plaque—
behind our back, in shale at highwall base
the rustic timber company pine-seedlings,
hostages of stupidity,
half-dead issue of our greed,
are a quarter century old.

Muriel Miller Dressler

Born in Kanawha County, West Virginia, poet Muriel Miller Dressler has roots firmly embedded in the region's mountains. Having seen the growth of the mining industry and the toll it took on the land and the people, she attempts in her poetry to establish a link between the tradition of the past and the progress toward the future. In her two collections of poetry, *Appalachia, My Land* (1973) and *Appalachia* (1977), Dressler conveys the dignity of the people of the region through her use of distinctive imagery and mountain dialect. Pride in her land and in her heritage is a frequent theme in her verse.

Go Tell the Children

Go tell the children the mountain is trembling,
An earth-moving monster is eating its way
Through grapevines and shumate and wild laurel thickets
And even Sweet William has fallen prey.

Go tell the children their true love is dying,
The whippoorwill's song no more shall they know;
Go tell the children to bow down in sorrow;
The fullness of mountains—of mountains must go!

Go tell the children to weep for the passing
Of redbuds and sarvis—a sight to be seen!
Tell them to hang down their heads in their sorrow
As they sing, "Green gravel, the grass is so green."

The flowers of the fringe tree are blacker than midnight,
The blue fruit now lies on the crust of dead earth;
No more shall white flowers hang down like fringes;
O, Go tell the children I weep at their birth!

Go tell the children that trailing arbutus
Lies in cold ashes of campfires once red,
That pipestem and spicebush now yield to the slaughter;
O, Go tell the children the mountain is dead!

From *Appalachia My Land* (Charleston, WV: Appalachian Center, Morris Harvey College, 1977). Reprinted by permission of the author.

David Whisnant

David Whisnant's work is frequently difficult to classify, as it combines sociology, mass psychology, history, and literary and social criticism in its wide-ranging analyses of Appalachian problems and proposed solutions. Born July 16, 1938, in Asheville, North Carolina, Whisnant received degrees from Georgia Institute of Technology (B.S.) and Duke University (A.M., Ph.D.). He has a prestigious record of publications, including three books on Appalachia. Two of these, *Modernizing the Mountaineer* (1981) and *All That Is Native and Fine* (1983), are among the most controversial works written about the region.

Modernizing the Mountaineer examines how agents outside Appalachia, particularly government-sponsored commissions, have made various efforts, forcible in many cases, to bring mountain society into line with "modern" standards. Whisnant's obvious distaste for what he considers hegemony has created some discussion. But his cogent and frequently powerful arguments merit serious attention.

Cultural Values and Regional Development

> We wake and find ourselves on a stair; there are stairs below us, which we seem to have ascended; there are stairs above us, many a one, which go upward and out of sight. . . .
>
>   Dream delivers us to dream, and there is no end to illusion. Life is a train of moods, like a string of beads, and as we pass through them they prove to be many-colored lenses which paint the world their own hue, and each shows only what lies in its focus.
>   —Ralph W. Emerson, "Experience" (1844)

Emerson's "many-colored lenses" image reminds us that our views of reality are at last inescapably personal. At the outset [of *Modernizing the Mountaineer*] I told how my own set of lenses and "train of moods"—or stages of personal growth, as a modern psychologist would have it—shaped my understanding of the particular reality I set out to comprehend and describe.

But views of reality are colored by more than merely *personal* "moods." We also see the world through the *collective* lens of culture. Most of us recognize that as a general principle, of course, but the importance of the principle in this particular context I perceived only gradually.

Initially I was compelled by two apparently disconnected clusters of images.

From *Modernizing the Mountaineer: People, Power, and Planning in Appalachia* (Appalachian Consortium Press, 1981; rev. ed. Knoxville: The University of Tennessee Press, 1994). Reprinted by permission of the author and publishers.

In one cluster there were hillbilly music, dance, and material culture—string bands and gospel singers, square dancers and cloggers, houses and barns, fences and chimneys, fireplaces and split-bottomed chairs. Some of those images came immediately from my own experience: a fiddler and a banjo picker in the neighborhood, the square dance team in our county high school, several thousand acres of mountain land to wander over behind our house. Others came indirectly: visits to my grandfather's Rutherford County, North Carolina, farm at 'lassy makin' time; hillbilly music on the "Carolina Farm Hour" every day at noon; WSM's "Grand Ole Opry" on Saturday night; and—when the weather was right—WWVA from Wheeling.

In the other cluster there were wasted and polluted streams; smog heavy in the valley and washing up the mountainsides; other kids' daddies who had to work "three to 'lebm" or graveyard; busloads of workers from Sunburst and Shelton Laurel, Big Ivy and Barnardsville, rolling into the textile mill parking lot where I sold papers before daylight.

For a long while after I began to write, the clusters remained separate, the cultural cluster usually in the background. The "developmental" cluster claimed most of my attention, as I read legislative hearings, planning documents, and consultants' studies, and struggled with the vocabulary and technical concepts of planners. But connections urged themselves upon me.

Church missionaries and settlement school workers most often turned out to have seen mountain people as their experience *disposed* them to, and to have "helped" as they were led by their own cultural lights. Beneath the vast technological superstructure of TVA, I perceived a substructure of cultural values and assumptions that controlled the agency more surely than the geomorphology of the Tennessee River Valley itself. The infrastructure planners of ARA and ARC—like their missionary and New Deal predecessors—could at last be understood better in cultural than in theoretical or technical terms. Like rotors in TVA's generators, they were whirled between twin poles of culture.

One pole was their own deeply imbedded mainstream culture—a conflicted amalgam of authoritarianism and libertarianism, individualism and paternalism, elitism and populism, nostalgia and futurism, self-help and social responsibility. The other was the ancient, tattered but treasured hand-me-down fabric of untenable cultural assumptions and judgments about mountain people. The "Appalachia" they sought to develop was, to some extent, an Appalachia created in their own minds—a mythic Appalachia, as Henry Shapiro's *Appalachia on Our Mind* has recently shown, held to as a cultural talisman by the rest of America.

As a variety of organic connections between culture and regional development continued to emerge, I at length concluded that *regional development must finally be understood as cultural drama rather than technocratic enterprise.* It is an arena in which the dynamics of conflict are set at the deepest spiritual, psychic, and cultural levels. Conflicts over the technical details of development theory and practice are at most secondary; they are the shadows on the walls of Plato's cave.

Cultural values and assumptions turn out to have controlled the development process in Appalachia in an astonishing number of its aspects. Of profoundest importance is the fact that the cultural values and predispositions shared by most planners and development agency bureaucrats have set the narrowest of limits upon their imagination; constricted the boundaries of their tolerance for social, economic, and political alternatives; and marked off the little that seemed to them "reasonable" or "sensible" from the much that did not. Thus the planning and development process turned out, over and over again, to be culturally narcissistic rather than *imaginative* and progressive.

In sum, the cultural drama of development as I have come to understand it is made up of four related aspects: (1) Development strategy is controlled by the cultural "set" of the developers themselves. (2) The dominance of that "set" renders the strategy insensitive to the cultural values of the "target population" (to use the contemporary phrase). (3) That insensitivity predisposes development programs to be culturally destructive. (4) Among those who plan and control development, a feigned reverence for and understanding of the affected culture is used as a cover for the essentially autocratic agendas of the developers.

George Ella Lyon

George Ella Lyon is a writer and speaker popular in Southern Appalachia. Upon our request she provided the following biographical information:

"I was born and grew up in Harlan, Kentucky, a coal mining town in the mountains. My first occupational goal was to be a neon-sign maker, and I guess I am still trying to make words that glow. I studied creative writing with Ruth Stone at Indiana University, where I did my dissertation on Virginia Woolf. In 1972 I began sending out a manuscript of poetry, and in 1983 my chapbook, *Mountain,* won the Lamont Hall award from Andrew Mountain Press. Since then I have made my living as a freelance writer and teacher, publishing a number of children's picture books (including *Come a Tide* and *Who Came Down That Road?*) and two novels for young readers (*Borrowed Children* and *Red Rover, Red Rover*). I live with my musician-husband and two sons in Lexington, Kentucky."

Progress

I reckon it was in the early Fifties
when they finally got the electric up at Smith.
I was hired to go behind the linemen
selling stoves, washers, frigidaires.

From *Appalachian Journal* 9.4 (Summer 1982), © *Appalachian Journal*/Appalachian State University. Used with permission.

Anyway, there was this one woman
I saw as I came around a bend
with her washtub set up by a poplar
singing like a bird at first light.

She seemed awful glad to see me—
took my hand in her soapy hand—
but it wasn't any washer that she wanted.
No sir, she wanted a hi-fi.

Paid cash, a hundred and some dollars,
set the cabinet on the dirt floor.
Full blast, Nashville filled the holler
and saved her all the drudgery of song.

Durwood Dunn

Historian Durwood Dunn is chairman of the Department of History and Political Science at Tennessee Wesleyan College, Athens, Tennessee. Born in 1943, Dunn received his education at the University of Tennessee at Knoxville (B.A., M.A., Ph.D.). He taught at Hiwassee College and the University of Tennessee before settling at Tennessee Wesleyan. His interest in Appalachian and Tennessee history and in American legal history has spawned several compelling books. Among these is *Cades Cove: The Life and Death of a Southern Appalachian Community, 1818–1937* (1988), winner of the Thomas Wolfe Memorial Literary Award. The article below is taken from this work. His most recent publication, *These Are Our Lives*, appeared in 1992. His book reviews and articles have appeared in journals such as the *American Historical Review,* the *Journal of American Folklore,* and the *Appalachian Journal.*

Death by Eminent Domain

Today the Great Smoky Mountains National Park is the most popular park in the nation, attracting 9.3 million visitors in 1985. Cades Cove is one of the greatest attractions of this park, preserving there, as the National Park Service maintains, an authentic living museum of native Southern Appalachian culture in the extant cabins and remaining structures. What is perhaps most intriguing to the cove's visitors, however, are the traces of forgotten homesteads, betrayed

From *Cades Cove: The Life and Death of a Southern Appalachian Community, 1818–1937,* © 1988 by The University of Tennessee Press. Reprinted by permission of the publisher.

each spring by jonquils, roses, and hyacinths appearing in profusion unexpectedly in the middle of open meadows.

By 1935 it was apparent to the Park Service that its policy of allowing the
cove to return to its wilderness state was a serious mistake. Cades Cove's
great beauty and charm had always been the contrast of its carefully cultivated fields and farms with the surrounding high mountains. A wilderness
cove, indistinguishable from the forests of its bordering wilderness, presented little of interest or scenic beauty to the tourist.

A solution to the problem of what to do with Cades Cove, now that it was
depopulated, appeared in a 1935 letter from Waldo G. Leland, permanent
secretary of the American Council of Learned Societies, to Arno B. Cammerer,
director of the National Park Service. Leland strongly urged that some effort be
made to both record and preserve the extant native culture and lifestyle of
the Great Smokies before the advent of millions of tourists erased this last
remaining vestige of Southern Appalachia.

Two lengthy studies for the National Park Service by Charles S. Grossman
and Hans Huth followed which carefully defined this culture and the best
means of preserving it. Here was yet another incident characteristic of a pattern of America's approach to Southern Appalachia so lucidly examined in
Henry D. Shapiro's *Appalachia on Our Mind.* Having fairly rid the cove of its
bothersome native inhabitants, the National Park Service sought national
authorities to define and reproduce their native culture so recently expired.

The results of these studies would have been completely satisfying to both
Mary Noailles Murfree and Horace Kephart because most of their enduring
stereotypes were clearly reflected in the final product. All modern structures,
particularly numerous homes of frame construction, were obliterated. The
single guiding principle was that anything which might remotely suggest
progress or advancement beyond the most primitive stages should be destroyed.
A sort of pioneer primitivism alone survived in the cove structures left standing.

It was as though, having destroyed the community of Cades Cove by eminent domain, the community's corpse was now to be mutilated beyond recognition. If the history of the cove had any meaning, it was simply that the
people followed regional and national patterns of development. Cove residents
witnessed many periods of progressive development in both the nineteenth
and twentieth centuries. They were neither the picturesque, superhuman, and
romanticized figures of Mary Noailles Murfree nor the wretched backward creatures living in depravity and degradation as represented by Horace Kephart.
Rather, they were in the final analysis representative of the broad mainstream of
nineteenth- and twentieth-century American culture and society from whence
they came: ordinary, decent citizens who often reacted collectively—and within
their limitations, courageously and responsibly—to the enormous economic
fluctuation, social change, and political disruption surrounding their lives in the
last two centuries within the American commonwealth.

In the peaceful cemetery of the old Primitive Baptist church lie the first
and last John Oliver—the founding settler and his great-grandson—some
sixty feet apart. Within these four generations of Olivers the community of

Cades Cove was born, flourished for a season, and died. Nothing can rob them now of their beloved cove or cherished community. To these sleeping patriarchs, the whole cove has become itself a larger graveyard for the community, since only their ghosts remember in minute detail the place names and lore of its streams and meadows, forgotten orchards and abandoned homesteads. With the passage of time, the collective consciousness of their community has dimmed to extinction, but among their descendants its afterglow still illumines Cades Cove.

Michael Joslin

Michael Joslin received his Ph.D. in English literature from the University of South Carolina. He presently teaches writing, literature, and photography at Lees-McRae College in Banner Elk, North Carolina. Since 1985 he has written feature articles for the *Johnson City Press* and illustrated them with his photographs. He also has had many photography exhibitions throughout the Southern Appalachian area. While living on a farm in the community of Buladean, North Carolina, he and Ruth Joslin published two books of articles and photographs of mountain people, places, and ways, all in an effort to remind us of a vanishing culture and the consequences of the loss, lest progress obscure entirely the natural roots and cultural heritage of the Southern Appalachians.

The Village Blacksmith

Under a spreading chestnut-tree
    The village smithy stands;
The smith, a mighty man is he,
    With large and sinewy hands;
And the muscles of his brawny arms
    Are strong as iron bands.

                                —Henry Wadsworth Longfellow

Much has changed since Longfellow wrote his enduring poem almost 150 years ago. The forge is no longer a center of town life, and large chestnut trees have disappeared, the victims of blight.

However, still today "large and sinewy hands" can be found to forge a horseshoe, and "brawny arms" to nail it to the horse's hoof.

Cut from the same cloth as Longfellow's exemplary hero is Vernon Buchanan, who travels winding mountain roads seeing that today's horses are shod as carefully as yesterday's.

From *Mountain People, Places and Ways,* Overmountain Press, 1991. Reprinted by permission of the author.

"Most people call me a horse-shoer. The word 'farrier' is not used much up here, but it would be the proper term I suppose," says Buchanan, who has practiced his trade, art, skill—"It's probably all three"—for more than twenty-five years.

"I used to travel from Beckley, West Virginia, to Knoxville, Tennessee, to Hickory, North Carolina, shoeing horses. Today I stick pretty much to Mitchell, Yancey, Avery, McDowell, and Madison counties in North Carolina," Buchanan says.

Because of the size of his territory, Buchanan drives his pickup truck from farm to farm, spending long, hot days with the horses and horsemen who rely on his expertise.

"I've got more than I can do. I'm not complaining, but sometimes I'm hesitant to answer the phone," he says.

While the smaller horseshoes can be bought ready-made for cold shoeing, the larger shoes must be forged by hand, hot-shoeing.

"You can put them to whatever hardness you want while you're forging. You can temper them to be soft or harder, whatever you want. It depends on how it'll be used," Buchanan says.

A picture of this modern blacksmith could well be used to illustrate Longfellow's poem. In his split apron, wielding tools that haven't changed in hundreds of years, and grasping the horse's hoof in his strong hands, Buchanan works with sweat glistening on his brow and without modern technology.

The basis of his work is the age-old relationship of man and horse.

"You've just got to get along with them. A horse can hurt you, not out of meanness but just because they're so big and so strong," Buchanan says.

"Patience has a lot to do with it. You've got to take the time that it takes for the horse, and each is different.

"Also, you can't be afraid of the horse. I'm not afraid of them, but I've got respect for horses," he says.

Gaining expertise in his work has been a lifelong process for Buchanan.

"I had horses when I was a kid. They had to have shoes, so I learned to do my own, and kinda branched out from there, got bigger and bigger.

"I spend a lot of time up in the Amish part of Ohio. I make two or three trips a year," he says. "You'll see a fellow out in a field. He'll have his hitch of six or eight horses, and his wife will have her hitch. The women can work them just as well as the men.

"The Amish have a lot bigger horses; the bigger they are, the better they like them," Buchanan explains. "Those long strides cover the field that much faster. In these mountains, a smaller horse will get over the hills a lot better than a big one, so we have smaller horses here.

"On Amish farms you hardly ever see a shoe on their work horses, but in this part there's so many rocks, and the ground's so rough, it breaks their feet up if they don't have shoes," he says. "Also, you get better traction with shoes."

Horses are plentiful in the mountain counties, where many farmers still use horse power to work their land. Getting horses shod correctly is important to these men who tend steep plots.

"There's a lot of people that can put a shoe on, but having the hoof trimmed just right and having the shoe fit just right are important," Buchanan says. "If it's not right, the shoe will come off.

"I'd shoe your horse just like I do mine, and I want mine to be shod the very best," he says.

With about twenty-five horses and mules of his own, Buchanan is never far from the creatures that have formed the framework for his life since he was a boy.

His knowledge of and rapport with the beasts is evident from the time he lays a gentling hand on one until he rasps smooth the hoof around the last shoe.

Each hoof is carefully cleaned out, nipped down, and shaved smooth and level before the shoe is fit. Each shoe is carefully shaped, flattened, and placed before a nail is touched. Each nail is set with extra care before being nailed in place.

"It's how far inside the hoof you get that's important," Buchanan says. "Too far, they'll definitely go lame, and you can set up tetanus. Usually as soon as it sets the hoof down, you can tell if it's bothering the horse."

When the horse is shod, Buchanan carefully cleans and wraps his files, then stows his equipment in the wooden cradle that travels with him.

While his tools are simple, his skills are not. Whether he's handling the large beasts in a way that soothes rather than annoys, snatching a horsefly from a quivering flank before the insect bites, or clinching the nails tight, the work is done well.

Longfellow's stalwart example of 150 years ago would be proud of his southern descendant, Vernon Buchanan, whose ways reflect the same dedication and care that made the village blacksmith a byword for reliability and industry.

Bernard Stallard

See volume 1, chapter 1, for biography.

Transition

Old ways of life are going from our hills,
It saddens most of us to see them go,
But then, a newer destiny fulfills
A promise, brighter than the life we know.
The looms and bull-tongued plows retire in death;
The sounds of zithers and of dulcimers
Fade with the accents of Elizabeth.
We watch and listen while the change occurs.
It makes us sad to see the old ways out,
But then there also goes a poverty
And ignorance we do so well to rout.

From *Appalachian Summer* (1975). Privately printed. Reprinted by permission of Frances Stallard.

We keep the better art, it seems to me.
These ancient hills rise high, forever strong,
To foster finer life and sweeter song.

Ricky Cox

Born in 1958, Ricky Cox was raised and now lives in Floyd County, Virginia. He earned an associate in applied science degree in machine technology at New River Community College, Dublin, Virginia, and worked for ten years as a machinist and tool-and-die maker before joining the English Department at Radford University, Radford, Virginia, as an instructor in 1990. Cox received a B.A. degree in history and an M.A. in English, both from Radford, and has taught freshman composition courses, American literature, and Appalachian folklore at Radford. He collects and sometimes restores antique tools and machinery. The critic Clive James has remarked ("The Voice of America," *New Yorker*, June 14, 1993) that for Mark Twain "there was no separation between machinery and poetry." Ricky Cox seems to share this opinion, even after the machinery has become junk.

Junk as Poetry

Before a symbol may appeal to the broadest possible audience, the limitations of time and space must be cast off. Otherwise, an object can have symbolic meaning only to the few who chance to observe a particular event at a particular place and time. The thing which most firmly binds a machine to a specific place and time is the function it was originally intended to perform. It is required, then, that a distance be somehow achieved between the machine and its original function. One way to do this is to select as symbols machinery which no longer has a function to perform, whether it has succumbed to, or outlived, the purpose for which it was intended. The common name for these metallic metaphors is junk.

Once the distracting clutter of regular practical function has been raked away by time or accident, machines are free to reveal the countless secrets entrusted to them by our next door neighbors and by nameless, faceless people now buried in Chicago or Des Moines or Detroit. Embedded in the caked grease and faded paint are bits and pieces of people's lives, for machines, like few other objects in American life, are repositories of dreams.

The details are mostly gone, erased by time and distance, but the outline of a grand story remains. There was once a man, or several men, who wanted to build a machine to do more and better, a machine to make farm work easier or trans-

From "Used Parts and the Poetic Impulse: Machines as Alternative Means of Expression," *Virginia English Bulletin* 38.2 (1988). Reprinted by permission of the author and *Virginia English Bulletin*.

portation more accessible to the common people. Perhaps he wanted to get rich, too, but that is beside the point. After many setbacks and disappointments, the dream becomes reality, and if the first one is the only one, or the first of ten million, it and each successor will carry with them a little of the mind and spirit that gave them substance. In *The American Scholar,* Emerson wrote of good books: "They impress us with the conviction that one nature wrote and the same reads." May it not be the same with a truck, behind whose proud lines and sturdy frame we perceive a mind that moves as our own?

Most of these pioneers set their names to their work, so that the hills are now dotted with monuments to J. I. Case, John Deere, and Henry Ford. Yet the great majority of the hands that made reality of grand visions belonged to men now nameless, even then faceless, and the dream is theirs also. A factory is built, and men come to work to find or finance their own dreams. At a county seat freight depot hundreds of miles away, another dreamer waits, able at last to buy a piece of equipment he thinks will help him finally get ahead. Their individual stories are lost, but some hint of them clings to objects once so much a part of their lives. We might search and question and fill in many of the gaps, but with no more than stands in front of us, we know that all these countless people lived and hoped and worked for something better. Here is the proof, a rusted hunk of dreams.

The dreams, perhaps, are visible only to another dreamer, but the long days spent chasing them are plainly recorded. There are dents and welded places that tell of bad luck and sledgehammer persuasion. Cracked water jackets and radiators remember some cold winter night and makeshift repairs bespeak a flat broke native genius.

For those who were familiar with a particular machine during its working life, it may be that the most popular function of junk as symbol, is junk as journal. Among the many used parts found in discarded machinery is a long-life battery which can jump start a hundred memories in an instant. In a culture described as oral, it seems only natural to make use of unconventional recording devices, things that bring to mind good friends and good times, triumphs and tragedies, and a multitude of other associations attached to things once a regular part of our immediate environment.

As symbols, machines lack the universality and clarity of words, yet they enjoy an advantage in that they appeal directly to the physical senses. The visual impact is obvious, as is the tactile, and usually a variety of identifiable aromas may be stirred up by removing appropriate parts or covers. You may learn, even, how old cars taste if you lie under one long enough. The single missing stimulus is sound, and it may be the one hardest to do without. Even though they may be eloquently mute, machines denied their voices are estranged from their primitive native tongue. I believe that the restorer of machines is keenly, if not consciously, aware of this silence, and that as a poet at heart he sounds his own voice by resurrecting one that would otherwise be stilled forever. Able to speak again, the machine tells anew the dreams once attached to it and adds a new verse to its song, that of the latest dreamer who would hear it sing once more. And for as long as it is able to speak, the reborn machine will tell their many names over and over, though it be in a strange tongue all men have hearkened to but none can fully understand.

It has been my intention here to present an aesthetic, as opposed to cultural, perspective on discarded machines, but I feel compelled to make an observation about the Appalachian affinity for broken, obsolete, or worn out things. Certainly this may be construed as frugality, but I believe that it represents also a wholeness in perspective that may be generally lacking in this country. To say that junk is ugly because it is not pretty indicates a difference of opinion, but to say that it is not pretty because it is old indicates a basic difference in philosophy. A culture which hides from itself the concept of growing old and can see no intrinsic value in inanimate things which are no longer productive has blinded itself to the cyclical nature of all things, manmade or otherwise. When we create a facade of perpetual newness by banishing old machines from the landscape are we not exercising the same rationale that banishes our old people to nursing homes? They cannot work; let us put them aside.

One day last fall, a friend of mine, James Bowman, was telling of having just seen the film *Deliverance* for the first time. Early in the film, in a scene set in a junkyard, one of the characters says something like, "I always wondered where everything ended up." It occurred to Mr. Bowman that, among all the coming and going and hustle and bustle of modern life, it is good to know, now and then, where something ends up. I think so too, and wonder if a poet might like that idea. If you see one today, tell him about it.

Work Cited

Emerson, Ralph Waldo. "The American Scholar." *The Portable Emerson*. New ed. Ed. Carl
    Bode. New York: Penguin, 1981.

Marilou Awiakta

See volume 1, chapter 3, for biography.

When Earth Becomes an "It"

When the people call Earth "Mother,"
they take with love
and with love give back
so that all may live.

This keynote poem for an address of the same title for the Governors' Interstate Indian Council,
    Nashville, Tennessee, August 1988, was reprinted in *Selu: Seeking the Corn-Mother's
    Wisdom* (Golden, CO: Fulcrum Press, 1993). Used by permission of the author and
    publisher.

When the people call Earth "it,"
they use her
consume her strength.
Then the people die.

Already the sun is hot
out of season.
Our mother's breast
is going dry.
She is taking all green
into her heart
and will not turn back
until we call her
by her name.

Charlotte Ross

Folklorist Charlotte Ross specializes in the history of the Appalachian region which has been her home since birth. She received her Ph.D. in folklore from the University of Pennsylvania and is now a professor in the communications department of Appalachian State University, Boone, North Carolina. A storyteller with a collection of 3,000 stories from the Appalachian region, she has completed a six-tape series of 147 stories which cover Appalachian history from the time immigrants arrived from Ireland through the 1980s. In 1985 she published a play, *From My Grandmother's Grandmother Unto Me,* which chronicles six generations of her family in Appalachia. The film adaptation was produced in 1988 by the Public Broadcasting System and starred Ross's daughter. In addition to her teaching, Ross also works with schoolchildren and conducts workshops for teachers on how to present Appalachia and its history.

Industrialization and the Attrition of Mountain Characteristics: A Fictional Study

The mountaineer who stood on his heights and watched the industrial revolution creep nigh was no stranger to the American reading public. He had been duly noted by travelers as early as 1784 (Smyth 79–84), christened "mountaineer" by 1824 (Harris 5), and thrust into prominence by Mary Noailles Murfree and John Fox, Jr., by the end of the nineteenth century.

From *Appalachian Literature: Critical Essays,* ed. Ruel E. Foster, MHC Publications, 1976.
Reprinted by permission of the author and publisher.

A spate of literary attention in the years that spanned the century's turning established him in the public mind as a completed stereotype. The depths of his character had been successfully mined, and the results distilled into generalities. The reading public knew the mountaineer as a tall, rangy Anglo-Saxon who was by blood and inclination an undiluted pioneer (Buck 50) with an eighteenth-century mind and an ever-ready rifle. Various authors had characterized him as proud, fiercely independent (Kephart 307), hospitable (Kephart 197), superstitious (Bradley 436–45), quick-tempered, vengeful (Ruth Lewis 21), hard-drinking (Mutzenberg 116), suspicious of strangers (Ruth Lewis 16), loyal to his clan (Fox 41), and patriotic, though abysmally ignorant of any government beyond the local level (Lewis 16).

He was, undoubtedly, all these things and more, but the dime novels of the 1890s, the moralistic fiction of the 1900s, and the many years of local color sketches, popular thrillers, and boisterous frontier humor had severely damaged his image. As a fictional stereotype, he fell just short of the ridiculous.

The development of the mountaineer as a subject for serious literary effort was further hampered by the public response to his environment. The stereotype occupied a mysterious, titillative region that attained near-fantasy status in the minds of many Americans. The Southern Highland region was eastern America's last unexplored territory, and it held all the fascination of the strange and far away. Horace Kephart had commented that, although he could find much information about Timbuktu in the public libraries of New York City, "about this housetop of eastern America they were strangely silent" (13). John C. Campbell, ending an arduous study of mountain life, described the region as "a land of promise, a land of romance, and a land about which, perhaps, more things are known that are not true than any part of our country" (xxi). The evocative incantation with which Stephen Vincent Benet described the mountains in the opening lines of the Luke Breckinridge section of *John Brown's Body* further established the southern highlands as an enchanted land (71).

Thus, the mountaineer had become a stock figure on a set stage; his world seemed timeless, changeless. He had come to the forefront of public attention because he and his homeland were anachronous, and there were very few who foresaw that they might not always remain so.

But, in that time between the wars, the mountaineer had already begun his inevitable journey into modern civilization. Industry, with its attendant materialism, was luring him into the valley mill towns or besieging him in the hills in the form of sawmills, mines, or shiny, intrusive rails. It was inevitable that he should succumb to these new lures, for poverty, caused by the disappearance of game and the overpopulation of the ridges, had begun to erode his Scotch-Irish thriftiness and his sense of self-sufficiency (Williams 86–97). As the barter system, which had been the hallmark of his agrarian society, was supplanted by hard cash, the impetus to bestir himself, to leave the fields and find a place in industry, grew stronger.

Poised as he was between the old world and the new, the mountaineer presented the ultimate literary opportunity: He was a figure of tragic proportions about to embark upon a ruinous but inevitable course. The scene was set for an American epic, but the old stereotype was still in vogue, and the moment passed.

It was to be many years before the mountaineer fully realized that the better attributes of his heritage had set him on a collision course with his new environment and hastened his disappearance as an identifiable southern type. His gradual realization of this fact is mirrored in the slowly accelerating development of the literary themes of exploitation and the attrition of native virtues due to industrialization. Between the early optimism of John Fox, Jr., who saw the advent of the coal industry as a boon to his area of Kentucky, and the cry of exploitation raised by Mary Lee Settle against that same industry in *Fight Night on a Sweet Saturday* lie fifty years of growing sensitivity to the mountaineer as a tragic figure "determined by heredity and tradition and doomed by the circumstances of his life to struggle hopelessly but heroically against the forces that ultimately destroyed him" (Williams 887).

The most compelling reason for the mountaineer's entry into industry was sheer economic necessity. Novelists who dealt successfully with this theme include Grace Lumpkin, James Still, and Hubert Skidmore.

In *To Make My Bread,* Lumpkin's Kirkland-McClures faced starvation one stormy winter. Snow had packed the ridges; credit had been denied at the country store; there was no shot for the guns, and the boys grew too weak to catch snowbound game by hand (28). Emma McClure had watched her children bend double from hunger pangs and known what it was almost to hate them, "because she could do nothing to help them in their misery" (31).

The marks of that winter were still strong upon the family when Small Hardy, the peddler, came with news of a cloth mill in Leesville where "poor folks are going to get rich" (39). The scenes in which the peddler speaks to the family about the mill towns where "the rivers flow with milk and honey and money grows on trees" (39), are executed in light and dark imagery reminiscent of Hawthorne.

The man is dark, hunchbacked, and small to match his name. Emanations of evil flow from him to John, Emma's youngest son, and he offers to buy John's puppy for its skin. Granpap Kirkland also resists the stranger's spell and casts small dark doubts over the peddler's glowing words. Granpap's instinctive aversion to living in a house that is not his, on land he could not hope to own, closes the discussion abruptly. But, when the stranger is gone, his words linger on.

Shortly thereafter, Granpap Kirkland is jailed for distilling. Returning to find the land sold and the sawmills approaching, Granpap senses the eventual dissolution of the family. He rebukes Emma, saying, "What if ye are poor, Emma, if ye have your own land?" (127).

Granpap's fears prove prophetic; when the lumber company begins to charge high rent on the cabin, the family moves to Leesville and the mills. Economically, there seemed to be no alternative.

Brack Baldridge's family in *River of Earth* is forced into the coal mines of Knott County, Kentucky, by the same sort of unrelenting economic necessity. Forced to move from a closed mining camp back to the farm, the Baldridges are drifting into starvation because Brack insists they must support his worthless kin. Ma, whose agrarian instincts tell her that the family's hope is in the land, burns down the house and moves her family into a tiny smokehouse where there is no room for Brack's kin. Then, just as her carefully nurtured garden seems promising, Brack gives away the food. The conflict between the agrarian Alpha, and Brack, who feels he cannot make a living farming, is heightened by poverty. Eventually Alpha acquiesces, and the family drifts back into the mining camps. Like the McClures, the Baldridges seem to have no viable economic alternative.

In Hubert Skidmore's *I Will Lift Up Mine Eyes,* the Cutlips are also ushered into industry by economic necessity. Repeated crop failures force this ordinary self-sufficient family, possessed of sturdy pioneer virtues, into the sawmill camp at Turkey Trot. Here, their resemblance to the Kirkland-McClures and the Baldridges ends.

The Cutlips still own land in the hills, and both parents are skillful farmers who have a great love for the land. Although their initial economic crisis was real and urgent, it was also temporary. There comes the inevitable day when they must decide when to go home. Maw has retained her agrarian heritage, and she is frightened by her diminishing control over her family and wants to get her children away from bad influences. But her husband, Nat, procrastinates and urges her to remain in the camps. Hoping that her children can obtain an education, she agrees to compromise.

Thus, the Cutlips represent a second pattern in the literary history of the mountaineer's involvement with industry: the family who consciously chose the mills or camps, hoping to educate the children, provide a few extras, or save money to buy land.

A third factor luring the mountaineer into the industrial world was a sort of masculine mystique. The mountaineer's attitude toward tough, dangerous outdoor jobs was rather like that of a modern youngster toward firemen, railroad engineers, or astronauts.

It was this fascination which held Nat Cutlip to his dangerous job as driver long after he had earned the money to return home and impelled Wilma Dykeman's character Tom Thurston in *The Far Family* to risk his financial security and his household calm by erecting a sawmill in his wife's beloved woods. Brack Baldridge in *River of Earth* and Burn and Gib McQueen in *The Far Family* had much the same feeling about mining, and W. E. Blackhurst's three novels are a celebration of the riotous, brawling life of the lumber camps.

Janice Holt Giles's character Hod Pierce, and Harriette Arnow's Clovis Nevels find themselves emotionally tied to the army and to war work in Detroit's automobile industry, respectively, by the satisfaction they derive from being successful, contributing parts of a larger whole. Thus, they become the fictional representatives of several generations of mountain youths who have found homes in the army or migrated between "Deetroit" and the hills of home.

In *Dunbar's Cove* we find compelling expression of that mysterious attraction of power and danger which lured mountain men into certain types of industry. Knox Dunbar tries to explain the appeal of the construction industry to his father, as he resists the older man's inducements to come home and fight the TVA. Looking from the observation tower across the vast dam site, he says, "That's mine, Papa. My work. I'm a dam-builder. I do my part on a bulldozer but all of it is mine, just like I laid every pour of concrete, hammered every piece of sheet steel into the ground to build the coffer-dams. I've made it my work, just like the cove is yours. That's why I can't go back. . . . It's my life, Papa" (Deal 314).

In *The Far Family,* Clay Thurston directs a number of similar comments toward his nephew, Senator Phil Cortland, as he tries to convince him of the desirability of physical involvement with one's work. "A man's got to work," he says. "What the hell good is a man if he's not doing something, building something, taking his part?" (Dykeman 305).

A fourth pattern through which the characters come into contact with industrialization is depicted in the physical invasion of industry into the isolated countryside. Novels in this category include DuBose Heyward's *Angel,* which features the powerful, relentless thrust of a modern highway through sparsely settled ridge country; and *To Make My Bread* and *Trees of Heaven,* which picture the locust-like devastation caused by invading sawmills. H. H. Kroll's *Darker Grows the Valley,* Borden Deal's *Dunbar's Cove,* and Ben Haas's *The Last Valley* also feature the intrusion of modern industrial society into remote coves, but in these novels the isolated older culture is legislated away. Eminent domain is the ultimate enemy; against it Matthew Dunbar's moral indignation makes only puny inroads (see Deal, chs. 3–11), and Kroll's marvelous Granny Hope Clinch, who was born a Republican and says she is destined to be "drowned one by WPA Roosevelt" (Kroll 376), can defeat it only by willing her own death.

Whatever the method of its introduction, contact between the mountaineer and industrial society was disastrous for the mountaineer. A few years of exposure to the new culture served to reduce him to the social stature of a poor white. He learned that pioneer virtues were a liability in his new environment, yet, without them, he lacked center and was quickly subjected to erosion in his family and personal life. Thus, for the first time, the mountain man deserved that derogatory epithet from the sandy ridges of Alabama; he had become a "hill-billy" (Williams 1359).

In *John Brown's Body,* Stephen Vincent Benét presented a picture of the mountaineer in a discordant clash with a rapidly changing world:

> They are our last frontier.
> They shot the railway-train when it first came,
> And when the Fords first came, they shot the Fords.

It could not save them. They are dying now
Or being educated, which is the same.
One need not weep romantic tears for them,
But when the last moonshiner buys his radio,
And the last, lost, wild-rabbit of a girl
Is civilized with a mail-order dress,
Something will pass that was American
And all the movies will not bring it back. (Benét 72)

The average mountaineer would have thought the passage offensive, inaccurate, and overly romanticized; yet, it was strangely prophetic. It took the 1927 stereotype of the mountaineer and, through gross overstatement, achieved the ridiculous. Thus, it foreshadowed the literary low we have reached with *The Beverly Hillbillies, The Real McCoys,* and *Hee-Haw* (Lee 1970).

It is significant that Benét, who gives an otherwise favorable characterization of Luke Breckinridge and his mountain counterparts, chose to employ both slapstick comedy and maudlin sentiment only when he tried to juxtapose the mountaineer and industrialization.

The theme of attrition of mountain culture due to industrialization presents the Appalachian author with his most difficult task. It is easier to have a character shoot at a railway train or ask a passing motorist what he grows to feed the thing than to show the impact of these changes upon his insular society.

Among those authors who have dealt successfully with the theme of attrition are Lucy Furman, Sherwood Anderson, the Chapmans, Hubert Skidmore, James Still, Jesse Stuart, DuBose Heyward, Harriette Arnow, Mary Lee Settle, Grace Lumpkin, Janice Holt Giles, Henry Harrison Kroll, Olive Dargan, Borden Deal, Ben Haas, and Wilma Dykeman.

Of all the industries treated, the textile industry appears to have had the most dehumanizing effect upon the mountaineer. In *To Make My Bread,* Grace Lumpkin suggests that the mountaineer's character and background make peaceful integration into the highly structured life of a mill village almost an impossibility.

Independence, pride, guilelessness, and native courtesy prove hazardous in Leesville. Basil is quickly corrupted by his lust for money and social position, Granpap is devastated by the age restrictions placed on mill employment, and Emma is discouraged by the production rate pay scale.

Since the family is not eligible for a mill house and must move in with relatives, Granpap returns home and resumes blockading. Emma, however, must stay and face the myriad daily humiliations and marginal existence of a mill worker. John and Bonnie are placed in classes with younger children and quickly become targets for the school bullies. Only John's undeserved reputation as a fighter, born of pain and desperation, makes life tolerable. His degradation is completed when Emma sends a note to school apologizing for his fighting.

Ill health and the Depression finally solidify the family's roles. John loses his job because his innate sense of justice leads him to question existing social conditions. Emma dies of pellagra, her bones almost literally ground to make their bread, and Bonnie, with her sweet voice, becomes a focus for the new labor movement. John's slow drift toward Communism is accelerated by Bonnie's death as a martyr in the clash between the workers and the strikebreakers.

Thus the dissolution is complete. Each person from the southern mountains is hampered by his inability to accept a position at the bottom of the heap. Unable to forego their independence, the Kirkland-McClures are destined for trouble.

Olive Tilford Dargan and Sherwood Anderson have created heroines outside the usual mode of mountain fiction. Neither Ishmalee Waycaster nor Kit Brandon is the typical heroine. Both flee from the land into the factory towns for reasons as much idealized as practical. Dargan's unfinished characters fade into the heavy background of social propaganda. Anderson's Kit Brandon, perhaps his most appealing heroine, initially enjoys feeling "little and lost" in the singing roar of the mill. It is Agnes, her revolutionary friend, who awakens Kit to the exploitation of the mountain family. "Look. We are like sheep numbered."

DuBose Heyward's *Angel* also contains a sketch of a mountain family's disintegration in a mill town. As the Kents leave Beartown for the valley, they are filled with good will and high hopes for the children's education. Myra promises to write and in a wild rush of generosity halts the caravan to return to the knob and give Angel the family's one valuable possession, a cow (198).

A few years later the Kents visit Beartown in a dilapidated Ford. As they preen in their cheap finery, Myra chatters about their good times and high living. All of the children have been taken out of school and put to work because "Times are so good now an' money's comin' so fast, we're takin' life while we kin" (200). The family goes to movies or dances every night because the parents want to have their fling before they begin saving, and the once frugal Myra considers soiled clothing disposable and feeds her family only canned food because she can't be bothered with a garden patch. Discussing their combined family income of three hundred and fifty dollars a month, Myra scornfully recalls that it once took her fifteen years to save three hundred dollars. Angel's attention is caught by Annie's persistent cough. "They got her in the steam room now," Myra explains, "an hit givens 'em a ticklin' in the chest" (200).

Slowly Angel realized that this visit is not purely social. Just as she turns to offer Myra the cow, Angel is forestalled by Myra's embarrassed demand, "We'd better take the cow back with weuns," she says. "Hit costs so much buyin' this condensed milk in cans" (206). Later, alone in the barn, Angel decides that she no longer wants to visit the towns.

W. E. Blackhurst's novels *Of Men and a Mighty Mountain* and *Sawdust in Your Eyes* are essentially a celebration of the rollicking life of the lumber camps. Yet, interspersed among the raves are sad small commentaries about the mountains and their people. A mountain man called Cheat speaks of the devastation left by the sawmills (Blackhurst 2), and a young lady (69) and the local sheriff (73) recall the devastation left by the lumberjacks. Poverty, crime, and the attrition of native virtues are revealed by a mill man who is deeply in debt to the company store (33), by a body never found because missing men were commonplace (97), and by a man who will speak of the camps only if he can remain anonymous (106).

In *The Far Family,* Martha McQueen Thurston opposes her husband Tom when he begins sawmilling in her beloved woods. Her rationale is almost pantheistic as she begs Tom not to "take and take from the land and never give back" (Dykeman 182).

The destruction of the woods leads to Tom Thurston's death and the family's economic difficulties. It also divides the children into two camps: the materialistic and the spiritual. Some thirty years after the woods are gone, the children meet for their mother's funeral and trace the family's dissolution to the destruction of the land (347).

For the Cutlips of *I Will Lift Up Mine Eyes,* attrition begins as their loaded wagon rolls into Turkey Trot and they are met with cries of "Ridge-runners." The first humiliation is quickly followed by others. The children are set upon by local toughs, Maw is exploited by her neighbors, and John is expelled from school. As Maw's control over the family diminishes, John becomes wild and immoral and eventually drifts into the mill. Because Nat Cutlip likes his dangerous job of snaking logs, he keeps postponing their return to the farm. He urges Maw to adapt to town life and insists that she be less thrifty. After his death, Maw takes Ben and Effie and escapes to the farm.

In *River of Earth,* interludes of peace and hope alternate with periods of despair. Alpha is willing to wrest a scant living from the earth in order to give her children a secure home life. Whenever the mines close and the family returns to the land, Alpha blooms, and the house is filled with laughter and plans for the future. But her husband, Brack, who "was born to dig coal" (Still 241), moves the family whenever he hears of an opening in the mines.

Largess and mobility are as instinctive to Brack as wanting a home is to Alpha, and he inevitably wins. In the mining camps, Alpha's bright hopes fade. Her children go uneducated and are subjected to evil influences, and she serves as an unwilling hostess to Brack's cousins.

When the Blackjack mine closes, Alpha loses the ultimate battle. Rather than return to the land, Brack plans to move his family to another state where it is rumored that "mines are working." Alpha's worst fears are realized; she and her children have become like Walking John Gay, "traipsing and trafficking, looking the world over" (52).

As the novel ends, the son who wanted to be a horse doctor and swore that he would never be a miner seems fated to fulfill a stranger's prophecy. "Whate'er you're aiming to be, you'll end snagging jackrock" (227).

In *Fight Night on a Sweet Saturday,* Hannah McKarkle, granddaughter of a coal mine operator, comes home to West Virginia in response to her brother's random, drunken cry for succor. Arriving in Canona, Hannah finds that Johnny's dissolute night has ended with his death in a fracas at the local jail.

Searching for the ghosts that haunted Johnny, she traces his last movements through the tawdry alley nightlife and the empty suburban sociality of Canona and ends at the county jail facing the mountain man who says he killed Johnny for "the cut of his jib" (Settle 130).

Gripping the bars, a grief-stricken and numb Hannah asks why. She is answered by Abraham Lincoln Andrew Jackson Catlett, a "distant cousin stranger" who got himself arrested hoping his family would be eligible for public assistance without him. Out of their mutual sorrow, and in the voice one usually reserves for children, Catlett gives his cousin Hannah the answers she has evaded all her life.

When she leaves the jail, Hannah drives, not to her parents' home in an exclusive residential area, but to Jake Catlett's mountain cabin on a knob that overlooks the country club on one side, and the devastated strip-mined earth on the other. There she meets the elder Catlett who lost his land to the strip miners and eventually lost his mining job to automation. As she delivers Jake's messages to his family, Hannah is struck by her resemblance to the oldest daughter, Essie. She realizes then that "the only thing that made us strangers was not a deep difference in blood, but an accident, long past, of the inheritance of hill land and the inheritance of bottom land" (132).

Jake also serves as an introduction to another social phenomenon which dealt harshly with mountain culture: migration. The Catletts sold their hill farm above Beulah to the advancing coal mines and became miners, secure in the belief that their strength and industry could always provide for the family. When they lost their jobs, they found themselves stranded in a hostile environment. Although they were still in the West Virginia hills, the area was rapidly becoming suburban, and the posh new country club below them was symbolic of a world to which they could not adjust.

The Tussies of Jesse Stuart's *Trees of Heaven* also illustrate that the cultural shock of migration should be measured *not* in miles, but in terms of alienation. When Anse Buchman ejects the Tussies from the land they love but do not own, the family moves to a town a few miles away. There Boliver changes from a happy loafer into a drunken idler, the women must take in laundry, and the two sons drift away from the family unit. Thus, the Tussies' only positive values, their carefree attitudes and their family solidarity, are threatened by the move.

Although almost every novel about industry also dealt with migration, two modern novelists best portray the psychological, moral, and cultural displacement of the migrant.

In *The Dollmaker,* Harriette Arnow contrasts the stable, codebound lifestyle of the mountains with the fast-paced but unstructured life of Detroit's wartime economy. Rawboned Gertie Nevels, her land-loving son Reuben, and her imaginative, elfin daughter Cassie are unable to cope with contemporary civilization because they are unwilling to adjust, as Gertie says "leastways not too good" (105).

Subjected to scorn and derision in the city, all the Nevels yearn for the respect and sense of belonging they knew in the mountains. Without these, Clovis loses his self-respect, Gertie prostitutes her talent and loses all hope of saving enough for a farm, and the remaining children "adjust" to an inferior existence. Only Cassie, who dies, and Reuben, who runs away, escape that corrosive loss of integrity common to the mountaineer in the industrial North.

In Wilma Dykeman's *The Far Family,* the descendants of the tall woman, Lydia McQueen, rally for a family crisis and remain for a funeral. Ivy Thurston Cortland, the family's touchstone, is torn between the two remaining poles of her life, her brother and her son.

Clay Thurston and Phil Cortland represent two different ways by which the mountaineer can make a place for himself in a modern industrial society. Phil Cortland is a United States senator who, despite his youth and his years outside the region, is fairly successful in bridging the gap between the mountains and the modern world.

Clay Thurston, a builder and construction worker, has been displaced by a machine. Stunned by the loss of his job and the breakup of his marriage, he returns home hoping to find the life he remembers from childhood: "being in the woods, a man's world, clean and simple" (Dykeman 31).

Missing the masculine satisfaction of his work, Clay searches desperately for the "great hunter" status he enjoyed as a young man. Since his boyhood friends have left the area, Clay finds hunting companions among the dissolute dregs of local society. After a drinking companion's death, Clay awaits trial. He has learned the bitterest lesson awaiting the modern migrant mountaineer: you can't go home again.

His friends are gone; his family unit is no longer capable of the day-to-day closeness of childhood; the woods are despoiled; and he is an outsider in the local village. Desperately, he demands of Ivy, "And what happened, Ivy? The greenness is gone. The woods aren't there, the water's ugly. What happened to it all?" (347). Toward the end of the novel, Clay's dissolution becomes complete, and he drives off a cliff in a last wild surge of power.

Whatever praises one might sing to our new industrial society must be tempered with the realization that we have lost and are yet losing our pioneers before the onward march of progress. And, as the poet says, "Something will pass that was American and all the movies will not bring it back" (Benét 72).

Works Cited

Anderson, Sherwood. *Kit Brandon.* New York: Scribner's, 1936.

Arnow, Harriette. *The Dollmaker.* New York: Macmillan, 1954.

Benét, Stephen Vincent. *John Brown's Body.* New York: Farrar and Rinehart, 1928.

Blackhurst, W. E. *Of Men and a Mighty Mountain.* Parsons, WV: McClain Printing, 1965.

———. *Riders of the Flood.* Parsons, WV: McClain Printing, 1954.

———. *Sawdust In Your Eyes.* Parsons, WV: McClain Printing, 1963.

Bradley, W. A. "In Shakespeare's America," *Harper's Magazine* 121 (Aug. 1915). 435–45.

Buck, Charles Neville. *Call of the Cumberland.* New York: Grosset and Dunlap, 1913.

Campbell, John C. *The Southern Highlander and His Homeland.* New York: Russell Sage Foundation, 1921.

Dargan, Olive Tilford. *Call Home the Heart.* New York: Longmans, Green and Co., 1932.

Deal, Borden. *Dunbar's Cove.* London: Hutchinson and Co., 1958.

Dykeman, Wilma. *The Far Family.* New York: Holt, Rinehart and Winston, 1966.

Fox, John, Jr. *Bluegrass and Rhododendron.* New York: Charles Scribner's Sons, 1901.

———. *The Heart of the Hills.* New York: Charles Scribner's Sons, 1913.

Giles, Janice Holt. *The Enduring Hills.* Philadelphia: Westminster Press, 1950.

Harris, Isabella D. "The Southern Mountaineer in American Fiction, 1824–1910." Diss. Duke University, 1948.

Heyward, DuBose. *Angel.* New York: George H. Doran Co., 1926.

Kephart, Horace. *Our Southern Highlands.* New York: Macmillan, 1921.

Kroll, Henry Harrison. *Darker Grows the Valley.* New York: Bobbs-Merrill, 1947.

Lewis, Helen. "Fatalism or the Coal Industry?" *Mountain Life and Work* 46 (Dec. 1970): 4–15.

Lewis, Ruth Fretwell. "The Southern Mountaineer in Fiction." Master's thesis, U of Virginia, 1929.

Lumpkin, Grace. *To Make My Bread.* New York: Macaulay , 1932.

Mutzenberg, Charles G. *Kentucky's Famous Feuds and Tragedies.* New York: R. F. Fenno and Co., 1917.

Settle, Mary Lee. *Fight Night on a Sweet Saturday.* New York: Viking, 1964.

Skidmore, Hubert. *I Will Lift Up Mine Eyes.* New York: Book League of America, 1936.

Smyth, J. F. D. *A Tour of the United States of America.* Dublin: G. Perrin, 1784.

Still, James. *River of Earth.* New York: Viking, 1940.

Williams, Cratis D. "The Southern Mountaineer in Fact and Fiction." Diss. New York University, 1961.

Chapter 6

Majority and Minority

Introduction

The Appalachian region is typically thought of as an ethnically homogeneous region. However, in the region's history many races crossed paths, and each left its mark on the culture in some way.

The various Indian tribes who contested Appalachia's abundant hunting grounds represented a certain cultural diversity. The first white settlers brought different cultural traditions, and since the settlement period the Appalachians have seen all manner of immigrants move steadily into and through the area. Though never a major slave-holding area, or perhaps because of that fact, the mountains became the home of some African Americans, as a number of black settlements emerged.

While Native and African Americans are the most prominent minorities, others play parts in Appalachia's history. Perhaps most curious among these is the Rugby settlement in East Tennessee, a utopian community of English second sons. Another anomaly in the racial history of the region is the mysterious Melungeons. Italians and inhabitants of the former Austro-Hungarian Empire came to work on the railroads and in the mines. Cheap labor has always been in demand in Appalachia, and this fact lured members of many ethnic groups. Appalachia is a crossroads, and as such has been a focus for the meeting of cultures. The shifting patterns of domination and immigration make Appalachia a complex and intriguing place to study.

Carl Lambert
(as told to Karen French Owl)

The following stories were told by Carl Lambert, a noted Cherokee historian and storyteller, to his niece, Karen French Owl, whose first writing was for the *Cherokee Perspective*. The mother of two daughters and grandmother of two granddaughters, Karen French Owl teaches special education at Cherokee High School in Cherokee, North Carolina.

Cherokee Heritage and Folklore

Story #1

Cherokees believed highly in the little people. They lived in certain areas, and the Cherokees more or less were forbidden to go into the areas because they were inhabited by the little people. Right at the upper end of the Big Cove section in the gorges is one of those places. Jerry W. told me about a story his father told him. His father was Owen W., brother to Joe W., up in the Big Cove. Their father and mother told them not to go up into the gorges because it was inhabited by the little people. One time the old folks were away from home, and they decided to go up there and see for themselves. They said it was a clear day and there was not a cloud in the sky. When they went up into this area in the gorges, they thought they were struck by lightning or something. They were stunned by something. When they came to, they got out of there. They did not see any little people, but they did not have to be told to stay away from there anymore.

Story #4

At the 32,000 Acre Tract where Gene O. lives, there is a creek that goes by his house, Fish Trap Branch. There was an Indian who lived between Gene O. and the Tuckaseigee River. The Indian's house burned down; he built it back, and it burned down again. So, he went to see some Indian medicine man on Conley's Creek. He told him about the situation. The medicine man told him he would have to move the house over because he had built the house in the path where the little people came down off the mountain to the

From *The Cherokee Perspective*, ed. Laurence French and Jim Hornbuckle, Appalachian Consortium Press, 1981. Reprinted by permission of the publisher.

Tuckaseigee River to fish, and the little people were the ones burning his house down. So he moved it to a different location. And it still stands. It was the third house that was built, and it was being burned down by the little people because it was in their path to the river.

Story #9

The storyteller was one of the most important people in the village. Before Sequoyah invented the alphabet to where they could write stuff down, at all the various festivals and stuff that they had during the year, the storyteller repeated all these stories to the younger people. And, of course, someone who had some special talent who could remember and who could tell things accurately was one. They would take lessons under the old storyteller. One of the things they did, they did not exaggerate. Usually when we tell things today, every time someone tells it, it gets a little bigger.

They did not have any way to write it down. These things had to be told accurately. They had to be told exactly the same way every time. The stories were passed down from one storyteller to another. This is how we got some of our history.

Anecdote #1

The Cherokees spun off from some of the Indians on the lakes: the Iroquois, Mohawks, and Senecas. They did not come directly from the lakes down here. That is one reason the Cherokees were so far advanced. In moving, they naturally came in contact with other tribes and probably intermarried. They probably picked up some of the culture of the different tribes. The Catawbas were just south of us. Some of the good pottery making came from them. The Catawbas were sitting on a good clay bed. The Cherokees did not have too much good clay to make their pottery. They made pottery, but it wasn't the same. There were the Overhill Cherokees and Middle and Lower Cherokees. When you compared the pottery, the Lower Cherokees made better pottery. This was because they had better clay to work with, and they were right next door to the Catawbas who were the best potters.

Anecdote #2

The Middle Cherokees were not affected by change as quickly as the Overhill or Lower Cherokees. The migration of the white settlers came from Virginia by Bristol and the Tennessee Valley. The English settling in came from Charleston, South Carolina, and came up through that area into the Piedmont and Georgia. The Lower Cherokees were more in contact with whites.

Even before the white settlers came, the tribes were fighting the Lower and Overhill Cherokees much more than these in here. This was because they were in a pocket and were protected by the Overhill and Lower Cherokees. It was too much trouble for a war party of any size to get very far. They would have to come through either the Overhill or Lower Cherokees to get in here. The Middle Cherokees were not changed very much. The Lower Cherokees were not understood by most of the other Cherokees, but their language was a bit different. They pronounced their words different. They were down there with the Catawbas and the Creeks and a lot of the names in North Georgia were Creek in origin, not Cherokee.

Anecdote #3

When DeSoto came through here in 1540 near Franklin, Indians were living in log cabins. Evidently, when they got into this area they had settled, and they decided that was it and started building homes and farming. They set down roots here. But the Cherokees, like other tribes, at first must have been a nomadic tribe. There is nothing to prove that they came directly down here from the lakes. There are some theories that they might have gone down into Central America and then wandered back up into this area. They may have wandered around literally thousands of miles before coming here to put roots down.

Anecdote #5

One legend the Cherokees had concerned a place in Brevard. Indians had been living there for over ten thousand years. The legend had it there was a blond group of people of smaller stature than the Cherokees. When they came, they were a group of people with blonde hair who lived in that area in Brevard. It was definitely a different origin of people, different from the Cherokees.

Anecdote #6

The Judaculla Rock about Cullowhee is the largest rock with picture writing in the United States. We do not know the origin of the rock. It might have been there before the Cherokees came. There is a legend about a giant named Judaculla who was supposed to live up there at the top of Balsam. Up above Caney Fork in Tuckaseigee, there are some fields that are known today as the Judaculla oil fields. That is where he did his farming, right up on top of the mountain. He was supposed to live up on the top of Balsam Mountains. The oil fields are there today. There are some bushes and shrubs growing there now since the Blue Ridge Parkway took it over. The mountaineers used to range their cattle up there. They used to talk about the Judaculla oil fields.

Anecdote #7

The myth of the Cherokees in the Mooney book must be the correct myth on creation passed down through Swimmer from our ancestors.

Anecdote #8

Most Indian tribes in general are very creative. This is inherited. The Indians had to be close to the land. They had to make use of whatever material was available to them. They utilized the white oak and cane. Some of the northern tribes used maple and ash and some other woods native to that area for making their baskets.

Indians were quite adaptable to their environment. If they had to go into a strange territory, they could easily adapt to that area. The Indians were natural conservationists. Their whole livelihood depended on their being conservationists, not killing off all the game or just using part of the animal. They used all of it. They knew they had to have a constant source of game and fish. They only took what they needed. They never killed more game than they could use or caught more fish than they were able to use. They knew they would have to come back another day or another month for more. They used fish traps to catch fish. They would use a dugout canoe to chase the fish into the trap. They would take out the big fish and throw back the smaller fish. That was the Indians' thinking; they [were] always looking to the future, instead of taking everything in sight. They designed their fish traps so that they would only catch the big fish and let the small ones go on through. But, once in a while, something would get caught in the traps, and they would catch the smaller ones.

Anecdote #9

That was one of the things that spooked the Indians when the white settlers came. There was not enough land. It was just that their guns killed off all the game and what they did not kill, they spooked with their guns. It took the Indians longer, and they had to go farther away from home to get their meat. This made the Indians more angry than them taking the land; it was the fact they were destroying the Indians' food supply.

Anecdote #10

Two hundred years ago the whites were surprised to see the Indians with gardens and fruit trees. They were living quite modern two hundred years ago. One village at that time had two hundred houses, one hundred on one side of the river and one hundred on the other. They had cattle and horses. Some whites ate with one chief whose wife even churned butter. The Cherokees had adopted a lot of the white man's ways. One of the reasons was because they were not nomadic; they were staying put, putting roots down where they were.

The idea they got where the women do all the work around the village was because it took a lot of able-bodied men to go out and hunt and bring in food everyday. The rest of them were out patrolling the borders to keep out intruders. This had to be younger people or older people, and the women were about the only ones left in the village. It was not because they wanted their women to do the work; it was just that the women were the only ones left to do the work around the home. Tending the garden and making baskets and pottery was hard work. And, some of the women also were looking after the older people who were unable to take care of themselves. The Cherokees are one of the more progressive tribes and have always been.

Theda Perdue

Theda Perdue's research focuses on the history of minorities, numerical and political, in the Appalachians, especially women and Native and African Americans. A native of Georgia, Perdue received her undergraduate degree from Mercer University and completed her Ph.D. at the University of Georgia in 1976. Since 1988 she has been professor of history at the University of Kentucky. Perdue is author of *Slavery and the Evolution of Cherokee Society, 1540–1866* (1978) and *Cherokee Editor: The Writings of Elias Boudinot* (1983) as well as other books and numerous articles. The work included here examines the history of the two subjugated races of the region in terms of how they dealt with both white settlers and each other.

Red and Black in the Southern Appalachians

The first black Appalachians did not live under the control of white planters, railroad builders, lumber companies, or mine operators; instead, they lived within the domain of the Cherokee Indians. The Cherokee Nation extended from its spiritual center at Kituwah, near present-day Bryson City, North Carolina, into what has become the states of South Carolina, Georgia, Alabama, Tennessee, Kentucky, West Virginia, and Virginia as well as North

From *Blacks in Appalachia*, ed. William Turner and Edward Cabbell, University Press of Kentucky, 1985. Reproduced by permission of the publishers.

Carolina. Much of this vast territory was hunting ground, but Cherokee villages lined the riverbanks of Western North Carolina, eastern Tennessee, northern Georgia, and northwestern South Carolina. The Cherokee were agriculturalists long before the arrival of whites and blacks, but they practiced only subsistence farming. Restrained by a belief system which condemned producing more than was necessary for survival, these Cherokees made no attempt to farm on a commercial scale which might have demanded slave labor. Cherokee society was relatively egalitarian compared with European society and with some African societies; the only distinctions derived from superior knowledge or skill. European contact dramatically changed Cherokee society—its economy, its political structure, and its attitudes—and the transformation of Cherokee society profoundly affected black Appalachians.

The Cherokee discovered that the capture of black slaves was particularly profitable, and by the American Revolution most Cherokees traded almost exclusively in black slaves. The Indians stole slaves from settlers in one location and sold them to planters living on another part of the frontier, rarely keeping black servants for their own use. Whether Cherokees abducted slaves or lured them away with the promise of freedom, the capture of Africans quickly replaced the capture of other Indians when the market for Indian slaves disappeared.

The most notorious Cherokee kidnapper of slaves was Chief Benge, one of the Chickamaugan warriors who refused to make peace with the Americans until 1794. On his last raid into southwestern Virginia, Benge captured Susanna and Elizabeth Livingston and three black slaves and attempted to transport them back to northwestern Alabama where the Chickamaugans resided. While on the trail, Benge queried Elizabeth about the slaveholders who lived on the North Holston River, particularly a General Shelby, and told the white women that he would "pay him a visit during the ensuing summer and take away all of his Negroes." On the third day after the raid, the Virginia militia attacked the abductors and killed Benge and most of his comrades. Colonel Arthur Campbell, the military officer of the area, wrote Governor Henry Lee of Virginia: "I send the scalp of Captain Benge, that noted murderer . . . to your excellency. . . . as proof that he is no more." The death of Benge marked the end of such brash slave raids (Addington 126).

Some Africans who came into the possession of the Indians were not captured but had instead sought refuge among the Cherokees, whose mountainous territory discouraged all except the most avid slave catchers. The treaty signed between the British and Cherokees in London in 1730 contained a provision for the return of these fugitives. "If any negroes shall run away into the woods from their English masters, the Cherokees shall endeavor to apprehend them and bring them to the plantation from which they ran away, or to the Governor, and for every slave so apprehended and brought back, the Indian that brings him shall receive a gun and a matchcoat" (Addington 190; Hewatt 2:8). In 1763 whites agreed to pay Indians one musket and three blankets, the equivalent of thirty-five deerskins, for each black slave captured and returned (Willis).

The fear that runaways might establish maroon communities in the relative safety of the Cherokees' mountains motivated slaveholders to offer such lavish rewards for the recovery of their slaves. In 1725 a prominent South Carolina planter expressed concern that some slaves had become well acquainted with the language, the customs, and the hill country of the Cherokees. The possibility that slaves and Indians might join forces against the whites made the colonists shudder. In 1712, Alexander Spotswood of Virginia wrote the Board of Trade that he feared "the insurrection of our own Negroes and the Invasions of the Indians." The dread of such an alliance continued throughout the colonial period and gave rise to "law and order" political parties. John Stuart's North Carolina rivals, for example, successfully capitalized on this anxiety because, as Stuart pointed out in 1775, "nothing can be more alarming to the Carolinas than the idea of an attack from Indians and Negroes" (Saunders 1:886 and 10:118; Nash 295). The fear of raids by maroons also partly shaped colonial Indian policy:

> In our Quarrels with the *Indians,* however proper and necessary it may be to give them Correction, it can never be our interest to extirpate them, or to force them from their Lands: their Grounds would be soon taken up by runaway *Negroes* from our Settlements, whose Numbers would daily increase and quickly become more formidable Enemies than *Indians* can ever be, as they speak our Language and would never be at a Loss for Intelligence. (Milligan-Johnston 136)

This fear was not wholly unfounded, as the following deposition given in 1751 by Richard Smith, the white trader at Keewee, demonstrates:

> Three runaway Negroes of Mr. Gray's told the Indians as they said that the white people were coming up to destroy them all, and that they had got some Creek Indians to assist them so to do. Which obtained belief and the more for that the old Warriors of Keewee said some Negroes had applied to him, and told him that there was in all Plantations many Negroes more than white people, and that for the Sake of Liberty, they would join him. (McDowell 291–92)

The colonists went to great lengths to prevent conspiracies of Indians and slaves. They soon discovered that the most effective way to accomplish their goals was to create suspicion, hatred, and hostility between the two peoples. The colonists not only employed Indians to find escaped slaves but also used blacks in military campaigns against Indians. In 1715, during the Yamassee war, a company of black militiamen participated in the invasion of the Cherokee Nation and remained after other troops departed to assist the Cherokees in an attack against the Creeks. After the Yamassee war the colonists ceased using black soldiers, although the South Carolina General Assembly during the Cherokee war of 1760 defeated by only one vote a bill to arm five hundred blacks. Nevertheless, slaves continued to contribute to the war effort in other ways, and more than two hundred blacks served as wagoners and scouts for Colonel James Grant's expedition against the Cherokees in 1761 (Porter 56–58; Willis 106).

In another move to prevent the development of congenial relationships between Africans and Indians, the southern colonies enjoined whites from taking their slaves into Cherokee territory. Trade regulations imposed by both Georgia and South Carolina under various administrations almost always made it illegal for the traders to employ blacks in their dealings with the Indians (McDowell 88, 136, 199; Alden 19, 210; Rothrock 3–18).

Stringent efforts to keep Africans and Native Americans separate and hostile sometimes failed. When red and black men successfully resisted or overcame the misconception fostered by whites, they probably recognized certain cultural affinities between themselves. Both emphasized living harmoniously with nature and maintaining ritual purity; both attached great importance to kinship in their social organization; and both were accustomed to an economy based on subsistence agriculture.

African and Cherokee relationships to their environments reflected similar attitudes toward the physical world. The spiritual merged with the environmental. Common everyday activities, such as getting up in the morning, hunting, embarking on a journey, and particularly curing illness, assumed for both races a religious significance, and even topographical features were invested with religious meanings. Africans associated mountains and hills as well as caves and holes with spirits and divinities, while Cherokees viewed streams and rivers as roads to the underworld and "deep pools in the river and about lonely passes in the high mountains" as the haunts of the *Uktena,* a great serpent with supernatural powers (Hudson; Mooney 240–52, 264, 270; Mbiti 72, 80).

Just as in Cherokee society, kinship rather than economics ruled the lives of most Africans. Kinship groups governed marital customs and relationships between individuals, settled most disputes, and enabled individuals to exercise their personal rights. Kinship was also a major factor in shaping the nature of both indigenous West African slavery and aboriginal Cherokee bondage. A slave generally lacked kinship ties, and he therefore lacked the personal rights and claim to humanity which stemmed from kinship (Mbiti 135–38; Grace 7).

Cherokees acted upon their assumptions about blacks, and when they founded their republic in 1827, the Cherokees excluded blacks from participation in the government. The founding fathers granted all adult males access to the ballot box except "negroes, and descendants of white and Indian men by negro women who may have been set free." The Constitution restricted office holding to people untainted by African ancestry: "No person who is of negro or mulatto parentage, either by the father or mother side, shall be eligible to hold any office or trust under this Government." The Cherokees also sought to discourage free blacks from moving into the Nation and enacted a statute warning "that all free negroes coming into the

Cherokee Nation under any pretence whatsoever, shall be viewed and treated, in every respect as intruders, and shall not be allowed to reside in the Cherokee Nation without a permit" (*Cherokee Phoenix and Indians' Advocate*).

By the time the Cherokees had established their republic, the use of black slaves on plantations had become a feature of their society. In part, the United States government was responsible for the introduction of plantation slavery. Following the Revolution, American Indian policy focused on the pacification and "civilization" of southern tribes. In compliance with the "civilization" program, Cherokees adopted the white man's implements and farming techniques, and individuals who had substantial capital to invest soon came to need extra hands. Because of the government's pacification policy, Cherokee planters could not satisfy their demand for labor by capturing members of their tribes, and few Cherokees worked for wages because the tribe's common ownership of land enabled every Indian to farm for himself. Therefore, the Cherokee upper class followed the example of its white mentors and began using African bondsmen. While most Cherokee masters owned fewer than ten slaves, and on the eve of removal, 92 percent of the Cherokees held no slaves at all, a few Cherokees developed extensive plantations in the broad valleys of eastern Tennessee, northeastern Alabama, and northern Georgia. The most famous, Joseph Vann, lived in a magnificent red brick, white-columned mansion which still stands near Chatsworth, Georgia. He owned 110 slaves in 1835, cultivated three hundred acres, and operated a ferry, steamboat, mill, and tavern (Perdue 110–28).

In the 1830s, the United States government forced the Cherokees to relinquish the fertile valleys of their homeland and move west of the Mississippi River to what is today the state of Oklahoma. Many slaves accompanied their masters on this sorrowful migration, which has become known as the Trail of Tears. The only Cherokees who remained in the Southern Appalachians were those who lived along the Oconaluftee River high in the Smoky Mountains. And among those Cherokees lived at least one black slave. In the 1840s, Charles Lanman visited the North Carolina Cherokees and spoke with Cudjo, who had belonged to Chief Yonaguska, or "Drowning Bear," before his death. Cudjo told Lanman that Yonaguska "never allowed himself to be called master, for he said Cudjo was his brother, and not his slave" (Lanman 418). Perhaps Yonaguska treated Cudjo as his brother because the mountainous region gave him no opportunity to exploit his slave.

Since removal, interaction between blacks and Indians in the Southern Appalachians has been limited, but their experiences in some ways have been similar. Until recently, legal discrimination made both groups second-class citizens. For example, only in the 1950s did North Carolina repeal legislation prohibiting marriage between blacks or Indians and whites. Educational and social discrimination affirmed this second-class status. Generally offered only menial jobs at wages below those paid whites, blacks and Indians have also been victims of economic discrimination. Indians, of course, had a land base, which blacks lacked, but frequently the land served as an invitation or provocation to further exploitation. Nevertheless, the Cherokees have continued to view themselves as radically different from blacks and their situation as significantly better than that of blacks. Such an attitude is the legacy of three centuries of hostility and fear. Perhaps if an atmosphere of cooperation and trust pervades the next three centuries, a new legacy will come into being.

Works Cited

Addington, Luther F. "Chief Benge's Last Raid." *Historical Society of Southwest Virginia* 2 (1966).

Alden, John Richard. *John Stuart and the Southern Colonial Frontier, 1754–1775.* New York: Gordian, 1944.

Cherokee Phoenix and Indians' Advocate, 21 Feb. and 13 Apr. 1828.

Grace, John. *Domestic Slavery in West Africa.* New York: Mueller, 1975.

Hewatt, Alexander. *An Historical Account of the Rise and Progress of the Colonies of South Carolina and Georgia.* 2 vols. London, 1779.

Hudson, Charles. *The Southeastern Indians.* Knoxville: U of Tennessee P, 1976.

Lanman, Charles. *Adventures in the Wilds of the United States and British American Provinces.* Philadelphia, 1856.

McDowell, William L. *Documents, 1750–1754.* Columbia, SC: South Carolina Archives Dept., 1958.

Mbiti, John S. *African Religions and Philosophy.* New York: Praeger, 1969.

Milligan-Johnston, George. "A Short Description of the Province of South Carolina." *Colonial South Carolina: Two Contemporary Descriptions.* Ed. Chapman J. Milling. Columbia: U of South Carolina P, 1951.

Mooney, James. *Myths of the Cherokee and Sacred Formulas of the Cherokees. Seventh and Nineteenth Annual Reports of the Bureau of American Ethnology.* Nashville, TN: C. and R. Elder—Booksellers, 1982.

Nash, Gary B. *Red, White, and Black: The Peoples of Early America.* Englewood Cliffs, NJ: Prentice-Hall, 1974.

Perdue, Theda. "Cherokee Planters: The Development of Plantation Slavery before Removal." *The Cherokee Indian Nation: A Troubled History.* Ed. Duane H. King. Knoxville: U of Tennessee P, 1979. 110–28.

Porter, Kenneth W. "Negroes on the Southern Frontier, 1670–1763." *Journal of Negro History* 33 (Spring 1948). 53–78.

Rothrock, Mary U. "Carolina Traders among the Overhill Traders, 1690–1760." *East Tennessee Historical Society Publications* 1 (1929): 3–18.

Saunders, William L., ed. *The Colonial Records of North Carolina.* N.p., n.d.

Willis, William S., Jr. "Divide and Rule: Red, White, and Black in the Southeast." *Red, White, and Black: Symposium on Indians in the Old South.* Ed. Charles M. Hudson. Athens: U of Georgia P, 1971.

Cherokee Poetry

Long before white settlers appeared in the New World with established genres of literature, Native Americans had been creating their own poetry and passing it on from generation to generation. The oral tradition is still alive, made more poignant by the threat to it posed by modern mechanical civilization, as the following poems by Cherokees clearly reveal.

D. Chiltoskie

The New Indians

The New Indians
We're here, we're strong
We've been suppressed too long
Now it's our time, to rise, to speak out
And to be heard.
The white men
They've tried to change and mold us
After them, but our spirits are too strong.
The New Indians
We're tired of being pushed, shoved,
Lied to, spit upon, and pitied.
The New Indians
Yes, it's our turn now
They can't stop us, we've got to be heard.
The white men
They've got to listen to us now
And they will!!

From *The Cherokee Perspective,* ed. Laurence French and Jim Hornbuckle, Appalachian Consortium Press, 1981. Reprinted by permission of the publisher.

Pam Taylor

I Am Indian, I

I suppose some people believe,
That we should have no race,
That the beauty of my deep bronze skin,
And the blackness of my hair,
Should carry no pride.
But I don't believe this is the truth,
Because . . .
Just as the Great Spirit
Created the
Fair skin of the Europeans,
The black skin of the Negro,
He created me Red.
So as long as there is air to breathe,
Water to drink,
And a place to rest,
I will look!
I will walk!
I will talk!
As an American Indian.

Tears

Columbus, "discovered"
Washington, "stressed"
Lincoln, "fought"
Jackson, "possessed"
and the
Redman, "wept."

John Ehle

See volume 1, chapter 2, for biography.

The Rise and Fall of the Cherokee Nation

A romantic concept of Indians evolved in the years following their removal
from the Southeast. The Cherokees were generally pictured as living peacefully in their mountain home—though fewer than one in five lived in mountain areas; their possession of black slaves was omitted from such portrayals;
their shamans were exonerated; their propensity for warfare was replaced
with peaceful coexistence with Creeks, Choctaws, Chickasaws, and the rest.
As individuals they were pictured as being free to work out individual relationships with nature. During this period, to be a white man and to have
taken part in the Indian wars became reprehensible, and apologies and ex-
cuses made by the veterans of Indian wars added to the embellishments. For
instance, a letter often quoted as accurately describing the events of Cherokee removal in 1838 and 1839 was written in 1890, fifty years later, by a
veteran of the United States Cavalry, John G. Burnett, who on his eightieth
birthday sought to assure his grandchildren of his own purity of past actions:

> The removal of the Cherokee Indians from their life long homes in the
> year 1838 found me a young man in the prime of life and a private sol-
> dier in the American Army. Being acquainted with many of the Indians
> and able to fluently speak their language, I was sent as interpreter into the
> Smoky Mountain Country in May, 1838, and witnessed the execution of
> the most brutal order in the History of American Warfare. I saw the help-
> less Cherokees arrested and dragged from their homes, and driven at the
> bayonet point into the stockades. And in the chill of a drizzling rain on an
> October morning I saw them loaded like cattle or sheep into six hun-
> dred and forty-five wagons and started toward the west.
>
> One can never forget the sadness and solemnity of that morning. Chief
> John Ross led in prayer and when the bugle sounded and the wagons
> started rolling many of the children rose to their feet and waved their
> little hands good-bye to their mountain homes, knowing they were leaving
> them forever. Many of these helpless people did not have blankets and
> many of them had been driven from home barefooted. . . .
>
> The long painful journey to the west ended March 26th, 1839, with
> four thousand silent graves reaching from the foothills of the Smoky

From *Trail of Tears,* © 1988 by John Ehle. Used by permission of Doubleday, a division of
Bantam Doubleday Dell Publishing Group, Inc.

Mountains to what is known as Indian territory in the West. And covet-
ousness on the part of the white race was the cause of all that the Cherokees had to suffer. . . .

The doom of the Cherokee was sealed, Washington, D.C. had de-
creed that they must be driven West, and their lands given to the
white man, and in May 1838 an Army of four thousand regulars, and
three thousand volunteer soldiers under command of General Winfield
Scott, marched into the Indian country and wrote the blackest chapter
on the pages of American History. . . .

Murder is murder and somebody must answer, somebody must explain
the streams of blood that flowed in the Indian country in the summer of
1838. Somebody must explain the four thousand silent graves that mark
the trail of the Cherokees to their exile. I wish I could forget it all, but the
picture of six hundred and forty five wagons lumbering over the frozen
ground with their Cargo of suffering humanity still lingers in my
memory.

Let the Historian of a future day tell the sad story with its sighs,
its tears and dying groans. Let the great Judge of all the earth weigh
our actions and reward us according to our work.

Children—Thus ends my promised birthday story.

This December the 11th 1890.

The exaggerations and factual errors of Burnett and others are regrettable.
They are damaging mainly to the reputation of the federal government. That
mighty institution is vulnerable in this case, certainly. The government was
wrestling in the first half of the nineteenth century with two grave problems, slavery and Indian rights; the first was solved by the bloodiest war ever
fought on the continent, and the second by a method of feints and dives and
promises and evasions. The government's inconsistencies bother public conscience. Even so, this method was less costly in human terms than an outright war, the alternative Indians would have found more understandable and
which would have been consistent with their own history; to them land belonged to the people who possessed it, who won it by force of arms. Jackson's
position was extreme, but his successor continued it; and his opposition party,
the Whigs, elected four years after he left office, made no changes in it.

One looks back nostalgically to the earlier days when Washington and
Jefferson believed a cultural adaptation was possible. Even then, however,
the policy makers did not rest easy. Thomas Jefferson wrote to Governor
William H. Harrison in 1803, "Should any tribe be foolhardy enough to take
up the hatchet at any time, the seizing the whole country of that tribe, and
driving them across the Mississippi, as the only condition of peace, would be
an example to others, and a furtherance of our final consolidation."

A practical alternative to Indian removal never came before the government. The alternative of leaving the body of the continent in Indian hands

was unacceptable. It was also unacceptable to leave it in French or British hands. One possible solution in the Cherokee case, which received little attention, was made by the federal agent, Return J. Meigs:

> The point had been reached where the Cherokee people should begin to fight their own battles of life, and that any further contributions to their support, either in the shape of provisions or tools, would have only a tendency to render them more dependent upon the Government and less competent to take care of themselves. Those who were already advanced in the arts of civilized life should be the tutors of the more ignorant. They possessed a territory of perhaps 10,000,000 acres of land, principally in the States of Georgia, North Carolina, and Tennessee, for the occupation of which they could enumerate a little more than 10,000 souls or 2,000 families. If they were to become an agricultural and pastoral people, an assignment of 640 acres of land to each family would be all and more than they could occupy with advantage to themselves. Such an allotment would consume but 1,280,000 acres, leaving more than 8,000,000 acres of surplus land which might and ought to be sold for their benefit, and the proceeds applied to their needs in the erection of houses, fences, and the clearing and breaking up of their land for cultivation. The authority and laws of the several States within whose limits they resided should become operative upon them, and they should be vested with the rights, privileges, and immunities of citizens of those States.

A word of praise might be bestowed on Old England, in that they were often protective of Indian rights. Prior to the American Revolution, the English king had placed Indian lands off limits to further settlement. Understandably, predictably, land speculators were furious over this policy. One might go so far as to wonder if "Give me liberty or give me death, but in any case give me Kentucky," was the battle cry in some circles.

Compared with France and Spain, England since Queen Elizabeth had been protective of Indian rights. Consider Spain. When the Spanish conquered Mexico, there were twenty million Indians living there; in the remainder of North America, including Canada, there were two million. Spain's policies of brutal slavery and outright extermination, combined with diseases, reduced the twenty million to fewer than two million population.

Effie Waller Smith

David Deskins plays a dual role as circuit court clerk of Pike County, Kentucky, and as literary scholar. He pursues his interest in Afro-American writer Effie Waller Smith when away from the courthouse. In 1987 Deskins began independent research on Smith's writings and her life, research that he continues today. He aspires to publish an intensive literary biography tracing her life and literary career. His publications include an introduction to *The Collected Works of Effie Waller Smith* (Oxford UP, 1991). In addition, Deskins has published a book on astronomy and a history of Pike County, Kentucky.

As Deskins reports in the *Collected Works,* little is known about Smith's life. She was born in 1879 on a farm on Chloe Creek about four miles from Pikeville. After attending local segregated schools, she went to the Kentucky Normal School for Colored Persons in Frankfort in 1900 and 1901 and then taught for sixteen years in Kentucky and East Tennessee. She died in Wisconsin in 1960. Her works include *Songs of the Months* (1904), *Rosemary and Pansies* (1909), and *Rhymes from the Cumberlands* (1909), from which the following representative poem is taken. Unabashedly affirming the beauty of the mountains and the inhabitants, Smith apparently chose to avoid writing about some of the sadder aspects of her experience.

My Native Mountains

I love my native mountains,
    The dear old Cumberland,
Rockribbed and everlasting,
    How great they are, and grand!

I love each skyward reaching peak,
    Each grassy glade and dale,
Each moss-and-fern-clad precipice
    Each lovely flower-decked vale.

I love each vine-hung rock glen,
    I love each dark ravine
Though there may hide the catamount
    And wild dog sly and mean.

From *Rhymes from the Cumberlands,* 1909. Reprinted in *Appalachian Heritage* 19.4 (Fall 1991), © *Appalachian Heritage*/Berea College. Reprinted by permission of *Appalachian Heritage* and David Deskins.

I love my mountains' forest
　　Varied and beautiful
I love her springs and waterfalls,
　　So pure and wonderful.

I love her richly plumaged birds
　　The pheasant and the jay,
The merry scarlet tanager,
　　The woodpeck bright and gay.

How oft among these mountains
　　Has the silvery music clear
From the lark's throat cheered the traveler,
　　And the honest mountaineer.

But more than these old mountains
　　Which with wonder I revere
I love with true devotion
　　The people who live here.

So here's with love sincere and dear
　　For her sons of brawn and worth;
For her daughters pure and lovely,
　　The fairest types of earth.

Richard B. Drake

Richard Drake teaches history and political science at Berea College in Berea, Kentucky. Born in Ames, Iowa, in 1925, he went on to earn degrees from Doane College, Crete, Nebraska (A.B.); the University of Chicago (M.A.); and Emory University, where he completed a Ph.D. in history. The author of *Mountaineers and Americans* (1976), Drake also contributes articles and reviews to journals such as *Negro History Bulletin,* the *Journal of Southern History,* and the *Appalachian Journal.* In addition to teaching and research, Drake served as editor of *Appalachian Notes* from 1973 to 1980.

Slavery in Appalachia: Review of
Mountain Masters, Slavery, and the Sectional Crisis
in Western North Carolina by John C. Inscoe

Well, Burke County, North Carolina, has done it again! First it was Edward
Phifer's excellent study, "Slavery in Microcosm," which appeared in the *Journal of Southern History* in 1962. Dr. Phifer was a local surgeon, but his skills
as a historian were such that he gave us the best in-depth, countywide study
of slavery and slave-owning that has been available for thirty years. Then
came John E. Fleming, a Burke County black who became my student at
Berea, then went off to Howard University for his doctorate involving a remarkable *Roots*-like study of his family and his ancestor, Tamishan. (See "An
Appalachian Afro-American Family," page 9 of this issue [*Appalachian Heritage,* Fall 1991].) Now comes another Burke County native, John C. Inscoe,
who went to the University of North Carolina at Chapel Hill for his train-
ing, and now has broadened our understanding of Appalachian slavery with
his insightful study, *Mountain Masters.* Inscoe, a professor at the University
of Georgia, is editor of the *Georgia Historical Quarterly* and has served as guest
editor of the *Journal of Southern History.*

Inscoe's coverage in this book stretches beyond Burke into all of Western
North Carolina, and even into the whole world the slave owners made. The
connections were political, economic, and matrimonial. Inscoe's picture of
Western North Carolina's slave-owning elite finds a predominantly rural
community well integrated into the larger market system of the antebellum
South. Many mountain masters were professional men; many others were in
business. But this elite was invested in land and slaves, and was tied intimately to the Old South's system of power and wealth. In fact, according to
Inscoe, western Carolina's principal politicians were leading southerners and
secessionists. Senator Thomas L. Clingman is Inscoe's principal example of a
mountain secessionist and passionate defender of slavery. Another is William Holland Thomas of Jackson County.

Inscoe's efforts are clearly revisionist; Inscoe penetrates into debatable territory, especially when he attempts to build a case that slavery in western
Carolina was remarkably moderate. His evidence for a benign mountain slavery involves, first of all, masters who made substantial efforts to preserve
slave families despite economic difficulties, as well as evidence of considerate
treatment. Another line of his argument relates to the strong, even enthusiastic support of secession by non-slaveholding whites, along with the general lack of protest in the region against the system by North Carolina's slaves
themselves. Such an interpretation flies in the face of the recent, massive, and
impressive historiography that has appeared since Kenneth Stampp's book, *The
Peculiar Institution,* appeared in 1956.

From *Appalachian Heritage,* Fall 1991, © *Appalachian Heritage*/Berea College. Reprinted by
   permission.

I am prepared to accept Inscoe's point that slavery may have been "more mild" in Western North Carolina, but it appears clear that many varieties of slavery existed in the United States in the antebellum period. Wherever slavery has emerged, it has had remarkable variations, as between Latin America and North America, which Frank Tannenbaum pointed out in the 1940s, or between the Deep South and the Border South in the United States.

Even within the southern mountains, the world of slavery presented wide variations. In the cotton-growing Tennessee Valley counties of northern Alabama, the plantation-slave system was nearly as fully developed as in any other of the Cotton Kingdom. Yet in a ten-county area surrounding Parkersburg, (West) Virginia, blacks and slaves were almost totally absent. The Shenandoah Valley counties in Virginia, furthermore, were so open to "hostile penetration" from both the free states and the large free black population of Maryland, that running away was an immense problem, and Shenandoah slave-owners were always apprehensive and suspicious of subversion, an important variable when compared with more "secure" areas.

Apparently Western North Carolina was a still different area within slavery. Non-slaveholding whites, following the traditional political pattern of deference, generally supported the decisions of their social betters and political leaders. The slave system seemed secure there, even essential, and when northern Republican agitation threatened the system's security, surely most people, slave owners and non-slaveholders alike, supported what appeared to be the best defense of slavery, secession.

The picture that Inscoe presents corroborates the recent research done by historians at Western Carolina University in their history of Jackson County, North Carolina. Most of the mountain population supported secession and the slave system in Jackson, as in Burke, Buncombe, and other counties. But what of the counties such as Madison where the slaveholding elite was such a tiny minority, and where local animosities became so excited by secession that guerrilla encounters quickly emerged, culminating in the notorious Shelton Laurel massacre?

Many of us were hoping that Inscoe's study would become a "classic" and would need little modification in the light of the available research. Although the study is a fine one, even an important one, the picture of slavery and slaveholding it presents needs further refining. The author, for example, has made little effort to understand why antislavery agitation was so weak in North Carolina by the 1850s. If the Barnes-Dumond explanation of southern antislavery is valid, as corroborated by the work of Clement Eaton, antislavery spokesmen in North Carolina had long since been driven from the state by a society increasingly intolerant of any debate over its "peculiar institution." The picture presented by Barnes, Dumond, Eaton, and others, sees North Carolina antislavery advocates driven first to East Tennessee (as Elihu Embree was), then into the Old Northwest, where these antislavery southerners became leading abolitionists—John Rankin, David Nelson, Gideon Blackburn, and others.

Inscoe's picture of mountain slavery and slave owners is partly corrective, for surely Western North Carolina had little in common with West Virginia, which successfully seceded from secession in 1863, and with East Tennessee, which might have seceded from Tennessee had she been better located. East Tennessee was quickly in rebellion against secession in 1861. Thus the southern mountain experience with secession was diverse. Some areas of the southern mountains were loyal to the Confederacy, at least at first, and even appeared satisfied with the slave system.

History is full of deep riddles, and one of the most significant in American and Southern Appalachian history has been that of Negro chattel slavery. But history is a process. Never, it appears, is any final book written that displays the whole truth. Historians are, after all, only human. When the past we are trying to recreate involves a riddle as mysterious as the impact of slavery in a country dedicated to freedom and human rights, it will take the best efforts of many generations of historians before a generally agreed-upon picture emerges. We have clearly not yet reached that place in our researches on the slavery of the mountain South.

But many modern scholars hold that slavery, in whatever form, was slavery and thus inherently a tyrannical denial of basic human rights. To them, Inscoe's effort to depict Western North Carolina slavery as moderate is most irritating. Yet mountain slavery in North Carolina was a different slavery from the slavery in Louisiana or the Alabama Black Belt.

Rather than cursing the research done, what slavery's scholars need to do is to appeal to Inscoe and others to do further research. In fact, the two active historians of slavery from Burke County, John C. Inscoe and John E. Fleming, one black and the other white, may be in the best position to provide us with that fuller picture of the impact of the "peculiar institution" upon mountain society.

Garry Barker

See volume 1, chapter 3, for biography.

My Grandfather Belonged to the Ku Klux Klan

My grandfather belonged to the Ku Klux Klan
On Mauck Ridge, Kentucky, 1921.

From *Bitter Creek Breakdown* (Berea, KY: Hollytree Press, 1991). Reprinted by permission of the author and publisher.

When a gang of booted, hooded horsemen
Rode the ridgetop
Latter day Morgan's Raiders
Who howled, shot,
Struck fear (and fascination)
Into children's hearts.

But Granddaddy and his rogue companions
Rode and shot just for recreation
Because in all of Elliott County, 1921,
There were

No Blacks
No Jews
No Catholics.

So Granddaddy and the boys
Sat in Willie Cox's barn all night
Drank moonshine
Played poker
Swapped knives
And brought along the kids.

My five year old father
Thought the Klan was a civic club.

Same ritual
Same bizarre trappings
And ceremony
As those men who meet every Tuesday night
At Mae's Restaurant
To drink coffee
Tell jokes
And get away from the house for an hour or two.

Granddaddy belonged to the Klan
For five years or more
Until somebody figured out that
Wearing a hood

Packing a pistol
And riding around cold in the dark
Wasn't as much fun as
A rocking chair by the fireplace
Whiskey from a glass

Barefooted
So your corns wouldn't hurt.

And that it didn't make much sense
To hate
A feller you'd never
Even met.

Lynwood Montell

Lynwood Montell, professor of history and folk studies as well as director of the Center for Intercultural and Folk Studies at Western Kentucky University in Bowling Green, was born in Tompkinsville, Kentucky, in 1931. After taking A.B. degrees at Western Kentucky and Indiana University, Montell completed his Ph.D. in folklore at Indiana in 1964 and began his career as a teacher and scholar. Montell has focused on the social and historical traditions of Appalachians. His works in folk research include *Ghosts Along the Cumberland* (1975), examining stories and rituals of death, and *Killings* (1986), which investigates the unwritten system of justice in the hills. *The Saga of Coe Ridge* (1970) is more historical in nature. The black inhabitants of Coe Ridge in the Cumberland Mountains were descended for the most part from former slaves in the region. The insular settlement, an anomaly in the region, in time became a haven for refugees of all sorts, minorities by circumstance if not by birthright. The excerpt here illustrates the problems this desegregated group confronted when, in a rare instance, it came in conflict with the world around it.

The White Gals

White women came to live among the Coe Negroes from 1885 to 1920, the turbulent middle years of the colony's history. Their presence coincides roughly with the days of feuding, and with the early years of moonshining and bootlegging when murder and violence gripped the colony and produced the genesis of the colony's internal sickness and ultimate extinction. These white girls were young and pretty, so it is said, and under normal circumstances easily could have found suitable mates in their own society. But cer-

From *The Saga of Coe Ridge: A Study in Oral History,* © 1970 by The University of Tennessee Press. Reprinted by permission of the publisher.

tain personal factors drove the girls away from the white man's society and into the realm of the legendary Negro colony on Coe Ridge.

The backgrounds of these young women were not identical by any means. Virginia Warren and Julie Newton came from the finest homes and had well-respected parents. The girls "went bad," however, and were driven from home by their own people. Two other girls, Sue Ann Barton and Patricia Smith, originated from a poor white background where society apparently cared little about moral standards—as a matter of fact, Sue Ann and Patricia were introduced by their parents to life in the Coe colony.[1]

The white people who had homes surrounding the Coe colony were apparently apathetic toward the presence of white women in Zeketown. The white oral traditions collected on this situation contained very few derogatory comments about the habits of these white women, and no words of condonation. The few comments that were offered never pointed the finger of guilt at the Negroes, but always pointed at the white women, whom the white informants considered one rung lower than the Negroes on the social ladder. Even the Negro informants displayed a languid attitude about their ancestral relations with the white women in the Coe colony. It is apparent that these informants accepted the days of cohabitation in Zeketown as a once common thing, perhaps deriving justification for the practice from earlier times when the slave masters used the Negro girls as they saw fit.

Molly and Nan

During their visits to the homes of Yaller John and Joe Coe,[2] in the late 1880s, Calvin and Little John met and courted two white girls from the Mud Camp community. Cal's sweetheart was Molly Ballard, a daughter of Vince Ballard, and Little John's girl was Nan Anderson, daughter of Walter Anderson. Barely in their teens, both girls lived at the mouth of Mud Camp Creek, near Cloyd's Landing in Cumberland County.[3] Cal and John became acquainted with Molly and Nan while working in the woods in the vicinity of the girls' houses; the men may have occasionally boarded at one or both of the homes.[4] Soon thereafter, Molly and Nan would slip away from their homes to meet Cal and Little John at the home of Sam Smith, a white neighbor whose wife, Bell, perpetuated the whole affair by letting the four rendezvous in her kitchen anytime they desired.[5]

Although Calvin was a grown man, about twenty-five years old, Little John was no more than sixteen. In the words of Mrs. Cornelius Allen (Little John's daughter), "His Uncle Cal led him astray. You know how a boy will worship his uncle. Well, that's the way it was with my father and Calvin."[6] After a few weeks of these secret meetings in the Smith home, the four decided to elope to Indiana where they could be married. It is generally felt that they were going to Indianapolis, but Little John's daughter emphatically clarified the matter: "Now let me set you straight on something! They were not going to Indianapolis! They were going to Jeffersonville; just far enough into Indiana to get married."

The whole plan of flight backfired in Glasgow, the nearest train station some forty-five miles from Zeketown. The four lovers went to the home of a Negro friend in Glasgow and there spent the night. The next morning they were apprehended at the railroad station. A white informant recalled their arrest:

> And they got on the train there in Glasgow. But they'd stayed all night, you know—no travel, no way of traveling much then, and they had to go to Glasgow and stay all night and catch a train out.
>
> So the next morning, why, the girls they wore veils over their faces to keep anybody from knowing they 'uz white, you know. But this colored (they stayed in a colored man's house, and of course they had to let him know everything). And they went to the depot then to get on the train, and why, he went out and got the officers, and they went and got them.[7]

Most of the informants did not agree that the police were notified by the Negro host. Tim Coe, for example, placed the entire blame on a tiny bee, which got behind the veil over one of the girls' faces. In fright, she knocked the veil from her face and revealed white flesh. George Allred, quoting Calvin Coe himself, related the incident in this manner: "They said they'd got away with them women . . . but them women had on veils. One of them kindly raised up the veil to scratch her face, and this colored feller saw her and he went and told the law that them colored fellers wuz running off with them white women, and they arrested Calvin and John."

The wind is blamed in the account given by Mrs. Susie Taylor Moore: "And they bought black veils, and them girls put them on, and they got on the train to leave. And it happened the wind blowed up one of the girls' veils and they seen they was white, and they arrested them right there and brought the girls back home."[8]

The four were taken to the Glasgow jail. Molly and Nan were sent home on the next stage, according to Tim Coe, and Cal and John were released on bail put up by Boles and Botts, two Glasgow attorneys. The *Chronicles* claims, however, that the two stood trial and were freed after John paid a fifty-dollar fine for drawing a gun on an officer. Barren County official records for 1889 give an account of the whole event. The Glasgow city attorney brought charge on July 20, 1889, against John Coe, Calvin Coe, and John Coe, the latter (Yaller John) being completely neglected by oral tradition. Their charge was for unlawfully assembling "themselves together for the purpose of causing the marriage of a white woman to a Negro man." Bail was set at $200 each. That same day they went before the county judge for trial. Their sentence was affixed at a fine of $150 each and fifty days each in the Barren County jail. They were released from jail in September, 1889.[9]

Notes

1. Virginia Warren, Julie Newton, Sue Ann Barton, and Patricia Smith are pseudonyms, used in this text to avoid any possibility of invasion of privacy.

2. Shortly after 1880, Old John and his brother, Joe, married Tennessee and Tilda Black, sisters from the Mud Camp community of Cumberland County, according to Mrs. Cornelius Allen, 24 Jan. 1964.

3. The Ballards lived at what was then called the Hunter Place, now owned by Jim Butler, according to Bart Ballard, the brother of Molly, on 12 Oct. 1963.

4. Mrs. Susie Taylor Moore claimed: "They jist said they wuz talkin' to two white girls. They was a-boardin' there at that place, and they got to talking to them two white girls."

5. The kitchen episode was described in an unrecorded interview by Cornelius V. Allen, 12 Oct. 1963, and by Bart Ballard, on that same date.

6. Statement made on 12 Oct. 1963. Little John was nine years old in 1880, according to the 1880 Cumberland County Census. Mrs. Allen was three years in error about her father's age, for he was nineteen when the attempted elopement occurred in 1889. This discrepancy in dates is explained when Barren County Court records are cited later in this chapter.

7. Mrs. Etta Short, in *Chronicles of the Coe Colony*, by Samuel Coe (Kansas City, KS: privately printed, 1930), 63, corroborates this testimony by stating that the four had spent the previous night in Glasgow. *The Chronicles*, according to Montell, are "the most important work dealing with Coe Ridge" (*The Saga of Coe Ridge: A Study in Oral History* [Knoxville: U of Tennessee P, 1970], 7). Written by Samuel Coe, a black man in collaboration with a white, the *Chronicles* "are extremely prejudiced against the white race. . . . For the most part oral traditions . . . closely parallel those of *The Chronicles*, yet none of the informants had read that work."

8. The *Chronicles*, 64, claims that one of the girls took off her gloves while eating, thus revealing white skin. The scene at the Glasgow train station has proved to be quite elastic. Certain accepted "historical truths" associated with the event are nothing more than a series of motifs which serve to give that portion of the legend its cohesiveness. It is not known whether one of the girls' gloves fell down to reveal a white arm, a bee got under her veil, the wind blew the veil up, or if she raised her veil to scratch her face. The folk who relate this portion of the legend apparently call upon such motifs to give the story its elasticity. Historians and folklorists need to be aware of the possibility that the folk may improvise history in order to preserve its core of veracity.

9. The trial is described in the *Chronicles*, 64. The official record, found in Commonwealth Order Book 4, Barren County, KY, 1889, p. 79, contains no mention of Boles and Botts, or of John drawing a gun on an officer.

Rita Bradley

Rita Bradley earned a master's degree in communicative disorders from East Tennessee State University in 1989. She works as a speech-language pathologist at the Pine Ridge Health Care Center in Elizabethton, Tennessee. Through the years she has told her children that their ancestors "sailed on the ships from Africa and sailed on the ships of Europe and met the ships when they came ashore."

I Y'am What I Y'am

You call me Black when my skin is tan,
my daughter is golden and my son's hair is bronze.

I'm supposed to be Soul yet I love country
music, cowboy hats, boots, blue jeans and
hoedowns.

I'm proud of my African ancestry but am
sick inside at being denied my Scotch-Irish
heritage. I'm one-third Cherokee Indian,
happy about it, and look it.

I feel secure among the mountains. Nothing
is more beautiful than the nearby
ranges tipped with clouds. I love
mountain crafts, mountain people and
babbling mountain streams.

Oh for my spirit to be allowed to soar
free. How I long for full acknowledgment
as a true, intricate part of the
mountain scene.

I am here, I belong here, Appalachia is
mine and I am Appalachia's.

From *Now and Then* 3.1 (Winter 1986). Reprinted by permission of the author and *Now and Then.*

Edward J. Cabbell

Edward J. Cabbell is, in his own words, "an African-Appalachian." Born and raised in the mountain community of Eckman, West Virginia, Cabbell attended Concord College in Athens, West Virginia, and took a master's degree at Appalachian State University, becoming the first black to receive a degree in Appalachian studies. Today he is an adjunct professor at Concord College and serves on many commissions and committees related to civil rights and ethnic heritage, including the Black Appalachian Advisory Council. He is affiliated with the Highlander Research and Education Center, New Market, Tennessee, and coordinates the John Henry Festival, a celebration of the black Appalachian tradition. "Black Diamonds" is part of Cabbell's ongoing research, in which he attempts to discover and document the African-Appalachian experience.

Black Diamonds: The Search for Blacks in Appalachian Literature and Writing

Unlike white Appalachian literature, which has been discovered and rediscovered many times, black Appalachian literature has yet to be revealed and appreciated. Scholars, teachers, and writers have failed to focus on the black experience in Appalachia. When they do, they generally view the number of blacks in the southern mountains as inconsequential and treat their existence and plight as peripheral, but see them as having had relative social and economic equality. Thus, literature, the chief interpretive agent for understanding the history and culture of any region or locale, has failed adequately to explore the black Appalachian experience.

In an attempt to discover as much of the black experience in Appalachian literature as possible, I first sought, located, and identified blacks as central characters in over twenty Appalachian-related novels. Hopefully the novels selected will introduce you to an awareness and understanding of blacks in Appalachian literature.

These selected novels basically deal with violent racial relationships, juvenile fantasies, and slavery. Most of them were written by white authors and were strangely inferior and rather disappointing in comparison to these writers' other novels. Their quest for a peculiar accuracy rather than richness of imagination made most of them lack significance, depth, and force. Second-rate Faulknerian intrusions are extremely distracting in these stark and sensitive novels that produce a sense of sadness, defeat, and decay. The best-

From *Blacks in Appalachia*, ed. William Turner and Edward Cabbell, University Press of Kentucky, 1985. Reproduced by permission of the publisher.

written characters are white, although the black characters are usually full of determination, moral convictions, and exaggerated loyalties to whites in their struggles for black survival. Readers, particularly black readers, are likely to become baffled and disillusioned with the treatment of blacks in these novels.

Violent race relations is the most familiar fictional subject for black characters in Appalachian literature. In such stories we usually find an act of violence being committed against a young black male falsely accused by an angry mob of an act against the virtue of a white female. Through a series of flashbacks, the mob scene usually emerges as the best-written and most effective scene in the novel. Moreover, the mixture of "peckerwoods," aristocrats, northern-style liberals, and black victims is much more the material for Deep South literature than the literature of the southern mountains. As a result most of the novels are classified as southern rather than Appalachian.

William Nathaniel Harben was one of the first authors to use blacks as central characters in a novel based on an act of violent racial relations. In *Mam' Linda* (Harper, 1907), Harben focuses on a faithful black mammy and her "no count" son in a story of prejudice, lynching bands, politics, and romance in Georgia. A young white attorney tenaciously defends the mammy's son who is unjustly accused of murder. In doing so, he overcomes the tradition of prejudice as he fights lawlessness and outwits the lynching bands.

Almost fifty years later we find Byron Reece's *The Hawk and the Sun* (Dutton, 1955) dealing with the lynching of a lame black named Dandelion for an act he did not commit against the virtue of Miss Ella, a small southern town bookseller. The impact of the mob scene upon the citizens of the town, however, is the focus of this novel permeated with southern atmosphere.

In *Shadow of My Brothers* (Holt, 1966), Davis Grubb tells the story of a black boy who "leers" at a white woman in a grocery store and is murdered that night by her husband and police accomplices. The murderer, Loy Wilson, is revealed as a Virginia aristocrat gone to bad seed in the southern hill country.

Often these stories take on a convincing tone of reality. Indeed, some of them are true accounts. Robert Bowen's *Tall in the Sight of God* (John F. Blair, 1958) is an autobiographical account of a black family from Wilkes County, North Carolina. Elizabeth Forbush's *Savage Sundown* (Pinnacle, 1980) is based on an actual incident in northeastern Georgia in 1912 that resulted in the banishment of blacks from the area. James von Streeter also tells a true story about five black children in Tennessee in his juvenile novel *Home Is Over the Mountain* (Garrard, 1972).

Lettie Rogers' *Birthright* (Simon and Schuster, 1957) is biographical in tone. It focuses on a young and pretty teacher who is dismissed because of her stand on racial problems in a small town. Even Lisa Alther's *Original Sins* (Knopf, 1980) uses five protagonists (four white and one black) in a turgid narrative that suggests that being southern is a handicap in the South as well as in the North. The ill-fated protagonists are sketched with a biographical flair that links us with reality in a tell-all book that might be more successful as a fantasy.

Joining these accounts of searches for pride and independence in the

Appalachian South are Isabel McMeekin's two stories of her invincible Juba in *Journey Cake* (Messner, 1942) and *Juba's New Moon* (Messner, 1949). Willa Cather deals with the slave relations in the hills in her *Sapphira and the Slave Girl* (Knopf, 1940), as does John Upchurch in *The Slave Stealers* (Weybright & Talley, 1968). Jane Curry's *Daybreakers* (Harcourt, 1970) allows children (two black and one white) to discover a fantasy world outside their milltown in West Virginia.

While these novels are interesting in many ways, they do not generally reveal a perception of black life in the southern mountains in the tradition of good, solid Appalachian literature. John Ehle comes closer to this perception than any other Appalachian novelist in his portrayal of Jordan Cummings in *Move Over Mountain* (Morrow, 1957). Cummings and nearly all the rest of the characters in this perceptive story are black. Presented as a very strong and good workman but quick to anger, Cummings finds it difficult to hold a job. He desires to take his wife and two sons north but decides not to leave his home in the hills of North Carolina. This is the literary tradition that separates Appalachian literature from southern literature. Ehle goes even further with black Appalachian character theme development in *The Journey of August King* (Harper, 1971). Williamsburg, a young slave girl, is running away to the North and freedom in this novel. She meets August King, a mountain man, who is forced to confront the belief that her freedom is his freedom, too. In order to reach this conclusion, he takes a journey within himself that reveals the classic essence of race relationships in the mountain South. Even the six black novelists with Appalachian-related manuscripts reveal no larger sense of this most engaging topic. In fact, one black author does not even deal with black characters in his novel.

William Demby's *Beetlecreek* (Rinehart, 1950) and Virginia Hamilton's *M. C. Higgins, The Great* (Dell, 1974) are without doubt the best novels by blacks with black Appalachian themes. The traditional Appalachian themes of individualism and self-reliance, traditionalism, fatalism, and, to a lesser extent, fundamentalism surface vividly within these well-written novels. Demby's *Beetlecreek* is basically a character sketch of Bill Trapp, an elderly white man who lives a solitary life near the black section of Beetlecreek, West Virginia. Johnny, a black youth from Pittsburgh, introduces Bill to the people nearby. Bill's shell is cracked, and he decides to give an integrated party for the local youth. Ugly sex rumors spread after the party. Bill is led toward tragedy. This is a very good story, but strangely it lacks the significance and depth of an outstanding novel. However, Demby, born in Pittsburgh and spending his early youth in Clarksburg, West Virginia, has an impressive achievement with *Beetlecreek*.

Virginia Hamilton, an outstanding writer of juvenile fiction, provides an interesting example of black Appalachian literature in *M. C. Higgins, The Great*. This winner of the Newberry Medal and the National Book Award is a moving story. M. C. Higgins sits on a forty-foot pole near his home on Sarah's Mountain (named after a runaway slave and ancestress). Through two strangers, M. C. grows to understand that both choice and action are within his power to escape the wounds of strip mining in the rolling hills of Appalachian Ohio.

Frank Yerby, an extremely popular black writer, provides a typical Yerby account of a nineteen-year-old white girl who flees to Augusta, Georgia, from the Carolina hills when her father decides to sell her into marriage to a sixty-five-year-old man of means to pay his drinking debts. However, Yerby's *A Woman Called Fancy* (Dial 1951) does not even resemble his popular novels *The Saracen Blade, The Vixen,* and *The Foxes of Harrow.*

Jesse Hill Ford's *The Liberation of Lord Byron Jones* (Atlantic Monthly P, 1965) is a well-written but complicated story told in a complicated way from the viewpoint of too many characters. Essentially, it is a story about a black undertaker in the Tennessee hill country who is forced to divorce his wife because of her open affair with a white policeman. The best-written character in the novel is white—Oman Hedgepath, the lawyer who accepts Jones's divorce suit.

John O. Killens provides an interesting account of the legend of John Henry in his *A Man Ain't Nothing but a Man* (Little, Brown, 1975). However, even this well-written account does not seem to provide the depth and significance that this great legend deserves.

Juliette Holley, a lesser-known writer, provides an interesting account of the world as seen through the eyes of a young black boy in the coalfields of her native West Virginia in *Jamie Lemme See* (Commonwealth P, 1975). Although not a powerful story, Holley's account is well worth reading.

Prior to his death, Alex Haley was writing a novel entitled *Henning, Tennessee.* Named for his hometown, the story deals with a man raising his grandson to be a "mountain man" in Appalachia. Haley has long revealed numerous aspects of rural black life that would make fascinating material for good Appalachian literature. I sincerely hope that Margaret Walker, Sonia Sanchez, Nikki Giovanni, Ishmael Reed, Julia Fields, and Norman Jordan, all major black writers with Appalachian roots, will also choose to deal with their native southern mountains in their novels, plays, and poetry in the near future. There is a dire need for their creative expressions about this region long neglected in American ethnic and geographic literature.

Primary nonfiction steps are being taken into uncovering the general history of blacks in the southern mountains. *Blacks in Appalachia* (UP of Kentucky, 1985), coedited by William H. Turner and myself, presents a diverse group of scholars and writers and their views on various aspects of the black experience in Appalachia. Although much of the material deals with black Appalachian coal miners, the material ranges from the perspectives of Booker T. Washington and Carter G. Woodson to the studies of coal mine company towns by David A. Corbin, biracial unionism studies by Richard S. Straw, and the personal accounts by Reginald Millner and Pearl Cornett. The selected readings are quite useful in black studies as well as Appalachian studies.

Minnie Holley Barnes is writing some very interesting oral history accounts of her native southwestern Virginia through her *Glimpses of Tazewell through the Holley Heritage* (Commonwealth P, 1977). Her work joins Charles W. Cansler's *Three Generations: The Story of a Colored Family in East Tennessee* (Kingsport P, 1939) and William Lynwood Montell's *The Saga of Coe Ridge*

(U of Tennessee P, 1970) in combining local history, black history, and oral history for educational as well as entertaining reading. Nevertheless, today no comprehensive monograph has appeared of depth and significance to reveal a major insight into the essence of the black experience in Appalachia. The John Henry Memorial Foundation, based in Princeton, West Virginia, which I founded in 1969, is working very hard to remedy this situation. However, due to a lack of adequate funding our collecting and releasing of information on blacks in Appalachia has been rather sporadic. We have released a bibliography of primary and secondary sources on black Appalachia. Students in my Appalachian studies classes at Concord College (Athens, West Virginia) occasionally emerge with creative ideas and projects that include a *Black Appalachian Trivia* game. With time and increased support, I expect to see some real black diamonds emerge within the arena of black Appalachian studies.

Jo Carson

In Johnson City, Tennessee, Jo Carson learned the art of storytelling from her family of raconteurs. A poet, playwright, and essayist, Carson also writes short stories and works for children. Carson has delighted audiences across the country and in Europe with readings from her works both in person and as a commentator on National Public Radio's "All Things Considered." Carson's *Daytrips* (1989) received the Kesselring Award for best play of the year by a new playwright and has had successful runs in Los Angeles and New York. Her acclaimed *Stories I Ain't Told Nobody Yet* (1989) is a collection of performance material used in her one-woman shows. Her play, *A Preacher with a Horse to Ride* (1990), which centers on Theodore Dreiser's 1931 investigation of Kentucky coal strikes, won a Rogers L. Stevens Award in 1993 and was published in 1994. She has also written a play called *The Bear Facts,* which won an NEA Playwriting Fellowship in 1993, featuring Davy Crockett's encounter with bears. Her most recent publication is *The Great Shaking* (1994), a children's book about the New Madrid earthquakes of 1811–12.

Crows

The kitchen table had a summer setting,
Padget's chair by the far window
so he could see the cherry tree
and when the crows got thick enough,
he could pick up his double barreled gun
aim between bites of yellow squash and lima beans

and blast a few of them to hell
as he put it. Padget had no love for crows.
Not much more for children,
his own dead of accidents or bad luck,
but his brother's sons were welcome
and with those sons came children,
me among them, to wonder at the man
who shot crows during Mamie's suppers.

Lump lived there too. She was blind.
Lump was the name she said was hers,
said she had no other,
said she had been born a slave
and Padget's daddy took her in.
Said she'd carried the afterbirth
to the hogs when Padget was born.
This was knowledge gathered over several visits.
She looked old enough to have been Egyptian
which was the oldest thing I could think of then.
She lived upstairs.
I carried up her supper and iced tea.

"Lump?"
"Tell Padget not to shoot no crows this time."
Padget shot the crows because they ate his corn.
"Him and the crows ruins the cherries. Tell him
there's more crows than cherries. Tell him
there's more corn than crows. Tell him
to spread them dead crows out in his field."
It was the most she'd ever said to me.
I waited, hoping for secrets she had to know.
None came so I waited to be excused.
She turned her ancient face to the evening light.
"Don't study me."
It was the closest I ever came to Egypt.
"Them that studies old age too close
will live to see it."

From *Appalachian Journal* 14.4, © *Appalachian Journal*/Appalachian State University. Used with permission.

R. T. Smith

R. T. Smith is Alumni Writer-in-Residence at Auburn University and coeditor of the *Southern Humanities Review*. He grew up in Georgia and North Carolina and attended Georgia Tech, the University of North Carolina at Charlotte, and Appalachian State University. Among several volumes of his poetry are *The Names of Trees* (1991) and *The Cardinal Heart* (1991). In 1987 he was presented the Zoe Kincaid Brock Award for *Birch-Light*, and in 1988 the Alabama Governor's Award for achievement by an artist. He is keenly interested in the poetry of Ireland, having studied in that country and having had poetry published in *Poetry Ireland Review* and *The Irish Times*.

Yonosa House

She stroked molten tones
from the heart-carved maple dulcimer.
My grandma did.
She sat like a noble sack of bones
withered within coarse skin,
rocking to snake or corn tunes,
music of passing seasons.
She sang the old songs.

Her old woman's Tuscarora uncut hair
hung like waxed flax ready to spin
till she wove it to night braids,
and two tight-knotted ropes
lay like lanyards on her shoulders.
On my young mind she wove
the myths of the race
in fevered patterns, feathery colors:
Sound of snow, kiss of rock,
the feel of bruised birch bark,
the call of the circling hawk.

Her knotted hands showing slow blue rivers
jerked nervously through cornbread frying,
pressed fern patterns on butter pats,
brewed sassafras tea in the hearth.
She wore her lore and old age home.

From *From the High Dive*, Water Mark Press, 1983. Reprinted by permission of the author.

They buried Yonosa in a doeskin skirt,
beads and braids, but featherless.
I cut hearts on her coffin lid,
wind-slain maple like the dulcimer.
The mountain was holy enough for Yonosa.
We kept our promise and raised no stone.
She sank like a root to be red Georgia clay.
No Baptist churchyard caught her bones.
I thank her hands when the maple leaves turn,
hear her chants in the thrush's song.

Don Johnson

See volume 1, chapter 3, for biography.

Raymond Pierce's Vietnamese Wife

couldn't understand milk gravy,
how her mother-in-law could brown
biscuits, keeping their insides white
and flaky, and her family transform
them into sodden lumps of dough
and warm liquid. She could not
fathom the distance and space
in her new life: vacant acres
of land between towns,
the squat brick ranches
shadowed by empty-windowed farmhouses
abandoned and allowed to fall.

Afternoons, she would cry
on the floor of the walk-in closet,
her husband's shirts crowded
along the wall like ghostly applicants
for visas. When he found her there
he couldn't understand the tears.

From *Watauga Drawdown*, Overmountain Press, 1990. Reprinted by permission of the author.

She had so much, now. In 'Nam
her people slept and ate in a room
no bigger than that closet.

When he drove her out to the lake,
he pointed at blank water, saying,
"I was born there, a hundred feet
down," thinking she would not
understand a valley flooded
so there would be no more floods.
But she did understand, as she
stared at the water's sheen
baring no hint of village, only sky
and the deep mountain of green.

Margaret Ripley Wolfe

Margaret Ripley Wolfe, a native of Hawkins County, Tennessee, is professor of history at East Tennessee State University, where she has taught
since 1969. She completed her B.S. and M.A. degrees at ETSU and subsequently earned her doctorate in American history at the University of Kentucky, where she was a Haggin Fellow during 1972–73. An American social
historian by training, much of her research has focused on the South and
Southern Appalachia; her work has found a wide range of scholarly and
professional outlets. Among her publications is *Kingsport, Tennessee: A
Planned American City* (1987), which challenges some commonly held notions about Appalachia. She is also the author of *Daughters of Canaan: A
Saga of Southern Women* (1995). A nationally and internationally known
scholar, listed in *Who's Who of American Women,* Dr. Wolfe's ancestry is
intricately tied to the Appalachian region. "Some of my relatives," she quips,
"arrived in East Tennessee more than two hundred years ago, and others
of them were already here waiting." She resides in Hawkins County, with
her husband and daughter, on a farm that her family has owned for more
than a century.
    Anyone wishing to review the extensive notes of the following article
should see the original article, referenced below.

Aliens in Southern Appalachia, 1900–1920:
The Italian Experience in Wise County, Virginia

The development of bituminous coal mining in Southern Appalachia coincided with the arrival in the United States of millions of immigrants from Southern and Eastern Europe. Before 1900 operators had depended on native whites and blacks for their labor force. Between 1900 and 1907, however, "new" immigrants in considerable numbers entered the coalfields of Alabama, Virginia, and West Virginia. According to a report of the Dillingham Commission, foreign-born workers represented three-tenths of the labor force in these states during this period. The South Italian was the largest ethnic group, comprising over 30 percent of the foreign-born and more than 8 percent of the total number of all employees. The possibilities for Italian laborers in this area of the country had been recognized as early as 1906 by Gino Speranza, an American-Italian lawyer with the Society for the Protection of Italian Immigrants in New York City. He had remarked on the "unusually good opportunity to study the question of Italian non-farming labor in the South" and urged finding "means for preventing forced labor among Italians in the South without closing a market which seems particularly well adapted for the Italian laborer." The Italian immigrants in the coal camps of Wise County, Virginia, from 1900 to 1920, offer a microcosm for the study of foreign labor in Southern Appalachia.

The principal coal mines in Wise County in 1900 were around Big Stone Gap. Because of the mountainous terrain, the area had been severely retarded in industrial and urban development, and the native culture survived on a meager agricultural base. Prior to the establishment of the coal camps, Wise County had a sparse population. Mine operators were confronted not only by a shortage of native laborers, but those that they employed were poor in quality and uninterested in underground work. The operators claimed that a generation earlier the residents of the county had been "at least two hundred years behind the civilization of the more densely populated sections of the United States." The Stonega Company, the largest mining operation in Wise County, with home offices in Philadelphia, therefore began recruiting foreign labor, newly arrived in the country, or native labor elsewhere in the United States.

The first aliens to enter the Big Stone Gap field were Hungarians from the Pocahontas Field of McDowell, Mercer, Mingo, and Logan counties in West Virginia and Tazewell County in Virginia. They found employment with the Virginia Coal and Iron Company (later the Stonega Coal and Coke Company) at Stonega in 1896. Within the next few years Italians, mostly from southern Italy, followed the Hungarians into the area, but never seriously challenged the dominance of that group among foreign-born elements. The Immigration Commission reported that the first Italians in the Big

From *Virginia Magazine of History and Biography* 87.4 (1979): 455–72. Reprinted by permission of the author and publisher.

Stone Gap field arrived at Norton in 1900 and entered the mines in considerable numbers around 1902. By 1907, 650 were at work in and about the mines. That particular study also indicated that Italian men were migratory and that only a small proportion had families with them. With the high degree of transience in the coal camps, thousands of different Italians may have worked the mines of Wise County from 1900 to 1920.

Government records, probably generally correct, contain some errors. Italians had actually arrived in Wise County before 1900, a fact recorded by the native Appalachians who noted their lawlessness. The *Big Stone Gap Post* reported in May 1898 that an Italian named Rossa had been a participant in a Sunday morning shootout at Stonega that left one man dead and five or six wounded. By the end of 1900, this same newspaper referred to "the Italian Colony" at Stonega and accused Italians there of being the aggressors in a shooting scrape on Christmas Day, resulting in the death of one man and the injury of another.

Italians with the Stonega Company experienced exceptional treatment compared to foreign laborers employed by some companies in the Southern Appalachians. There is no evidence indicating that this particular company abused the foreigners in its service; on the contrary, company officials made every reasonable effort to keep earning as well as working and living conditions at a level to retain foreign labor. Housing received perpetual attention. Stonega officials not only concerned themselves with the original construction but also tried to maintain and improve dwellings. One candid official reported that

> Twenty-three box houses located at what is called 'Slabtown,' in the upper part of Osaka town, were remodeled and set on brick foundations in November and December 1915. These houses were always unfit for habitation, and only part of them were occupied by a low class of labor previous to remodeling. The houses as finished, with fences and garden plots, are particularly attractive to the foreigners, and this has been made a district for foreign miners working in the Roda mines, and is popular with this class of labor.

Stonega officials also displayed a concern for the health and safety of miners and their families that was unique for the area and time. Not only did they maintain a company hospital at Stonega staffed by a well-trained company doctor, sometimes assisted by other physicians, but they also established mine-safety programs. In 1915, according to the annual report, "The Engineering Department . . . with the assistance of the Medical Department has advanced the cause of 'Safety First' this year." There had been "Complete isolation of contagious diseases, guarding of electric circuits and moving parts of machinery, posting of warning notices and a thorough training of First Aid Teams at all plants." Race entered into the safety crusade, as the company had nineteen white first-aid teams and three colored. The latter existed for the benefit of blacks, and all whites, including foreigners, were to be saved by the other nineteen.

Education likewise received attention. Stonega town, established by 1897, had schools in operation as early as the 1898–99 school term. The *Big Stone Gap Post* reported in June 1899 that the company had provided the teacher's salary for a six-month supplemental term at the white school and paid the entire salary of the teacher at the black school. By August of the same year, the white school building had been enlarged by an additional room to meet the demands of an increasing population. The company financed all the improvements, relying on the school board of Wise County to reimburse it when its treasury would permit. According to the *Post* reporter, the addition to the building was "a decided improvement" and gave it the appearance of an "academy."

Recognizing the religious needs of foreign workers as well as more mundane requirements for existence, the company arranged for Catholic priests to live in the camps and constructed houses for the clergy and churches for the congregation. In 1906 Charles G. Duffy, a Stonega official, reminded the abbot at St. Bernard, Alabama, of the company's efforts after the Reverend Bernard Menges had ordered a priest popular with the Hungarians to another locality. "Now this would be a hardship on our coalfield, and unfair to the companies because of the great shortage of labor in this locality," he lamented. "The Coal Companies throughout this region, and particularly the Stonega Company, were the pioneers in encouraging church work in this part of Virginia. The new house for the Priest, which is just about completed, is a very nice one, and better than the original plan called for." The abbot responded within two weeks, explained his action, and concluded that the company's interests would not suffer. As an apparent afterthought, Menges penciled the following: "The spiritual interests of the congregation will also be taken care of." He also promised Duffy that the popular priest, Father Anthony Hoch, would "use his best influence among the Hungarians at Stonega to have them remain where they were."

In spite of the efforts of the Stonega Company to secure and retain foreign labor, which were exemplary, it enjoyed no long-term success and incurred considerable expense. Newly recruited labor often abandoned the Stonega mines once they were in the area and found employment with rival operators to avoid repaying transportation charges. Even those who stayed long enough to enjoy the benevolent paternalism of the company could not be retained. The high degree of transience in the camps impeded the development of the type of group identity necessary to sustain a sense of community, and the limited opportunities for upward mobility discouraged individual adaptation.

The outbreak of World War I further aggravated the circumstances confronting the Stonega Company and other firms that had come to rely on unskilled immigrant laborers. First, the entry of the United States into the war necessitated enlarging the military forces and expanding industry, thereby intensifying the already-existing labor shortage in the country. Second, hostilities in Europe virtually halted emigration, depriving American industrialists of their principal nondomestic source. Nonetheless, officials of the Stonega Company reported continual efforts to secure foreigners. Desperate for a better quality of labor, after relying during World War I on illiterate

Alabama blacks, who had "little interest or pride in their employment," they sent a representative through Ohio and Michigan in 1920 searching for foreign-born workers, but without success.

Although coal operators were primarily responsible for the presence of Italians in Southern Appalachia, railroad contractors lured others to the region; noteworthy in this endeavor was George L. Carter of the Carolina, Clinchfield and Ohio Railroad. In 1902, Carter and his associates purchased the property of the Ohio Railway and Charleston Railway Company and organized the South and Western Railway Company, specifically planned to implement the development of Southwest Virginia and Eastern Kentucky coalfields. The completion of the road, known as the Clinchfield, marked a new era in railroad construction. Where other roads had gone around mountain barriers, the Clinchfield cut through them. Throughout almost its entire length, from Spartanburg, South Carolina, to Elkhorn City, Kentucky, it traversed a rugged mountain country, cutting through the intervening ridges with a high standard of construction and easy grades which fit it for the carriage of immense tonnage. This remarkable engineering feat owed its success largely to Italian immigrant labor. Apparently all of the contractors, but definitely the Meadows Company and the Spruce Pine Carolina Company, employed labor agents, some Italians, who routed new arrivals in northern port cities to jobs in the southern mountains. They procured thousands of Italians, many just off the boat, unable to speak English, anxious for work, and ignorant of their destination when they fell in with the agents. When the railroad was completed, some of the Italians who survived the construction moved into the coalfields of southwestern Virginia and eastern Kentucky; others made their way to northern cities.

The Italian experience with the construction of the Clinchfield Railroad represented a somber chapter in the annals of Southern Appalachian history. Destruction of the Clinchfield contract labor records leaves much of the story recounted only in the myths and legends of the mountains. Nonetheless, enough concrete facts remain to provide convincing testimony of the cruelties and injustices suffered by Italian laborers. Some evidence survives in the form of unmarked graves along the railroad right-of-way and in scattered churchyards paralleling the construction route; the most convincing, however, survives in diplomatic correspondence.

On June 20, 1906, Italian Consul G. C. Montagna lodged a formal protest with Secretary of State Elihu Root, complaining of the harsh treatment of Italian laborers by the Spruce Pine Carolina Company at Marion, North Carolina. The listed abuses included using armed guards, forcing Italians to work underground when they had contracted to work above ground, whipping them, compelling them to buy all supplies at the company store thus securing the return of all the wages, and withholding mail from families of the employees. Montagna filed this protest after Italians who had escaped from the company sought the help of the consul in securing back pay and the possessions they had left behind. Montagna had then commissioned an investigation by Gino Speranza, who was aided by the Italian Consular agent in Charleston, South Carolina, and United States District Attorney Alfred Holton. Their findings supported the complaints of approximately two hundred Italians who escaped, leaving behind about fifteen hundred of their countrymen.

The incident that immediately preceded the diplomatic protest, a bloody row, occurred on May 14, 1906, at Marion. Local law enforcement officials in the employ of the Spruce Pine Carolina Company organized a posse and launched an armed attack on the Italian camp, leaving two dead and five severely wounded. Nine uninjured Italians were jailed. They were eventually tried, found innocent, and released. The leaders of the attack were indicted for manslaughter, and warrants were issued against some agents of the Carolina Company. After several conferences between Italian officials and representatives of the South and Western Railroad (early name for the Clinchfield), the company agreed to pay indemnities to the heirs of the dead and all the Italians who were innocent victims of the incident on May 14. The company also promised to dismiss and never again employ those agents who had been guilty of ill-treatment of Italian laborers.

The outrageous cruelties by the Spruce Pine Carolina Company did not repeat themselves elsewhere on the construction line and did not represent official policy of Carter and his associates. Speranza, in fact, did not want the South closed to Italian laborers. "Indeed," he said, "I personally should like to have Italians sent to work for the Carolina Company especially in its Clinchport (Virginia) section where conditions are almost ideal." This is not to say that there were not other isolated incidents of cruelty by inhumane labor bosses. Working conditions varied from one location to another on the route, depending on the contractor, as did the reception of Italians by the native mountaineers.

The environment of railroad work camps was uncertain, the nature of the work taking a fierce toll in human lives. Sophisticated construction machinery had not come into use, and, except for blasting and some mule-drawn carts and drag pans, picks and shovels cut the road through the mountains. Internal fights also cost lives. Reid Queen, Sr., Little Switzerland, North Carolina, who worked on the Clinchfield construction project, recalled one altercation among Italians. Fifteen or so men had hired one of their countrymen to prepare their meals. One evening they returned from work to find him drunk and no signs of supper. An explosion of Italian temperament resulted in the execution of the cook, who was tied to a tree and shot.

Not only did Italian laborers in Southern Appalachia suffer abuses at the hands of their American employers, but their tragedy was further complicated by their own countrymen, who sometimes delivered them into the hands of harsh taskmasters. There is no doubt that the padrone system operated in Southern Appalachia. The Spruce Pine Carolina Company employed Jim Mazzone to recruit Italians in New York. Mazzone, however, became irritated with his associates when they failed to provide transportation funds for him, and he emerged as a leader of the discontented Italians at Marion,

North Carolina. Gino Speranza also found the padrone in operation in West
Virginia. Responding to complaints of Italians there, he visited Kelly's
Camp in Kanawha County. Kelly, an Italian contractor despite his name,
had vowed "by the national tricolor," in a letter to the Italian consul in New
York, that there were no Italians in his area of West Virginia. Speranza, after
walking railroad ties and riding a mule to reach the isolated camp, found
several Italians at work. The foreman, Kelly's partner, who greeted him was
a "Neapolitan of splendid physique." Italians in West Virginia were held by
force after transportation had been advanced; beatings had occurred and
workers had disappeared mysteriously.

Records of labor abuses during these years in Southern Appalachia remained
to overshadow the benevolent paternalism of such organizations as the Stonega
Company. Even the most humane employers shared in the greater tragedy, however, for railroad construction and mining development at the turn of the twentieth century marked the beginning of capitalistic rape of Southern Appalachia
by northern investors. Just as the northern capitalists exploited the mineral resources of Appalachia, they also exploited its natives and its adopted children.
Interestingly enough, the transplanted southern Italians and the natives of
Southern Appalachia possessed certain common characteristics: they were
victims of geography and related political developments; they seemed to
share a penchant for violence and lawlessness; they engaged in similar economic pursuits; they lagged behind their national counterparts in educational opportunities; and a resemblance existed between their general levels
of sociological development. The great irony lay, however, in the fact that
South Italian immigrants had broken the bonds of a retarded society, migrated to America in search of opportunity, and been lured to Southern Appalachia, only to find themselves in a locale exhibiting many of the characteristics from which they had fled.

The South Italians who filtered into the Appalachians from northern ports
of entry found themselves in a rugged mountainous area not unlike their native region. The political remoteness of rural eastern Kentucky and southwestern Virginia resembled the second-class status of southern Italy, dominated by the more prosperous, highly industrialized North. Southern Italy,
under the monarchy, according to one historian, "received treatment more
appropriate for a colony or appendage." In the 1880s, Baron Sidney Sonnino
had reminded parliament that the government had not made any significant
move to improve living and working conditions for southern Italians. After
the turn of the century, diplomat-historian Luigi Villari noted in a published
work: "The North has made a great advance in wealth, trade, and education,
while the South is almost stationary."

The native of the Southern Appalachians was as helpless in the face of
encroaching northern capitalism and the related economic and political developments as the South Italian under the monarchy. Coal company officials
recognized the cultural retardation and victimized the mountaineer. Harry
M. Caudill, in his "biography" of eastern Kentucky, noted that outsiders

who followed the railroads into the Cumberland Plateau viewed the mountaineer as "a sort of latter-day border pioneer, summed up in the expression 'our contemporary ancestors.'" Caudill observed that the mountaineer still lived in a manner "not strikingly different from that of his forefathers forty years after the first settlements." Agents for coal companies who persuaded the natives to sign over mineral rights to their land exploited this weakness. Caudill described such a transaction:

> On one side of the rude table sat an astute trader, more often than not a graduate of a fine college and a man experienced in the large business world. He was thoroughly aware of the implications of the transaction and of the immense wealth which he was in the process of acquiring. Across the table on a puncheon bench sat a man and a woman out of a different age. Still remarkably close to the frontier of a century before, neither of them possessed more than the rudiments of an education.

Given these circumstances, the coal company officials likewise were able to impose their political will in local, state, and congressional elections.

In view of the political and economic subjugation of South Italians and Southern Appalachian mountaineers, it was not surprising that locally they gloried in a savage individualism that often spent itself in lawlessness and violence. In Southern Appalachia the lawless element of native mountaineers and Italian immigrants constituted a small minority of the population, but often their deeds were so flamboyant that they received disproportionate attention. Well known were the myths, legends, and some of the facts of Italian criminality in the mother country and in American cities. Less well known, perhaps, were such deeds in remote rural and small-town America. Local journalists in Wise County, Virginia, celebrated the shootings and knifings in the Italian colony at Stonega around the turn of the century and noted with delight a somewhat unique occurrence in 1904. On a payday in January, two Italians shared a keg of beer. The resulting merriment led to the disfigurement of one when the other attempted to carve a map of Italy on his head. In the Virginia-Tennessee state-line town of Bristol, bordering on the southwestern Virginia coalfields, newspapermen likewise observed the lawless nature of Italians. They reported in 1908 that Mike Scarpina, an interpreter and restaurant owner, was arraigned for carrying a concealed weapon. He pleaded guilty and paid a find of $25.00 and court costs of $9.60. Bristol newspapermen also followed the activities of Italians as far away as Memphis and reported a dreaded Black Hand incident there in 1909.

Local journalists who took delight in publicizing the lawlessness of the wild-spirited Latins reported with equal alacrity the same trait in their fellow mountaineers. Before capitalism unleashed itself in full fury, law and order had languished; and even the coal operators were helpless in curbing many of the bloody feuds and skirmishes. One native reminisced that gunplay had been common on the main street of Norton, Virginia, where glass chimneys on street lights had to be replaced about once a week because they were usually shot out on Saturday nights. In 1889 the town had boasted one church and eight saloons. A reliable merchant reported in 1895 that a gang of robbers had been preying on wagoners en route to the railroad station at Norton. The editor of the *Big Stone Gap Post* added: "Pound Gap has always been a bad place; over a dozen people have been killed there since the war . . . moonshine whiskey is plentiful on both sides of the state line at one dollar per gallon." Two weeks later the editor asked how long this situation would be tolerated. Not even the lives of law officers were safe in some areas of Southern Appalachia, as evidenced by the murder of Tom Osborne, sergeant of the Norton police, by a black man on July 15, 1895. The area newspaper recorded the circumstances: "The colored people of the town were having a dance in the suburbs, and Osborne had gone there to see that the peace was preserved." The murderer was not apprehended until eight days later. Even as late as the 1920s, ambushes were commonplace and attempts on law enforcement officials continued. In August 1923, an unknown "bushwhacker" blasted away at a Norton policeman while he was waiting for a car reportedly loaded with moonshine whiskey. The bullet passed through this hat, missing his scalp by less than an inch. The officer returned to town and changed his hat, apparently undisturbed by his experience.

The Appalachian natives and Italian immigrants not only shared a lawless nature but also had followed similar economic pursuits prior to their exposure to capitalism. The natives of Wise County were pre-industrial, small-scale merchants and farmers before the introduction of modern industry. In eastern Kentucky, according to Caudill, "From all over the plateau there trooped in motley gangs of rawboned mountaineers with their bonneted wives and barefoot children, to seek jobs in the mines. Initially most of them were sharecroppers whose lessening returns from the soil had brought them to a point only a few jumps ahead of starvation." Of the foreign-born who settled in the southern United States, the Dillingham Commission reported that nearly three-fourths of the total had been engaged in farming or farm labor prior to emigration. Of 1,072 South Italians investigated, 78.4 percent had been involved in farming or farm labor, 5.1 in mining, 5.3 in general labor, 1.1 in manufacturing, 7.2 in hand trades, and 2.9 in other occupations.

Estimated agrarian or agrarian-based income of Appalachian natives before the introduction of northern capitalism and that of South Italians around the time of the mass migration to America suggested the relative poverty of both groups in comparison to their more prosperous countrymen. Some wretched dirt farmers in the southern mountains harvested no more than ten to fifteen bushels of corn per acre. A census of agriculture conducted as late as 1930 revealed that the Appalachian region contained the highest percentage of low-income farms in the nation, some returning annual incomes of less than $600. An official report by the Italian government indicated that the annual income for the head of a household possessing a small house with a piece of land might be $273, while his expenses amounted to $295. According to a popular Italian saying, "If it had not been for immigration, we in Italy would have had to resort to violence in order to make a living."

The South Italians who had the vitality to emigrate to America renounced their traditional agrarianism, as did Appalachian natives who left their small farms for the coal camps. Nonetheless, it was doubtful that either group substantially bettered the relative quality of their existence when they entered the service of the coal barons. In the coal and coke industries of Virginia and West Virginia, employees fell into three general categories—miners, coke drawers, and company men. Pay for miners and coke drawers depended on piece work, while all other employees, inside or outside, received a stated wage per day. Daily earnings in the South for a majority of native whites, blacks, and South Italians amounted to between $2.00 and $2.50 per day. Steady employment depended on generally good economic conditions. The average annual income of 230 foreign-born male heads of families in Virginia and West Virginia in the decade after 1900 stood at $500; South Italians, $456. Furthermore, the remoteness of the camps from cities limited the opportunities of foreign-born wives to supplement the family income by working as domestics. The Italians who settled in southwestern Virginia were employed mainly as coke drawers and outside laborers, with very few in the mines because of their fear of the dangers associated with underground work—which speaks well for their instinctive intelligence, a trait they shared with native Appalachians "who looked with disdain and distrust at anything they did not understand."

Whatever the advantages of instinct, a significant minority of native Americans and Italians in Wise County lacked many of the benefits of formal education. The census of 1910 revealed that 15.4 percent of the native white male population of voting age was illiterate, 20.5 of the foreign-born white, and 34.0 of the black. This report did not provide a breakdown by national group. Ten years later the situation of the foreign-born and blacks had further deteriorated. The efforts of the coal companies clearly had benefited the native whites and either had impeded or stabilized the condition of other groups. In 1920, 11.9 percent of the native white males, aged twenty-one and over, were illiterate; 32.6 of the foreign-born; and 37.9 of the black.

The significance of these figures is subject to speculation. Several possibilities should be considered. While the coal companies supported compulsory education and longer school terms, constructed school buildings, and hired teachers, it might be assumed that their efforts were directed more toward native whites than the foreign-born and blacks. Existing evidence indicates, however, that opportunities were not denied these groups. In Stonega, the Virginia Iron and Coal Company paid substantial percentages of the salaries for teachers and erected a modern school building for whites. Blacks, properly segregated according to the standards of the time, had their own school staffed wholly at company expense. Officials of this company argued for longer school terms, and in May 1902 could boast the first nine-month school term in Wise County. A year later, they expressed regret when the state legislature failed to muster the votes to enact a compulsory education bill and cited a statement by the Virginia superintendent of public instruction that not 10 percent of the children in mining districts attended school, "growing up in ignorance to be a future menace to society and the state." At the same time, according to Caudill, "the overwhelming majority of the people possessed little concept of the role of learning in the building and nurturing of civilization." Parents prided themselves on their accomplishment if they kept their children in school through the eighth grade.

Mobility and alienation may provide further explanation for the rising illiteracy of blacks and foreign-born. Those who benefited from educational opportunities may have fled the mountains, leaving behind the less able and the more recent arrivals. Immigrant and black parents may have believed that their economic situation prevented them from educating their children or that the established society scorned them. Natives often ridiculed the speech of the foreign-born and pretended that they could not understand them when they attempted to converse in English. Under such circumstances, parents may have found it easier to keep their children at home. Whatever the explanation for the rising illiteracy among foreign-born and blacks, the disparity in literacy between native whites and foreign-born was not nearly so great in 1910 as a decade later.

Physically drained by the difficult labor and struggling to eke out an existence, immigrants could hardly be expected on concentrate on intellectual pursuits. Gino Speranza found a seventeen-year-old Italian orphan in Kanawha County, West Virginia, whose penmanship was unusually good. The youth volunteered that he had completed the third grade in Italy and added, "I used to write well, but shoveling makes my hand shake." Labor and living conditions for immigrants in Wise County, Virginia, although difficult, appeared to have been generally superior tho those in West Virginia at that particular time.

Prior to the establishment of company towns in Wise County, public education there had lagged behind the progressive areas in this country and was comparable with that in Abruzzi and Molise. One observer, traveling in Italy, commented on "narrow, dark, damp rooms, without water or toilets . . . the pupils exposed to the bitter mountain winds because the windows lack panes." Such conditions were not unheard of in Appalachia at mid-twentieth century and were undoubtedly more common at the beginning of the century. In 1960 Caudill spoke at an eighth-grade commencement in a coal-camp school. "The seven graduates," he wrote, "received their diplomas in the dilapidated two-room building which had sheltered two generations of their forebears. A shower sent a little torrent of water through the ancient roof onto one of the scarred desks. The worn windows rattled in their frames and the paper decorations which had been prepared by the seventh graders fluttered in drafts admitted by the long-unpainted walls."

Education has been viewed by sociologists and historians as one means of facilitating assimilation and upward mobility. If this process remained slow in Southern Appalachia, and other opportunities were likewise lacking, then northern urban environments were more favorable for assimilation than rural and small-town southern settings. Most Italians who took up residence in American cities developed a group consciousness, formed benevolent societies and clubs, and forged a sense of community. This resulted in their adjustment to new conditions and their subsequent social and geographical mobility out of the tenement districts. If contemporary sociological studies of South Italians and mountaineers of Southern Appalachia have any applicability to past generations, the natives encountered by Italian immigrants to Southern Appalachia between 1900 and 1920 were not unlike countrymen that they had left behind in Italy. Edward C. Banfield, in his study of a poverty-stricken South Italian village during the early 1950s, found the peasants tradition-bound, fatalistic, family oriented, and victimized by *la miseria.* He contended that the appalling conditions there could be explained largely "by the inability of the villagers to act together for the common good or, indeed, for any end transcending the immediate, material interest of the nuclear family." Jack E. Weller, basing his observations on thirteen years of residence as an outsider, identified remarkably similar characteristics of the Southern Appalachian natives. He pointed to individualism, traditionalism, fatalism, and family orientation. According to Weller, "The members of a family . . . are bound to one another by ties of emotional dependence which tend to increase insecurity. In a sense, the family is not so much a mutually supporting group, in which each member gives himself for the other, as it is a group in which each member demands support from the others." Assuming that Italians who migrated from southern Italy had been motivated by a drive to escape hopeless conditions, they could hardly be expected to tarry long in a region that suffered from the same backwardness.

Apparently the Italians who remained in Appalachia assimilated without difficulty. Few in number, they developed no exaggerated sense of group consciousness and, therefore, posed no obvious threat to the mountaineers. Instead their attitudes blended with the pervasive mountain mentality, which in turn helped to bind them all to conditions of poverty. Given the significance of family ties to Italian aliens prior to emigration and the role played by the family unit and ethnic community in assimilation into American society, some effort must be made to assess these factors in reference to Italians in Wise County. Records of baptisms, deaths, and marriages, maintained by Catholic priests at Sacred Heart in Stonega from 1900 to 1920, while leaving much to be desired, nonetheless offered some interesting insights. This congregation represented the largest community of Catholic immigrants in Wise County during this period. Several Italian family units lived in Wise County; most married adults had entered into their contracts before they came into the area; intermarriage with other ethnic groups, native and foreign, was not unheard of, but most of the Italians married within their own community; and very few deaths, natural or accidental, occurred during this period among the Italians who were affiliated with this congregation, suggesting that the incidence of industrial and mining fatalities was not disproportionate for this ethnic group.

Although the Italians who maintained their ties with Catholicism may have been exceptional, their lives revealed a degree of group consciousness. Marriage and baptismal records showed no concrete evidence of any Italian female having married a non-Italian male between 1900 and 1920. Italian males, however, married native Appalachian females, and some had married native Americans from other parts of the country before coming to Appalachia. The Italian male influence in such unions was evident, the children being baptized in the church of their fathers even when the mothers were Protestant. A few families forged close ties, brothers of one family marrying sisters from another and Catholic Italians becoming godparents for each other's children. When deaths occurred, the Italian community felt duty-bound to bury its own—often in its segregated cemeteries.

Italian family ties and some measure of group consciousness can be documented, but the degree of sophistication in Wise County hardly compared with such developments in northern urban ethnic communities. Furthermore, the Italian experience in the coal camps of Wise County was more likely to foster such developments, minor as they were, than that of their counterparts in isolated areas of West Virginia and in the railroad construction camps throughout Southern Appalachia. Italians in this region of the United States were not able to develop political influence between 1900 and 1920 or protect their personal rights. Instead they were forced, by their sheer helplessness, to depend on Italian aid societies in large northern cities and the Italian consular agents.

Although the native whites and the Italians shared the experience of hardships and certain cultural characteristics, extreme differences existed in the areas of religion and ethnicity. The Italians who came to Wise County broke the bonds of a highly formalized Catholicism. Furthermore, because of their relative numerical weakness, they did not possess the advantage of a neighborhood Italian Catholic church. Those who continued to practice the old religion had at their disposal the services of Benedictine priests from St. Bernard's Abbey, Cullman, Alabama, but many of these priests were Germans who directed their principal attention to the more numerous Hungarian immigrants. The Reverend Clarence Meyer, who worked in the Appalachian coalfields during the 1920s, reported that, although "there was not much formalism in the profession of their faith as the opportunity to practice their faith formally was limited," Italians still "considered it a must to have their children baptized and to marry and be buried in a Catholic rite." The spirit of the frontier evinced itself in religion as practiced in the mountains. One priest in Wise County entered the following in his baptismal records: "Child was baptized in woods/ Mile above Appalachia (town)/ Had no time to take name/ Waving to the train coming/ Received name on the 17th of December 1904."

Coupled with the breaking of ties to a highly ritualistic church, Italians found themselves surrounded by rock-ribbed Protestant fundamentalists, mostly Baptists and Methodists, who considered themselves the elect, caring little for the fine delineations between other religious groups. Father Ambrose Reger, one of the priests who worked in the mountains, caught the spirit of the Protestant attitude toward Catholics as revealed in the following: "Some Catholic miners had come to Coalport (Kentucky), and one of them asked a native whether there were any Catholics in Middlesboro. The good man said he didn't know for sure, but wouldn't be surprised if there were—Middlesboro being such a tough town."

The difference in religion between natives and immigrants represented no small matter, but different ethnic backgrounds, and all that that meant, loomed as a more serious problem for the newcomers. Natives of Appalachia prided themselves on their English and Scotch-Irish ancestry and on their peculiar kind of culture molded and perpetuated in the remote mountain valleys. Open hostilities flared when Italian laborers entered the region, including such brutal incidents as that at Marion, North Carolina, and those in the hollows of West Virginia. That these episodes did not repeat themselves in Wise County should be attributed to the general concern of company operators for the well-being of their employees and the fact that Italians were so few that natives did not view them as a threat. Nonetheless, the natives, whatever their class, considered themselves superior to the newcomers by virtue of birth and long residence in the area. Italian immigrants or other newcomers were not allowed to forget that they were aliens in a strange land.

Discrimination against foreigners in Wise County and in Southwest Virginia and East Tennessee was often subtle, characterized by snide remarks about lawlessness and the inferiority of the newcomers. The editor of the Johnson City, Tennessee, *Comet*, endorsing the efforts of the Carolina, Clinchfield and Ohio Railroad, which was involved in a crusade to return native southerners to their birthplaces after having used Italian labor to lay the tracks over which they could be transported, voiced prevailing sentiments: "The foreigner is all right. Frequently he makes a good citizen and leaves behind him a family of strong, good American people. But we have a hankering and a yearning for our own, the men and women born in our own air, from our own soil and of our own stock."

The generalization that southerners disliked blacks as a race but liked them as individuals might well be paraphrased to explain the Southern Appalachian attitude toward Italian immigrants. The *Big Stone Gap Post*, the same newspaper that in the 1920s carried an editorial favoring restricting immigration and supporting the Ku Klux Klan, printed a front-page obituary for Tony Nard on December 5, 1923. Nard had lived on a small farm near Big Stone Gap for the past twenty-five years. As eulogized, "He was a familiar character in and around Big Stone Gap where his honest dealing and devoted friendship won for himself and family many friends in this section." Another immigrant, Colisco Francisco Anatonio, who worked as a laborer on the Clinchfield construction project, settled at Ross Camp Ground, a farming community near Kingsport, Tennessee. Clipse, renamed by the local postmaster, stood only five feet, a portly man with strong features. He became an asset to the community, where he was affectionately known to some and derisively to others as "Frank Tally." Local farmers sought him as a laborer because of his reputation as a builder of good, strong fences. Yet his children sometimes suffered the taunts of their classmates.

The desire of Italians to escape a backward society is evident in their emigration from their native country. Their relative retardation as pre-industrial people in an industrial world, and their similarities to and differences from the natives of Southern Appalachia, shaped their experience in Virginia from 1900 to 1920. The Italians found themselves caught in the vacuum of a cultural clash, as northern capitalism crept over the remote mountain valleys. In a progressive sense, the concept of northern capitalism represented a superior cultural phenomenon when compared to the pre-industrial, agrarian orientation of Appalachian natives and Italian immigrants. The appearance of northern capitalism in Southern Appalachia made native mountaineers short-term beneficiaries and long-time victims. The present-mindedness, individualism, and poverty-produced fatalism of the local people left them virtually helpless to contend with the forces of modernization. Although the personal characteristics of the natives of Appalachia matched many of those which have been identified in Southern Italian society, they did not mold the lives of Italian immigrants who rose above the circumstances of their birth to seek better lives elsewhere. Although Italian immigrants sometimes suffered abuses and injustices in Southern Appalachia, they had the presence of mind to defend themselves even if they were dependent on the Italian consulate and northern immigrant aid societies. Failing to develop a high degree of group consciousness in the southern mountains, they nonetheless, as individuals, rejected in America a society remarkably similar to that in Europe from which they had escaped.

Amy Tipton Gray

A native of Johnson City, Tennessee, Amy Tipton Gray received her B.S. and M.S. at East Tennessee State University. She is currently the coordinator of the Writing Center at Caldwell Community College in Hudson, North Carolina, where she teaches classes in math, the arts, and country music history. Her poems have appeared in magazines such as *Now and Then*. In 1988 Gray's poem "Hillbilly Vampire" was awarded honorable mention by the Appalachian Writers Association in their annual competition. A collection of her poems under the same title, *The Hillbilly Vampire* (1989), satirizes the exploitation of the Appalachian South by ethnologists.

No Minority

There is no name
  (so she was told)
  for what you are.

Two generations into town
  is one too far.

One generation still
  retains some authenticity:
  a measure of—veracity.
Legitimacy, if you will.

It's either or—it's town or hill.

Just listen to the way you speak.

You bought a book to learn to play.
You took a class to learn to dance.
That hardly is the mountain way.

No. There isn't any more to say.
There is no name for what you are.

It is, however, plain to see
  that you are no
  minority.

From *The Hillbilly Vampire,* Rowan Mountain Press, 1989. Reprinted by permission of
Rowan Mountain Press.

Harry Brown

Harry Brown is a graduate of Davidson College. He received an M.A. from Appalachian State University and a Ph.D. from Ohio University. Since 1970 he has been a member of the English Department of Eastern Kentucky University, in Richmond, where he now teaches courses in modern American literature and poetry writing. His verse has appeared in publications such as *Kansas Quarterly, Southern Humanities Review,* and *Kentucky Poetry Review.* He was coeditor of *God's Plenty: Modern Kentucky Writers* (1990), and he has published two collections of poems, *Paint Lick Idyll* (1989) and *Measuring Man* (1989).

Different Shades of Green

Yesterday we picked greens upon
Greens upon greens from our salad garden
To cook and freeze for winter evenings.
The only green we snubbed was careless weed,
Alias lamb's-quarter, which some relish
But we refuse on principle because
This hoggish potherb tries to take
Every inch of our garden plot.
Because most greens are never exclusive at heart
We mix them in the kitchen sink to rinse
Before they're dropped in the cooker to simmer
With fresh spring onions for half an hour or more.
Thus there they lay: kale, a greyish green;
And light green mustard leaves, stronger than kale
On the tongue but not in blood and bone;
Collards from the southern cabbage tree
The color of kale but again not so rich;
Savoy spinach leaves, the loveliest
I think of all our salad garden,
From wide, dark green roses whose glossy petals
Wrinkle and bulge in no design but their own.
Slightly mottled, dull and a little rough,
The largest leaves were Seven Top,
For turnips grow fastest of all the greens.
For that reason perhaps in this world whose soul

From *Appalachian Heritage* 14.3 (1986), © *Appalachian Heritage*/Berea College. Reprinted by permission of the author and the publisher.

Steps to the *law of supply and demand*
Turnip greens (and tubers) are least elite
Among gourmet connoisseurs and chefs.
But we rebel against
Most populous is least
And sometimes like to feast
On a dish of turnip greens
Seasoned with cracklings
Or served with chine.

George Scarbrough

See volume 1, chapter 1, for biography.

Implication

Near Chestua in Polk
In a high field at the top
Of a low-crowned mountain, a chain
Drawn through a rusty eye
Summoned me out, and a voice,

Speaking from once lingual
Ground, accosted me as I took
Apples from an autumn tree
As stooped as an old willow,
And left my tracks stepped

Deep in mud by the mouth
Of the open well as I fled the presence
Of implication. On Wilnouty, I found
A trilobitic stone with the look
Of language on it, and in a dry

Biblical county stood like a man
With a slab ordained to be interpreted

From *Invitation to Kim,* Iris Press, 1989. Reprinted by permission of the author and publisher.

To a beleaguered people, but covered
It back with red leaves for safe-
Keeping on the mountain.

At the end of a trail on Whitspur
I came to the runnered house drawn sheer
With the cliff's thousand-foot drop,
And saw through a sliding pane
The Crazy Man reading a book

At his table while behind him
A branch of gum glowed like crown-
Fire in the rough room. I leaned
Close to the glass. *Pascal's*
Pensées, the title said.

I wanted to knock, to be asked in,
To have the din of a word with him:
Inquire what he made of the book,
How the haws were on the pinnacle,
Where there were muscadines.

But I had been warned of intrusion,
Cautioned against interference. How
Admonition has always persuaded me
To little: to eschew the wild thought,
The errant study: to keep clear

Of implication in a litigious
County filled with quarreling voices
And hateful judgments. I stormed
The day my friend was shot down on
His doorstone in the presence

Of his wife and children.
"Politics makes enemies," my father said.
"Leave well enough alone." He strode to the door
And back again and back to the door.
Silhouetted there, he spoke, turning:

"Little landlords sweep with a clean
Broom," he said, meaning more than murder,
His eyes lively with anger.
"Keep your mouth shut, boy.
We have no portion here."

Chapter 7

Feuds and Violence

Introduction

Although the "outsider" easily associates Appalachia with "feudin' and fightin'," Appalachia may not be substantially more violence-prone than the rest of the country. Violence thought endemic to Appalachia is in truth representative of the violence found throughout the nation. However, the region has a mythos built around not only its fighting heroes but also its desperados, bad men, and killers.

In some cases fighting becomes a tradition, a situation which manifests itself in the *feud*. A classic model of the vicious cycle, the feud originates in the lawless atmosphere of the frontier, where personal squabbles are settled through bloodshed, and acts of revenge and retribution continue until the original cause of the conflict, as in the case of the Hatfields and McCoys, is lost to history.

Wide publicity accorded the Hatfield-McCoy feud and other "troubles" has given rise to the general perception of the brutal redneck and to the quality that John Shelton Reed, noted student of southern culture, identifies as "meanness." But it must be kept in mind that traditionally violence in Appalachia has functioned as part of a personal code of honor and integrity. Unlike inner-city violence, which is motivated almost exclusively by greed, violence in the hills more often is rooted in personal codes received from the community and from the individual's forebears. Traditional Appalachian violence, however deplorable, has provided a certain continuity and exercised restraint over the wild impulses of the mountaineers.

Otis K. Rice

A graduate of Morris Harvey College (now the University of Charleston), Otis K. Rice earned a master's degree at West Virginia University and a Ph.D. at the University of Kentucky. For nineteen years he worked in the Kanawha County, West Virginia, public school system before joining the history department at West Virginia Institute of Technology in Montgomery, West Virginia. Rice is perhaps best known for his historical account of one of the oldest family feuds in the South, *The Hatfields and the McCoys* (1978). He contributes articles and reviews to historical journals and has served on the editorial board of *West Virginia History*. Rice has explained his focus on regional and local history as a means to "illuminate our national experience." In 1987 he was named professor emeritus at West Virginia Institute of Technology.

New Year's Day 1888

Until the autumn of 1887, the Hatfield-McCoy feud remained primarily a family vendetta, waged without effective intervention by the constituted authorities of either Pike or Logan counties. The election of Governor Buckner and his support of the proposals of Perry Cline, however, lifted the feud into the political sphere. Although Buckner's motives were unquestionably altruistic, his intercession did not herald a new evidence of the majesty of the law or of swift and certain justice. Rather, through the machinations of Cline and his associates, it resulted in an infusion of the cheapest and most corrupt kind of politics. Other feuds of the Kentucky mountains had repeatedly shown that when legal authority failed to stand above the warring factions and aligned itself with one side or the other, it intensified and prolonged the troubles. Without any doubt, the politicization of the Hatfield-McCoy feud and the efforts of Cline to turn it to personal advantage forced it into one of its most violent periods.

Although the Hatfields had no confidence in Cline and other Kentucky authorities and little expectation of justice, much less of mercy, at the hands of a Pike County court, they might have done well to allow matters to settle for a time. Already Governor Wilson's reaction to the letter of Frank Phillips and the reports of Cline's venality held forth the possibility that he would not honor the extradition request from Kentucky. Moreover, the exposure of Cline's duplicity might have undermined some of his influence with Governor Buckner. The threat remained, nevertheless, that Pike County friends of

From *The Hatfields and McCoys,* University Press of Kentucky, 1985. Reproduced by permission of the publisher.

the McCoys or bounty hunters might engage in extralegal methods to arrest the Hatfields and take them to Kentucky for trial. The Hatfields had no intention of allowing that to happen.

Early in the morning of a cold, crisp January 1, 1888, Devil Anse, Jim Vance, and Cap Hatfield decided to take the initiative. They dispatched Johnse and Tom Chambers, also known as Tom Mitchell, to round up the clansmen, some of whom, either because of fear of arrest or a desire to avoid further entanglement in the feud, were hiding in the hills. Johnse's wife, Nancy, had left him, and he was temporarily free to participate in the activities of his family.

The first recruit was the easily influenced Ellison Mounts, reputedly the son of Ellison Hatfield. Over six feet tall and weighing more than 180 pounds, the twenty-four-year-old Mounts seemed the archetype of the wiry, athletic mountaineer. With his light blond hair and dull gray eyes, he was generally called "Cotton Top." His boyhood had been spent "in the usual pursuits of a rude, unrully [sic] country boy, in fishing, hunting, roving about the neighborhood and engaging with boon companions in Sabbath-breaking, petty pilfering, and all the multifarious pursuits known to the average ungoverned country boy." Barely literate, his "education in vice" had been "very thorough," and he participated in his first murder in 1882 after the McCoy brothers killed his father in the election-day troubles on Blackberry Creek.[1]

At Dow Steele's, on Island Creek, Johnse, Chambers, and Mounts met Devil Anse and his sons, Cap and Robert E. Lee, or Bob, who was a mere youth. According to Mounts, they continued on to the homes of Henry Vance, Floyd Hatfield, and other supporters and finally arrived at the cabin of Jim Vance. There Devil Anse, Cap, and Vance held a council and presumably came to the conclusion that they must eliminate Randolph McCoy and members of his family who might present damaging evidence against them if they were extradited to Pike County for trial. As Jim Vance explained, with agreement from Cap and Johnse, the Hatfields had "become tired of dodging the officers of the law, and wished to be able to sleep at home beside better bed fellows than Winchester rifles, and to occasionally take off their boots when they went to bed."

Once the plans were announced, the men unanimously expressed their willingness to participate in them. Ironically, the only one to hold back was Devil Anse, who declared that he was too sick to take part and that he would turn over the leadership to Vance. No one questioned the sincerity of Devil Anse's explanation, and all agreed to accept Vance as their leader. They included Cap, Johnse, Bob, and Elliott Hatfield (the last a son of Ellison and a nephew of Devil Anse), Tom Chambers, Ellison Mounts, Charles Gillespie, and French, or Doc, Ellis. Vance sought to impress upon his followers the importance of absolute fidelity to the plan. Raising his arms above his head, he declared, "May hell be my heaven; I will kill the man that goes back on me tonight, if powder will burn."[2]

With unity and firmness of purpose, the band of nine well-armed men advanced up the Tug Fork. Between four and five o'clock in the afternoon, they stopped at Cap Hatfield's for supper. Darkness was coming on fast, but a full moon appeared. Concealing themselves as much as possible, the men proceeded to Poundmill Run and crossed a ridge to Peter Branch and Blackberry Creek. Their route, almost identical to that taken by Wall Hatfield and the Mahon brothers the night following the attack upon Ellison Hatfield by the McCoys, undoubtedly brought back bitter memories and steeled them in their resolve to remove a potential threat to them. Passing Jerry Hatfield's, the site of the fateful 1882 election, they swung up Hatfield Branch to the crest of a mountain and emerged on Blackberry Fork of Pond Creek. When they had gone about a mile, they tied their horses, and Cap, Johnse, and Vance put on masks. From there they advanced silently toward Randolph McCoy's house, which stood on a flat of heavily wooded hillside.[3]

According to the plan of attack, the nine men surrounded the McCoy dwelling, a double log house with a roofed passageway connecting the two parts. Cap and Mounts stationed themselves at the back door of the kitchen, and Bob and Elliott Hatfield covered the kitchen door that opened upon the passageway. Johnse and Vance watched the entrance from the passageway to the main house, and Chambers, Gillespie, and Ellis stood guard over the front entrance.

After they had taken their positions, Jim Vance called for the McCoys to come out of the house and surrender as prisoners of war. His demand awakened Calvin McCoy, the twenty-five-year-old son of Randolph, who was sleeping in the upstairs of the main part of the house. Calvin hastily put on his trousers and suspenders and hurried downstairs to warn his mother to remain quietly in bed. He then went back upstairs for a better vantage point for defense, while his father took up a position on the first floor.

About that time Johnse, ignoring the orders of Jim Vance to withhold fire until he gave the signal, shot into the McCoy house. His precipitous action was followed by a fusillade from the attackers and answered by rapid firing by the McCoys from the windows, with Calvin "shooting like lightning." Ironically, the first victim of the encounter was Johnse, who received a charge of bird shot in the shoulder.

In the midst of the shooting, Jim Vance and Tom Chambers undertook to set fire to the house. Vance ran to a side of the building that had no windows, where he saw some cotton drying. He struck a match to it and placed part of it in a joist hole and the remainder against the shutter of the door. Chambers, observing the new tactic, dashed to the woodpile and seized a large pine knot, which he ignited. With the blazing pine knot, he ran to the kitchen area, where he leaped upon a pile of logs and onto the roof. There he attempted to pry loose a shingle, with the intention of placing the burning pine knot in the loft. Before he could accomplish his purpose, someone fired a gun from the room below, blowing a hole in the roof and momentarily blinding Chambers. When he regained his composure and his sight, he saw that his numb and bloody hand had three fingers missing. He dropped the torch, rolled to the ground, and sped off as fast as he could to safety. The pine knot fell to the ground and smoldered harmlessly.

The fire that Vance had ignited at the door of the cabin, however, showed signs of spreading rapidly. Calvin McCoy called to his sisters, Josephine, Alifair, and Adelaide, to put it out, but Vance warned that if they came out he would shoot them. The girls tried to extinguish the flames with the water in the cabin, which they quickly exhausted, and then used the buttermilk in the churn, but to no avail. The fire spread and began to engulf the doorway.

About that time Alifair opened the kitchen door. She beheld the masked men but called out to Cap Hatfield that she recognized his voice. Cap and Johnse saw her at the same instant and called to Ellison Mounts, who was nearest her, to shoot her. Mounts fired and the girl collapsed on the ground near the doorway. Josephine called from the inside to ask whether her sister was hurt, but the incomprehensible moans of Alifair left no doubt that she had been mortally wounded. Sensing some tragedy, Calvin called down to find out what had happened. His answer came in Josephine's screams that the attackers had killed Alifair.

Upon hearing that Alifair had been shot, Sarah McCoy, her mother, rushed to the back door. Vance commanded her to go back and raised his rifle as if he would shoot her too. Sarah saw, however, that he had the wrong end turned toward her and continued toward her dying daughter. Vance bounded toward her and struck her with the butt of the rifle. For a moment she lay on the cold ground, stunned, groaning, and crying. Finally, she raised herself on her hands and knees and tried to crawl to Alifair.

According to Sarah McCoy's own account, she pleaded with the attackers, "For God's sake, let me go to my girl." Then, realizing the situation, she cried, "Oh, she's dead. For the love of God let me go to her." Sarah put out her hand until she could almost touch the feet of Alifair. Running down the doorsill, where Alifair had fallen, was blood from the girl's wounds. Johnse, who was standing against the outside wall of the kitchen, took his revolver in the hand which he could still use and beat Sarah over the head with it. She dropped to the ground, face down, and lay motionless.

Meanwhile, the fire continued to spread along the front and one side of the larger cabin. By then nearly overcome with smoke and realizing that the situation for the family was desperate, Calvin descended the ladder to the lower story and told his father that he would make a run for the corncrib and hold off the attackers while Randolph tried to run past them to safety. Calvin never made it to the corncrib. Surmising his plan, the Hatfields concentrated a murderous fire upon him, and he, too, met his death.

Calvin's bold scheme enabled Randolph to escape from the burning house. Grabbing extra cartridges, the older man, still vigorous at sixty-two years of age, dashed through the smoke and into the nearby woods. Knowing that pursuit would be foolhardy, the Hatfields had to content themselves with a mission only half-accomplished. In their frustration, they set fire to the McCoy smokehouse, which was filled with fresh meat from the fall slaughtering. They retired from the scene, blaming Johnse's impetuous firing for the failure of their plan and certain that the wrath of Randolph McCoy now would know no limits. Their new venture and the survival of witnesses left them more vulnerable than ever.[4]

Dejected, the Hatfield party mounted their horses for the ride home. Charley Gillespie's horse had broken loose during the attack, and he rode behind Cotton Top Mounts, who fainted from the loss of blood on the way. From the ridge above Blackberry Fork they could see the burning cabin and the trees outlined against the reddened sky. Faintly, in the distance, they could hear the wails of the McCoy girls, crying for help in their distress.

Behind them the Hatfields left a scene of unmitigated horror. Calvin and Alifair lay dead, and Sarah McCoy remained unconscious. When Randolph McCoy emerged from a pigpen, where he had taken refuge, he saw that his daughters Adelaide and Fanny, who were seventeen and fourteen years old, had built a small fire to protect their apparently dying mother from the penetrating cold. Randolph found Sarah with her arm and hip broken and her skull crushed. He saw the dead bodies of Calvin and Alifair, the latter with her long hair frozen to the ground. Even a less vindictive man than he might have vowed revenge at such a sight.

Shortly afterward, neighbors, attracted by the fearsome nighttime fire, arrived at the McCoy homestead. They placed Sarah on a cot and carried her to the home of her son Jim, who lived about a mile farther down Blackberry Fork. A few days later they bore the bodies of Calvin and Alifair to the McCoy cemetery, where they laid the two most recent victims of the feud to rest beside their three brothers—Tolbert, Pharmer, and Randolph, Jr.—who had been buried in a triple grave less than six years earlier.[5]

Left without a home and with sorrows and hatred weighing upon him, Randolph McCoy left Blackberry Fork. He moved Sarah, still valiantly clinging to life, by wagon to Pikeville and to the home of Perry Cline. There they found Rose Anna, who made the care of her mother her own reason for living. Two pictures of Randolph during the succeeding weeks have emerged. Truda McCoy describes him as a silent, morose, and broken man. Virgil C. Jones, however, states that, in contrast to the women of the family, who bore their grief in silence, "the wails of the father were uncontrolled" and that he frequented the streets of Pikeville cursing the Hatfields and threatening revenge. Perhaps both descriptions contain some truth, as both appear to be in keeping with aspects of McCoy's character.[6]

The violence of New Year's night of 1888 diverted some of the attention of the newspaper press from other feuds of the Kentucky mountains. Attracted by the sensational aspects of the events, but lacking reliable information, the press seized with avidity upon grossly inaccurate and often totally unfounded rumors. The *Louisville Courier-Journal* of January 8, 1888, like other Sunday newspapers of the week following the attack upon the McCoy family, carried a brief account based upon a letter written to State Senator A. H. Stewart by a friend in Pikeville. The *Courier-Journal* declared, "It appears that in 1882 parties led by a man named Hatfield, abducted three boys named McCoy, and conveyed them to West Virginia. A reward was offered for the arrest of the Hatfield party, and one of the gang was captured, who is now in the Pike County jail. On Sunday last others of the same party went to the residence of Randolph McCoy, in Pike County, and killed his wife, mother of the three boys mentioned, and his son, also set fire to the house, which, with its contents, was entirely consumed."

The newspaper article further stated, "Two little girls, daughters of McCoy, escaped, and succeeded in recovering the dead bodies from the flames. McCoy escaped in his night clothes under fire of the murderers, shooting as he went, but without effect so far as ascertained." The account noted, "The Pikeville jail is strongly guarded, but fears were entertained at the hour of writing that an attempt would be made to release the member of the gang [Selkirk McCoy] confined there."

Although it provided more accurate background material, the *Wheeling* (West Virginia) *Intelligencer* of January 9, 1888, drew upon a dispatch from Catlettsburg, carried by the *Cincinnati Inquirer*, for an equally erroneous version of the attack upon the McCoy dwelling. "A few nights since," the dispatch stated, "the Hatfield party visited the residence of Randolph McCoy and set fire to the house. Alafara, his eldest daughter, was the first to open the door and make her appearance, and in the glaring light she was shot dead by the fiends outside, who were concealed. His son Calvin next appeared, and he was shot dead. His wife made her appearance in escaping from the burning building and was shot through the head, and although she was still alive at last accounts she will die." Adding to the errors and simplifications, the account further declared, "Randall M'Coy escaped from the burning house with his shotgun, and although a volley was discharged at him he escaped unhurt, and opened fire upon the attacking party. He is known to have killed one of the gang by the name of Chambers, and, it is said, shot Cap Hatfield in the shoulder, and putting the rest to flight. So ends the chapter."

The *Intelligencer* added that $2,700 in rewards had been offered for members of the Hatfield clan charged with the murders of the three McCoys in 1882 but that "no one seems anxious to take them, as they are strongly barricaded in the wilds of West Virginia." Declaring that the outlaws had killed McCoy's wife, three of his sons, and a daughter, the writer also speculated that "retributive justice is now likely to follow, as their last acts have stirred up that whole section," but he observed that "if the Hatfields are ever taken, dead or alive, the men who undertake the job will experience some fun, as this set of West Virginia toughs is a determined and desperate band."

Remoteness from the scene of the tragedy only partly explained the inaccurate stories carried by the press. One of the most erroneous accounts appeared on January 12, 1888, in the *Big Sandy News* of Louisa, Kentucky, the closest newspaper. It reported that it had received "reliable information" from Pikeville that "Cap Hatfield was killed and that John[se] Hatfield and other members of the gang were badly wonded [*sic*] by Calvin McCoy and his father." It declared that Calvin "mortally wounded two of the squad before he was killed." The article also carried the mistaken news that "a seventeen-year-old daughter of McCoy [Adelaide] has become insane over the awful affair" and that "one of Johns [*sic*] Hatfield's arms was so badly lacerated and shattered that it has been amputated." After the type for the article was set up, the editor added later information to the effect that Cap had not been killed, but he injected another error by declaring that Chambers, rather than Selkirk McCoy, was then under heavy guard in the Pikeville jail.

Just as Perry Cline's activities introduced a political dimension to the Hatfield-McCoy feud, so the Hatfield attack upon the McCoys on the night of January 1, 1888, placed it in the journalistic sphere. The newspapers proved no more able than the politicians to bring truth to the surface and to promote a resolution of the turmoil that beset Pike and Logan counties. Yet, in the long run, both contributed to a conviction by the people that, for the good of the two states, the mountain dwellers would have to settle their differences by more peaceful means.

Notes

1. *Louisville Courier-Journal,* 18 Feb. 1890; Testimony of Ellison Mounts, *Commonwealth of Kentucky v. Plyant Mayhorn* [Mahon], Case #19601, Kentucky Court of Appeals.

2. For the members of the Hatfield party, see statements of Charles Gillespie, *Cincinnati Enquirer,* 14 Oct. 1888, and *Wheeling Intelligencer,* 17 Oct. 1888; and of Ellison Mounts, *Louisville Courier-Journal,* 18 Feb. 1890. Vance's words are noted in Virgil Carrington Jones's *The Hatfields and the McCoys* (Chapel Hill: U of North Carolina P, 1948), 95.

3. Jones, *Hatfields and McCoys,* 95–96.

4. For details of the attack upon the McCoy home, I have drawn primarily from the confession of Charles Gillespie, *Cincinnati Enquirer,* 14 Oct. 1888, and *Wheeling Intelligencer,* 17 Oct. 1888; the testimony of Sarah McCoy in *Commonwealth of Kentucky v. Ellison Mounts,* Case #19602, Kentucky Court of Appeals; the confession of Ellison Mounts, *Louisville Courier-Journal,* 18 Feb. 1890; and the account of Charles S. Howell, *Pittsburgh Times,* 1 Feb. 1888.

5. *Louisville Courier-Journal,* 18 Feb. 1890.

6. Truda W. McCoy, *The McCoys: Their Story as Told to the Author by Eyewitnesses and Descendants,* ed. Leonard Roberts (Pikeville, KY: Preservation Council Press, 1976), 148; Jones, *The Hatfields and the McCoys,* 102.

Roy Helton

Roy Helton was born in Washington, D.C., but spent a great deal of time in Pennsylvania and later in the Carolinas and Kentucky. His collection of poems is *Lonesome Water* (1930).

Old Christmas Morning:
A Kentucky Mountain Ballad

Where you coming from, Lomey Carter,
    So airly over the snow?
And what's them pretties you got in your hand,
    And where you aiming to go?

Step in, Honey: Old Christmas morning
    I ain't got nothing much;
Maybe a bite of sweetness and cornbread,
    A little ham meat and such.

But come in, Honey! Sally Anne Barton's
    Hungering after your face.
Wait till I light my candle up:
    Set down! There's your old place.

Now where you been so airly this morning?
    Graveyard, Sally Anne.
Up by the trace in the salt lick meadows
    Where Taulbe kilt my man.

Taulbe ain't to home this morning . . .
    I can't scratch up a light:
Dampness gets on the heads of the matches;
    But I'll blow up the embers bright.

Needn't trouble. I won't be stopping
    Going a long ways still.
You didn't see nothing, Lomey Carter,
    Up on the graveyard hill?

From *Appalachian Heritage* 6.4 (Fall 1978), © *Appalachian Heritage*/Berea College. Reprinted by permission.

What should I see there, Sally Anne Barton?
   Well, sperits do walk last night.
There were an elder bush a-blooming
   While the moon still give some light.

Yes, elder bushes, they bloom, Old Christmas,
   And critters kneel down in their straw.
Anything else up in the graveyard?
   One thing more I saw:

I saw my man with his head all bleeding
   Where Taulbe's shot went through.
What did he say?
            He stooped and kissed me.
   What did he say to you?

Said, Lord Jesus forguv your Taulbe;
   But he told me another word;
He said it soft when he stooped and kissed me.
   That were the last I heard.

Taulbe ain't to home this morning.
   I know that, Sally Anne,
For I kilt him, coming down through the meadow
   Where Taulbe kilt my man.

I met him upon the meadow trace
   When the moon were fainting fast,
And I had my dead man's rifle gun
   And I kilt him as he come past.

But I heard two shots.
               'Twas his was second:
   He shot me 'fore he died:
You'll find us at daybreak, Sally Anne Barton:
   I'm laying there dead at his side.

Pinckney Benedict

Born in Ronceverte, West Virginia, Pinckney Benedict grew up and continues to live on his family's dairy farm north of Lewisburg, West Virginia. He graduated magna cum laude from Princeton University in 1986 with a B.A. in English and received his M.F.A. degree in 1988 from the Writers' Workshop of the University of Iowa. After an appointment at the Hill School, a preparatory school in Pottstown, Pennsylvania, Benedict spent two years on the creative writing faculty of Oberlin College. His first short-story collection was *Town Smokes* (1987); his second, *The Wrecking Yard* (1992).

The Sutton Pie Safe

A blacksnake lay stretched out on the cracked slab of concrete near the diesel tank. It kept still in a spot of sun. It had drawn clear membranes across its eyes, had puffed its glistening scales a little, soaking up the heat of the day. It must have been three feet long.

"There's one, dad," I said, pointing at it. My father was staring at the old pole barn, listening to the birds in the loft as they chattered and swooped from one sagging rafter to another. The pole barn was leaning hard to one side, the west wall buckling under. The next big summer storm would probably knock it down. The winter had been hard, the snows heavy, and the weight had snapped the ridgepole. I wondered where we would put that summer's hay.

"Where is he?" my dad asked. He held the cut-down .410 in one hand, the short barrel cradled in the crook of his elbow, stock tight against his bare ribs. We were looking for copperheads to kill, but I thought maybe I could coax my dad into shooting the sleeping blacksnake. I loved the crack of the gun, the smell of sulphur from the opened breech. Again I pointed to the snake.

"Whew," he said, "that's a big one there. What do you figure, two, two and a half feet?" "Three," I said. "Three at least." He grunted.

"You gonna kill it?" I asked.

"Boys want to kill everything, don't they?" he said to me, grinning. Then, more seriously, "Not too good an idea to kill a blacksnake. They keep the mice down, the rats. Better than a cat, really, a good-sized blacksnake."

He stood, considering the unmoving snake, his lips pursed. He tapped the stock of the gun against his forearm. Behind us, past the line of willow trees near the house, I heard the crunch of gravel in the driveway. Somebody was driving up. We both turned to watch as the car stopped next to the smokehouse. It was a big car, Buick Riviera, and I could see that the metallic flake finish had taken a beating on the way up our lane.

© 1987 by Pinckney Benedict. Reprinted by permission of Ontario Review Press.

My father started forward, then stopped. A woman got out of the car, a tall woman in a blue sun dress. She looked over the car at us, half waved. She had honey-colored hair that hung to her shoulders, and beautiful, well-muscled arms. Her wave was uncertain. When I looked at my dad, he seemed embarrassed to have been caught without a shirt. He raised the gun in a salute, decided that wasn't right, lowered the gun and waved his other hand instead.

It was too far to talk without shouting, so we didn't say anything, and neither did the woman. We all stood there a minute longer. Then I started over toward her.

"Boy," my dad said. I stopped. "Don't you want to get that snake?" he said.

"Thought it wasn't good to kill blacksnakes," I said. I gestured toward the house. "Who is she?" I asked.

"Friend of your mother's," he said. His eyes were on her. She had turned from us, was at the screen porch. I could see her talking through the mesh to my mother, nodding her head. She had a purse in her hand, waved it to emphasize something she was saying. "Your mom'll take care of her," my dad said. The woman opened the porch door, entered. The blue sun dress was pretty much backless, and I watched her go. Once she was on the porch, she was no more than a silhouette.

"Sure is pretty," I said to my father. "Yeah," he said. He snapped the .410's safety off, stepped over to the diesel pump. The snake sensed his coming, turned hooded eyes on him. The sensitive tongue flicked from the curved mouth, testing the air, the warm concrete. For just a second, I saw the pink inner lining of the mouth, saw the rows of tiny, backward curving fangs. "When I was ten, just about your age," my dad said, leveling the gun at the snake, "my daddy killed a big old blacksnake out in our back yard."

The snake, with reluctance, started to crawl from the spot of sun. My dad steadied the gun on it with both hands. It was a short weapon, the barrel and stock both cut down. It couldn't have measured more than twenty inches overall. Easy to carry, quick to use: perfect for snake. "He killed that blacksnake, pegged the skin out, and give it to me for a belt," my dad said. He closed one eye, squeezed the trigger.

The shot tore the head off the snake. At the sound, a couple of barn swallows flew from the haymow, streaked around the barn, swept back into the dark loft. I watched the body of the snake vibrate and twitch, watched it crawl rapidly away from the place where it had died. It moved more quickly than I'd seen it move that afternoon. The blood was dark, darker than beets or raspberry juice. My dad snapped the bolt of the gun open, and the spent cartridge bounced on the concrete. When the snake's body twisted toward me, I stepped away from it.

My dad picked the snake up from the mess of its head. The dead snake, long and heavy, threw a couple of coils over his wrist. He shook them off, shook the body of the snake out straight, let it hang down from his hand. It was longer than one of his legs. "Wore that belt for a lot of years," he said, and I noticed that my ears were ringing. It took me a second to understand what he was talking about. "Wore it 'til it fell apart." He offered the snake to me, but I didn't want to touch it. He laughed.

"Let's go show your mother," he said, walking past me toward the house. I thought of the woman in the sun dress, wondered what she would think of the blacksnake. I followed my dad, watching the snake. Its movements were slowing now, lapsing into a rhythmic twitching along the whole length of its body.

As we passed the smokehouse and the parked Riviera, I asked him, "What's her name?" He looked at the car, back at me. I could hear my mother's voice, and the voice of the other woman, couldn't hear what they were saying.

"Hanson," he said. "Mrs. Hanson. Judge Hanson's wife." Judge Hanson was a circuit court judge in the county seat; he'd talked at my school once, a big man wearing a three-piece suit, even though the day had been hot. It seemed to me that his wife must be a good deal younger than he was.

The snake in my father's hand was motionless now, hung straight down toward the earth. His fingers were smeared with gore, and a line of blood streaked his chest.

"Why'd you kill the blacksnake?" I asked him. "After what you said, about rats and all?" I was still surprised he'd done it. He looked at me, and for a moment I didn't think he was going to answer me.

He reached for the doorknob with his free hand, twisted it. "Thought you'd know," he said. "My daddy made a belt for me. I'm gonna make one for you."

&

The woman in the sun dress, Mrs. Hanson, was talking to my mother when we entered the porch. "I was talking to Karen Spangler the other day," she said. My mother, sitting at the other end of the screen porch, nodded. Mrs. Spangler was one of our regular egg customers, came out about once every two weeks, just for a minute. Mrs. Hanson continued. "She says that you all have just the best eggs, and the Judge and I wondered if you might possibly . . ." She let the sentence trail off, turned to my father.

"Why, hello, Mr. Albright," she said. She saw the snake, but she had poise: she didn't react. My father nodded at her. "Mrs. Hanson," he said. He held the snake up for my mother to see. "Look here, Sara," he said. "Found this one sunning himself out near the diesel pump."

My mother stood. "You don't want to bring that thing on the porch, Jack," she said. She was a small woman, my mother, with quick movements, deft reactions. There was anger in her eyes.

"Thought I'd make a belt out of it for the boy," my dad said, ignoring her. He waved the snake, and a drop of blood fell from his hand to the floor. "You remember that old snakeskin belt I had?".

Mrs. Hanson came over to me, and I could smell her perfume. Her skin was tan, lightly freckled. "I don't think we've met," she said to me, like I was a man, and not just a boy. I tried to look her straight in the eye, found I couldn't. "No'm," I said. "Don't think we have."

"His name's Cates," my mother said. "He's ten." I didn't like it that she answered for me. Mrs. Hanson nodded, held out her hand. "Pleased to meet you, Cates," she said. I took her hand, shook it, realized I probably wasn't supposed to shake a lady's hand. I pulled back, noticed the grime under my fingernails, the dust on the backs of my hands. "Pleased," I said, and Mrs. Hanson gave out a laugh that was like nothing I'd ever heard from a woman before, loud and happy.

"You've a fine boy there," she said to my dad. I bent my head. To my father, my mother said, "Why don't you take that snake out of here, Jack. And get a shirt on. We've got company."

He darted a look at her. Then he waved the snake in the air, to point out to everybody what a fine, big blacksnake it was. He opened the screen door, leaned out, and dropped the snake in a coiled heap next to the steps. It looked almost alive lying there, the sheen of the sun still on the dark scales. "Mrs. Hanson," he said, and went on into the house. He let the door slam behind him, and I could hear him as he climbed the stairs inside.

Once he was gone, Mrs. Hanson seemed to settle back, to become more businesslike. "The Judge and I certainly would appreciate the opportunity to buy some of your eggs." She sat down in one of the cane bottom chairs we kept on the porch in summer, set her purse down beside her. "But Sara—may I call you Sara?" she asked, and my mother nodded. "Something else has brought me here as well." My mother sat forward in her chair, interested to hear. I leaned forward too, and Mrs. Hanson shot a glance my way. I could tell she wasn't sure she wanted me there.

"Sara," she said, "you have a Sutton pie safe." She pointed across the porch, and at first I thought she meant the upright freezer that stood there. Then I saw she was pointing at the old breadbox.

My mother looked at it. "Well, it's a pie safe," she said. "Sutton, I don't know—"

"Oh, yes, it's a Sutton," Mrs. Hanson said. "Mrs. Spangler told me so, and I can tell she was right." Mrs. Spangler, so far as I knew, had never said anything to us about a pie safe. Mrs. Hanson rose, knelt in front of the thing, touched first one part of it and then another.

"Here, you see," she said, pointing to the lower right corner of one of the pie safe's doors. We'd always called it a breadbox, kept all kinds of things in it: canned goods, my dad's ammunition and his reloading kit, things that needed to be kept cool in winter. The pie safe was made of cherry wood—you could tell even through the paint—with a pair of doors on the front. The doors had tin panels, and there were designs punched in the tin, swirls and circles and I don't know what all. I looked at the place where she was pointing. "SS" I saw, stamped into the wood. The letters were mostly filled with paint; I'd never noticed them before.

Mrs. Hanson patted the thing, picked a chip of paint off it. My mother and I watched her. "Of course," Mrs. Hanson said, "this paint will have to come off. Oh, a complete refinishing job, I imagine. How lovely!" She sounded thrilled. She ran her hands down the tin, feeling the holes where the metal-punch had gone through.

"Damn," she said, and I was surprised to hear her curse. "What's the matter?" my mother asked. Mrs. Hanson looked closely at the tin on the front of the pie safe. "It's been reversed," she said. "The tin panels on the front, you see how the holes were punched in? It wasn't put together that way, you know. When they punched this design in the tin, they poked it through from the back to the front, so the points were outside the pie safe."

"Oh," my mother said, sounding deflated. It sounded ridiculous to me. I couldn't figure why anyone would care which way the tin was put on the thing.

"Sometimes country people do that, reverse the tin panels," Mrs. Hanson said in a low voice, as if she weren't talking to country people. My mother didn't disagree. "Still, though," Mrs. Hanson said, "it is a Sutton, and I must have it. What will you take for it?"

I guess I should have known that she was angling to buy the thing all along, but still it surprised me. It surprised my mother too. "Take for it?" she said.

"Yes," Mrs. Hanson said, "it's our anniversary next week — mine and the Judge's — and I just know he would be thrilled with a Sutton piece. Especially one of the pie safes. Of course, I don't think it'll be possible to have it refinished by then, but he'll see the possibilities."

"I don't know," my mother said, and I couldn't believe she was considering the idea. "Is it worth a lot ?" It was an odd way to arrive at a price, and I laughed. Both women looked at me as if they had forgotten that I was on the porch with them. I wondered what my father would say when he came down from putting on a shirt.

Mrs. Hanson turned back to my mother. "Oh, yes," she said. "Samuel Sutton was quite a workman, very famous throughout the Valley. People are vying to buy his pieces. And here I've found one all for myself. And the Judge." Then, as if understanding that she wasn't being wise, she said, "Of course, the damage to it, the tin and all, that does lower the value a great deal. And the paint." My father had painted the breadbox, the pie safe, when it had been in the kitchen years ago, to match the walls. We'd since moved it out to the porch, when my mother picked up a free-standing cupboard she liked better.

"I don't know," my mother said. "After all, we don't use it much anymore, just let it sit out here. And if you really want it . . . " She sounded worried. She knew my father wasn't going to be pleased with the idea. "We should wait, ask my husband." Mrs. Hanson reached into her handbag, looking for her checkbook. I knew it wasn't going to be that easy.

"Didn't that belong to Granddad?" I asked my mother. She looked at me, didn't answer. "Dad's dad?" I said, pressing.

"It was in my husband's family," my mother said to Mrs. Hanson. "He might not like it."

"Could we say, then, three hundred dollars? Would that be possible?" Mrs. Hanson asked. She wasn't going to give up. Just then, my father opened the door and stepped out of the house onto the porch. He had washed his hands, put on a blue chambray shirt, one I'd given him for Christmas.

"Three hundred dollars?" my father said. "Three hundred dollars for what?" I saw my mother's face set into hard lines; she was determined to oppose him.

"She wants to buy the pie safe," my mother said. Her voice was soft, but not afraid.

My father walked over to the breadbox, struck the tin with two fingers. "This?" he said. "You're going to pay three hundred for this?" Both my mother and Mrs. Hanson nodded. "I think that's a fair price, Mr. Albright," Mrs. Hanson said. I noticed she didn't call him Jack.

"You could use it to get someone over to help you work on the barn," my mother said. My father didn't even look at her. I moved to his side.

"Didn't know the breadbox was for sale," he said. "Didn't know that it would be worth that much if it was for sale."

"My father owned that," he said. "Bought it for my mother, for this house, when they were first married." He turned to my mother. "You know that," he said.

"But what do we use it for, Jack?" she asked. "We use the barn. We need the barn. More than some pie safe."

My father put his hand on my shoulder. "You're not going to leave me anything, are you?" he said to my mother. She flushed, gestured at Mrs. Hanson. Mrs. Hanson managed to look unflustered.

My dad looked at Mrs. Hanson. Her calm seemed to infuriate him. "We aren't merchants," he said. "And this isn't a furniture shop." He turned to me. "Is it, boy?" I nodded, then shook my head no, not sure which was the correct response. "Mrs. Hanson," my mother began. You could tell she didn't like my father talking like that to Mrs. Hanson, who was a guest in her home.

"Don't apologize for me, Sara," my dad said. "Go ahead and sell the damn breadbox if you want, but just don't apologize for me." My mother opened her mouth, shut it again.

"Boy," he said to me, "you want a snakeskin belt like I was talking about? Like my daddy made?" He gestured out the porch door, to where the headless snake lay. A big fly, colored like blue glass, was crawling on the body.

"Yes, sir," I said, glad not to have to look at the high color rising in Mrs. Hanson's cheeks.

"You come out back with me, then, and I'll show you how to skin it, how to stretch the hide. How'd that be?" Neither my mother nor Mrs. Hanson said a word. My dad pushed me ahead of him, and I headed out the door.

As he came after me, he turned and spoke through the screen. "I'll tell you something, Mrs. Hanson," he said. "You ought not to try to buy what hasn't been put up for sale."

❧

Outside, my father groped in his pocket for a second, came up with his old Barlow knife, flicked the blade out. "You hold the snake for me," he said. "We'll take that skin right off him." He held out the body to me. I hesitated, reached out and took it.

It was heavy and rope-like, cool and limp in my hands. The scales were dry as sand. "Set it down there," my dad said, "and hold it stretched out tight." I set the snake down.

"Belly up," my dad said. "We don't want to mess up the scales on his back. That's what makes a snakeskin belt so nice, so shiny, them back scales." I rolled the snake. The scales on the sausage-like belly were light-colored, looked soft, and I prodded them with a forefinger. The skin rasped against my fingernail.

"Here we go," my father said, and pressed the blade of the knife against the belly of the snake. He always kept the knife razor-sharp, had a whetstone at the house he kept specially for it. I looked away. The knife made a sound as it went in; I thought I could hear him slicing through muscle, thought I could hear the small, cartilaginous ribs giving way under the blade.

Mrs. Hanson left the porch, and I could tell from the way she was walking that she must have gotten what she wanted. She moved with a bounce in her step. She looked over at us where we were kneeling, shook her hair back out of her face, smiled. My father paused in his cutting for a second when he heard the car door open. Mrs. Hanson backed the Buick around, headed back down the lane, toward the highway. A couple of low-hanging branches lashed the windshield as she went.

My mother stood on the porch, an outline behind the mesh of the screen, watching her go. When the car was out of sight, she turned and went back into the house.

My father gave a low laugh. When I looked at him, he was holding something gray between two fingers, dangled it back and forth in front of my face. "I'll be damned," he said. I looked down at the snake, the open stomach cavity, realized that he was holding a dead mouse by its tail. "No wonder that snake was so sleepy," my dad said. "He just ate." I stood, turned away from him.

"What's the matter?" he asked. I didn't answer. "You aren't gonna let that bother you," he said, and there was disdain in his voice. I put my arms over the top rail of the board fence around our yard, leaned my weight on it. I closed my eyes, saying nothing.

My father lowered his voice. "Thought you wanted that belt," he said. I wanted to turn to him, tell him that I did want the belt, just to give me a minute. I wasn't sure I could trust my voice not to break. "Guess not," he said.

Once again, I heard the sound of the knife, two quick cuts. I turned to look, saw that he had deftly sliced the body of the snake, had carved it into three nearly equal sections. It looked like pieces of bicycle tire lying there, bloody bicycle tire. My father rose, wiped his hands on his jeans.

"You think about that, boy," he said. "You think about that, next time you decide you want something." He walked past me, not toward the house, but toward the ruined barn.

Kathryn Stripling Byer

Kathryn Stripling Byer received her B.A. in English at Wesleyan College and completed her M.F.A. at the University of North Carolina–Greensboro. Her first collection of poetry, *Search Party* (1979), was followed by another, *Alma* (1983). *The Girl in the Midst of the Harvest* was published in the Associated Writing Program's award series for 1986. Byer has received a fellowship from the North Carolina Arts Council as well as from the National Endowment for the Arts. Her *Wildwood Flower: Poems* (1992) was chosen by the Academy of American Poets as the Lamont Poetry Selection for 1992. Her poems have also appeared in journals such as *Georgia Review, Southern Poetry Review,* and *Nimrod.* Byer is currently poet-in-residence at Western Carolina University in Cullowhee, North Carolina.

Chestnut Flat Mine

They say the fringe of her shawl clung
like lichen to creek rock
and under the laurel her sash looked
for all the sad world like a garter snake.

Farther on something so sheer
it was almost invisible floated away
on the Toe River. Red
said the woman who watched it go by,

baby-blue said her little girl stoning
the water with acorns. (Did he stroke
her silken leg after he'd unlaced
her tiny black shoe? Did he say Little

Darling, you're mine and what good
are your fancy ways now?) God Almighty,
the way they heard screams floating
downhill like what I imagine a town woman

wears underneath all her finery,
but when they came to the old mine by late
afternoon, they found only her gloves
thrown aside in the larkspur. Her dress

From *Wildwood Flower,* Louisiana State University Press, 1992. Reprinted by permission of the author.

was laid out like a corpse with a rose
in its lap, on its lily-white bosom
a bird's nest of wrinkles as if a man's
head had lain ever so gently there.

John Morefield

John Morefield was born in Lincoln County, Tennessee, and educated at Davidson College and the University of Florida. In addition to teaching English at Miami-Dade Junior College, the University of Florida, and, currently, East Tennessee State University, he has worked construction, sold wine, written environmental impact statements, waterproofed buildings, tended bar, and raised apples. His fiction has appeared in *The Stone Soldier: Prize College Stories, 1964, Florida Quarterly, In Place, Columbia* (his story "History Is Bunk" received that journal's Editor's Fiction Award in 1986), and others. He has written three novels; *Some Other Grief* is the second of these. A fourth novel, which concerns migrant farm workers in East Tennessee, is in progress.

"Skinning the Dog" comes from *Some Other Grief.* Set in East Tennessee during World War II, the story reveals all too clearly that violence was flourishing on the home front as well as the battle front. The protagonist, Coy Peake, like Iago in *Othello* and John Claggart in *Billy Budd*, raises the basic question of motiveless malignity. Is evil fundamentally a sickness or sin? Is it rooted in the environment or genes or both, or is it something forever beyond our understanding, something that, in the words of the story, "comes over us"? Most important, the story illustrates, as did the war itself, what grief awaits when decent people wait too long to confront violent acts in the making.

Skinning the Dog

One of the witnesses Quinn Jones summoned to strengthen his contention that Coy Peake was sane was Worley Lewis. Worley looked as uncomfortable in the witness box as a man could.

"Just what is your relationship with the defendant, Mr. Lewis?"

"I married his sister."

"So you've known Coy most of your life and known him closely for a good part of that time?"

From *Some Other Grief.* Printed by permission of the author.

"Yes, sir, I reckon so."

"You went to school with him, hunted and fished with him?"

"Yes, sir."

"He was at your wedding?"

"Yes, sir."

"What did he give you for a wedding present?"

Worley seemed surprised at the question. "Why, nothin, I don't reckon."

"Is Mr. Peake poor, then? Any poorer than anybody else on Tilson Creek?"

"Not no more'n nobody else, I don't reckon."

"Did other people give you wedding presents?"

"We didn't call em that, I don't reckon. But most folks give us sumpm or other."

"Like what?"

"Nothin costly, it seems like. Maybe a kittle. Or maybe a good feather piller. Sometimes it might of been sumpm they already had."

"But you didn't mind that, did you, since the thought is what counts?"

"Yes, sir, that's how I felt about it."

"Now you said most folks gave you something. What do you mean by 'most', exactly?"

"Well, I reckon everbody we knowed give us a present of some kind. Exceptin Coy."

"Hmm. Did he express any regret that he hadn't given you anything? Did he say it was because he was short of money right then, or something like that?"

Thornton finally stood up. "Your honor, Mr. Jones is wasting the time of this court. I fail to see how this line of questioning bears upon the case before it."

"Your honor, defense counsel has said he intends to fall back on the tired old insanity defense. Now, I don't believe for one minute that the sensible men and women of this jury will fall for that old line. Furthermore, I intend to make their job easier by establishing that Coy Peake is not insane but merely as mean as a snake. And that the vicious and heartless murder and dismemberment of the unfortunate Sarepta Simmons was done out of meanness, not madness."

"I'll overrule the objection."

"I'll ask you again, Mr. Lewis. Did Coy seem sorry that he hadn't given you a present?"

"No, sir, not a bit. He acted like he was proud of it. He showed a bunch of money around when folks was over at the house atter the weddin. He'd been off som'ers and had him a bunch of money, it looked like three or four hunderd dollars."

"Do you remember what he said?"

"He said it looked like he was the onliest one that never give us nothin, and him with all that money. He said he'd done give me his sister and he reckoned that was enough."

"And he seemed to want everybody to know that he had plenty of money and chose not to give you and his sister something just out of stinginess and meanness?"

"Objection."

"Sustained."

"Is there another word for it, Mr. Lewis?"

"I don't know what it would be."

"I don't either, my friend. Now then. You said you've hunted with Coy. Did you enjoy that?"

"No sir."

"Oh, don't you like to hunt?"

"I like to hunt pretty good. But I never did like to hunt with Coy."

"Why did you, then?"

Worley hesitated, looked even more uncomfortable, if that was possible. "Well, it was like . . . you see, I ain't no differnt from most other folks. I ain't no coward, but if—you see, if Coy was to come up to a feller and say he wanted him to come huntin with him, why you just done it. You didn't say no, I was aimin to work my apples today, or I was aimin to take my wife to the store, or nothin like that."

"Oh? Why not?"

"On account of you didn't know what he was liable to do."

"Did he ever do anything to you?"

"No, sir, he never did."

"Well then, why were you afraid of him? Because it sure sounds like you were. Did you ever know him to do anything to anybody on Tilson Creek?" Worley looked so intensely unhappy that Tommy Hardin, watching from his front-row seat, thought the man was going to be ill; he stared at the floor and shook his head. "Why were you afraid of him?"

Tommy thought: Wally's up against it now. Jones isn't fooling around this time. This time he's ready. The little pause in testimony here, which gave Jones time to step back from his witness, pace dramatically, walk in front of the jury box and look each man and woman in the eye, seemed to Tommy to be carefully thought out and prepared. But he was sure it did not seem so to the jury. They were totally absorbed by what they were hearing from Worley Lewis.

"Never mind that last question, Mr. Lewis. Let's go on to the story of the dog." He gestured at the jury. "These good people know very well that you and I have talked over your testimony beforehand. I know the story of the dog, and now I want you to tell it to these men and women, and I want to say in advance that I am sorry they have to hear it, just as I am sorry you have to tell it again." Worley seemed to beg with his eyes, but without any hope. "Go on, Mr. Lewis. It's almost over." Worley took a breath.

"Well, one evenin, I reckon two or three years ago, it were the day atter Thanksgiving, me and some of the other fellers was settin over behind the store and—"

"Behind the store? Would you explain?"

"Old Man—I mean Mr. Tilson that owns the store, he's got three or four logs layin on the ground down yonder behind and a place for a fire and sometimes fellers goes down there to set and talk before it gits too cold to. The apples were done picked and sold and hadn't nobody started in to prunin yet and they wadn't much to do. Times like that we'll set down and build a fire and talk about huntin and stuff."

"Did Coy usually join you?"

"Sometimes he did. I wouldn't say he usually did."

"But on this day he did."

"Yes sir. We was talkin about grouse and it happened Coy had this purty little bird dog bitch with him that he'd got back in the summer. He set down and scratched that dog's y'ers whilst we was a-talkin."

"Do you remember anything that was said?"

"Yes, sir. Buell Rice was tellin about when he was out huntin one day and got over on Turkey Creek wher he hadn't never hunted before, and he come up on this old man's yard that lives over there and the old man come out and got right ill with him, told him to git offen his land. 'Or I'll skin you alive!' the old man kep sayin; just stood there on his porch shakin one fist in the air and holdin his pants up with the other'n: 'I'll skin you alive! I'll skin you alive!' Buell was tellin about that, you see. And we had us a little laugh over that. And then Coy, he spoke up. He hadn't said nothin up till then."

"What did he say?"

"He said reckon what that would be like, to be skint alive. You reckon it's possible to skin somebody alive. And somebody said they hear'd the Indians done it to white people. And Coy said, 'I'd shore like to see that.' Them was his very words: 'I'd shore like to see that.' But nobody didn't pay him much mind."

"Then what happened?"

"Well, we went on talkin about huntin and stuff, and direckly somebody axed Coy how he liked that little bird dog bitch he had. And Coy thought about it a minute and he says, 'Boys, she ain't worth a tinker's dam.' And he went on about how she wouldn't hold a point and he couldn't kill no grouse with her atall and he reckoned he was gone to have to get shed of her and did anybody want her. Nobody said nothin."

"Nobody would take the dog? Was it that they didn't want her or were they just afraid of Coy?"

"I couldn't say about that. But wouldn't nobody take her. I wisht now *I* had of."

"Why is that, Mr. Lewis?"

"Coy went on about how that dog weren't no good and he couldn't give her away and all the time he was ascratchin her ye'rs and then he kindly turned the dog's face up to hisn and said, 'You know what I ort to do? I ort to skin you alive.'"

Somewhere along the way the listeners had sensed what was coming: there was not a sound in the courtroom, not a cough, not an audible breath, not a shuffle of a single foot.

"And then he done it." Now there were faint murmurs; Tommy heard himself make an involuntary sound, almost a whimper. No one seemed to notice.

"Mr. Lewis, what did you say? Did you say he did it?" Jones' voice was pained, almost faint. "Please explain." No one wanted to hear what Worley would say next, but nobody could turn away from it, either.

Worley was in it now, wanted to get it out and over with. "He tuk out his pocket knife and run it over a stone three or four times, then he grabbed that dog by one of her hind legs and flopped her over on her back. He run the blade of the knife under the hide on her belly and started workin it towards her head, same as you'd do skinnin a ground hog. He knowed what he was doin, just how to do it." Tommy had stopped believing what he was hearing, even as the detached journalistic part of his brain was already forming the words with which he would frame this testimony for tomorrow's paper. This was not part of a world he could recognize; and he had been on the trek up the mountain. He had been there, seen all, but this was beyond his imagination.

"And the dog was alive during the whole . . . procedure?"

"Yes sir. Till the hide was plumb offen her."

"What was she doing?"

"About what you'd expect. She was hollerin and floppin around. But Coy's mighty stout not to be no bigger'n he is, and I reckon she got weaker and weaker, till she couldn't put up much of a fight and you couldn't hear no sound comin out of her though she was still workin her jaws, tryin to holler." Tommy glanced at the jury; they were not watching Worley any more. They were staring at Coy where he sat beside his attorney. Where was Wally, anyway? Why was he allowing this to happen?

"What did Coy do when he was finished?"

"He just kindly stepped back, holdin the hide in one hand and the knife in t'other."

"I guess there was blood everywhere?"

"No, sir, they wasn't too much blood, Coy done such a good job of skinnin her. They were a kind of a red fillum over the dog, you might say."

"So he just stood there and watched the dog's dying agonies."

"Yes, sir, exceptin I don't reckon the dog would of died for a good while."

"So somebody finally put an end to this?"

Worley was deeply mortified, his voice muffled and low. "Not right away."

"You mean you and—how many other men? How many of you were there?"

"They was . . . five of us altogether."

"There were *five* men there? And not one of you made a move to stop this horror? Why, Mr. Lewis? Why?" Worley made some sound. "Was it because you were afraid? Afraid of Coy Peake?"

"Yes, sir, I reckon it was." Worley's voice was fainter than ever; Tommy tried to calculate what this admission must have cost him, what indeed the entire testimony must be taking out of him.

"I'm sure your fear was well founded," said Jones, his voice quiet and heavy with sympathy and sorrow. "How long did this go on?"

"I couldn't say exactly. After a bit Buell got out his own knife and went over to the dog. He opened the blade and kindly bent over—the dog didn't have the strength to run around no more; she was alayin on the ground jerkin—and put the blade out to her. But he stopped. He looked over at Coy and just stood like that. Fin'ly, Coy nodded his head and Buell went on and cut her thote."

"Was there any sign that Coy regretted even a little bit what he had done?"

Worley thought about this. "I don't know, he . . . he didn't say so right then, but . . . well, he took the dog and the hide with him. I thought he might just go off and leave it there and let Mr. Tilson bury it or sumpm. Nobody wouldn't have said nothin to him if he had. But he took dog and hide with him."

"Do you think he knew what he did was wrong?"

Thornton, long a non-presence, rose partially. "Objection."

"Sustained." But Jones was ready for him.

"All right. Then did he *say* anything to indicate that he knew what he did was wrong?"

"He said he didn't want us to tell it around, what he done. He said he didn't know why he done it or what come over him."

"Would you say he acted ashamed?"

"Objection."

"Overruled."

"Yes, sir, I'd say he acted ashamed for a minute."

"Hmm. To me, all this sounds like he knew this was wrong in the first place, before he ever did it." This was the essence of the insanity defense, Tommy was thinking: a flaw in the knowledge of right and wrong, an inability to distinguish between the two. "Is that what it means to you?"

"Objection."

"Sustained."

"Let me ask you something else, Mr. Lewis. Have you ever known any crazy people?"

"Well, they was one old man up the road when I was just a boy . . ."

"How old were you?"

"Well, he was there when I was borned, and I reckon I used to see him till I was fifteen or sixteen." Tommy glanced at Thornton, expecting him to jump up with another objection. But Thornton was listening intently, jotting down a note from time to time.

"And this old man was insane? Crazy? How do you know that?"

"Cause he got so bad that one day they come and got him."

"Who did?"

"Why, some fellers from the state. They had on white shirts and pants, and they run him down and tied him up and put him in that li'l ole truck they come in. I hear'd they tuk him to Knoxville and put him in the *in*sane asylum they got down yonder."

"No doubt that's what happened. You say he got so bad they came and got him. What did he do?"

"Well, for a long time he'd stand out in his yard—his wife was dead and his children was growed and off som'ers and didn't never come see him—and cuss at people walkin' by, didn't make no difference who they was. And by and by he got to wher he'd creep along in the ditch that run in front of his house whenever anybody'd walk by in the road. He quit saying stuff, but he'd crawl along beside whoever it was and kindly peep out at em till they was past. Fin'ly, they said he quit eatin hardly at all and they were scared he'd starve hisself to death."

"Then you've seen at least one genuinely crazy person in your life." Everybody knew what was coming next. "Mr. Lewis, do you think Coy Peake was crazy? Is crazy?" Everyone with the least knowledge of the law was looking at Thornton. Surely he must object. Jones was asking Worley to make a judgment he was in no way qualified to make. What was Thornton waiting for? But defense counsel merely sat, listening carefully to everything that was said.

What an incredible blunder, Tommy was thinking. They had all grossly overestimated Wally Thornton. For he had no business in a courtroom if he let a thing like this go by. For the people on the jury—notwithstanding what a big-city jury might respond to—were likely to give far more credence to someone they could recognize, feel equal or a little superior to, than they would to a psychiatrist full of talk about complexes and obsessions.

"Was he? Is he crazy, in your opinion?"

"No sir," said Worley, who seemed surprised at the question. Possibly Jones never thought he would be allowed to ask it. "I don't think he was."

Worley's had been the most damaging testimony yet, thought Tommy as Wally Thornton stepped up to cross-examine. He might as well throw it in; Coy's as good as fried already. The thing about the dog had hurt worse than any of the details about Sarepta. Everybody already knew what there was to know about that. It was old stuff, had lost its punch. But the dog. Wow. There's nothing he can do, he thought, watching in pity as Thornton approach Worley Lewis.

"That was some very interesting, uh, testimony, Mr. Lewis. I'm sure I join the jury and everyone else in this courtroom in my appreciation for your expert opinion of the mental state of the defendant."

"Defense counsel will refrain from sarcasm," said Judge Baines.

"Yes, sir. I will also refrain from asking why, if Mr. Lewis and his friends had Mr. Peake outnumbered four to one, he could not possibly have prevented what happened. You did say that, Mr. Lewis, didn't you? There were four of you and only one of him, about the same ratio I imagine of white-suited men to the one poor little crazy man you told us about a while ago?"

"Objection. The witness' courage or lack of it is not at issue here."

"Your honor will recall that I asked only how many men there were in addition to Mr. Peake."

"The witness may answer the question."

"Uh, they was five of us to his one."

"Oh?" said Thornton, looking puzzled. "I distinctly thought—wait a minute." He walked to the defense table and picked up a piece of paper. "You said—I believe I took this down accurately—'They was five of us altogether.' Is that right? Is that not what you said?"

"I meant they was five of us besides Coy."

"Oh. Besides Coy. But I don't believe the district attorney asked you how many there were *besides* Coy." He consulted the paper again. "The district attorney asked, 'How many of you were there?' Those were his exact words, unless the prosecution wishes to take issue with my recollection. All right then. In response to that question you said, 'They was five of us altogether.' *Altogether.* An interesting word for you to use. Five of you altogether. Of *us.*

Us, Mr. Lewis. That says to me that there was *us,* and then there was . . . Coy." The realization of what Thornton was up to began to dawn on Tommy. Perhaps he hadn't blundered at all. "It appears you thought of Coy as someone other than one of you. Would that be an accurate statement? *Was* Coy one of you, in the same way, say, that Buell Rice was one of you?"

"I reckon he weren't one of us, no sir."

"Good. Now we're getting somewhere. Why wasn't he? How was he different?"

"Your honor, defense counsel cannot conduct a direct examination of the witness."

"There's a thin line here," said the judge. "I'm not sure I can agree with you. Proceed for now, Mr. Thornton."

"How was he different? Was he . . . you know, Mr. Lewis, I found myself profoundly touched and moved by your story of the demented little man—the crazy man. What a sad tale that was, of the poor little outcast, lost and confused in a world he had ceased to understand. You know, I got the distinct impression from your telling of it that he had been able to function in the world at one time, that he wasn't always crazy, that there was a progression—"

"Your honor, surely we all see what defense counsel is up to. He simply cannot be allowed to attempt any comparison between that pitiful individual and the monster that is on trial here."

"And why not?" said Thornton, directing his reply to Jones. "The prosecution has sought to establish a contrast between that 'pitiful individual' as he calls him and my client. I am surely within my rights to refute the prosecution by attempting to establish that there are greater similarities between the two than might appear at first glance."

"The court will decide what your rights are, Mr. Thornton. But you are overruled, Mr. Jones. Please sit down."

"Mr. Lewis, elsewhere in your testimony you said," and once again Thornton consulted a piece of paper, "you quoted Coy by saying 'He didn't know what come over him.' *He didn't know what come over him.* Have you ever had occasion to say that? *Have* you ever said that?" Christ, what a gamble, thought Tommy. Or did he have some instinct to guide him?

"No, sir, I reckon not."

"Reckon not? Have you or haven't you?"

"No sir."

"How many times have you heard other people say it? Your neighbors, for instance?"

"Not too often."

"Not too often? Have you ever heard anyone else actually say those exact words?"

"No, sir."

"Would the Coy Peake you grew up with have said it? Would the Coy Peake of, say, ten years ago have said it? Would he have had any reason to say it?"

"No sir."

"He got worse, then, over the years. Is that accurate?"

"Yes . . . yes, sir, I reckon you could say he got worst."

"Just as the little man in the ditch got worse?"

"Yes, sir, I reckon so."

"Are you so sure now that Coy is not crazy? Isn't it just possible that you have been the unknowing witness to man's descent into the hell of madness?" Worley looked confused. "Don't you think Coy might have been going crazy—insane—before your very eyes and you couldn't see it? Isn't that possible, Mr. Lewis?"

"Yes, sir, I reckon that's possible."

"Thank you, that's all the questions I have for this witness."

Tommy sat back, well-nigh breathless with admiration. He'd never liked Wally much, maybe never would. But the guy had the makings of one hell of a trial lawyer. Makings hell. Jesus, to let Jones go on like that with the dog story and all the rest of it, never saying a word, apparently never doubting that he would turn the prosecution testimony to his own advantage—it must require nerves of steel and the kind of self-confidence—no, not that maybe, but an absolute belief, a knowledge, that anything you try is going to turn out right for you.

Jones seemed to hesitate when the judge asked if he had any redirect for Worley, but finally shook his head, looking considerably less confident than he had when the day began. It was after four, so court was adjourned.

The Ballad of Frankie Silver

Around Christmas-time of 1831, Frances Stewart Silver, called Frankie, was living with her husband, Charles Silver, at the mouth of the South Toe River, in what was then Burke County, North Carolina. On the evening of December 22, having chopped a big pile of hickory wood for the holidays, Charlie lay down with his baby on a sheepskin near the fire. While he dozed, Frankie struck him a glancing but almost decapitating blow with an axe, then, while he thrashed about the room, snatched up the child and threw herself into bed and pulled the covers over her. When he grew quiet, she arose and finished the job. She dismembered the body, burned portions of it, and hid the rest under the puncheon floor of the cabin and in a hollow sourwood tree outside. Then she "redd up" the room, scouring away some of the bloodstains, shaving away the deeper ones on wall and mantel with the axe, and went with her children to her mother-in-law's.

After a few days the neighbors began to inquire about Charlie. Frankie explained that he had left home to buy his Christmas whiskey and suggested that he had fallen into the river, drowned, and been frozen over. The more suspicious began a search, assisted, according to one tradition, by a Negro from Tennessee with a magic glass ball. Warm weather and a little dog were more efficacious than the glass ball. The puncheon floor and the other hiding places yielded their gruesome secret.

Frankie was tried at the March 1832 term of the Morganton Superior

Court, Judge John R. Donnell presiding. Records of the testimony revealing motives for the crime are scanty and inconclusive. Jealousy was apparently the one that impressed the jury. On the other hand, the clerk of the court that tried the case has been reported to have said, when an old man, that Frankie "would not have been convicted if the truth had been disclosed on the trial. . . . Silver mistreated his wife and she killed him in protection of herself." Whatever the truth may have been, she was convicted of murder and sentenced to be hanged. While her appeal to the Supreme Court was pending, she escaped from jail and made her getaway concealed in a load of hay but was speedily recaptured. She was hanged on Damon's Hill in Morganton on July 12, 1833—the "only white woman and with the exception of one Negress, the only woman ever capitally punished in North Carolina after it assumed the status of statehood."

This dreadful, dark and dismal day
Has swept all my glories away.
My sun goes down, my days are past,
And I must leave this world at last.

Oh, Lord, what will become of me?
I am condemned, you all now see.
To heaven or hell my soul must fly.
All in a moment when I die.

Judge Daniels has my sentence passed,
These prison walls I leave at last.
Nothing to cheer my drooping head
Until I am numbered with the dead.

But oh! that Dreadful Judge I fear.
Shall I that awful sentence hear?
'Depart you cursed down to hell
And forever there to dwell.'

I know that frightful ghosts I'll see
Gnawing their flesh in misery,
And then and there attended be
For murder in the first degree.

There shall I meet the mournful face
Whose blood I spilled upon this place.
With flaming eyes to me he'll say,
'Why did you take my life a way?'

The above background information on this version of "The Ballad of Frankie Silver" comes from *The Frank C. Brown Collection of North Carolina Folklore*, vol. 2, Duke University Press, 1952. The poem is reprinted by permission of the publisher.

His feeble hands fell gentle down,
His chattering tongue soon lost its sound.
To see his soul and body part
It strikes terror to my heart.

I took his blooming days away,
Left him no time to God to pray,
And if sins fall upon his head
Must I bear them in his stead?

The jealous thought that first gave strife
To make me take my husband's life.
For months and days I spent my time
Thinking how to commit this crime.

And on a dark and doleful night
I put his body out of sight;
With flames I tried to consume
But time would not admit it done.

You all see me and on me gaze.
Be careful how you spend your days,
And never commit this awful crime,
But try to serve your God in time.

My mind on solemn subjects roll.
My little child, God bless its soul.
All you that are of Adam's race,
Let not my faults this child disgrace.

Farewell, good people. You all now see
What my bad conduct's brought on me,
To die of shame and of disgrace
Before this world of human race.

Awful indeed to think on death,
In perfect health to lose my breath.
Farewell, my friend, I bid adieu.
Vengeance on me must now pursue.

Great God, how shall I be forgiven?
Not fit for earth, not fit for heaven;
But little time to pray to God,
For now I try that awful road.

Judith Fiene

Judith Fiene has been a social worker for thirty years. She received her M.S.S.W. degree from the Kent School of Social Work, University of Louis-ville. She was a psychiatric social worker in the Kentucky mental health sys-tem and worked with the Indiana Services to Crippled Children. After moving to Knoxville, Tennessee, in 1975, Dr. Fiene became the social-work supervisor at the University of Tennessee Hospital's Developmental and Genetics Center and continued field work with rural families with develop-mentally disabled children. She received her doctorate in social work from the University of Tennessee and serves as an associate professor there. Dr. Fiene's doctoral research was published as *The Social Reality of a Group of Rural, Low-Status, Appalachian Women: A Grounded Theory Study* (New York: Garland Press, 1993). Her current research interests include the percep-tions of social support by rural, battered women and alcohol use and stress among Appalachian working-class women.

Battered Women and the Legal System in Southern Appalachia

When abused women leave their batterers (albeit often temporarily) they find that they still have limited control over their own lives. Their first out-side contact is usually with a law enforcement agency. The need for orders of protection or charges of assault against the abuser bring the women into courts and into contact with lawyers and judges. When the women leave their batterers, some will seek sanctuary at a local shelter. Many of them en-ter the public welfare and public housing systems seeking the financial means and resources to live independently. In almost every case, except in shelter, the women must interact with systems designed and administered by men.

The following comments are taken from a report of the experiences of a group of Appalachian battered women as they interacted with law enforce-ment personnel, shelter workers, judiciary staff, and other community agents because they had been beaten. The material was gathered while I worked daily, for one month, as a volunteer at a rural women's shelter, taping ex-tended interviews with eight women and keeping a journal of conversations with other residents and staff. I also conducted a focus group interview with a battered women's support group in Knoxville, Tennessee.

From "The Appalachian Social Context and the Battering of Women," from *Practicing An-thropology* 15.3 (Summer 1993). Reprinted by permission of the Society for Applied Anthropology.

The Legal System

Whether women enter shelters or have other resources for leaving, most of them at some point must deal with the courts. Typically, abused women come to face male judges and often male attorneys. In some jurisdictions women's advocates are available to go to court with women. These advocates know which judges have seemed sympathetic and ready to give protective orders. Indeed the advocates' efficacy is dependent on finding benign members of the ruling system. Many of the women in this study made it clear that they see themselves as dealing with a male system where men receive preferential treatment.

In rural counties women may already know the names of magistrates and their reputations for dealing with violent men. Some judges are seen as always letting men off from serious charges. The women fear that the judge will not give them a protective order because they have not recently been injured, even when past violence has hospitalized the woman. Some of the women believe that men receive only a figurative slap on the wrist.

Going to court also means facing one's abuser. This may be the first time a woman has faced her partner since she had him arrested or left the home. Sometimes the women believe the abuser's perspective is given more credence by the court than is the clear evidence of the women's injuries. Anita reported, "Well let me tell you, if you live in North Carolina and go to get a warrant, and you're up there with nothin' but a robe on . . . and he starts cussin' as soon as the magistrate brings out the order for the warrant. And he [the judge] denies the warrant. And you're up here with a black eye, with blood running out of the side of your mouth, with no clothes on."

Even when an order of protection is issued, many women come to see it as a farce, even a joke the system plays on them. "I'll tell you about those orders of protection because I've got one, and I've had one. My husband tried to ram me with a car, . . . run us off the road. You know what our order of protection is? It's been postponed until December. . . . It's not worth the paper it's printed on. It's a bunch of garbage."

A second woman reports:

> He keeps reentering my home with the order of protection I have, and
> just like it is nothing. And really, to me, I don't think our judicial system
> is doing one thing for us women. The judicial system is a joke. Yeah, it is.
> Absolutely a joke. And I would like to stand before every judge in Knox
> and Sevier county and tell them that. There's no teeth in anything. I mean,
> I go to court, we have a date set, I go to court, he doesn't show up and
> they don't do one thing about it. And that's not right. It's like the victims are still being victimized by the person.

While abused women may become sanguine about their own lack of protection by social systems, they are distraught in regard to the dangers the abuser presents for their children and believe the courts fail to protect them adequately. Given the centrality of children to these women, their complete absorption in the caretaking role, this failure to protect appears to be the greatest injustice, and they feel helpless. Abusers often threaten their victims with "getting a lawyer and obtaining custody of the children." The experiences women encounter in custody hearings reinforce this threat. The women believe their experiences are trivialized when they perceive the court's attitude as "He's okay, he just beats up his wife (partner)." Mary talked about her court experience. "I tried to protect my child but it was the judge that put the children in my husband's hands and now they're being treated for sexual abuse. . . . And I fought, I fought to keep him (from) getting them. I said, how about (limiting) visitation. The judge said, oh no, you don't have enough proof, you don't have anything that proves he's capable of doing this. After he had done this to me for all these years. . . ." Another woman in a custody battle said, "Well, I'm in contempt of court because he hasn't seen them in two months and now he's filed a petition against me. . . . Honey, contempt of court means nothing. . . . But do you know what? Probably for a woman, they'll probably put you in jail. But a man, they will not, because it's a man judge."

One woman was able to utilize the champion system by finding a person with more power to intercede for her at court. This mother was trying to obtain custody of a teenage son who had been thrown out by his abusive father, but the ex-husband didn't show up in court. When the man did appear unexpectedly, a juvenile court officer was angered and wouldn't act, blocking the proceedings. The mother appealed to a third party in the community who had personal influence with the judge. The judge then interceded, signing the custody order.

Many of the women in this study were quite conscious of the inequity between men's power and women's resources. These women do not want special treatment, but they want their injuries to be taken seriously, not as isolated private events, but as important facts when considering questions of child custody, visitation, and support. They want to feel that they receive equal protection and justice in the courts. They want their right not to be battered to be recognized by the powerful social systems that influence their lives.

Pat Arnow and Norma Myers

In 1994 Pat Arnow became editor of *Southern Exposure.* Previously she edited *Now and Then,* the magazine published by the Center for Appalachian Studies and Services at East Tennessee State University. She is a writer and photographer whose essays, stories, book reviews, articles, and photos have been published by *Southern Exposure, Pacific News Service, Heresies,*

Liberty, North Carolina Arts Journal, Appalachian Journal, and other magazines, books, and newspapers. She co-authored a play, *Cancell'd Destiny* (with Christine Murdock and Steven Giles), which was produced by the Road Company of Johnson City, Tennessee, a professional touring theater promoting new work, and by the theater department at the Virginia Polytechnic Institute and State University in Blacksburg. Arnow is a native of Chicago and has lived in Appalachia since 1978.

Norma Myers is the assistant director of libraries for archives and special collections at East Tennessee State University. A native of northeastern Tennessee, she holds a master's degree in history from East Tennessee State University and a master's degree in library and information science from the University of Tennessee at Knoxville. She is a member of the Tennessee Historical Records Advisory Board.

Crime in Appalachia: The Search for Evidence

Appalachian and southern violence have been favorite hobby horses of writers and scholars for more than a hundred years. The latest foray comes from David Hackett Fischer in his extensive new history, *Albion's Seed: Four British Folkways in America* (New York: Oxford UP, 1989). In his section "The Origin and Persistence of Regional Cultures in the United States," Fischer offers data to support the argument that southerners and Appalachians are particularly violent. He shows elevated murder rates in the southern states. Although he fails to cite any references, we presume that he got the figures from the *Uniform Crime Report,* put out yearly by the FBI. But we don't know how he supports this statement: "Homicide rates were also high in northern cities with large populations of southern immigrants both black and white. But southern neighborhoods occupied by migrants from the north tended to have low homicide rates." This is not the kind of information contained in the *Uniform Crime Reports.* Nor does he explain the evidence for this unsettling argument: "Others argue that southern violence is mainly a legacy of ethnic or racial diversity. But some of the most violent communities in the southern highlands have no black residents at all, and are in ethnic terms among the most homogeneous in the nation. At the same time, many New England communities are ethnically diverse and yet comparatively peaceful."

At the Appalachian Studies Conference in Berea, Kentucky, in 1991, Fischer said that he quantified his evidence using teams of student researchers. He said they found "a pattern which is very special in southern violence of exceptionally high rates of prosecution for personal violence—cases of assault, that sort of thing—[and] exceptionally low levels of crimes against property, uniquely so . . . that's the evidence one has to deal with."

We'd like to deal with that evidence, but without better information

From *Now and Then* 8.2 (Summer 1991). Reprinted by permission.

about his sources, it's not easy. These statements demand empirical support, for a region's reputation rests in the balance. Thus, we undertook a modest study of readily available data. We looked at the latest available volume of *Uniform Crime Reports,* for 1989. The book reports numbers of murders, forcible rapes, aggravated assaults, and robbery, along with violent crime totals. The charts also list property crimes, including larceny-theft, burglary, and motor vehicle theft. All states, most cities of more than ten thousand residents, and some counties are listed. Breakdowns of reported crimes are given for region, but most of Appalachia is grouped with the rest of the South. Understanding this region's data requires a cross-sectional comparison.

We focused on cities since that was where we could find the most complete data. Given the small size of Appalachian cities and how spread out the metropolitan statistical areas are, we felt that information from these cities would provide a fair representation of what was going on in Appalachia in terms of crime. In addition, we believed that much of the population of Appalachian cities comes from a rural Appalachian background, which would reinforce our sample as a good one to understand overall crime rates in the southern mountains.

We compiled a listing of towns with more than ten thousand residents each and of metropolitan statistical areas (MSAs—cities or groups of cities of more than fifty thousand population) listed in West Virginia, east Tennessee, western North Carolina, southeastern Ohio, and western Maryland. We found no listing for cities in eastern Kentucky (except for Ashland, which is part of the Huntington, West Virginia, MSA) or northern Georgia (though Georgia is mentioned as part of the MSA of Chattanooga).

This gave us a list of twenty cities in the region with a [combined] population totaling 2.7 million. We compiled the totals of violent crimes and the totals of property crimes. We also listed murders and rapes separately (though they are also included in the violent crimes totals). For comparison, we located twenty cities of comparable population in the Midwest, Northeast, and West. We also compiled another listing of twenty comparable-sized cities of the South. Then we compared rates for the three sets of cities.

The selection of the comparison cities was not random; there weren't enough comparable-sized cities to use as a pool for a random sample. We did avoid any city within the Appalachian Regional Commission's extensive boundary of Appalachia. (We didn't include all the cities in the ARC territory in our Appalachian sample because that area takes in too much territory to make a meaningful statement about Appalachia; it includes much of the Carolina piedmont, upstate New York, and even Mississippi).

Our findings show that Appalachian cities are among the safest in the U.S., on the whole. The rates in the comparison U.S. cities are higher on all measures. The comparison cities of the South show the highest rates on all measures.

Because of the striking regional differences, we were inspired to look at the rates of two large cities that the Appalachian Regional Commission in-

Low Crime Rates in Appalachia's Cities

Selected Cities and Metropolitan Statistical Areas (MSAs), 1989	Total Population	Violent Crime Rate	Property Crime Rate	Murder Rate	Rape Rate
Appalachia	2,686,862	359.1	3,768.9	6.1	32.0
North, Midwest, and West	2,688,449	670.6	5,631.9	7.9	50.8
South	2,679,684	832.8	6,055.1	9.7	51.5
U.S. Total	248,239,000	663.1	5,077.9	8.7	38.1
West Virginia	1,857,000	146.7	2,216.2	6.5	18.7
Pittsburgh (MSA)	2,099,512	392.2	3,001.3	3.2	27.6
Birmingham (MSA)	929,861	788.2	4,720.9	15.5	44.3
MSAs U.S. Total	191,346,929	779.7	5,716.5	9.7	42.5

SOURCE: *Uniform Crime Reports for the United States,* 1989, by Federal Bureau of Investigation, U.S. Dept. of Justice, Washington, DC.

cludes as Appalachian. Pittsburgh and Birmingham, at the northern and southern end of the region, displayed striking differences that reinforced the findings of our selected samples. We also looked at the state totals for West Virginia, the only state that is totally Appalachian. The state has the lowest property crime rate in the U.S. and the sixth lowest violent crime rate in the nation.

David Hackett Fischer might be right about his assessment of violence in the South, but lumping the Southern Highlands in with the rest of the South may be doing this region a disservice. There *are* some parts of the region with exceptionally high murder rates. And even in West Virginia, with the lowest overall crime rate in the nation, the murder rate ranks only twenty-eighth at 6.5 per 100,000 population. Though the rate is still below the national average of 8.7, the murder rates are out of line with the low rates for other crimes in West Virginia.

These are disturbing figures and need further study. But focusing only on the small areas of Appalachia that do have exceptionally high murder rates obscures the nature of most of the region, with its remarkably low rates of both violent and property crime.

Note

Research assistance was provided by Charles Moore, Richard Blaustein, Carol Norris, Steven Patrick, and Steven Giles.

Bob Henry Baber

See volume I, chapter 5, for biography.

West Virginia Lowku

Federal statistics indicate
West Virginia has the highest percentage
of road fatalities
and the lowest crime rate.

I take this to mean
that the roads are crooked
and the people are straight.

From *Appalachian Journal* 13, no. 3 (Spring 1986): 287. Reprinted by permission of the author and publisher.

Peggy J. Cantrell

Peggy Cantrell, associate professor of psychology at East Tennessee State University, holds a Ph.D. in clinical psychology from the University of Southern Mississippi. Her experience includes a clinical psychology internship at St. Elizabeth's Hospital in Washington, D.C., and work in Southwest Virginia community mental health. Her research interests, focusing on gender-role issues and family violence, have yielded the only regionally based statistical evidence on the latter subject to date.

Rates of Family Violence and Incest in Southern Appalachia

When we think of violence, "family" is not the first word that comes to mind. Yet, his review of the literature led Richard Gelles in 1980 to describe the "American family as one of our country's most violent institutions" ("Violence" 878). Further, in 1992, the American Medical Associa-

---

Portions of this article are from the *Journal of Appalachian Studies* 6 (1994): 39–47. Reprinted by permission of the author and the publisher.

tion stated that more women are physically injured by family members each year than by car accidents, muggings, and stranger rape, *combined*. Millions of adults and children are injured by family members each year, leaving both short- and long-term physical and mental ill effects (Gelles, "Violence"; Gelles, *Family Violence*; Gelles and Cornell; Straus and Gelles).

Stereotypes portray Appalachia as more violent than other geographic regions of the U.S. However, archival research by Pat Arnow and Norma Myers on reported crimes challenges this assumption. According to FBI *Uniform Crime Reports*, Appalachian cities have lower levels of violent crime than comparably sized cities in other parts of the country (Arnow and Myers). A second aspect of the stereotype of Appalachia involves family relationships. That is, Appalachian families are stereotypically depicted as being more violent and/or incestuous than other families.

Though the national studies of the past decade have helped us better appreciate the levels of violence in families across the U.S. as a whole, there have been virtually no studies which focus on Appalachian families. Thus, I began a series of projects with the primary purpose of evaluating levels of intrafamily violence and incest in southern Appalachia. A secondary purpose was to delineate factors associated with the presence of family violence. This essay summarizes four projects spanning five years of data collection between 1986 and 1990.

For all of my projects, only families who had never been identified by an outside agency or practitioner as violent were included. In each case, the subject reporting on family behaviors was a young adult or adolescent family member. The first project utilized a random sample of freshmen and sophomores at a regional university, including 147 men and 286 women. Most were between eighteen and twenty years of age, single, Caucasian, and Protestant.

In the second and third projects, the entire sophomore high school population of a rural southwest Virginia county was utilized. Most of these students were sixteen years of age, single, Caucasian, and Protestant. Approximately 220 students participated in each project.

The final project focused on sexual histories of adult women, including, but not limited to, incestuous experiences. Two hundred and thirty-nine women, including members of a regional women's organization and university students, participated. Their ages ranged from 20 to 41 years, with a mean age of 30.33 years.

Participants completed questionnaires listing behaviors used during conflicts within families. Some of the behaviors were purely verbal, while others described physical exchanges. Those behaviors likely to cause pain in the recipient are considered violent. Examples of violent behaviors are pushing, shoving, grabbing, and slapping with an open hand. Those behaviors likely to cause injury are considered physically abusive. Behaviors which define physical abuse include kicking, biting, hitting with a hard object, hitting with a fist, beating up, using a knife or a gun (Straus). Participants also an-

swered demographic questions and questions about how their family functioned aside from conflict i.e., family closeness, communication, recreational
activities, etc.

The measure used in the fourth project was a sexual history questionnaire
modeled after that used by Finkelhor. The questionnaire includes items per-
taining to incest but does not exclusively focus on it.

The regional results follow the national trends reported by Straus and
Gelles (1990), but there are interesting points of departure. The rates of violence are similar, but the rate of more severe violence, or abuse, appears to be
significantly higher than that reported in national studies (Gelles and Cornell;
Straus and Gelles 1990). As in the national studies, the most commonly reported conflict behaviors were nonviolent, verbal negotiation, and verbal
abuse. However, violent behaviors were almost as common as the nonviolent
behaviors! Physical violence mother-to-subject was reported in more than 85
percent of the respondents, father-to-subject in 79 percent, father-to-mother
in 28 percent and mother-to-father in 27 percent.

To really capture the seriousness of interpersonal violence in families, it is
necessary to focus on those behaviors which are not only violent, but which
have a high potential for causing injury. When only the physically abusive
behaviors are examined, the reported rates are considerably lower, but still
alarming. Mother-to-father abuse was reported by 13.6 percent of the sample
and father-to-mother abuse by 12.4 percent. Twenty-two percent of the
sample reported mother-to-subject abuse and 20.1 percent reported father-
to-subject abuse.

In addition to the incidence of violent behaviors, I was also interested in
what factors were related to the presence of violence. One such factor was
parents' education level. When father's education level was 0–8 years or
when it was post college graduate, more subjects reported father-to-subject
abuse. More subjects reported father-to-mother abuse when father's education was 0–8 years, while fewer subjects did so when father's education level
was post college graduate. Mother's education level was significant in relation to father-to-mother abuse, with fewer subjects reporting abuse when
mother's education was college graduate, but more when mother's education
level was post college graduate. The upper levels of parents' education being
associated with abuse are findings unique to these regional studies. Elsewhere,
only lower levels of education are associated with higher levels of violence.

Subjects who indicated that their grandparents had been abusive reported
more violence in the current generation. This finding supports the adage that
"violence begets violence" as well as learning or modeling influences in the
cycle of family violence. It also emphasizes the need for prevention and early
intervention programs to disrupt the generational cycle of violence.

Father's employment status was significantly related to reported abuse,
with more subjects reporting abuse if father was unemployed. Unemployment increases family stress, a factor previously linked with family violence

(Voydanoff). Stress may arise from a variety of sources: economic, family disruption, social isolation, psychopathology. Abuse was more frequently reported in blended as opposed to biological families as well. Blended families may experience more stress.

Perhaps family stress also accounts for the relationship with parents' education and violence seen in the regional samples. Certainly low parent education is related to economic stress, but the highest levels of education may also be related to stress at the other end of the economic scale. Parents with the highest levels of education may be involved in high-stress careers and lifestyles which correlate with overall high stress. This is an interesting finding and hypothesis which warrant further study.

The inclusion of family process variables is unique to these projects and may be of use in identifying families at risk for violence for early intervention or prevention programs. Families who were described as being very rigid, with difficulty adapting to the changing needs of family members or demands from outside the family, and who were also enmeshed, demanding excessive closeness and loyalty from family members, were more often violent families. Certainly these are processes which could be targeted for family education or early intervention programs.

Switching from family violence to the results of the incest survey, we find alarming results as well. Although the father-daughter rates are comparable to those reported elsewhere (Russell), the other types of incestuous contact and the overall rate found in the regional sample are more than double those reported in the most respected national study to date (Russell). Thirty-eight percent of the regional women indicated that they had had at least one incestuous sexual experience before the age of eighteen years. In half of these cases, the other person involved was a brother. Uncles accounted for 27 percent of the reported incest (16 percent of the entire sample), and fathers accounted for 15 percent of the reports, or 4 percent of the entire sample (Peters and Cantrell).

All of the families across the local studies are nonclinical. That is, these families would not appear in any institutionally derived data on family violence because they have not been identified as such by the courts or human service agencies. Thus, the fact that already identified families were excluded, makes these figures even more astounding and disturbing.

Because these regional data are primarily based on adolescent family member reports and college samples, they should be considered preliminary. Though preliminary, these findings are the only body of empirically based data on the Appalachian region. Further, it would be expected that more broadly based samples which have greater demographic variety would show higher rather than lower rates of family violence. Being largely based on college student populations, these samples are going to include few families who are at the more extreme ends of social isolation, economic deprivation, and dysfunction. Additionally, the national samples did not necessarily exclude families who had known histories of family violence. Though it is surprising how much violence is revealed, we could also assume that subjects tend to underreport violence. In fact, Gelles maintains that family violence research may underestimate the incidence of family violence by as much as 50 percent (*Family Violence*)!

More extensive research is needed to unravel the puzzles of violence and incest in Appalachian families. Some features common in Appalachian families, i.e., the presence of extended family members, strong family networks, long-term rootedness in communities, and strong regional pride, would seem to be the types of factors which would facilitate resistance to family violence. Certainly deficits in these factors have been linked to violence elsewhere (Gelles and Cornell). Perhaps the Appalachian region has other cultural aspects exaggerated in the stereotype, including family structure (patriarchal, rigid, enmeshed) and social values (fierce independence, conservatism) which may contribute to domestic violence.

Ironically, the family is considered sacred in America and in Appalachia. Intrusions into the family by outsiders are resisted. Yet, until we know and understand the dark sides of family living, many individuals are going to continue to fall victim to their families rather than benefiting from the security and safety this institution should afford.

Works Cited

Arnow, Pat, and Norma Myers. "Crime in Appalachia: A Study of Cities." *Now and Then* 8, no. 2 (1990): 9–11.

Finkelhor, David. *Sexually Victimized Children.* New York: Free Press, 1978.

Gelles, Richard J. "Violence in the Family: A Review of the Research in the Seventies." *Journal of Marriage and the Family* 42 (1980): 873–85.

———. *Family Violence.* 2d ed. Newbury Park, CA: Sage, 1987.

Gelles, Richard J., and Claire P. Cornell. *Intimate Violence in Families.* 2d ed. Newbury Park, CA: Sage, 1990.

Peters, Debra K., and Peggy J. Cantrell. "Factors Distinguishing Samples of Lesbian and Heterosexual Women." *Journal of Homosexuality* 21, no. 4 (1991): 1–15.

Russell, Diana. "Incidence and Prevalence of Intrafamilial and Extrafamilial Sexual Abuse of Female Children." *Child Abuse and Neglect* 7 (1983): 133–46.

Straus, Murray A. "Measuring Intrafamily Conflict and Violence: The Conflict Tactics (CT) Scale." *Journal of Marriage and the Family* 41 (1979): 75–88.

Straus, Murray A., and Richard J. Gelles. *Physical Violence in American Families.* New Brunswick, NJ: Transaction Publishers, 1990.

Voydanoff, Patricia. "Economic Distress and Families." *Journal of Family Issues* 5 (1984): 273–88.

James G. Branscome
and James Y. Holloway

James G. Branscome is a native of Carroll County, Virginia, and a graduate of Berea College. A member of the Committee of Southern Churchmen, he has written extensively on Appalachia and the Tennessee Valley Authority.

James Y. Holloway is the founding editor of *Katallagete,* a journal of religious inquiry, published twice a year at Berea College. Also, he is McGaw Professor of Philosophy/Religion Emeritus, Berea College, Berea, Kentucky. He is the author of books and editor of anthologies about the South and southern Appalachia from a theological perspective.

Nonviolence and Violence in Appalachia

James G. Branscome

Consider Appalachian mountaineers. They are the "new world barbarians," Arnold Toynbee said—the only barbarians in history ever to attain civilization and then lose it. If they do not repent from their whiskey-crazed feuding, they should "perish," the *New York Times* said in a 1913 editorial. They are *Yesterday's People,* said the Reverend Jack Weller in a recent book by that title, a book that Appalachians rank as the most vicious and discriminatory ever written about them. Robert Coles, in a long review-article praising it, called the book "useful and affecting" and said it "belongs in the hands of all those—in the government, in the foundations, in the professions—concerned with the region." Writing last summer in *Southern Voices*, a journal of the Southern Regional Council, freelancer Lawrence Wright wrote that the people of Harlan County, Kentucky, had "lost the civilizing instinct to clean their nests." Not long ago the *Washington Post* refused to carry one episode of the "Doonesbury" cartoon strip on the grounds that it was "entirely too pointed and overstepped the bounds of decency;" yet that Watergate-exposé newspaper carries without censure Al Capp's "Li'l Abner" comic strip summing up hillbilly culture as "not readin, not worryin, not bathin!"

So one sits here in Appalachia thumbing through six fat manila folders that make up an "Anti-Hillbilly File," while the nation's media rush to Charleston, West Virginia, to paint a local textbook squabble—which in fact had to do with local control over schools more than anything else—into a new mural of the "monkey trials." Except this time, they mixed in coal miners as the dummies instead of William Jennings Bryan. Why these half-

From *Katallagete,* Winter 1974. Reprinted by permission.

truths, innuendoes, downright lies? Why, especially, from the world's, the nation's, the South's, "best" in media, academia, and the ministry of Jesus Christ? Why is it that otherwise sane people believe and write that mountaineers are the most apathetic people in the world, and yet somehow manage to believe and write that they are also the nation's most vicious and violent-prone people? Why "Bloody Harlan" and not also "*Bloody* Delano" and "*Bloody* Wounded Knee" and "*Bloody* Selma" and "*Bloody* Detroit" and "*Bloody* Attica?" and "*Bloody* Boston?" Why is it that Appalachians alone carry the burden of the violence *done against them*? And while suffering the stigma of being violent barbarians, why must they also suffer the spirit- and even life-choking propaganda (modern man's most eerie addition to violence) directed at their psyche?

The phenomenon is especially puzzling because mountaineers have performed most of their violent acts at our nation's urging. In fact, at its command. It was mountain folk who contributed to the winning of the Revolution with their victory in decisive battles at Kings Mountain and Guilford Court House. It was they who gave victory to Andrew Jackson in New Orleans, and rushed into the Battle of 1812 and the Mexican War. It was they, alone of southerners, who flew Union flags over their courthouses during the Civil War, displaying their loyalty to the nation, and put no less than 250,000 hill folk on the Yankee side in that battle. Only the industrial East exceeded mountaineers in total number in Teddy Roosevelt's charge into Cuba. In both World Wars, many mountain counties found draft boards unnecessary. West Virginia led the nation in per capita Vietnam deaths. Twenty-five West Virginians per 100,000 population were killed in that war, compared to seventeen for 100,000 nationally. These Ulster-bred settlers and their ancestors — haters of kings, bishops, and all those in authority—have reaped only scorn as their reward. Instead of plaques from the Pentagon, they get platitudes such as this one recently intoned by a major at Fort Knox: "They're awfully prone to desert and go AWOL." No matter that, at the nation's call, they have learned and practiced violence.

Despite the myths, and excepting their true-grit Americanisms in doing-in the Indians, mountaineers hung up their guns during the peace.

Appalachian counties, until the invasion of the industrial-technological complex, had among the lowest homicide rates in the nation. The people who had escaped into the hills to avoid tyranny were hardly interested in creating their own tyranny. So they wrote at Watauga, in eastern Tennessee, the first Constitution ever drafted by American-born whites. Even before the New England abolitionists were born, mountaineers were publishing antislavery newspapers and operating an underground railroad. Eli Embry was publishing the *Emancipator* in Jonesborough, Tennessee, even before William Lloyd Garrison had reached puberty. When the times demanded, mountain folks displayed an unusual talent for breaking away from the federal states and forming their own with names like the State of Franklin and West Virginia—all without slaughter. And, despite their modern liberal and outdoor dramatist detractors, the first U.S. Census showed them to have more reading and writing ability than their neighbors to the east. The Watauga Declaration, signed before the Revolution, contained the "X's" of only two men. Mountaineers, the facts indicate, have only one unforgivable trait: they never have believed, and probably never will believe, that "America" is a failure.

It should be pointed out, of course, in the interest of keeping the record straight, that the region is not a monolith, either culturally or economically. Its development has varied tremendously from one part of the mountains to the next, depending upon geography; availability of natural resources such as coal, timber, and water; and historical circumstances such as early settlement patterns and the choosing of sides in the Civil War. But the major factor in creating the complex social, economical, and political problems of today came with the gradual industrialization of the area over the past eighty years or so. The reaction of mountaineers to industrialization and technology is one of the most misunderstood and untold stories of American cultural history. It is in this encounter that mountaineers, for the sake of survival, have been forced to move against violence, mostly to lose.

James Y. Holloway

What may be the heart of the matter in the struggle against violence today begins—not necessarily chronologically—with who we are, where we stand, individually, specifically, concretely, in circumstance, about the violence in ourselves against those who are nearest to us. Not the decisions of a movement. Rather, each one deciding in one's own gut and head, not letting one's glands juice out a "group decision" after song, speeches, testimonies, and more songs. Rather, one, and by one: here, and there.

Maybe then a signal to Caesar? A signal passed into State (that is, Caesar's) policies? Doubtful, although it would be foolish to foreclose that possibility. In any case, Jacques Ellul's notions on the violence of the State as State, about "violence as necessity," confirms too much of my experience to believe seriously that nonviolence either ought to or can undertake to transfer a movement's convictions into Caesar's policies. It is a confusion of realms: of Caesar's, and Christ's. (After all, what State so recently bathed in the teachings of that greatest disciple of nonviolence just entered the community of "atomic devices"? Will anyone urge that that event nullifies the greatest disciple's teachings?) The State might just here and there glimpse in a refracted way witnesses to nonviolence, and might therefore be influenced to moderate its policies of violence. Sociologically, it would be ridiculous to deny that possibility. And that is to the good, so long as the State's moderation of overt violence does not produce in its wake a more subtle yet more effective form of violence by the State's dehumanizing dependencies and soul-crunching propagandas. But it never means that Caesar is "converted," or "transformed," or even "humanized," only that a witness at one time was an exception faintly heard by the State. In any event, such objectives can never be the goal of nonviolence, for nonviolent witness must always reckon with the opposite possibility: that the State today can digest nonviolent witness and spew out whenever and however to suit State purposes.

Ellul again: "the order of violence cannot be brought under moral judgment." (I underscore that Ellul's *Violence: Reflections from a Christian Perspective* [1969] is essential reading for this issue of *Katallagete*.) So the struggle against violence in our day is a specific and unique one; immediate to us: in bedroom or bar; with son, daughter, darlin' companion, even wife; in cocktail lounge, classroom, shop, committee meeting, supermarket, coffee-break, telephone call, hospital, bait store. We cannot be against violence or anything else—and certainly not in any "movement"—unless we recognize the almost limitless varieties and possibilities of violence in ourselves. Only then do we recognize the almost limitless varieties and possibilities, and shapes, forms, and levels of violence which rage outside and against us.

The struggle against violence today becomes a parable, but in fact a parable impossible *to be* by "doing" anything: only *being,* called by parables which are beyond us and which, therefore, most of us know only through the witness of others. Jesus: yes. Gandhi: yes. Others: yes, for we have seen their witnesses. A parable lived rather than actions "done," against all forms of violence—therefore a parable difficult *to be* in today's communal or community phrasings. Perhaps in our time only "incognito" (as Kierkegaard would phrase it; and, on this, see Ellul's *Hope in a Time of Abandonment* [1973]). The struggle against violence begins immediately and concretely where and how we are with the others nigh unto us at this moment, for it is only here that we experience violence for what it is in truth, in fact. It is only here that we have the basis for rejecting the many subtle and effective violences which silently yet ever so deadly make our *selves* and the ones who are nearest to us into abstractions, blanks, integers which buy soap or compute missile trajectories. There is no genuine struggle against violence in a wider context, in a movement context, unless the apprehension of and the temptation to violence is overcome in ourselves and against our neighbors. Otherwise, the wider context, the movement context, against violence becomes only one more abstraction that itself becomes violent.

The struggle against violence today—against, that is, the many ways our age has devised to debase, use, prostitute, make less-than-human, and murder us and those who are nearest to us—that struggle must always be concrete, unique to us and to where we are, and has nothing to do with Caesar's multidimensional schemings. Or rather, it ought not to have anything to do with what the State or any other complex is, or what they try to do to us. Instead, it has to do with who and how we are with the others who are nearest to us: with who we see in those who are nigh. When we see in the one who is neighbor only an abstraction, a blank that walks and talks but is not with and in us, since we are not with and in him, then we see in the neighbor only those multidimensional, well-known abstractions of racism, poverty, Vietnam, ecology, Watergate, inflation/deflation. And we react accordingly with those well-known violences which are characteristic of the policies of political messianism. We see in the one who is nigh to us the States' abstraction of him, so we debase him, pollute him, use him, commit adultery against him, kill him—in racism, poverty, Vietnam, ecology, Watergate, inflation/deflation: And there is no struggle against the violence in ourselves and against our specific deeds of violence against those who are near.

And thus does the latent totalitarianism of the State become actual, because the one bulwark against political messianism renders to Caesar the things that are God's. The ones who are near us become abstractions of the State, or the media, or of education, psychiatry, group-therapy, assorted liberation efforts, economics, technology, and movements. We join enthusiastically with our bodies and our money in their judgment about what "to do" about the abstractions by more legislation, investigations, antipersonnel missiles, Chevrolets-for-America, Masters-and-Johnson, Burger Kings, and Ban Roll-On.

Such is the quality of our age in which the struggle against violence takes place: the violence of "doing" something, *being* no-thing.

&

The confession at the outset of these reflections is that, from personal experiences and encounters in the '40s and '50s as well as the '60s, to this day I do not know what nonviolence means as a movement.

When this is said, however, it becomes necessary to emphasize again what was urged some paragraphs back. This not to condone, excuse, justify, say less, wink at, violence which *in any form* necessarily diminishes *in any way* one's humanity. For one thing, the past thirty years demonstrate how the complex which now energizes America "digests" (that is, assimilates) violence so efficiently. (What I mean, as an example, is the final insignificance, for those most intimately concerned, of the ghetto rebellions and Far Left desperations of the mid- and late '60s.) More concretely, for another, what is meant is that Christ defines our humanity (not we, his). It is Jesus in us and in those nigh to us who rejects the State's abstraction of us, and our neighbor. He is God's gift which frees us from the grip of violence's necessity— and especially the necessity to justify, as a sanction of Christ's, violence by the State or The Revolution.

Works Cited

Ellul, Jacques. *Hope in Time of Abandonment.* New York: Seabury P, 1973.
———. *Violence: Reflections from a Christian Perspective.* New York: Seabury P, 1969.

Chapter 8

Exile, Return, and Sense of Place

Introduction

Appalachia is perhaps one of the few places in the country where the concept of homeland still has great vitality. For those raised among them, the mountains are the *Heimat*, in the true German sense of the word, with its connotations of an inexpressible quality which is both a gift to and a claim upon its constituents.

Why, then, do many Appalachians leave if the place is so important to them? Some leave simply as a matter of preference. Many blacks abandoned the post–Civil War South in search of basic freedoms. Others, black and white, responded to the push and pull of economic forces, and for those who leave willingly, leaving becomes exile. Some young people, like Thomas Wolfe, quit the small town for personal quests of education and discovery, proclaiming that one can't go home again. Yet Wolfe continually acknowledged the tug of home in his fiction. Some flee the law to be returned home by extradition. Others, such as those described by Abraham Verghese in *My Own Country*, return home seeking the consolation of family after contracting AIDS in major cities. Homesickness is a familiar Appalachian malady as illustrated by Gertie Nevels in the classic Appalachian novel *The Dollmaker*. Thus the motif of the Return forms an important part of Appalachian creative expression reaching back to the earliest known literature.

Of course, many Appalachians stay in place, perpetuating Appalachia's distinctive characteristics and maintaining a sense of continuity in the face of perpetual change. For them, life in the Appalachians provides the solid ground upon which to make one's stand for better or worse. What both expatriate and die-hard share is a respect and love for the land and its people, and a sense, however lost or beguiled, of home.

Nikki Giovanni

A native of Knoxville, Tennessee, Nikki Giovanni moved with her family to Cincinnati when she was two years old. She earned her B.A. at Fisk University, Nashville, Tennessee, where she graduated with honors. She also attended the University of Pennsylvania School of Social Work and Columbia University's School of the Arts. Giovanni was an associate professor of English at Rutgers University and later a professor of creative writing at Mount St. Joseph-on-the-Ohio, Mount St. Joseph, Ohio. A prominent figure in the 1960s black literary renaissance, Giovanni has earned an international reputation as a poet, essayist, and lecturer. Her first three books of poetry, *Black Feeling, Black Talk* (1968), *Black Judgement* (1968), and *Re: Creation* (1970), aimed to awaken people to the beauty of blackness by blending introspection with social and political activism. The autobiographical *Gemini* (1971) was nominated for the 1973 National Book Award. The birth of her son Thomas in 1969 precipitated a shift in focus from revolution to family, and Giovanni began to write children's poetry while continuing to write for adults. The poems in *Those Who Ride the Night Winds* (1983) reveal a heightened self-knowledge and imagination as well as a continuing concern for political awareness. In 1987 Giovanni moved to Virginia Polytechnic Institute and State University under the Commonwealth Visiting Professor program and elected to remain and teach as well as continue writing.

Knoxville, Tennessee

I always like summer
best
you can eat fresh corn
from daddy's garden
and okra
and greens
and cabbage
and lots of
barbecue
and buttermilk
and homemade ice-cream
at the church picnic
and listen to
gospel music
outside
at the church

From *Black Feeling, Black Talk, Black Judgement* (Quill Publishers, 1970). © 1970 by Nikki Giovanni. Reprinted by permission of the author.

homecoming
and go to the mountains with
your grandmother
and go barefooted
and be warm
all the time
not only when you go to bed
and sleep

Gurney Norman

Gurney Norman is one of the leading writers of Southern Appalachia. Born in Grundy, Virginia, he grew up in Hazard in the eastern Kentucky coalfields. He was educated at the University of Kentucky and at Stanford University, where, as a Wallace Stegner Fellow, he studied short-story writing with Frank O'Connor.

Norman is the author of *Divine Right's Trip,* which was first published in segments in *The Last Whole Earth Catalog* (1971) and of *Kinfolks: The Wilgus Stories* (1977), a book of short stories including "Fat Monroe," which was made into a movie featuring Ned Beatty. He is also the author of narratives for three documentary programs on Kentucky and Appalachian history for Kentucky Educational Television. Professor of English at the University of Kentucky, he is also an instructor for the Hindman Settlement School Appalachian Writers Workshop conducted annually at Hindman, Kentucky. Norman is noted as much as a teacher of writing as he is as an author.

Norman's novel *Divine Right's Trip* follows the title hero as he makes an emotional and intellectual odyssey from boyhood to manhood and from exile to return. The following selection from that novel depicts the hero's response to the first sight of familiar ground.

Where Daniel Boone Stood

Big Hill

In the section of Kentucky where the bluegrass and the eastern mountains meet, near Berea, one of the major landmarks is Big Hill. There are several distinctive hills and knobs and rises in the vicinity, but Big Hill is the dominant land mass for several miles around. For travelers on U.S. 421, the bottom of Big Hill represents the precise dividing line between the flat lands

From *Divine Right's Trip* (Frankfort, KY: Gnomon Press, 1990). Reprinted by permission of the publisher.

and the branch of the Appalachian Mountains known as the Cumberland Plateau. At the bottom, the traveler headed west is entering the Kentucky bluegrass country. From the top, he faces a range of hills flowing south and east for more than a hundred miles, until they are finally broken by the broad agriculture valleys of southwestern Virginia and East Tennessee.

Big Hill is a special place upon the ground, and it was an important feature in the landscape of D. R.'s mind as well, because it reminded him so much of his father, and Daniel Boone. The Boone legend in Kentucky, or one version of it anyway, has it that it was from Big Hill that Boone got his first look at the lush central Kentucky plain, the fabled garden spot that had been the object of his fantasy and quest. When D. R. would ride over Big Hill with his father, his father never failed to make some reference to Boone and the Wilderness Road. D. R. had no idea how many times that might have been, but surely it was in the thousands. When his father left the coal country of Kentucky in the fifties and moved the family to Cincinnati, they came home every weekend for the next year, and almost every weekend for two years after that. And they always passed over Big Hill on their way to the homeplace up in Finley County.

His father would say, "Right here now David's where old Boone got his first look at his new country. Stopped right over there by that mailbox, could see as far as he could see." He would grin then, and wait for David to respond. He made the joke two times every weekend, coming and going, but somehow it was always funny. David would begin to anticipate it miles before his father would say it, like a story he knew but never got tired of hearing. His father would say, "Yes sir, old Boone leaned his gun against that very mailbox yonder, and looked all around."

One time when Boone leaned his gun against the mailbox he found a letter in it from John L. Lewis that said DON'T COME TO KENTUCKY, BOYS, THE WORK'S TOO HARD AND THERE'S TOO DAMN LITTLE PAY. Another time there was a letter to Daniel from his brother Squire that said, "If you see a boy named David Ray Collier out in them woods, you send him home, he's too young to roam."

David said, "There was not."

"Oh yes there was too," said his father.

His father's name was Royce. Royce Collier. And in those days, before his mother's second marriage to Wallace Davenport, Collier was David Ray's last name too.

"Oh yes," said Royce. "Squire sent that very letter to Daniel Boone. You ask Doyle here if he didn't."

Doyle, the assistant driver and chief mechànic for the old Pontiac, only twenty-four then, tall and lean, fresh out of the Army, sitting in the front seat beside Marcella, would nod and say that it was so, and that if David didn't believe it he could just ask Royce there. And round and round it would go, two men supporting each other's teasing lie, and sometimes it was funny and David would laugh, and sometimes they would tease too far and hurt David's feelings, and then he would sit back into the crowd of cousins in the rear seat and pout the rest of the way to the homeplace.

Recollection

That car of Daddy's was an old Pontiac he bought with the first wages he ever earned in Cincinnati. It had over a hundred thousand miles on it when he got it, but he never hesitated to take off in it for Kentucky. The first year we lived up there we never missed a weekend going home. Fifty-two round trips in a year, over two hundred miles each way, six, seven, sometimes eight and nine people in it every run. Every Friday as soon as Daddy'd get home from work we'd load up and head out, and drive six straight hours south on old U.S. 25, through Lexington and Richmond, east into the hills on 421, then down state route 666 to the homeplace in Finley County. In the wintertime it would be dark before we even set out, but in the summers the light would hold 'til almost Richmond, and I remember the programs that came on the radio about that time of day. My daddy played the guitar some, and he loved hillbilly music, and so at six o'clock he'd tune in the Hillbilly Hit Parade out of WCKY in Cincinnati. I remember it started and ended with somebody's fierce picking of the "Steel Guitar Rag," and then when it was over Wayne Rainey and Lonnie Glossen would come on, trying to sell harmonica instruction courses. Wayne and Lonnie were good musicians too, and when they'd get wound up Daddy would get excited and start to sing along with them, and bounce around in his seat and beat on the steering wheel with his hand. He'd cut up like that for miles and miles. He'd tickle us all so much we'd forget how uncomfortable we were, piled on top of one another in the back seat of that old car. On Fridays you wouldn't mind being uncomfortable because you knew you were on your way to someplace you really wanted to be a lot, but on Sundays you'd feel so blue about having to leave the homeplace to go back to Cincinnati there wasn't any way in the world to get comfortable and Daddy would have to stop every hour or so and let people out to stretch. We hated it, coming back, but then it was only five more days 'til we'd go down home again, and we cheered ourselves up with that thought. The five days would drag by but finally Friday would get there. Daddy would come in from work, clean up a little and then there we'd be, on the road again. About six hours later we'd turn off at Mrs. Godsey's store and drive up Trace Fork to the homeplace.

It would be midnight by the time we'd get there and Grandma and Granddad would be in bed asleep. Granddad never let anything keep him from getting his sleep, but if Grandma was feeling well she'd get up and come in the kitchen and hug us all and start taking cornbread and beans and cold mashed potatoes out of the oven and setting them on the table. Daddy would say here now Mommy, you quit that, we've all done and eat. But Grandma would keep hauling out the food and before long we'd all be seated at the table, me and Daddy and Marcella and Doyle and usually some of Doyle's kinfolks would be with us and they'd sit down too and there we'd all be, in the middle of the night at Grandma's house, eating cold beans and potatoes and blackberry jam on that good cold cornbread.

Then it wouldn't seem like half an hour 'til there we'd be again, sitting at the table, Granddad with us this time, the beans and potatoes hot now, the pork hot, the beets hot, the cornbread hot, the cobbler hot, and the milk cold as ice from sitting all night in the spring house. That would be Saturday dinner. Sunday dinner was always chicken and gravy and cole slaw with beans and potatoes, a big pone of biscuit instead of cornbread, and ice tea for those that didn't want milk.

Sunday dinner was considered the best meal of the week at the homeplace but I never did like it after we moved away because it was after Sunday dinner that we always had to load up in the Pontiac again and go back to Cincinnati. I was always too sad to eat much on Sundays, and what little I would eat I'd usually throw up as soon as we got back on the road. At dinnertime on Saturday I'd eat like a starved horse, thinking: twenty-four hours. Twenty-four whole hours to romp around the pasture and the woods, then in the evenings to hang around with my grandfather while he went about his chores. On Saturday that twenty-four hours stretched away forever, but when it was over and it was time to leave it would all seem like some strange little fifteen-second dream.

When it was time to go, Grandma and Granddad would follow us out to the car and stand around while we got in. Then Daddy would start the motor, back up to the coal pile, fight the steering wheel 'til the wheels turned, then ease forward down the lane, pausing in front of Grandma and Granddad for a final good-bye. I always wanted to cry at that point but I never did, except once as we were leaving, at the last second, as a surprise, Grandma tossed a Payday candy bar to me through the window and hit me in the eye. I let out a terrific squawl, and cried 'til it was time to get out of the car and puke. I held my eye and screeched like I was mortally wounded, but the thing nobody knew was that I wasn't really crying about being hit in the eye at all. All that was just an excuse for this other kind of crying I wanted to do, which I did plenty of on that occasion. I suffered pretty bad that trip 'til we got back down around Big Hill and Daddy started carrying on about Daniel Boone again. Daddy always made me laugh on Big Hill, and passing over it tonight I could feel that old familiar laugh sensation start to rumble in my guts again.

P. J. Laska

Born in 1938 the son of a West Virginia coal miner, P. J. Laska is professor, poet, and novelist. He served four years in the U.S. Air Force before beginning a college career that culminated in a Ph.D. from the University of Rochester in 1968. He then taught philosophy at colleges including York University in Ontario, Canada, and the University of Arizona. Laska's first book of poems, *D.C. Images and Other Poems* (1975) received a National Book Award nomination. In addition to several more volumes of poetry, Laska wrote a novel, *The Day the Eighties Began* (1991). A contributor of poetry to anthologies such as *Soupbean: An Anthology of Contemporary Appalachian Literature* (1977), Laska also contributes articles to journals including the *Minnesota Review* and *Southern Exposure*. Laska has cited William Carlos Williams and the Imagist movement as the basis for his development as a poet.

The Hillbilly Odyssey

It began veiled and immovable,
like mountains
in the morning mist.
Early sight
was that of a blind baby
with a sense of fate.
Old fears
labeled existential
clobbered them right away.

In debt up to their necks
those black lung checks
came too late
to save the families bustin up.
Some ran away
and joined the Army.
Some went up North
looking for jobs,
while big city culture snickered
at those hillbilly white socks.

In those days nothing worked
but self-hypnosis
and Dale Carnegie speech lessons:
If they could stop stuttering
they figured they could speak
and that would be a step
in the right direction.
Then when the world turns round
and forward comes back,
they bend but don't crack.
They don't let up,
they just keep on
beginning again.

© by P. J. Laska. From *Songs & Dances* (Prince, WV: The Unrealist Press, 1977), 21. Reprinted by permission of the author.

Phillip J. Obermiller

and Michael E. Maloney

The relevance of this article is underscored by the passage in November 1992 of a Cincinnati ordinance which singled out Appalachians for protection against discrimination.

Phillip Obermiller received his Ph.D. in sociology from the Union Institute in 1982. From 1982 to 1992, he taught at Northern Kentucky University, Highland Heights, where he was an associate professor of sociology. He is currently a Center Associate at the University of Kentucky's Appalachian Center. Obermiller is a founding member of the Appalachian Studies Association and of the Urban Appalachian Council in Cincinnati. A former officer and board member of the council, he remains an active member of its research committee.

Michael E. Maloney is a native of Breathitt County, Kentucky, and an urban consultant for the Appalachian People's Service Organization, Cincinnati. He teaches Appalachian studies at Xavier University, Cincinnati, and Chatfield College, Saint Martin, Ohio.

Living City, Feeling Country: The Current State and Future Prospects of Urban Appalachians

The term "urban Appalachian" was coined in the early 1970s by Appalachians living in midwestern cities to describe themselves after they realized that the term "Appalachian migrant" was no longer appropriate. Most of these people were not migrants in the sense that they had moved recently from one region to another, or in the sense that applies to migrant farm workers.

"Urban Appalachian" became the favored term to describe those people and their descendants who had come from the Appalachian region to live and work in cities outside of Appalachia. The original migrants are referred to as first-generation migrants, their children as second-generation migrants, their grandchildren as the third generation, and so on. The term "urban Appalachian" is also used at times to characterize the population of urban centers within Appalachia such as Knoxville or Pittsburgh, but this usage is less frequent.

As used in this chapter, the term "urban Appalachian" includes both migrants to cities outside of the Appalachian region and their descendants of whatever generation. For simplicity we shall refer to the first and second generations as the early generations, and to the third, fourth, and following generations as the subsequent generations.

The phenomenon of Appalachian migration has been well documented

From *Appalachia: Social Context Past and Present,* 3d ed., ed. Bruce Ergood and Bruce E. Kuhre, Kendall-Hunt, 1991. Reprinted by permission of the authors.

over the past twenty years. From 1940 to 1960, more than seven million people, including most of the rural youth, left Appalachia, while only three million people moved into the region during the same period. Thus the region lost four million people during what is referred to by James S. Brown (1962) as "the Great Migration." This mass migration not only depleted the population of Appalachia, but also had the effect of creating large communities of urban Appalachians in metropolitan centers outside of the region (McCoy and Brown). The cities receiving much of this migration were located primarily in Ohio, Indiana, Illinois, and Michigan. During the 1980s, with the decline of employment in the manufacturing industries in the Rustbelt and the growth of labor and service employment in the Sunbelt, Appalachian migration streams shifted away from the midwestern states towards states in the South and West (Obermiller and Oldendick, "Moving On").

Much has been written about the social problems, emergent ethnicity, and class status of urban Appalachians. The social problems faced in Appalachian communities are being addressed through cultural, advocacy, and self-help organizations in several cities (Maloney, "Prospects"; Wagner, "Too Few Tomorrows"). Much of the literature on urban Appalachians produced over the past two decades focuses on their emergence as a new urban ethnic group (Obermiller, "The Question"; Philliber, *Appalachian Migrants*). More recently researchers have gone beyond the issue of ethnicity to investigate the position of Appalachians in the urban social class structure (Obermiller, "Labeling Urban Appalachians"; Philliber, "The Future of Appalachians").

Most urban Appalachians have now lived outside of the region for all of, or the greater portion of, their lives. Since millions of Appalachians have made the transition from rural newcomers to long-term residents of urban neighborhoods, new questions are being asked. Given the fact that over three decades have gone by since the peak years of Appalachian migration, how are these people and their children faring in the cities? How do they compare on key social indicators with other urban groups? Are Appalachians assimilating into urban culture or returning to the region? What are some of the key social policy questions they have raised for urban administrators and politicians?

This essay will attempt to shed some light on these questions. To do so, it will be necessary to draw on various studies that use a variety of methods. The Cincinnati metropolitan area has an extensive history of Appalachian immigration and an equally extensive repertoire of current social research on urban Appalachians. Although the studies we refer to focus on Appalachians in the urban counties of northern Kentucky and southwestern Ohio, we believe that the findings can be extrapolated to urban Appalachians living in similar metropolitan areas outside the region.

We shall proceed by first discussing the demographic information we have on first- and second-generation urban Appalachians. We then consider the conditions affecting subsequent generations of Appalachians. We conclude with an analysis that looks beyond the current status of urban Appalachians to the issues that will affect them in the decade of the 1990s.

The Early Generations: A Demographic Profile

In both 1980 and 1989, questions were placed on the Greater Cincinnati Survey that allowed for identification of first- and second-generation urban Appalachians. The surveys used a random-digit dialing technique to contact approximately one thousand respondents in Hamilton County, Ohio, the county in which Cincinnati is located. The sampling procedure and response rate allowed for confidence intervals ranging between 3 and 5 percent for each question. The respondents were divided into three comparison groups: white non-Appalachians (white), black non-Appalachians (black), and white Appalachians (Appalachian). Because of their relatively small numbers in the sample (2.3%) and their ambiguous status, black Appalachians were not included in either the black or Appalachian cohort (cf. Philliber and Obermiller, "Black Appalachian Migrants").

The early generations of urban Appalachians make up a substantial portion of Hamilton County's population. In 1980 they constituted a quarter of the people living in the county; nine years later they still accounted for one in five of the county's residents. Although migration has slowed, natural increase is adding to the urban Appalachian cohort and, taking into consideration the third and fourth generations, we estimate that the Appalachian component may be as much as 40 percent of the county's total population.

First- and second-generation urban Appalachians are about evenly split in terms of cohort size, but, as one would expect, have different age dynamics. The average age of first generation Appalachians in 1989 was 49, while the average age for the second generation was 43. Although the longitudinal data indicate that Appalachians are aging faster than non-Appalachians and that the first generation is aging more slowly than the second generation, we must be cautious in interpreting these figures. First of all, since our sample is comprised of only the first two generations of Appalachians, the Appalachians appear to be older than the non-Appalachians cohort because the latter does not select out particular generations for analysis. Second, because first-generation Appalachians naturally have a higher mortality rate than the second generation, their average ages appear to be rising more slowly over time.

Despite these cautions, the data indicate clearly that first- and second-generation Appalachians form a large cohort that is substantially above the average age of the non-Appalachian groups in the county. In 1989 the average age of blacks was 39, of whites 43, and of Appalachians 46. The early migrants and their children are growing old, and this fact will have a strong effect on the interpretation of the other Appalachian demographic characteristics.

The ratio of men to women in the urban Appalachian community is shifting over time to a higher proportion of women. By 1989, 61 percent of Appalachians surveyed were women and 39 percent were men. This is coherent with an aging population in which men tend to die at an earlier age than women.

The fact that migration has slowed and Appalachians are long-term residents in urban areas is documented in the 1989 figures on length of residence. For blacks the average length of residence in the county was 29, for whites it was 32, and for Appalachians it was 31. Since 1980 this represents a slight increase for blacks, a modest increase for whites, and a large increase for Appalachians. Again, this change can be linked to the age factor; since Appalachians tend to be older overall, they have had a greater opportunity to establish a longer residency period. Nonetheless, it is important to note that Appalachians are long-term urban residents with very few recent migrants among them; only 3.5 percent had lived in the county two years or less, and 67.3 percent had lived there twenty-one years or more.

From another perspective on residency, Appalachians are becoming more urban over time. In 1980, 68.6 percent of the Appalachian respondents lived in the suburban areas of the county surrounding the city of Cincinnati, and only 31.4 percent were city dwellers. By 1989 a significant shift had taken place, with 44.4 percent living in the city and 55.6 percent living in the balance of the county. The comparative statistics show that the proportions of blacks and Appalachians living in the Cincinnati part of Hamilton County have shown large increases in the period between 1980 and 1989. Cincinnati is becoming a city with a growing minority population that is mostly black and Appalachian.

The data on marital status and household size indicate that the urban Appalachian family remains a strong social unit. Appalachians are more likely to be married or widowed than either blacks or whites. Conversely, they are much less likely to have never married than either of the other two groups. The fact that over seven in ten Appalachian respondents reported that they were married can be attributed in part to the higher average age of this group. However, this argument is diminished somewhat by the fact that urban Appalachian divorce rates are about one-third those reported by blacks and on a par with those reported by whites.

The average household size for Appalachians (3.1) remained constant over the nine-year period of the two surveys, and is about the same as that for blacks and whites. The average number of adults in Appalachian households (2.3) has grown slightly from 1980 to 1989, while decreasing for the other two groups. The average number of children under age eighteen in Appalachian households (.77) has declined between 1980 and 1989, and is lower than that of either blacks or whites. The larger number of adults and smaller number of children in Appalachian households is consistent with the higher average age of the household members.

Urban Appalachians are the least likely among the three groups to report no religious affiliation. Seventy percent of those surveyed reported being Protestant, but nearly 20 percent reported being Catholic, a substantial gain in the latter category since 1980. The proportion of Protestants among Appalachians and blacks is similar, and these groups are distinctly different from the whites, half of whom are Catholic and two-fifths of whom are Protestant.

Educational attainment has improved for urban Appalachians in the interval between the two surveys. In 1989 Appalachians had fewer high school dropouts (17% vs. 27%) and more students in college and graduates from college (45% vs. 36%) than in 1980. However, in 1989 Appalachians held the same relative status in educational attainment as they had in 1980, that is, they fared better than blacks but worse than other whites. The data on educational attainment show that blacks are more likely to drop out of high school and college than Appalachians, while whites are more likely to complete high school and college than Appalachians. When the sample is confined to Appalachians living in inner-city neighborhoods, their educational outcomes are even worse than those for urban blacks (Obermiller and Oldendick, "Urban Appalachian Health").

The overall occupational status of urban Appalachians declined between 1980 and 1989. During this period, Appalachians gained in the number of sales and clerical jobs they held (+14%), but lost ground in the job categories of craftspersons (-10%) and operatives (-7%). Unfortunately, significant employment growth for Appalachians came in the lowest occupational category, that of laborers and service workers (+12%). Blacks also showed substantial growth in the labor and service category, while the growth in this area of employment was only half as large for whites.

The rate of unemployment among Appalachians has dropped slightly from 1980, but is well over double those reported for both whites and blacks in the 1989 survey. This last statistic must be tempered with the knowledge that many Appalachians work outside of the standard employer-employee relationship; they work for themselves in the informal economy doing home maintenance, roofing, hauling, appliance and auto repair, providing child care, and selling goods at flea markets. These individuals may not consider themselves "employed" in the traditional sense, but they are working hard to maintain their family's income.

Between 1980 and 1989, the number of Appalachian families with total incomes of less than $20,000 a year declined, and the number with annual incomes over $30,000 a year rose. However, in the middle-income category, $20,000 to $30,000, Applachian families lost ground. Overall Appalachian representation across the family income categories is on a par with whites and significantly better than figures for black families. Although this pattern may vary between inner-city and suburban neighborhoods, it has remained constant at the county level from 1980 and 1989. A significant portion of Appalachian family income is provided by women, some four-fifths of whom are in the labor force.

The Subsequent Generation: Prospects for the Future

The situation of subsequent generations of urban Appalachians can be described in a more qualitative fashion. A minority has obtained a college education, moved away from blue-collar Appalachian neighborhoods, and largely assimilated into a large urban culture. Others have moved from the old neighborhoods but maintain blue-collar lifestyles, including their extended family and a group of Appalachian friends as their primary social network. Most urban Appalachians, however, continue to live in working-class neighborhoods whose principal residents are other white Appalachians.

Appalachian neighborhoods vary greatly in their locations within the metropolitan area and in the socioeconomic status of their residents. Some are inner-city neighborhoods characterized by multifamily rental units and high rates of underemployment, unemployment, and poverty. These communities are affected by the social problems typical of such areas: high rates of crime and delinquency, teen pregnancy, substance abuse, child neglect, and family violence. While it is common to think of these neighborhoods as slums, it is more useful to think of them as low-income ethnic neighborhoods or urban villages (Gans). An urban village is an area of low-cost housing in which a group, usually immigrants, rebuilds the family, community, and economic structures that were debilitated by migration. Life in the urban village is more familiar to the earlier generations of Appalachian migrants than to the subsequent generations.

William Philliber (*Appalachian Migrants*) found that the majority of urban Appalachians in Cincinnati do not live in inner-city neighborhoods. Most live in working-class communities, some of which are located in the suburbs. Appalachians also make up a significant part of the population of small towns and cities that surround metropolitan core cities like Cincinnati (Obermiller and Maloney, in press).

Education is a critical issue for the Appalachians of the subsequent generations. Early migrants could obtain manufacturing jobs that merely required physical dexterity and some mechanical aptitude. In an era when most jobs with reasonable salaries require advanced skills, urban Appalachian students drop out of high school in large numbers (Maloney and Borman). Many reasons have been advanced to explain the high rates of school failures and dropouts among urban Appalachians (Maloney et. al.). School administrators point to absenteeism and a lack of interest in education among Appalachian parents. Appalachians regard urban public school systems as large, impersonal bureaucracies with little cultural sensitivity. Whatever the explanation, the fact remains that urban Appalachians in Ohio drop out of school at rates even higher than those of other cultural and racial minorities.

The early generations of Appalachians arrived in the cities during an era of industrial expansion and strong unions; semiskilled jobs were plentiful, wages were rising, and health and retirement benefits were generally available. Because of this blue-collar background, urban Appalachians of the subsequent generations have been devastated by the decline of the automobile, steel, and other manufacturing industries in the Midwest. These workers and their families have adapted in a variety of ways. Some have gone back to the mountains, but this option is limited by the lack of work and housing in rural Appalachia. Others have moved to the urban growth centers of the South and the West in search of work. Some of those who stayed found replacement jobs in the industrial sector, but many have been forced to settle for lower-paying jobs in the service sector of the formal economy or to resort to work in the informal economy. Family income is maintained by increasing the number of workers; spouses and children all take jobs to supplement the household budget.

Family networks are still heavily used to find employment or to provide a temporary place to live while job searching. Those lacking family support may go on public assistance or get help from their church or a local social agency, but this is considered a strategy of last resort. Appalachians living in inner-city areas who have lost the support of their families and neighbor-hood social welfare agencies can be found living on the streets, in shelters for the homeless, and in the lines at soup kitchens.

As with education and employment, health conditions among the subse-quent generations vary greatly. Urban Appalachians in poverty have high rates of coronary heart disease, diabetes, and work-related disabilities. Their children suffer from lack of perinatal care, poor nutrition, and the effects of urban pollu-tion. Sexually transmitted diseases affect many Appalachian teenagers. Among all generations of urban Appalachians, injuries related to work are common, as are illnesses due to stress and diet such as diabetes, hypertension, and heart dis-ease (Obermiller and Oldendick, "Urban Appalachian Health").

A key question concerning the subsequent generations is whether they are losing their Appalachian identity and assimilating into the cultural main-stream. With some exceptions, most urban Appalachians are concentrated in blue-collar enclaves, in urban neighborhoods, suburban communities, and small town settings. Because of their numbers, they often form the majority population in these places. In addition to living near relatives and other people with an Appalachian background, they associate with their own kind at work, in their churches, labor unions, civic associations, schools, and in lo-cal bars and restaurants. Their music, dance, crafts, and artistic traditions are constantly being renewed through arts and crafts festivals, bluegrass preserva-tion societies, records, tapes, films, and radio programs. Although there are more Appalachians in Ohio's Miami Valley (Cincinnati, Hamilton, Middletown, Dayton, Xenia, Troy) than in all of eastern Kentucky, the residents of these towns make use of the easy access to their homeplaces and kinfolk in the moun-tains. To a certain extent, urban Appalachians resemble Mexican-Americans in the southwestern U.S. who gain cultural support from visits or frequent com-munication with their home districts in rural Mexico.

Most studies of migrant groups find that ethnic identity begins to dwindle with the third generation (Philliber, "The Future of Appalachians"). However, the process of assimilation is slowed by ethnic organizations with strong leader-ship that promotes the cultural heritage and the political concerns of the group. It is also hindered by the presence of discrimination and the perception by the group of exclusion from the economic and social mainstream. We believe that all the factors we have cited are limiting the absorption of Appalachians into the dominant urban society. There is no danger of the disappearance of Appala-chians from the social map of urban America in the 1990s.

Comments and Policy Recommendations

We now turn to an analysis of data on urban Appalachians and a commentary on the social policy and program implications of this information. In discussing the data we again take care to distinguish among urban Appalachians by both age (early generations vs. subsequent generations) and by socioeconomic status (suburban vs. inner-city).

The early generations of urban Appalachians are clearly an aging population. During the 1990s their concerns can be expected to move away from a focus on education and employment and turn to health care. Moreover, many urban Appalachians are aging in place rather than returning to the region for retirement (Obermiller and Maloney, "Looking for Appalachians in Pittsburgh"). On the contrary, many elderly Appalachians are being moved from the region by their urban kinfolk to metropolitan areas where access to health care facilities, nursing homes, retirement communities, and the potential for in-home care is much more abundant.

The aging of the early generations also has implications for urban Appalachian women, the traditional caregivers in the Appalachian cultural milieu. At a time when the number of children per household is beginning to fall, and women's educational attainment and labor force participation have begun to rise, care for the elderly will become a larger part of the responsibilities in Appalachian households. Much of this duty will devolve upon the women in the household.

From a policy standpoint, the aging of the urban Appalachian population will require more resources in the areas of health care and geriatric services. From a programmatic point of view, social welfare organizations will need to be concerned not only with the Appalachian elderly but also with their caregivers, who for the most part will be working women.

Among the subsequent generations, adult education and job training will continue to be important issues. The longitudinal data show urban Appalachians losing way on a socioeconomic treadmill; even as their educational attainment improves, the demand for education in the labor force increases at a higher rate. This explains why members of the early generations who have increased their rates of high school completion are gradually slipping into lower-status job categories over time. In these families, a stable income can be maintained only by maximizing the number of workers in the family. If the cost of living increases while family size remains stable, many working-class urban Appalachians will slip into poverty.

The situation for inner-city Appalachians is even more grim. Half of the adults in these neighborhoods have no more than a high school education, school dropout rates range as high as 75 percent, and youth unemployment is a serious problem. While social problems abide in these neighborhoods, the urban Appalachian community is not without resources to deal with them. In Cincinnati, community schools have been founded to provide on-site G.E.D. programs, adult education courses, and college-level classes. The

Appalachian extended family has been battered but not broken as a social unit. It still provides the social and economic resources necessary for its members to survive in an urban setting.

Policy makers need to focus not only on the problems in the urban Appalachian community, but also on its inherent strengths. Every effort should be made to recognize and reinforce the successful survival mechanisms that are operating in low-income Appalachian neighborhoods. Academic and job training projects, for example, should be designed to bolster Appalachian family interaction and local community schooling initiatives. Social welfare programs should support local initiatives among urban Appalachians, rather than attempt to supplant them.

School reform is a critical issue among urban Appalachians (cf. Maloney, "Urban Appalachians and School"). For the inner-city school systems, stemming the drop-out rates among Appalachian youth continues to be a concern for most of the community but relatively few school administrators. In suburban areas, some school systems have better retention rates among Appalachian youth, but these students generally finish in the bottom half of their graduating classes. One programmatic suggestion that has yet to be widely implemented is the inclusion of Appalachian studies units in both teacher-training sessions and school curricula.

Another area of concern implicit in the comparative survey data gathered in Cincinnati and its environs is the relationship between the urban Appalachians, blacks, and whites. As we have noted, blacks and Appalachians are the two largest minorities in the city, yet non-Appalachian whites hold most of the economic and political power in Cincinnati. The black community is frustrated, fearing the loss of hard-won legislative and constitutional gains. Urban blacks are leery of sharing meager power and resources with their Appalachian neighbors; unless new means of cooperation are developed between these two groups, increasing conflict over power and resource allocation will occur.

The policy direction is clear: municipal governments in cities like Cincinnati need to hold mediation sessions with black and Appalachian leaders to discuss cooperation in conflict resolution and resource allocation. Specific areas for mediation include control of community agencies and the allocation of employment and training funds. In the area of education, black leaders favor school desegregation plans that entail district-wide busing, while urban Appalachians favor community control of neighborhood schools with local attendance. Resolution of these differences would allow both groups to focus on the quality of education they seek for their children.

Not all issues polarize urban blacks and Appalachians. For instance, they frequently hold similar agendas in opposing police brutality and the displacement of low-income families from their neighborhoods. They share concerns about the inclusion of minority studies in school curricula and about the effects of heavy industrial pollution on their children (cf. Lower Price Hill Task Force). Urban Appalachians and their black neighbors have great potential for either conflict or cooperation. The coming decade may well decide which strategy will prevail.

Conclusion

In the coming years, urban Appalachians will continue to deal with issues they have wrestled with in the past, in particular education and employment. Establishing cooperative relations with other racial or ethnic minorities will continue to be a priority in an era of shrinking resources. New concerns will include a stronger emphasis on health care for the elderly population and the very young. Adult education and job retraining will take on increased importance as the decade advances.

The urban Appalachians we have studied do not lack the resources necessary to deal with the changing urban scene. They are maintaining relatively strong family bonds, supporting and using their own cultural institutions and organizations, and devising new ways to deal with old problems. The future for urban Appalachians holds the promise of both great struggles and great successes.

Works Cited

Brown, James S., and George A. Hillery. "The Great Migration, 1940–1960." *The Southern Appalachian Region: A Survey.* Ed. Thomas R. Ford. Lexington: U of Kentucky P, 1962.

Gans, Herbert. *The Urban Villagers.* Glencoe, IL: Free Press, 1962.

Lower Price Hill Task Force. *Report on Health, Education, and Pollution in Lower Price Hill.* Cincinnati, OH: Urban Appalachian Council, 1990.

Maloney, Michael E. "The Prospects for Urban Appalachians." *The Invisible Minority.* Ed. Philliber and McCoy.

———. "Urban Appalachians and School Reform." Paper presented at annual meeting of Central States Anthropology Association, 1990. Mimeographed.

Maloney, Michael E., and Kathryn M. Borman. "Effects of School and Schooling Upon Appalachian Children in Cincinnati." *Too Few Tomorrows.* Ed. Obermiller and Philliber. 89–98.

Maloney, Michael E., et al. *The Moraine School District: A Report.* Cincinnati: Applied Information Resources, 1989.

McCoy, Clyde B., and James S. Brown. "Applachian Migration to Midwestern Cities." *The Invisible Minority.* Ed. Philliber and McCoy.

Obermiller, Phillip J. "'Ain't Goin' Back': The Aging of Appalachian Migrants in Urban Neighborhoods." *Change in the Mountains: Elderly Migration in Appalachia.* Ed. Graham Rowles and John Watkins. Lexington, KY: Sanders-Brown, Center on Aging, 1991. 97–108.

———. "Labeling Urban Appalachians." *Too Few Tomorrows.* Ed. Obermiller and Philliber. 35–42.

———. "The Question of Appalachian Ethnicity." *The Invisible Minority.* Ed. Philliber and McCoy.

Obermiller, Phillip J., and Michael E. Maloney. "Looking for Appalachians in Pittsburgh: Seeking Deliverance, Finding the Deer Hunter." *Pittsburgh History* 73 (1990): 160–70.

Obermiller, Phillip J., and Robert W. Oldendick. "Moving On: Recent Patterns of Appala-
    chian Migration." *To Few Tomorrows*. Ed. Obermiller and Philliber.
———. "Urban Appalachian Health Concerns." *Mountain to Metropolis: Appalachian Migrants
    in American Cities*. Ed. Kathryn Borman and Phillip Obermiller. Westport, CT: Burgin
    and Garvey, 1994. 51–60.
Obermiller, Phillip J., and William W. Philliber, eds. *Too Few Tomorrows: Urban Appala-
    chians in the 1980s*. Boone, NC: Appalachian Consortium P, 1987.
Philliber, William W. *Appalachian Migrants in Urban America: Cultural Conflict or Ethnic Group
    Formation?* New York: Praeger, 1981.
———. "The Future of Appalachians in Urban Areas." *Too Few Tomorrows*. Ed. Obermiller
    and Philliber. 117–21.
Philliber, William W., and Clyde B. McCoy, eds. *The Invisible Minority: Urban Appalachians*.
    Lexington: UP of Kentucky, 1981.
Philliber, William W., and Obermiller. "Black Appalachian Migrants: The Issue of Dual
    Minority Status." *Too Few Tomorrows*. Ed. Obermiller and Philliber.
Wagner, Thomas E. "Too Few Tomorrows." *Too Few Tomorrows*. Ed. Obermiller and Philliber.

Jim Wayne Miller

Jim Wayne Miller is a poet, essayist, professor of German, and student of the history and literature of his native Appalachian South. Born in Western North Carolina, he studied at Berea College and at Vanderbilt University, and has lived in Bowling Green, Kentucky, since 1963. He is a member of Western Kentucky University's Department of Modern Languages and Intercultural Studies. His books include *Dialogue with a Dead Man* (1974); *The Mountains Have Come Closer* (1980); *Vein of Words* (1984); *Nostalgia for 70* (1986); and *His First, Best Country* (1993). He has edited an anthology of Appalachian literature for secondary schools (*I Have a Place*, 1981), as well as Jesse Stuart's *Songs of a Mountain Plowman* (1986) and James Still's collected poems, *The Wolfpen Poems* (1986). Miller is a celebrated teacher of writing as well as a lecturer and workshop leader.

The Brier Losing Touch with His Traditions

Once he was a chairmaker.
People up north discovered him.
They said he was "an authentic mountain craftsman."

From *The Mountains Have Come Closer,* Appalachian Consortium Press, 1980. Reprinted by
    permission of the author and publisher.

People came and made pictures of him working,
wrote him up in the newspapers.
He got famous.
Got a lot of orders for his chairs.

When he moved up to Cincinnati
so he could be closer to his market
(besides, a lot of his people lived there now)
he found out he was a Brier.

And when his customers found out
he was using an electric lathe and power drill
just to keep up with all the orders,
they said he was losing touch with his traditions.
His orders fell off something awful.
He figured it had been a bad mistake
to let the magazine people take those pictures
of him with his power tools, clean-shaven,
wearing a flowered sport shirt and drip-dry pants.

So he moved back down to east Kentucky.
Had himself a brochure printed up
with a picture of him using his hand lathe,
bearded, barefoot, in faded overalls.
Then when folks would come from the magazines,
he'd get rid of them before suppertime
so he could put on his shoes, his flowered sport shirt
and double-knit pants, and open a can of beer
and watch the six-thirty news on tv
out of New York and Washington.

He had to have some time to be himself.

John B. Stephenson

Sociologist John Stephenson is concerned with understanding the nature of community and with regional development. He has attempted to identify and provide solutions to such problems in his books *Shiloh: A Mountain Community* (1968), *Appalachia in the Sixties* (1972), and *Ford—A Village in the West Highlands of Scotland* (1984). Stephenson was born in 1937 and raised in Staunton, Virginia, facts which account for his focus upon the Appalachian region. He received degrees from the College of William and Mary (B.A.) as well as from the University of North Carolina at Chapel Hill (M.A., Ph.D.).

Shiloh

"Shiloh" is a cluster of several neighborhoods ranging around a single main road in a rural Western North Carolina county. The cluster is sufficiently integrated by kinship, friendship, and economic ties that it is thought of by residents—as well as by outsiders—as a single community. The origin of the community appears to be lost entirely to history. More than likely it was settled by whites of varied nationality in the 1700s, some of whom might have arrived there by way of the North Carolina Piedmont, though some of whom may have traveled south along the Blue Ridge spine. It is extremely doubtful that this small area was ever completely isolated from the rest of the country in terms of its contacts, although it may have been relatively uninfluenced by what went on elsewhere until the late nineteenth and early twentieth centuries, when timber interests and missionaries moved in to harvest trees and souls, respectively.

Change surged upon Shiloh as a consequence of World War II, when roads were built and improved, schools were upgraded and consolidated, the extent of farming declined, employment in mining and manufacturing began and increased, and communications from the outside grew in quantity and nature as a result of the coming of automobiles (in the 1940s and 1950s), telephones (in the 1960s), and television (in the 1950s).

By 1965 I identified the coming in of outsiders as no more important than the passing through of tourists and the occasional summer visitor interested in a second home. These I saw as another source of the "modernizing" influence of the outside world on this relatively unknown and nondistinctive mountain place. On the other side of the ridge there was, I knew, an entire summer settlement of Floridians in another cove, but I did not foresee clearly what would happen on the Shiloh side of the mountain. Nor did I completely appreciate what lay behind the resettling of this nearby cove and what its effects on local structures and culture were.

When I drove into Shiloh in 1980, however, the first observation I wrote in my notes concerned the real estate billboards decorating the approach to the community. They were new, as was the sign which pointed to the campground and recreation area that did not exist on my earlier visits. Driving down the main road, I noticed that a branch office of a national realty chain had opened since my last trip to Shiloh, and that the store had changed hands. I was surprised to see a new Presbyterian church, not far from the old one, which apparently was still functioning, and then a brick building that boasted a new volunteer fire department.

A few new homes could be seen from this road, but otherwise the housing looked much like it had fifteen years before. When I explored the off-roads, I discovered that what could be seen from the main road was entirely mislead-

From "Escape to the Periphery: Commodifying Place in Rural Appalachia," *Appalachian Journal* 11.3 (Spring 1984), © *Appalachian Journal*/Appalachian State University. Used with permission.

ing; there were numerous new homes up the coves, as well as new mobile homes and greatly improved older residences of long standing. Further down the main road, I saw signs marking new tract developments, one of which was built around a championship golf course on the edge of which had been built a new Bavarian restaurant (owned by natives of Bavaria, I might add).

With the aid of the son of one of my former key informants, I mapped the entire community, identifying the occupants of every dwelling for comparison to a similar map I had made fifteen years earlier. And with the help of the son of another informant, I extracted information on land ownership in the township covering a thirteen-year span. I interviewed the new realtor and examined the records of property sales in that office. I talked to numerous newcomers and longer-term residents.

The story of change in Shiloh in 1980, I learned quickly, had to do with the resettlement of the community by persons whose origins were outside the mountains and indeed outside North Carolina altogether.

I found that while my friend John Henry Sommers had moved his household from down on the creek up to the main road, an internationally known concert pianist and her physician son-in-law and his family had moved from an eastern city to a place down on that same creek. John Henry was proud of his new location, pointing to the town sign in his front yard and remarking that "You can't hardly get more downtown than that." The pianist's household was equally proud of its new homestead up under the trees and out of sight of the entire community.

I learned that the deaf-mute old man who once made a rockerless rocking chair for me was enjoying life in Morganton, North Carolina, while his old ramshackle house off the beaten path toward the upper end of the creek had been bought and completely remodeled, complete with white picket fence, by a retired couple from Miami.

I discovered that Bowman's store had been bought by a couple from the city of Baltimore, who had read about the property in a nationally distributed realty catalog. During all his years in the General Electric plant, the man had dreamed about being a country storekeeper, and now his dream was a reality.

Ironically, the farther I drove from the highly visible areas near the main road, the more likely I was to witness the transformation of the community. For people like John Henry, moving to the highway was an escape from marginality and the social class put-downs associated with life down the creek. To the newcomer physician, the attorney, and all the retired couples from the cities, the realization of their anti-urban ideal was measurable by the distance away from the highway. So as the John Henrys moved in closer to what they saw as a progressive, civilized life, the urbanites took their places, both literally and figuratively. Crumbling foundations of old houses were shored up, rusting roofs were replaced, weatherbeaten boards were made shiny with paint, and new mailboxes were erected bearing family names unfamiliar both to me and to the natives.

Statistics confirmed what the eye could see. The tax records for 1980,

Shiloh Township, 1968 and 1980
Owners of Taxable Property by Nativity and Residence Category

Nativity	1968	1980	1968–80 Increase	1968–80 % Increase	% Total Increase
Township Native	521	532	11	2.1	2.6
County Native	27	86	59	218.5	14.2
Non-Native			[325]		[78.3]
Full-time Resident	59	148	89	150.8	21.4
Part-time Resident	69	171	102	147.8	24.6
Non-Resident	403	537	134	33.2	32.3
Unknown and Other	27	47	20	74.1	4.8
TOTAL	1,106	1,521	415	37.5	99.9

Source: County Tax Records for 1968 and 1980, coded by Christopher Chrisawn, lifelong native resident

when compared with those for 1968, showed that the total number of parcels of land had increased, while the average size of each had decreased. They also showed that the value of the land had skyrocketed over this thirteen-year period. And they told that the proportion of properties belonging to owners who were not native to the township or the county had grown strikingly.

The tax records showed, for example, that the number of property owners had increased from 1,106 in 1986 to 1,521 in 1980 (see table). *Seventy-eight percent of this increase was made up of non-natives.* In 1968, the proportion of taxpayers who were natives of the township was already low at 47.1 percent; by 1980, the figure had fallen to 35.0 percent.

When the category of "non-native" was broken into subcategories, the numbers became even more interesting. The owners were first divided into "resident" and "nonresident," and the residents were further classified as "full-time" and "part-time." The largest percentage increase occurred among full-time residents, followed closely by part-time residents. Far and away the smallest percentage increase was among township natives, who increased their ownership by only eleven properties, or 2.1 percent. In short, native ownership was giving way to outside ownership, and the fastest growing category of new owners were those who bought property in order to take up full-time residence.

Who were the newcomers, and for what reason had they come to Shiloh? Some, of course, were speculators who did not live there and never intended to. They hoped simply to enjoy financial gain. Others had bought property to enjoy short holidays, sometimes renting out their otherwise unoccupied houses in order to help meet the mortgage payments. Others had built or bought homes to which to retire; some of them had reached retirement and lived in Shiloh year-round. The remaining category was also full-time residents; these were the year-round dwellers with intentions of permanent residence, who came to work in the vicinity and find a better life for themselves and their families. They were typically of working and childrearing age.

The ownership statistics from tax records showed what had already been revealed to me in a visit with the realty office. Sixty pieces of property worth a total of $1 million had been sold by the company since it opened its doors four years earlier. Where were the buyers from? The realtor opened a desk drawer and read off the home addresses of the clients: twenty-three from Florida, three from New York, two from Mississippi, and one each from such places as Connecticut, Vermont, New Jersey, Ohio, Michigan, Pennsylvania, Illinois, Missouri, Indiana, Maryland, and Lexington, Kentucky. Eleven were from North Carolina, of whom five were from the county and only one from the township.

What reasons did people give for buying places in Shiloh? Generally, it had to do with the fulfillment of a dream—not always the same dream, but some kind of imagined improvement in the quality of life. People said they were tired of the city—the danger, the traffic, the noise, the racial situation. People said they had been in places like this while on vacation, and they had in mind to live out their retirement days in a kind of unending extension of long-awaited, full-time leisurely inactivity. People said they came here for solace and retreat, to get close to the land and be with real people. A few people said they came here to help the sick, the poor, the unlettered, the disorganized, and those deficient in high culture. All these people said they liked the place and, in varying degrees, the people, and that they felt at home here.

What they had bought was, both literally and figuratively, a place. (A place, one might say, on Fantasy Mountain.) From whom was the land being purchased? Much of it was in the hands of land speculators and developers. Ironically, most of the so-called "spec" property was handled by a native son who had sold his father's grocery business to devote more time to more interesting commercial pursuits. This was Craig Bowman, who was exceedingly bright—bright enough to know where the money was and insightful enough to see exactly what was happening as a result of his own actions.

Craig knows that the land values in this township have risen faster than elsewhere in the county; that this is referred to as the "Gold Coast" of the county. According to him, land sales have surpassed Pensacola. "Many people," he says, "have sold out to outsiders at what to them is a high price and have bought over in McDowell County or in Burke, changing their lifestyles." Craig buys land and sells it for profit. I asked him what the local people think about what he's doing. He says, "The local people always want to know whether the people I'm selling to will be nice people. So far, they've been satisfied." Then he became pensive: "I would trade all the money for the way it was in the mid-fifties, but it's too late. There's an old saying: don't crap in your own backyard. But we've done it, and I've helped. We all justify land development by saying if we didn't do it, somebody else would. Sooner or later, nobody but a few of us who can afford it will be left here." As if to prove his point, he later introduced me to a man named Ed by saying, "I want you to meet a member of a dying breed—a native."

The breed is not dying, of course, but it is becoming outnumbered. The natives who have not moved to Piedmont, North Carolina, or to Los Angeles and other out-of-state cities are still finding employment within commuting distance, at places such as Baxter Laboratories, American Thread, Hickory Springs, Blue Bell, Glen Raven, Armored Garments, the golf course, the Highway Department, and the Forest Service. They still fish and go to church and observe Decoration Day and visit back and forth in ways reminiscent of Shiloh in 1965.

But the structure of community life is tangibly different, and subtle cultural changes have not gone unnoticed. None but the most hopelessly romantic would deny that many of these changes represent community improvements, although there is a great deal of ambivalence expressed by natives. In 1965, Shiloh experienced near-trauma in creating a community improvement organization because no one would agree to be nominated as chairman. In fact, there were no community organizations except for the churches and a softball team, and the only reason the community improvement group came into being was because of the efforts of a minister from Ohio. Now there is a volunteer fire department, organized by newcomers but run jointly by newcomers and natives. There is a program for senior citizens, organized by newcomers. The new church was begun at the instigation of one man from "outside." A monthly music appreciation group was organized— again by newcomers. Child development and health services have improved because of the initiative of a physician who moved into Shiloh. He has also maintained an imaginative program of assistance to problem families, coupled with housing improvement. Last, but certainly not least, there is now a community center in Shiloh, an unthinkable development fifteen years ago, which has been accomplished mainly through the efforts of newcomers. (A YMCA-sponsored youth program was the next program in the works in 1980; this idea was being promoted mainly by the wife of a recently arrived chiropractor.)

Relations between the newcomers and the natives vary greatly, but, in the main, the attitude is one of mutual tolerance, a keeping of distance, a muted disdain. Most of the newcomers expressed to me the feeling that they were well-accepted by the natives, but they admitted that they rarely associated with them except in public places such as the stores and in meetings. They had ideas about local culture which were not especially complimentary. ("Nobody will ever act together down here." "They're not taught things about responsibility and motivation." "They don't know the world outside this little place." "The low level of education is appalling." "I didn't realize the apathy of the people." "They don't know about things so they don't want them." "People are afraid to say anything for fear it will come back on them. We need to introduce the democratic process here.") The newcomers say that people are friendly, but they don't socialize. They do not take meals with natives, for example, and they do not golf with them.

The private feelings of some of the newcomers are, in fact, so negative that they doubt the wisdom of the changes they have made: the false imagery of romantic Appalachia is occasionally revealed to them. In another community near Shiloh, a woman who had bought an old farm place wrote to her son:

> It is so gloomy here and I hate it!!! I wish I was in the city where I could hear the cars and smell all that pollution. Also maybe there would be decent TV reception and there would be somebody to talk to. These southern people make me feel inferior as hell and I don't know why. I'm going to try to be happy and make the best of the situation but I can guarantee it—unless there is a huge change in my feelings—I am going back to Bean Town [Boston] and I don't care who wants to stay here. It's too lonesome here!

The farm was sold, by the way, to another urban refugee the next year.

The natives do not hide their feelings well. One man, attempting to put his new neighbors in a good light, said, minimally, "They speak. And I speak to them." Another says that some are better than others:

> Some of these outsiders is all right and others is just plumb hateful. They're unfriendly, don't want you to set foot on their land but want to roam all over yours. I sold a man ten acres above me here; I wisht I hadn't. I needed the money. It's been sold twice since then and I never met the man that owns it now. He *might* be one of those hateful ones.

Another native talks about how the outsiders stick to themselves. He does have one close friend who is an outsider (he says, "He ain't no smarter than I am"), but as for most of them, he says simply that "the Florida people has about taken over." When I asked Hope Sommers if she knew of any other terms people used for the newcomers, she said, simply, "land-takers."

A retiree from Miami, watching the sun set from his front porch while he broke with local custom and drank a beer openly in front of God and his neighbors, said that he had found the local way of life different from his, but not surprisingly different. He said people were easy to get along with. "We don't have any problems. It's live and let live. Nobody sticks their nose in your business." That may be all he asks for, coming from Miami, but I asked him how he thought local people felt about outsiders like himself. His answer was accurate and perceptive: "They like the money from Florida people, but then they resent them."

We see in this one small Appalachian community a case of rural invasion and succession. Local families are leaving Shiloh in search of improved lives in towns and cities, and urban refugees are taking their places in the country, also in search of better ways of living. The machinery of this complex exchange is oiled and operated by a combination of local and outside entrepreneurs—all brokers of one kind or another. And the consequence is an uneasy acceptance of change on the part of natives—an eagerness to take the money and run, coupled with as yet ill-formed questions about messes of pottage. The changes involve getting the community organized, forming more substantial community associations than Shiloh has ever known, paving over local customs with the thoughts and habits and energy of urban sophisticates who came here to look at the scenery, lift up the benighted, and get away from the high prices and urban confusion they left behind.

While the natives may struggle with ambivalence toward their new neighbors, the newcomers seem on the whole quite happy with their decisions to relocate to Shiloh. While they may be aware of the distance at which they are kept by the natives, that pattern of distancing is nothing new to them, and it is more than acceptable as a part of community life; it is probably even preferred over the alternative. For the most part, the newcomers *feel* accepted, and they *feel* at home. The full-time residents have made commitments to this place. It is now *their* place. They feel affection for it and love its physical aspects, and they want to care for it and "improve" it.

There can be little doubt that the newcomers' influence on Shiloh is making it a better community in many respects, if we measure community vitality by the degree of locality-based association and mutual problem-solving. If, on the other hand, we were to define the strength of community in terms of shared identity or shared sense of place, the picture in Shiloh is more confusing. My impression is that the newcomers may now have a stronger sense of place than do the natives, who are uncertain what is happening to their place. One native, in attempting to analyze what was taking place in Shiloh, said unsentimentally, "You've got to have progress, but after you reach a point, you lose what you had and you can't get it back."

The place has changed, every native seems to agree. One commented that "neighborhoods are not as closely knit. Life is faster paced. People don't keep up with each other—they don't care that much." Another, describing what he meant by saying that the pace of life had changed, said, "Decisions are made quickly now. It used to take three days to decide whether to cut your hay. And you don't make deals on handshakes anymore, either." These are people reporting their perceptions of culture change, changes in a place they are not certain is even theirs anymore, a place becoming so filled with outsiders that some of the natives are feeling a bit crowded. Mountain humor, as humor everywhere, often has an edge to it, as when one man said to me, "If you're thinking about moving down into here, I'd say you'd better hurry while you can still wedge in."

As Shiloh changes into whatever it is to become, it will slip quietly into that future with the aid of *native* as well as external land brokers and culture brokers. Craig Bowman is an example of the local land broker who learns to live with episodic waves of nostalgia. Jim Hartley is a culture broker who plays a role in the transition because he understands the old Shiloh and the newcomers equally. Jim has lived in California as much as he has lived in Shiloh. There are California plates on his pickup. There is a surfboard lying in the yard—probably the only one in the county—and it belongs to a native. Jim wants to stay permanently in the valley, but he leaves the door open to opportunities elsewhere, just in case things do not work out here. He could probably live anywhere, make a decent living as a builder/carpenter, and be happy. Everyone knows Jim, native and newcomer, and everyone likes him. Jim does not suffer from nostalgia; he is not tormented by images of a departed past. He represents the kind of cultural and interpersonal linkage which will make the transition of community identity a relatively smooth one.

What is happening in Shiloh, while it is not universal, is taking place in a number of other settings. Howard Newby, for example, has published thoughtful studies of the effects of incomers in farm villages of East Anglia. Boyd Gibbons has written a poignant account of the responses of natives to development efforts on Wye Island, Maryland. . . . The selling of land proceeds apace, although without much study, along the entire Blue Ridge spine in eastern America. And the consequences of the marketing of a romanticized sense of place are felt today in many parts of Highland Scotland, including the village of Ford in Argyll.[1] My scant familiarity with studies in Wales suggests that parallel changes have been and are taking place there.[2]

What is happening to local communities as a result of this commodification of peripheral places? One might call it "rural gentrification," but it is not quite that. Today's newcomers are not members of the gentry, by and large. They range from professional class to working class, and the majority are hardworking white-collar, managerial, and subprofessional.

Likewise, what is happening is similar in some respects to invasion and succession, except that the ethnic and class nature of these invaders is quite different from the classic case of Chicago; nor is there anything faintly resembling concentric zones; nor are the consequences anything like what the Chicago model would predict.

The process really involves an exchange of places, in which young rural aspirants to a better life flee to the cities while urban refugees flee to the countryside for the same reason. In both cases, new lives are sought by persons unhappy with their present sense of place. Sense of place lends itself to the commodity form just as readily as any object, so that place becomes imaged, hyped, brokered, and marketed, just as do rock singers, cigarettes, automobiles, and politicians. Success is promised the young in the cities, and rustic peace is assured all who come to the countryside—peace and a chance to uplift the benighted.

The long-term consequences for community cannot be discerned fully; indeed, they are still developing. In the case of Shiloh it is certain that basic community structures have been affected but certainly not altogether negatively. Whether new divisions within the community will erupt into overt conflict which tears apart the fragile structures of daily life remains to be seen. The transformation in Shiloh has been peaceable, but latent divisiveness remains a subliminal threat to community vitality. Presently, it exists at the level of mutually understood—and so far amiable—hypocrisy. This is partly because what resistance the natives feel is kept under control by a stronger ethic which prizes courtesy and the maintenance of smooth social relationships at almost all costs. There is also an almost total absence in this community of experience with organizational forms through which to mobilize resistance.

The phenomenon of escape to the periphery will probably continue for as long as city dwellers find urban areas unsatisfactory places to live. Most of the forces which influence this movement of people are so far beyond the ability of local communities to control them that they will probably continue to respond in the same ways that we respond to changes in the weather: they will accommodate as best they are able.

The need for a satisfying sense of place appears to be strong at present, for whatever reasons. And where there is a need which can be identified, marketing ingenuity and investment capital are not far behind. These conclusions lead me to speculate that for some time to come, we will have ample opportunity to study the phenomenon of escape to the periphery and its consequences for rural communities.

Notes

1. The effects of incomers to a Scottish village are described at some length in John Stephenson, *Ford: A Village in the West Highlands of Scotland* (Lexington: UP of Kentucky, 1984).
2. Professor Ronald Frankenburg's classic study, *Village on the Border,* indicated as much long before many of the rest of us could see the significance of such changes.

Work Cited

Gibbons, Boyd. *Wye Island: The True Story of an American Community's Struggle to Preserve Its Way of Life.* Baltimore: Penguin Books, 1979.

Jeff Daniel Marion

See volume 1, chapter 4, for biography.

Ebbing and Flowing Spring

Coming back you almost
expect to find the dipper
gourd hung there by the latch.
Matilda always kept it hidden
inside the white-washed shed,

From *Vigils: Selected Poems,* Appalachian Consortium Press, 1990. Reprinted by permission of the publisher.

now a springhouse of the cool
darkness & two rusting milk cans.
"Dip and drink," she'd say,
"It's best when the water is rising."
A coldness slowly cradled
in the mottled gourd.
Hourly some secret clock
spilled its time in water,
rising momentarily only
to ebb back into trickle.
You waited while
Matilda's stories flowed back,
seeds & seasons, names & signs,
almanac of all her days.
How her great-great-grandfather
claimed this land, gift
of a Cherokee chief
who called it "spring of many risings."
Moons & years & generations
& now Matilda alone.
You listen.
It's a quiet beginning
but before you know it
the water's up & around you
flowing by.
You reach for the dipper
that's gone, then
remember to use your hands
as a cup for the cold
that aches & lingers.
This is what you have come for.
Drink.

Lisa Koger

Lisa Koger graduated from West Virginia University (B.S.) in Morgantown and the University of Tennessee at Knoxville (M.S.). She received her M.F.A. degree from the University of Iowa in 1989. A freelance writer and lecturer in fiction and poetry writing, she also teaches writing workshops. Her collection of short stories, *Farlanburg Stories* (1990), explores the lifestyles and attitudes in a typical small southern town. She currently lives in Somerset, Kentucky.

Extended Learning

Della Sayer had promised to teach Vacation Bible School the first through the fifth of August, but when Frank phoned to say he and his family would be coming for a visit that same week, she regretted her promise and decided to wiggle out of it. It wasn't that she didn't want to help her class make macaroni sculptures or pop-up Jesuses. Frank was her son, her only child, and he hadn't been home in two years. He was married to a dentist named Marjorie, a quiet, fragile-wristed woman with lovely teeth. Della looked forward to spending time with her son and his wife, but it was her grandson, eight-year-old T. Barry, she really wanted to see.

Della lived alone on a farm seven miles south of Farlanburg. It was no longer a real farm in the working sense now that her husband Royce was dead, but there were enough cows to keep the weeds down and a few chickens that occasionally scratched up enough energy to drop an egg in the grass. The nearest neighbors, the Peevys, lived more than a mile away, which meant Della could hoe her garden in her nightgown if she wanted, and there was no one whose permission she had to ask.

During the summer she took her bath when evening first began to trickle into the hollow, then she sat on her back porch and reveled in the beauty of her flowers and the smell of her own clean skin. She liked to watch the shadows creep up the hills, over rock, fence, and thicket, climbing higher, covering ridge tops, until her world was submerged in darkness and the moon looked like the sun seen from the bottom of a clear blue lake. At the same time each night, if the dogs behaved themselves and didn't start their infernal yapping, a whippoorwill slipped out of the woods and sang on a hillside rock. Della would yawn and think her farm a dandy place to live and the best place in the world to visit, and she would climb the stairs to bed surprised she didn't have company more often.

Frank and his family arrived on a Sunday night, exhausted from being on the road two days. They pulled their Volvo into Della's barn lot a little after ten o'clock and left a white trail of Styrofoam cups and empty food containers behind them as they lugged suitcases through the dewy, moonlit yard. Della met them on the porch, arms open wide. "Frank!" she said. "Son!"

"Hello, Mom," said Frank. He was a tall man with thinning hair and poor posture. He had a well-trimmed beard and a Ph.D. from Purdue University, and had been a forestry professor at Oklahoma State University for the past eleven years. In photographs taken of him during professional meetings or departmental wingdings, he appeared bright-eyed and very distinguished, Della thought. But the Frank who came to her house always arrived bleary-eyed, with bugs on his windshield, and he acted as if some essential part of himself had been overlooked in the packing and left behind.

From "The Druther Stage," *Farlanburg Stories,* W. W. Norton Co, 1990. Reprinted by permission of the publisher.

Della kissed her son and hugged him tightly, then turned and embraced Marjorie, who had lifted her foot and was frowning at something on the bottom of her left shoe.

"What is it?" asked Della, and Marjorie showed her.

"Ornery dogs," Della said. "Sorry about that."

While Frank headed back to the car for more suitcases, Marjorie stepped off the porch and wiped her sandal in the grass.

"Where's T. Barry?" Della asked.

"Asleep," said Frank. "I'll get him."

Della was disappointed but tried not to show it. She could count on one hand the number of times she had seen her grandson. She often wondered if she would even recognize him if she met him on the street. She talked to him on the phone every couple of weeks, but it was hard to tell much about a person when you asked, "What're you doing?" and he said, "Talking to you."

"You need to bring the boy out here to see me more often," she said every time she called Frank.

"Road runs two ways," he reminded her.

He was right, Della knew, but the older she got, the less she felt like traveling. How could she tell her son, who had half his life ahead of him, that although she was in good health and not afraid of dying, she didn't want to do it in a strange bed several hundred miles from home?

As Frank carried T. Barry through the yard, Della was surprised and a little sad to see how much he'd grown. Gently, she picked up her grandson's bare foot and kissed it, then stood aside and let Frank pass. As she carried the suitcases into the downstairs guest bedroom, she wondered what it was like to come home after two years. Did home still *feel* like home, was it a place you were instinctively drawn to, or did you come because you thought you ought to, because the navigator in you happened to remember the way?

At eleven o'clock the next morning, Frank and Marjorie were still asleep. Della, who had been up since five, sat on the back porch steps enjoying the sun. Beside her sat T. Barry, hands on his knees, a wrinkled bag full of hickory nuts in his lap. She scooped a handful from the bag, tapped one with her hammer, then dropped the kernel into her grandson's open mouth. "So," she said. "Tell me again what the T. stands for. Is it Terrence or Tutwyler? My memory's not as good as it used to be, you understand."

The boy chewed steadily and looked at Della out of clear, deep-set gray eyes. He was a quiet kid with thick, blond hair cut so his head appeared peanut-shaped and difficult to balance. His arms and legs were remarkably unscarred and new looking as though he hadn't figured out what to do with himself from the neck down. "Thurman," he said, shyly. "You know that."

Della nodded and cracked another nut. "Maybe. Or maybe I just wanted to see if *you* did. I knew a man once, a pitiful fellow, who got kicked in the head by a horse and couldn't remember his own name. He went crazy trying to think of it, so they locked him in a corncrib and kept him there till he died."

T. Barry frowned and studied Della's crib. "I don't believe that. It's against the law to lock someone in a corncrib."

"They abolished that law," said Della. "I guess you're not familiar with the Corncrib Act."

T. Barry bit down hard on an unshelled nut. "What's 'abolish'?"

"It means to do away with, to get rid of. Don't worry about it, though. I still think you're plenty smart."

"I'm in the Extended Learning Program. It's a thing for smart kids at my school."

"Oh," said Della. "Are you smart?"

T. Barry shrugged. "Smart enough not to believe everything you tell me. Mama and Daddy say you have a bad habit of making things up."

Della laughed. "They'll probably tell you there's no such thing as the Corncrib Act." She shook her head. "I don't know why grown-ups are ornery and try to keep things from kids."

T. Barry rolled a nut with the toe of his shoe. "Is it true about that crazy man? Tell me the truth."

"Of course it is."

"What's his name, then?"

"Can't say."

"Why not?"

"Because if he didn't know it," said Della, "how do you expect me to?"

The day turned out to be a scorcher. By three o'clock that afternoon the temperature had reached the mid-nineties, and the cows had wandered off the hills and stood under the apple trees below the house, chewing cuds and flicking matted tails at the flies. Della suggested they all pile into her car and go for a drive to enjoy the countryside, maybe get an ice cream cone, her treat, but no one seemed especially wild about that idea.

"Don't think you have to entertain us," said Frank. "You just go on and do your thing, and so will we, and that way we can all relax."

Della stood in her kitchen, rolling and cutting egg noodles, Frank's favorite dish when he was a child. In those days, he liked to fish and hunt, and he spent hours wandering over the hills. He'd come home with burrs in his socks and a craving for noodles, and Della would fix them once or twice a week. Now, he insisted they weren't worth the trouble it took to make them.

Frank was asleep, Marjorie was reading, and T. Barry lay stretched out on the living room floor doing his homework, which was necessary, Marjorie explained, if he was to be competitive come fall with the other kids in his class.

"Homework," Della said to herself as she picked up a big knife and sliced off sections from the roll of noodle dough. Frank had never done homework during the summer, and as far as school went, he had certainly done all right. He had made good grades in high school and had earned a scholarship to the state university. Four years had turned into six, six into ten; more than half his life had been spent in school. He had knocked off all the rough edges, but in the process, something else had been knocked off, too. Della loved her son dearly and was proud of his accomplishments, but there were moments when she was struck by the unmotherly thought that, at some point, he had turned into one of the most boring people she knew.

Tuesday evening, Della wanted to invite the neighbor's children, the Peevys, for a wiener roast, but when she asked Frank to gather wood and cut sticks, she discovered that neither he nor Marjorie approved of wieners because of the ingredients added to the meat. Della listened and shook her head in pretend dismay while Frank went on about the general laxity of the Food and Drug Administration. "Will you all eat chicken?" she asked.

The next morning Frank announced that he and Marjorie planned to drive to Clendenin to see the new Jack Nicholson movie. Della wanted to take T. Barry out to his great-uncle Harve's farm, but he didn't seem all that keen on going, so she dropped that. After Frank and Marjorie left, she sat down on her lumpy couch in the living room. T. Barry lay half asleep in the recliner, his silence as measured as the metronomic ticking of the clock. "What do we want to do?" she asked him, and he said it didn't matter.

"Of course it does!" said Della. "Everything matters," but even as she said it, she had doubts. "Help me think," she said. "We could go on an adventure."

"I don't want to go on an adventure," he said, yawning and turning on his side.

"You just think you don't," Della said, trying to rouse him with her cheerfulness. "I know a place back on the ridge where there are blackberries as big around as my finger."

T. Barry gripped both armrests and scowled.

Della tried to persuade him by promising to bake a cobbler, and when that didn't work she told him she'd take him to see a haunted house.

"I don't believe in ghosts," he said.

"You might if you saw one," Della said kindly. She scooted a foot stool beside the recliner and sat down. "Do you believe in bird lice?"

He nodded.

"I do, too," said Della. "My eyes are bad now, so I can't see them, but I don't doubt that they're there. I believe in dragons, dead Ed Sullivan, Jesus Christ, and the Easter bunny. And I believe that if little boys don't run and have fun and climb trees while they're still little boys, they'll wake up one day and be old men before they know how." She held out her hand. "Come with me."

T. Barry leaned over the edge of the chair and picked up a copy of *TV Guide*.

Della looked at her grandson. He was already much older than she'd thought. She hurried into the kitchen and dug her Polaroid out of a drawer, then went to the hall closet to get her purse. When she returned, she was waving a five-dollar bill. "Do you believe in this?"

T. Barry stared at the money.

"Come with me," said Della, "and it's yours."

As they walked the narrow dirt road up the hollow, Della pointed out various places of interest. "This is where your dad caught his first fish. Over there, in the middle of that sumac, sits the diesel motor and edger from your grandpa's sawmill." They saw several deer tracks, surprised a quail, and even discovered some ginseng. It was almost four o'clock when they headed back. They had no berries, but Della carried more than a dozen snapshots, proof of the outdoor experience they had shared. The adventure had cost her almost nine dollars, but she didn't regret the expense. He had waded, skipped rocks, and caught minnows, and Della had an especially nice shot of him on a grapevine, looking, if not thrilled, at least pleasant, on his joyless ride through the air.

That night, his last night on the farm, T. Barry was tired and went to bed early. He was still asleep when Frank carried him out the next morning at dawn. The night drained away, but a heavy fog still filled the hollow. Della hugged her son and Marjorie. "Don't stay away so long," she said, and they promised they wouldn't.

Della went to the Vacation Bible School Wiener Roast and Parents Program that evening. She had not missed it in fifteen years. When the singing was over, the crowd moved outside, and Della joined them. She pulled a lawn chair next to the fire and sat beside the pastor's wife, Mary Sue.

"So," said Mary Sue. "How was your son's visit?" She looked tired. Bible School took its toll on the teachers.

"Good," said Della. "Same as always. How did things go this week for you?"

Mary Sue gazed at the kids screeching and playing in the churchyard. "I don't know," she said. "Sometimes I think we're just wasting our time. There are days when I wonder whether they take anything home at the end of the week besides their cookies and their crafts."

As the sun sank behind the hills, Della watched a group of boys chase each other with hot marshmallows, their laughter rising like sparks through the summer air. "They're kids," she said. "Maybe that's enough."

Fred Chappell

Fred Chappell was born in Canton, North Carolina, in 1936. From 1957 to 1960 he worked as general manager and then as credit manager for two Canton furniture stores. He earned his B.A. and M.A. degrees at Duke University. Chappell has taught English at the University of North Carolina at Greensboro since 1964. A nationally acclaimed poet and novelist, Chappell often draws on childhood memories to write about mountain experience.

His first novel *It Is Time, Lord* (1963), published before completing his master's degree, is noted for its complex narrative structure. *The Inkling* (1965), *Dagon* (1968), and *The Gaudy Place* (1973) explore the theme of the destruction of the personality. Chappell's best-known work and winner of the Bollingen Prize is *Midquest*, a four-volume poetic autobiography that concerned the author's thirty-fifth birthday. As indicated in the title of one of his major works, *I Am One of You Forever* (1985), Chappell, like Faulkner and Welty, gives overwhelming evidence of the lasting bond with the people and place of his birth.

A Prayer for the Mountains

Let these peaks have happened.

The hawk-haunted knobs and hollers,
The blind coves, blind as meditation, the white
Rock-face, the laurel hells, the terraced pasture ridge
With its broom sedge combed back by wind:
Let these have taken place, let them be place.

And where Rich Fork drops uprushing against
Its tabled stones, let the gray trout
Idle below, its dim plectrum a shadow
That marks the stone's clear shadow.

In the slow glade where sunlight comes through
In circlets and moves from leaf to fallen leaf
Like a tribe of shining bees, let
The milk-flecked fawn lie unseen, unfearing.

Let me lie there too and share the sleep
Of the cool ground's mildest children.

From *Sources,* Louisiana State University Press, 1985. Reprinted by permission of the publisher.

Index

Weeks-Townsend Memorial Library
Union College
Barbourville, KY 40906